Management of Technology and Innovation in Japan

Cornelius Herstatt
Christoph Stockstrom
Hugo Tschirky
Akio Nagahira

Editors

Management of Technology and Innovation in Japan

**With 89 Figures
and 28 Tables**

Springer

Prof. Dr. Cornelius Herstatt
Christoph Stockstrom
TU Hamburg-Harburg
Institut für Technologie- und Innovationsmanagement
Schwarzenbergstrasse 95
21073 Hamburg
Germany
E-mail: c.herstatt@tu-harburg.de
E-mail: stockstrom@tu-harburg.de

Prof. Dr. Dr. Hugo Tschirky
ETH Zürich
Technology and Innovation Management
Kreuzplatz 5
8032 Zurich
Switzerland
E-mail: htschirky@ethz.ch

Prof. Dr. Akio Nagahira
Tohoku University
Graduate School of Engineering
Management of Science and Technology (MOST)
04 Aza-Aoba, Aramaki, Aoba-ku, Sendai City,
Miyagi Prefecture 980-8579, Japan
E-mail: nagahira-akio@nifty.com

Cataloging-in-Publication Data
Library of Congress Control Number: 2005936155

ISBN-10 3-540-25326-2   Springer Berlin Heidelberg New York
ISBN-13 978-3-540-25326-6   Springer Berlin Heidelberg New York

Springer is a part of Springer Science+Business Media
springeronline.com

© Springer-Verlag Berlin Heidelberg 2006
Printed in Germany

Cover design: design & production GmbH
Production: Helmut Petri
Printing: Strauss Offsetdruck

SPIN 11408376   Printed on acid-free paper – 43/3153 – 5 4 3 2 1 0

Preface and Introduction

What Makes this Book Unique?

No crystal ball is required to safely predict, that in the future – even more than in the past – mastered innovativeness will be a primary criterion distinguishing successful from unsuccessful companies. At the latest since Michael Porter's study on the competitiveness of nations, the same criterion holds even for the evaluation of entire countries and national economies. Despite the innumerable number of publications and recommendations on innovation, competitive innovativeness is still a rare competency. The latest publication of UNICE – the European Industry Organization representing 20 million large, midsize and small companies – speaks a clear language: Europe qualifies to roughly 60% (70%) of the innovation strength of the US (Japan). The record unemployment in many EU countries does not contradict this message.

A main reason may be given by the fact that becoming an innovative organization means increased openness towards the new and more tolerance towards risks and failures, both challenging the inherently difficult management art of cultural change. Further, lacking innovativeness is often related to legal and fiscal barriers which rather hinder than foster innovative activities. Yet another reason to explain Europe's notorious innovation gap refers to insufficient financial R&D resources on the company as well as on the national level. As a result, for example, high-ranking decisions on the level of the European Commission are taken to increase R&D expenditures in the European Union from roughly 2% to 3% of GNP. Also, the EC recognizes that the identified potential shortage of researchers, particularly in Science, Engineering, and Technology, will pose a serious threat to the EU's innovative strength. Finally the promotion of a framework program for research and technological development ought to be continued in order to enhance competitiveness of companies and national economies. Such kinds of arguments are also strongly supported by UNICE.

Such arguments may certainly be parts of a solution to Europe's precarious economic situation but they lack an essential focus on companies' reality: Innovativeness is not only the result of sufficient resources and favorable external conditions. Rather, the capability to effectively transform available resources under given circumstances into marketable products and services determines to a large extent a company's competitive innovativeness. This specific management competence is often referred to as Management of Technology and Innovation (MOT). In a broad sense, it aims at mastering the technology-driven innovation process directed towards binding higher-ranking business objectives. This generic task includes the entire scope of management decisions on technology and innovation strategies, R&D structures, competencies, processes, make-or-buy options, strategic alliances or acquiring start-up's. In other words: Qualified MOT competence has the potential to leverage or even multiply given R&D resources. MOT, having its origin mainly in the United States and being still a young discipline of management, is gradually gaining acceptance by major European Universities.

In Japan, as compared to Europe the situation is quite different. Despite its economic stagnation during the last decade Japan has maintained the leading position in R&D spending at a level of 3.35 % of GDP for the year 2002 followed by the US with 3.08 %. This amounts to a total sum of R&D spending in Japan, which is only slightly below Europe in spite of the EU's double-sized population. The same holds for the number of researches and patents. And in strong contrast to Europe, MOT has become a top issue on the agenda of governmental institutions and industrial organizations in Japan. Whereas the Ministry of Education, Culture, Sports, Science and Technology (MEXT) is strongly promoting MOT education at 40 universities, focused MOT support is initiated by the Ministry of Economy, Trade and Industry (METI) and the National Institute for Science and Technology Policy (NISTEP). In other words: Aiming at maintaining a sustained innovation leadership position Japan is adding MOT competence to its traditional innovation capability with the potential and expectation to further increase its innovation contingent competitiveness.

This "double focus" of Japans technology and innovation policy gave reason for the edition of this book at hand. Japan's unparalleled economic development since the Meiji Restoration has since been the main theme of countless publications. They all try to shed light on motives and factors which might explain the rapid evolution of a country, which is not at all blessed with natural resources or a vast agricultural base, into the second largest economic power in the world. Such attempts are made for example by Edwin O. Reischauer, the former American Ambassador to Japan: In his opinion the multiplication of the standard of living many times over since the beginning of the twentieth century has only been possible because of intensified industrialization.

The main driver of this development was the ambition to catch up with the West following the vision 和魂洋才 ("wakon yosai") which is often interpreted as "Japanese Spirit, Western Technology". It consisted of a rapid adoption of Western achievements usually followed by adaptation to the Japanese way of life and subsequent perfection. It is reported for example that within two decades of the black ships' arrival, Japan boasted its first bakery (1860), photo shop (1862), telephone (1869), beer brewery (1869), cinema (1870), daily newspaper (1870), and public lavatory (1871).

There are distinct exceptions to this pattern of knowledge adoption. According to Eiichi Maruyama, today's roots of high tech image technology can be traced back to 浮世絵 (ukiyoe) referring to the ancient Japanese art of making multicolor wood block prints. Producing wood block prints requires mastering high precision engraving work since deluxe versions consist of up to 50 or 60 blocks using powder of gold and silver foil in addition to ordinary dyes on embossed paper. The attachment of the Japanese to high resolution color printing technology seems to be conserved in the art of micro lithography to fabricate for example the 256-megabit DRAM, where exposures are required using different masks with resolutions of submicron accuracy. In this field, Japan is the front-runner. The image technology of Japan is also leading the world in other aspects, such as high definition television called "Hi Vision". Liquid crystal displays boast an over-whelming market share, and Japan also assumes a leading role in the development of 40" plasma displays for next generation wall-hanging type TVs.

The industrialization of Japan had to be export-oriented, due to its dependence on foreign energy resources, which is the highest in the world. At the same time, this vital dependence - being a main reason for existential fear of uncertainty - ini-tiated a strong motivation towards new technological energy solutions to gradually lower that risk.

An interesting question relates to the origin of Japan's successful industrializa-tion. It seems that naturally given conditions play a crucial role. Japan is perma-nently threatened by natural menaces. Typhoons, earthquakes and to a certain ex-tent tsunamis are scary phenomena of everyday life. Their occurrence is not necessarily a surprise anymore. It means that the Japanese have been "condi-tioned" over millenniums to live with insecurity and uncertainty and have obvi-ously developed a survival will to brave permanent threats. It also seems that this individual and collective disposition to survive is representing a reason to over-come economic crises as well. In this context it is interesting to observe that the Japanese economy adjusted to drastically changing environments like the first and the second oil-crisis as well as the steep appreciation of the yen relatively well compared to other industrialized countries. It might further support the view that the dominant Japanese core competence consists of collectively well solving exis-tential problems such as the rapid industrialization following the Meiji restoration or economic recovery after World War II. Certainly another reason for the adapta-bility of Japan and its economy lies in the massive increase in productivity, which has been far higher than in many other industrialized countries. But also the ability of Japanese manufacturers to develop high-quality products fast is an important aspect in this context, of course.

Japan is in many respects impressing economic and societal development car-ries explicit cultural imprints of Shintoism, Buddhism and Confucianism. Shin-toism being the native religion is directed towards harmony with nature. Inherent to Shintoism is the belief, that inexplicable or highly respectable appearances are expressions of a kami (god). Therefore, worshipping at these kamis' shrines, espe-cially in times of personal sorrow represents an important way of finding relief from adverse feelings. Also, Shinto rituals require states of absolute physical and mental purity. It is in fact a level of purity which is not experienced by Western people. For this reason, there are qualified opinions from Japanese industrialists that today's ultra high level of clean room production would not have emerged without the almost passionate sense of purity indispensable for true Shinto prac-tice. Buddhism's basic beliefs are quite different. Buddhist teachings aim at ways of living which ease getting along with everyday's toilsomeness and therefore also contribute to find a rationale for accepting given living conditions. Confucianism finally is not a religion in our sense but rather a compilation of moral rules. They typically ask for respectfulness towards older people and loyalty towards higher-ranking people and complimentary responsible care for subordinates. Confucian-ism is considered to have established a disciplined structure of a "vertical society" with consequences such as cohesive organizational culture and identification with common objectives. Likewise the Japanese pronounced sense of community is enhancing the inner coherence of groups.

This book at hand does not at all attempt to reveal additional explanations of Japan's historical, economic, and societal uniqueness. What it does though, is to focus on the concrete particularity of current Japanese ways of coping with technological change and innovation. In this respect, it will give profound insights into Japanese ways of managing technological change and innovation, looking at various relevant levels such as strategy, processes, organization, culture, and project management.

This approach to current Japanese MOT reality within cultural, economic and societal complexity makes this book unique. The research findings will allow first conclusions, on the one side to what extent the pattern "adopt-adapt-perfect" has altered the originally Western based MOT concepts. On the other side, the revealed MOT practice in Japan represents potential opportunities of learning from proverbial Japanese perfection achievements.

The book is addressed to Managers responsible for product development, new business development, Marketing, or market research as well as Scientists, lecturers, and students of Technology and Innovation Management. It is intended to broaden and deepen the understanding of the way technology management is organized and innovation processes are managed in Japan. This is based on the assumption that Japan's innovation system, which contains very specific features and constitutes an integral part of its competitiveness, is distinct from other national innovation systems and thus offers possibilities of learning for others, despite cultural or social differences.

How Is this Book Organized?

This book is about how leading Japanese companies including Toyota, Canon, Sony, Sanyo, Shimano or Asahi-Glass manage technology and innovation referring to strategic, structural, process-related, and project-management related issues. Most articles are written by Japanese researchers, among these prominent colleagues like Takahiro Fujimoto (University of Tokyo), Kiyonori Sakakibara (Keio University) or Kentaro Nobeoka (Kobe University), being extremely familiar with the current situation of such companies. Further a number of contributions are devoted to discussing what European and US companies can learn from Japanese Companies applying Technology and Innovation Management related techniques and methods. Moreover, we look at how Japanese Culture affects the Management of Technology and Innovation in companies such as the ones mentioned above, as well as at how Western companies may profit from these perspectives. This book is an edited collection, and the chapters together cover various aspects of Technology and Innovation Management in the Japanese context. All contributions add significantly to the state-of-the-art knowledge in diverse areas, and the authors deliver valuable insights into Japanese management approaches.

The book is organized in five parts, starting with a chapter on strategy, followed by chapters on organization, processes, cultural aspects and implementation

We will briefly summarize the content of each chapter as follows:

Part I: Strategic Aspects

Sakakibara and Matsumoto address the issue of appropriating returns from innovation activities. They show how engineering of the product architecture may lead to inter-firm differences in appropriability and illustrate how Canon has been able to frequently shift added value between its devices and consumables in the copier and ink jet printer business. The authors suggest that Canon's efforts for high appropriability have a historical background and that flexible change in product architecture is the key to its success.

Takeishi and Aoshima study Shimano, a manufacturer of bicycle components, and show how Shimano has been able to perform well in an industry that is hit by recession and in which most companies experience considerable difficulties. Looking into its corporate history, the authors analyze how Shimano's innovation and component integration activities have allowed it to capture a position that may be described as the "Intel of the bicycle industry". Finally, the address the challenges lying ahead of Shimano and comment on how innovation may continue to be a driver of its corporate success.

Kusunoki investigates how innovations may overcome commoditization in an industry and allow companies to regain customers' willingness to pay. He stresses that conventional thinking, explicitly or implicitly assuming that innovations are dimensional phenomena, may be ineffective for creating differentiation and promoting consumers' willingness to pay. Moreover, he argues that innovations along particular dimensions may do more harm than good for de-commoditization and firms preoccupied with such "dimensional thinking" of innovation may be entrapped even more into commoditization.

Tomita and Fujimoto stress the increasing sophistication and diversification of customer needs. They show how companies are required to look beyond their customers, who are often intermediate users and have to consider the needs of end users, i.e. their customers' customers. Analyzing the case of LUMIFLON, the authors define the downstream of the value chain as a "customer system," and argue how an effective NPD pattern in a "customer system"-oriented manner should be through designed.

Part II: Process Aspects

Harryson describes the origins of the know-who based innovation process, which was born in Japan, but is increasingly applied throughout Asia. It aims at enhanced speed of innovation and reduced R&D risk through new processes that are no longer limited to intracorporate know-how, but leverage instead global know-who. Drawing on examples from Canon and Sony he shows how targeted acquisition of external expertise may be combined with an organic approach to internal resource deployment for enhanced innovation performance in the network system as a whole.

Beise argues that successful Japanese innovation management is not only rooted in general management techniques, strong relationships to suppliers and other commonly cited factors. He identifies the Japanese market context as an important driver for many globally successful innovations originating from Japanese companies. It is shown how characteristics such as a large domestic market at an early stage of the technology life cycle or a high penetration rate in the growth phase of the diffusion, and product designs or technological trajectories that were favored in Japan and later became economically advantageous worldwide have contributed to lower manufacturing costs or market knowledge and thereby benefited Japanese companies.

Yasumoto and Fujimoto explore how Japanese firms successfully employ product technologies and associated product development capabilities in oversea markets. They analyze how close interfirm relationships between Japanese firms contribute to successful product/process development at home and how these close relationships may hinder Japanese firms from sufficiently exploiting technologies and capabilities in oversea markets. Drawing on the example of Japanese mobile phone handset manufacturers in the US, they show how interface capabilities, firm-specific interaction routines that enable the firm to assimilate significant knowledge from partner firms, could help Japanese firms to exploit accumulated technologies and associated product development capabilities in close interfirm relationships in oversea markets.

Herstatt et al. report on the results of a large-scale study about typical front-end-related innovation practices in 553 Japanese mechanical and electrical engineering companies. They explore typical activities concerning the generation and assessment of new product ideas, the reduction of technological as well as market uncertainty and front end planning. The authors also report on differences between successful and unsuccessful companies and show that front-end-related activities such as customer integration during idea assessment, systematic translation and integration of customer requirements as well as systematic planning contribute to project success.

Haak analyzes the Toyota production system and examines how its different components have evolved into a process heavily contributing to Toyota's global success. He identifies the central factors, which have influenced the development of the key features of the Toyota production system. In addition he addresses the issue of whether the dynamism, i.e. the constant process innovation and change inherent in the Toyota production system, forms the basis for its flexibility which ensures that the system can survive in the face of rapidly changing competition and market constellations.

Part III: Organizational Aspects

Nobeoka proposes a conceptual framework for multi-project management organization and describes the processes involved in changing from a heavyweight product manager organization to a multi-project management organization. He illustrates his argument by analyzing the reorganization of Toyota in 1992 and 1993, which was the most fundamental change in the product development organization that Toyota ever implemented in the last 30 years. He concludes that organizations should aim at achieving both cross-functional coordination and inter-project coordination simultaneously and, using the Toyota example, shows how the apparent contradiction between these two goals may be solved.

In a case study of automobile part suppliers and manufacturers, Ge and Fujimoto investigate under what conditions suppliers are involved in new product development. In their analysis the authors distinguish between different patterns. Of interaction which they not only ascribe to relation-specific skills but identify the attributes of the auto parts in question as an important factor influencing the nature of interaction. They use product architecture reasoning to highlight the attributes of auto parts and derive and recommendations for supplier-manufacturer interaction in new product development.

Herstatt et al. investigate new product development (NPD) processes and planning in 15 Japanese companies. They explore how these companies structure their NPD processes and conduct their planning activities in order to strike a balance between the needs for efficiency and flexibility, which often carry opposing implications for organizing and managing new product development projects. They find that while the majority of the companies build their NPD efforts on a similar process model, they also employ diverse procedures to achieve their aims. In addition, the authors recognize a strong inclination towards planning R&D activities, which is shared by all companies involved in the project.

Part IV: Cultural Aspects

Nakata and Im address the issue of emerging competition for Japanese companies arising from neighboring firms in South Korea. They focus on a comparison of Japanese and Korean companies in terms of new product advantage. Their survey of more than 200 innovation managers in both countries shows that while cross-functional integration, new product team proficiency, and initiation tasks are critical antecedents of, or contributors to, new product advantage, the effects differ between Japan and Korea.

Reger investigates how European, American, and Japanese companies differ with regard to the degree and ways of internationalization of their R&D activities.

Based on a survey of more than 200 companies he shows that Japanese companies undertook less internationalized R&D activities compared to North American and Western European corporations. Also Japanese and North American companies are shown to strongly follow a concept of generating technology at home, while Western European companies give more room to build up centers of excellence and own competences in R&D units abroad.

Gerybadze also addresses the issue of international R&D and knowledge generation activities. He shows how this process is characterized by a simultaneous increase in intensity and speed of innovation, rise of international sourcing strategies for R&D, a greater emphasis on application and demand-pull, and an increasing emphasis on open innovation. He also highlights the cognitive and strategic differences in the way the innovation process in addressed in Japan and Western Europe to analyze the different strategies adopted by the companies from these differing cultural backgrounds.

Herstatt, Verworn and Nagahira investigate how Japanese and German companies reduce project-related uncertainty during the early phases of the innovation process. While most of the companies in the sample successfully reduced uncertainty, the authors identify different approaches by the Japanese and German companies respectively. In conclusion, the authors outline that there is no general best solution to this problem and argue for a careful consideration of influencing factors such as corporate culture when establishing these activities.

Part V: Implementational Aspects

Drawing on his extensive experience as a practitioner, Mori describes how the environment for IP management faced by Japanese companies is in the midst of considerable change. He highlights the substantial legal activity in the area of IP protection that has recently been taking place as well as the huge importance, which IP management has gained among Japanese firms. To substantiate the need for further changes, he explores the objectives of IP management, using leading examples of IP-intensive Japanese companies like Hitachi, Canon, Seiko Epson, and Olympus.

Trauffler and Tschirky describe the elaboration and implementation of basic strategic technology management concepts in a Japanese technology intensive company, which were proposed and put into action during an academic consulting project where researchers form the Swiss Federal Institute of Technology, Zurich – Chair of Technology and Innovation Management – collaborated with the company for a of period of more than eighteen months. In doing so, the authors report how MoT concepts were elaborated and implemented in a company that previously did not have any such concepts in use and describe which MoT activities were introduced and implemented and in which order. They also provide a generalized and practitioner-oriented procedure derived from the experiences of this particular case.

This book would have not been possible to realize without the support of the authors from Japan, the US and Germany, and we want to strongly express our gratitude for this effort.

Hamburg/Zurich/Tokyo, September 2005

Cornelius Herstatt and Christoph Stockstrom,
Hugo Tschirky,
and Akio Nagahira

序　文

この本の特徴はなにか？

未来におけるイノベーションを安全に予測するために預言者が使う水晶玉は必要ではない。過去においてはもちろん、未来でも、イノベーション能力に長けていることが負組の企業と成功企業を区別する主要な基準になるだろう。国家間の競争優勢性に関するマイケル・ポーターの研究以来、その基準は国家全体と国家経済の評価にも使われている。数えきれないほどのイノベーションに関する発表や提案にもかかわらず、競争的な革新性は未だに稀有な能力である。UNICE（2,000万社の大企業及び中小企業を代表する欧州の産業組織）の最新発表は、次のようにはっきりと述べている。欧州は米国(日本)のイノベーションの強さの6〜7割位しか持たない。多くのEU諸国における失業率はこのこととは矛盾してはいないのである。

　この主要原因は次の事実により得られるかもしれない。革新的な組織となるのは新たなものに対する公開性と危機や失敗に対しての寛容性を増大させることを意味する。この公開性と寛容性の両者とも本質的に企業文化の変化に関する経営技術の困難性に対する挑戦である。さらに、イノベーションの欠如はイノベーションを促進させるよりはむしろ妨害する要因として働きがちな法的かつ財務的障害としばしば関連している。そして、欧州の悪名高いイノベーションのギャップを説明するもう一つの理由は、企業のみならず国家レベルでの財政上のR&D資金不足のせいだとされている。その結果、例えば、欧州委員会の意思決定によりEUにおけるR&D資金はGNPの約2％から3％まで増加されている。また、欧州委員会は潜在的な研究者、特に科学、工学、技術における研究者の不足はEUのイノベーションの強さにおける深刻な脅威をもたらすことを十分認識している。最後に、研究や技術開発のための構造プログラムの振興は企業や国家経済の競争力を向上させるために維持されるべきである。このような主張も、また、UNICEにより強力に支持されているのである。

　確かにこのような主張は不安定なヨーロッパの現実の経済状況に対する解決法となるかもしれないが、企業の現実に焦点をあてるという本質的な点が欠けている。イノベーションは十分な資源と有利な外部の状況だけで果たされるものではない。むしろ、与えられた状況下で、可能な資源を効率的に製品やサービスへと変換させる能力が企業のイノベーション競争力の大きな部分を占める。この特有の経営能力はしばしばMOT（技術とイノベーションのマネジメント）に関係している。広い意味で、MOTはより高い水準の事業目標と結びついた技術主導型イノベーションを習得することを目的としている。言い換えれば、MOTは技術およびイノベーショ

ン戦略、R&D組織論、企業能力、プロセス、make or buy の選択、戦略的
提携又はベンチャー企業の買収、等のすべての経営上の意思決定を含んで
いるのである。すなわち、権限を付与されたMOT的能力は、企業の潜在
能力を向上させ、固有のR&D資源に影響を与え、あまつさえ増加さえさ
せる可能性を有している。主に米国で起こり、未だに経営の新学問である
MOTは、徐々に欧州の主要大学に受け入れられつつある。

　日本においては、欧州と比べその状況はかなり異なる。過去20年間の経
済的沈滞にも関わらず、日本は2002年のGDPの3.35％をR&D部門で費やし
ており、R&D投資においてトップを維持している。米国は3.08％でその次
である。日本のR&D投資の合計は欧州のの人口が日本の人口の倍である
のにも関わらず、欧州よりわずかに下回っている程度に過ぎないし、研究
と特許の件数は日本と欧州は同数である。そして、欧州とは反対に日本に
おけるMOTは日本の政府機関や産業組織の最重要な課題となっている。
文部科学省（MEXT）が日本国内の40の大学でMOT教育を推進させている
一方で、MOTプログラム自体への支援は経済産業省（METI）や科学技術
政策研究所（NISTEP）により始められている。すなわち、日本のR&D活
動を世界トップレベルとして維持するためには、伝統的なイノベーション
能力に加えて、MOT能力を付加することによってイノベーション競争力
がさらに増加するのではないかという可能性と期待感が高いのである。

　日本の技術およびイノベーション政策という二つを焦点とすることがこ
の本の出版の理由である。明治時代以来、日本の経済成長は数えられない
ほど多くの研究発表の主要テーマとなってきた。それらはほとんどが天然
資源や農業基盤が脆弱でありながら、世界第2の経済大国となった日本の
急進的な成長の秘密を解き明かしたいという強烈な動機を有している。こ
のような日本の発展の秘密解明の例として元駐日米国大使であったエドウ
ィン・O・ライシャワー大使は、次のように述べている。彼は、日本の2
０世紀初以来生活水準の向上は徹底した工業振興策のみによって可能とな
ったとする。しかし、この成長の中心的な原動力は、「日本の精神を保ち
つつも、西洋の技術を積極的に取り入れる」としばしば訳される「和魂洋
才」のビジョンに従って西洋に追いつくという野心的な試みであった。そ
れは日本の生活様式に西洋技術を急進的に適用することであり、その後の
成果で効果は証明された。1853年の米国のペリー艦隊の日本への来航
(「黒船」) 後の20年間で、日本は、最初の製パン（1860）、写真館
（1862）、電話機（1869）、ビール工場（1869）、映画館（1870）、日刊
新聞（1870）、そして公共トイレ（1871）などをつぎつぎと開始したこと
がその実例して報告されている。

　しかしながら、日本の知識採用のこのようなパタンに明白な例外があ
る。丸山栄一（Eiichi Maruyama）によると、現在のハイテク映像技術の根
幹は多様な色で作られた江戸時代の日本の版木印刷によって作成された浮
世絵と深く関係しているとされる。版木印刷は高い精密度の彫刻技術が必
要であり、豪華な印刷には染められた飾り紙と金と銀の粉末を使った50〜

60個の版木によって構成される。こうした日本の伝統的な高解像度の印刷技術の応用は、例えば256MBiteの DRAMを製造するマイクロ・リソグラフィーの技術において見事に応用されているという。256MBite DRAMは超微細精密度で異なるマスクパターン毎に露光技術によって転写されていく。この分野の技術ではかって日本は先頭を走っていた。また、日本の映像技術はほかに「ハイ・ビジョン」と呼ばれる高品位テレビといわれる部門においても世界のトップクラスである。LCD(液晶ディスプレイ)は韓国、台湾に逆転を許したが、それでも有力な市場占有率の一角を占めている。また、日本は次世代壁掛け形テレビといわれている４０インチのプラズマ・ディスプレイの開発において先頭を走っている。

　　日本の工業化は、世界一の国外のエネルギー資源依存国であったことから、必然的に輸出指向形の加工貿易とならざるを得なかった。同時に、この致命的ともいえる国外への資源依存は次第に資源依存リスクを下げるための新たなエネルギー技術の開発による解決への強力な動機を生み出した。

　　日本の急進的な工業化の成功の起源に関しては面白い説が提唱されている。そこでは、日本の立地条件が重要な役割を果たしていると思われる。日本は昔から自然災害に脅かされてきた。台風、地震そして津波は恐ろしい日常の自然現象であり、日本人にとってはその発生は驚くにはあたらない。このことは日本人が長い間不安定と不確実を克服するために環境に適合してきた結果、永久的な脅威に対抗する生存のための知恵を明確に発達させてきたことを説明している。また、生存のためのこの個人および集団としての気質は経済的危機を克服した理由を説明しているように思われる。この本において、日本経済が第一次、第二次の2回のオイル・ショックのみならず、他の工業化国家と比較して、相対的に円の急速な価値上昇のような環境変化に果敢に対応したことを探求していることは、興味をそそるところである。日本の他国に抜きん出た中核能力は明治時代以来の急速な成長や世界二次大戦後の経済回復のような現実的な問題を集団的に上手く解決することであるという見方を裏付けているように思われる。日本及びその経済の適応力に関する別の理由は多くの工業国よりはるかに高い生産性の大規模な増加である。もちろん、早くてよい品質のものを開発する日本の製造業者の能力もこの本でとりあげている重要な側面である。

　　経済及び社会的な成長で多くの関心を浴びている日本は神道、仏教、そして儒教などの明白な文化的内面性を印象付ける。日本の本来の宗教である神道は自然との調和に向けられている。神道の本質は、説明することが困難ではあるが、尊敬すべき神（Kami）と呼ばれる存在に対する信頼である。したがって、特に悲しい時に、神社で祈るのは神に救いを求める重要な方法である。また、神道の儀式は完璧な体と精神的な純粋性を必要とする。実際の純粋さの水準は西洋人が経験できないことである。このような理由で、真の神道の実践のため無くてはならない強い純粋さがなくては現在の高いレベルのクリーン・ルームでの生産はできなかったと日本の産

業人たちは語っている。仏教の基本的な思想は大きく異なっている。仏教の教えは毎日の苦労から抜け出すことを目的としており、その結果、与えられた生活状況を受け入れるための理論的根拠を示すのに寄与する。最後に儒教は我々の感覚においては宗教ではなくて、むしろ道徳的な規則を編集したものである。儒教は高齢者に対する尊敬と支配層に対する忠誠心と下部層に対する責任感ある管理を求める。儒教は公共の目的のための結合力ある組織的文化や一体化を確立し、安定的構造の「垂直的社会」をもたらしたと考えられている。同様に、日本人の共同意識として説明されている点は日本人内部の結束力の強さを高めている。

この本は日本の歴史的、経済的および社会的特徴の付加的説明をすることを目的としてはいない。しかしながら、技術的な変化やイノベーションに関する現在の日本の具体的な特徴に注目している。この点で、我々は技術的変化とイノベーションに対する日本の経営手法、戦略、プロセス、組織、文化、そしてプロジェクト運用のような多様な関連レベルの観察方法を通じて深い洞察を得るはずだ。

文化的、経済的、そして社会的な複雑性の中での現在の日本のMOTの実態に近づくのがこの本の特徴である。この研究では、まず「採択―適用―完成」の基本パターンが本質的に西洋のMOT概念を変形させてきたという結論を得られる。他方で、日本において明らかになったMOTの実践は、よく知られている日本人の完璧主義からの潜在的な学習機会を表している。

この本は製品開発、新事業開発、マーケティング、市場調査の責任者のみならず、研究者、講師、そして技術とイノベーションを勉強する学生のために書かれている。この本は日本での技術経営手法とイノベーションプロセスを幅広く、かつ、深く理解するのに役に立つはずである。この本は、日本のイノベーションシステムが固有の特徴を有し、競争優勢の重要な部分を構成しているという理解に基づいて書かれている。日本のイノベーションシステムを他国のイノベーションシステムとは区別し、文化的又は社会的な違いにも関わらず、学習の可能性を提供するものである。

Table of Contents

Part I: Strategic Aspects

Part II: Process Aspects

Part III: Organizational Aspects

Part IV: Cultural Aspects

Part V: Implementational Aspects

List of Contributing Authors

Yaichi Aoshima

Associate Professor
Institute of Innovation Research
Hitotsubashi University, Tokyo, Japan

Marian Beise

Senior Research Associate
Faculty of Business, Department of Management
City University of Hong Kong, Kowloon, Hong Kong
SAR of the People's Republic of China

Takahiro Fujimoto

Full Professor and Director
Manufacturing Management Research Center
Faculty of Economics
University of Tokyo, Japan

Dongsheng Ge

Research Assistant
Manufacturing Management Research Center
Faculty of Economics
University of Tokyo, Japan

Alexander Gerybadze

Full Professor and Director
Chair of International Management and Innovation
University of Hohenheim, Stuttgart, Germany

René Haak

Deputy Director and Manager
Business & Economics Group
German Institute for Japanese Studies, Tokyo, Japan

Sigvald J. Harryson

Assistant Professor
Program Director of Managing Growth through Innovation
Baltic Business School, Kalmar, Sweden

Cornelius Herstatt

Full Professor and Director
Institute for Technology and Innovation Management
Technical University of Hamburg-Harburg, Germany

Subin Im

Assistant Professor of Marketing
College of Business
San Francisco State University, USA

Ken Kusunoki

Associate Professor
Graduate School of International Corporate Strategy
Hitotsubashi University, Tokyo, Japan

Yoichi Matsumoto

Graduate Student of the Doctoral Program
Graduate School of Media and Governance
Keio University, Fujisawa, Japan

Yonoshin Mori

Director
Arthur D. Little (Japan), Inc., Tokyo, Japan

Akio Nagahira

Full Professor
Institute for Management of Science and Technology
Tohoku University, Sendai, Japan

Cheryl Nakata

Associate Professor of Marketing and International
Business
College of Business Administration
University of Illinois-Chicago, USA

Kentaro Nobeoka

Full Professor
Research Institute for Economics and Business Ad-
ministration
Kobe University, Japan

Guido Reger

Full Professor and Director
Brandenburg Institute for Entrepreneurship and Small
and Medium-Sized Enterprises (BIEM)
University of Potsdam, Germany

Kiyonori Sakakibara

Full Professor
Graduate School of Media and Governance
Keio University, Fujisawa, Japan

Christoph Stockstrom

Research Assistant
Institute for Technology and Innovation Management
Technical University of Hamburg-Harburg, Germany

Osamu Takahashi

Assistant Professor
Graduate school of Art and Design
Tohoku University of Art and Design, Yamagata, Ja-
pan

Akira Takeishi

Associate Professor
Institute of Innovation Research
Hitotsubashi University, Tokyo, Japan

Junichi Tomita   Research Assistant
                             Manufacturing Management Research Center
                             Faculty of Economics
                             University of Tokyo, Japan

Gaston Trauffler   Research Assistant
                             Management, Technology, and Economics Department
                             Swiss Federal Institute of Technology Zurich, Switzerland

Hugo Tschirky   Professor emeritus
                             Management, Technology, and Economics Department
                             Swiss Federal Institute of Technology Zurich, Switzerland

Birgit Verworn   PhD, Technology Consultant
                             Association of German Engineers, Düsseldorf, Germany

Masanori Yasumoto   Associate Professor
                             Faculty of Economics
                             Shinshu University, Matsumoto, Japan

Part I: Strategic Aspects

Designing the Product Architecture for High Appropriability: The Case of Canon

Kiyonori Sakakibara and Yoichi Matsumoto

The Issue of Appropriability

For both manufacturing and service sectors, key success factors for firms to grow are implementing innovations and acquiring the returns from the innovations. The innovator's capability of getting the returns from his innovations is called "appropriability of innovations." The purpose of this paper is to discuss the issue of appropriability of innovations by examining the specific example of Canon Corporation of Japan.

When any innovation is successfully implemented, spillovers from the innovation are inevitable in most cases, and invite free riders. In other words, an innovator alone cannot monopolize the returns from his/her innovation. Thus, it is important to minimize the spillover, which ultimately improves the appropriability of innovation.

The collaborative papers on this subject by economists Klevorick, Levin, Nelson and Winter (Levin et al. 1987; Klevorick et al. 1995) are well known. Their study, which employs a questionnaire survey, is known as the Yale Survey. Having been inspired by the Yale Survey, Japanese economists also published comparable study results (Goto and Nagata 1997; Cohen et al. 2002). Among management researchers, Teece (1986), von Hippel (1990) and others picked up the subject as well.

Previous studies have concluded that appropriability varies between different industries or product categories. For example, it is relatively easier for science-based industries such as the pharmaceutical industry to harvest the benefits from own innovation than for other industries because patents often protect the products. However, the appropriability varies not only between industries. Competing companies within the same industry can realize different levels of appropriability of innovations based on their strategies. From this perspective, the appropriability of innovations is subject to managerial decision-making.

For example, two manufacturers which have roughly equal product market shares and compete head to head may show different profitability if one has a key device and the other does not. Sharp Corporation's high profitability in the business of liquid crystal display TVs is a case in point. Its profitability is estimated to be higher than Sony's, for example, because Sharp possesses the liquid crystal display technology and manufactures in-house, while Sony does not.

Although in-house manufacturing of devices, particularly key devices, is a way to increase the appropriability, it is not a bulletproof strategy. Dell is a case in point. In the personal computer business, Dell does not manufacture any devices and components and uses an outsourcing strategy for high appropriability. Michael Dell, the founder of Dell, envisioned a way to create value through innovative distribution and marketing rather than through manufacturing. He has succeeded in developing a business model that enables high appropriability in that business area.

Characteristics of the Business Performance of Canon

In the section that follows Canon Corporation of Japan is used as a best-practice case that exemplifies high appropriability among competitors. It is a highly successful company: the latest business performance as of December 2003 shows sales on a consolidated basis of Y319.8 billion, an operating profit of Y45.44 billion, and operating margin before tax of 14.2% and an after tax profitability of 5-8% which makes Canon one of the most profitable Japanese manufacturing firms.

Canon has 3 major business groups. The first and central group is the camera product group. A successful diversification created the second competence, the business machine product group. The third area, the optical and other products group, aims for specialized market segments.

As for the contribution to corporate performance, the business machine product group is the most significant contributor to the overall profitability of Canon. This group currently accounts for 70% of consolidated sales and 107% of profitability (the contribution to the overall profitability exceeds 100% because in 2003 the profitability of the optical and other products group was negative). Operating margins by business are camera 19.3%, business machine 21.4%, and optical and other -2.8%. Although all groups are major players in the respective markets, the high operating margin of the business machine product group is noteworthy.

Why is the business machine product group so profitable? Both camera and business machine products hold significant world market shares, contributing to the high profitability. However, having great market share alone is insufficient to describe why the profitability of the business machine product group is higher than that of the others. What is unique to the business machine product group is that after-sales support and consumable supplies, besides the up front sales of products, are powerful sources of profit. It is a distinctive structure for profit making. The questions at hand are what the distinctive structure for profit making is, how Canon has been able to establish it, and whether or not any companies that manufacture the same product types automatically achieve high profitability.

Profitability of the Business Machine Product Group

Two representative products of the business machine product group include copying machines and inkjet printers. The domestic market share of copying machines in terms of shipment unit shows Canon at 29.7%, Ricoh at 29.5%, and Fuji-Xerox at 22.0%. As the top 3 manufacturers hold over 80% of the market, it is clear that these three dominate the domestic market (*Nikkei Sangyo Shinbun*, August 13, 2003). As for the ink jet printer, the domestic market share is in an oligopoly situation controlled by Seiko Epson (50.8%) and Canon (41.7%) (*Nikkei Sangyo Shinbun*, July 29, 2003).

If the operating margin trends of 4 representative manufacturers of business machines (Canon, Ricoh, Seiko Epson and Fuji Xerox) are compared in the latest 5 years, it shows that Canon has been the only company with a return on sales consistently higher than 10%. As the content of business machine operations in each company varies, it is not possible to precisely conduct a comparative analysis. Nonetheless, it is safe to conclude that Canon consistently demonstrates higher profitability than competitors.

Cartridge Technology that Sustains Copier's High Profitability

In order to understand the uniquely high profitability of Canon's business machine products group, it is helpful to take a look at the example of its small-size personal copier, which found family and personal uses.

Canon developed the first-in-the-world personal copier PC-10 in 1982. The market loved the model, and it contributed greatly to the company's growth. The distinctive feature of this small-scale personal copier is Canon's home grown "cartridge technology." The cartridge technology combined the central functions of the copier, packaging, image development device, charger, photoconductive drum, consumable toner, and cleaner functions into one cartridge. Then the all-in-one cartridge is replaced with toner's expiration. The unique technology of Canon eliminated periodical inspections and toner refills, and enabled the development of the personal copier market for the first time in the world. As Canon's advertisement stated, "simple-maintenance and support-free" became possible. Also, the technology made the product significantly more compact. The cartridge method was successfully transferred to laser-beam printer (LBP) product lines.

Prior to the PC-10 the plain-paper copiers, or PPCs, were for business organizations only, and the countrywide network of after-sales service providers supported maintenance of the installed equipment. It was a norm that copiers came with maintenance services. Photoconductive drums needed to be replaced when they reached their expiration; toners needed to be replenished and disposed; charger's wires tended to attract dust and therefore needed to be cleaned periodically; cleaners needed to be replaced; and so on. In other words, using PPCs necessitated periodical checks, maintenance, replacement of consumables, and timely repairs when needed. Those conditions were undesirable for family or personal uses. It was either unfeasible to establish such a network to support family and personal users or unprofitable to do so. With the cartridge technology Canon made it possible to bring PPCs to the family and personal market without the traditional service network.

The cartridge technology, which allowed for simple-maintenance and support-free products, was technically significant, but it was not everything. Canon's all-in-one cartridge did not only represent a consumable, but also contained central functions of a copier, proprietary technologies and patents, within it.

As everyone knows, there is a black cartridge in a Canon copier. Because it is an encapsulated type, detailed contents are not identifiable. It contains both, high-precision central mechanisms, such as the image development device, and value-added consumable items. Intuitively speaking, the cartridge in a Canon copier is "a black box that contains technology and profit." The other part of the copier, in contrast, is a low value-added plastic case and both mechanically and technologically simple. It is, so to speak, "a chassis."

By continuously introducing new products employing the same cartridge technology, Canon limits exposures of its own technology and maintains the highly profitable structure of the product line. The company considers the profitability of each product as a viable technical issue to be addressed during the development and engineering phase.

The Origin of the Idea

The idea that the profitability structure of products is based on development and engineering issues originates from the successes and lessons in Canon's camera business.

Canon was originally established as an R&D and manufacturing company of 35 mm high-quality cameras in 1933 when there was no sufficient technology to manufacture cameras in Japan. Its initial slogan was "Defeat Leica." Leica was the name of the world's best camera manufactured in Germany. It is widely recognized that Leica was the model for the modern camera.

From the beginning the company focused solely on developing and manufacturing high-quality cameras and gained its reputation. In 1961 "Canonet" with an automatic exposure mechanism became very popular, which contributed to the development of the mid-class camera market and caused the subsequent explosive growth of Canon.

In 1962 the former President Takeshi Mitarai, Chief Technology Officer Hiroshi Suzukawa and Keizo Yamaji, a technician in the lens division, took a trip to the United States to strengthen the North American camera sales and learn ways to diversify the camera business. They received an unexpected welcoming at the Eastman Kodak headquarters in Rochester, New York. Yamaji described the Kodak visit as follows ("My Resume" on *Nihon Keizai Shinbun*, March 14, 1997):

> When we visited several of the major Eastman Kodak facilities, they brought us fancy lunches and dinners to welcome us. I asked, "Why is this?" "Cameras that you manufacture are film burners," was the response.

The sales of film grow exponentially in relation with the cumulative camera sales. I understood completely. It would be hard to start a new film business, but I would like to engage in consumables. Because of this experience we decided to sell all consumables when we entered into a copier business.

Yamaji became the first manager of the product development department in the new business division upon returning from the American tour and played an important role in developing new products towards diversification. This was when he was 34 years old. Meanwhile, what did "film burners" mean? It literally meant that cameras burnt rolls of film. Thanks to mass production of good camera, people would take a lot of pictures and burn a lot of films. As a film manufacturer Canon's success was a pleasure. As employees of a camera manufacturer, they must have had mixed feelings about it. This experience ultimately led the company to business machine products, the first of which were copiers.

This episode was told as an anecdote of the historical visit to Kodak. However, the same situation actually existed in Japan. Canon employees must have known about the attractiveness of consumables because the sales of domestic film manufacturers, such as Fuji Film, skyrocketed when the sales of Canon cameras went well. In fact, the business performance of domestic film manufacturers outstripped that of camera manufacturers at some point.

For this reason, Canon engineers already apprehended that the development of copier products was not simply making "a box," but a new business model with a different profit-making structure than that of cameras. In short, it was the idea of making a machine that used consumables, and that using the consumables was an important element of the company business.

The idea of exploring consumables and the technological breakthrough of Canon's image development device together brought about the development of the unique cartridge. The former Managing Director Masashi Kiuchi was responsible for the breakthrough of the image development device, and the former Vice President Hiroshi Tanaka was responsible for the development of the cartridge technology. The use of a cartridge in copiers was then duplicated in the development of the printing head of bubble jet printers. Hiroshi Tanaka was the leader in that project as well.

When reexamining Canon's copiers with this historical background in mind, we can see a striking similarity between the association of a cartridge in a copier and that of a film in a camera. It is not only the similarity in appearance but also the similarity in naming. The name "cartridge technology" used in copiers must have come from the terminology used in the camera technology. The similarity of naming in both copier's cartridge and camera's film cartridge is not coincidental. It is a result of conscious efforts.

In a nutshell, during copier development, Canon was aiming for a new business model that could bundle camera and film cartridge into one business, so to speak. And it did succeed in realizing the model. This idea was further developed in its printer business. We will describe this continued effort in the following section.

Therefore, it does not suffice to say, "the copier business is profitable because it involves consumables," as it does not take into consideration that Canon has developed the unique technology based on its historical background.

Analysis of the Ink Jet Printer Business in Japan

In this section an intensive study of Canon's ink jet printer business in the Japanese market is used to look at appropriability of innovation. The development of ink jet printer products and the market trends during the 1990s are at the center of attention. First, however, we need to succinctly learn about the ink jet printer technology.

Characteristics of the Technology

There are broadly two printer types – the impact type and the non-impact type. An example of the former kind is the dot-matrix printer and examples of the latter kind are thermal and electro photographic printers. Ink jet printers also constitute a non-impact printer type.

Ink jet printer technology is complicated. The printer is a kind of precision machinery; however, dealing with raw materials of ink requires the latest knowledge in chemistry. Determining an unclogging flow of ink requires knowledge of hydrodynamics. Measuring ink droplet formation necessitates knowledge of ultrasound and charged particle dynamics. Furthermore, electronics circuits, computer software, and semiconductor technologies are needed. Thus, ink jet printers are a conglomerate of multiple technologies (Okubo 1999).

Ink jet printers can employ one of several printing methods. The most influential ones are the Bubble Jet method of Canon and the piezoelectric method of Seiko Epson. The Bubble Jet (BJ) method in brief is a mechanism that uses thermal energy to extract ink. Heated ink at the nozzle is gasified and produces bubbles. The expansion of the bubbles pushes ink out from the discharge spout. When the heater temperature drops, the bubbles constrict and the pushed ink turns liquid as it flows out. When the bubbles at the nozzle disappear, ink is newly supplied via the capillary phenomenon. On the other hand, the piezoelectric method uses energized electric voltage to extract ink. It employs piezoelectric elements, which vibrate when voltage is superimposed, to insert pressure in the cavity (ink compartment) and extract ink. The application of this method is the Mach Jet (MJ) method of Seiko Epson.

Although there are methodological differences, the basic mechanism of ink jet printing is simply spraying ink on paper. Because of its simplicity there are several advantages. Typical advantages among many include that plain paper can be used, letter quality is high, print speed is high, and product costs are low. Also, color application is relatively easy and operation noise levels are low because it is non-impact. However, there are shortcomings due to the simplicity of the process, such as clogging ink, the interfusion of bubbles in ink channels, and the erosion of head material by ink. The improvement of inks and cleaning of the nozzle surface have remedied these shortcomings. Making the ink head disposable was another solution Canon employed although this led to the problem of increasing running cost (Takahashi and Irie 1999).

Both methods exhibit different advantages and disadvantages. For example, the head used for the BJ method can be mass-produced through an etching process similar to the production process of semiconductors. Thus the cost per head is low. However, the use of heat limits the number of ink types that can be used for the BJ method. On the other hand, the head used for the MJ method must be produced mechanically leading to a higher cost per unit than for the BJ head. However, the mechanical extraction of ink by the MJ method allows for a greater variety of ink types to be used and for better ink control which is advantageous in printing super-high-resolution color images such as photographs.

New Product Introduction Race

In this section we look at the history of ink jet printers from the inception of the market and the new product introduction competition along the technology curve. We use mainly the discussion set forth by Masaya Miyazaki (2002). This is the most detailed and exhaustive paper about ink jet printer among numerous other papers and case studies (Yoneyama 1996; Miyazaki 1999, 2001; Fujiwara 2002).

Canon BJ-10v

Product development of ink jet printers for PCs began around 1980 when Seiko Epson's dot impact printer dominated both the overseas and the domestic markets. The early versions of ink jet printers were selling as "a quiet replacement" for dot impact printers. Until 1990 it was a product for a niche market. It was the Canon BJ-10v that broke out of this positioning to create a new market segment for ink jet printers. It was revolutionary in that it aimed at the personal market segment that had been served by dot impact and thermoelectric printers before. Over 4 million units of the BJ-10v were sold, which became the funding source that kick started the ink jet printer business as an independent business unit.

The BJ-10v used the bubble jet head that had been deployed in the previous two models. Thus the revolutionary aspect resided outside of technology. The BJ-10v was an A4-size personal notebook printer that could be battery powered and carried around. It stood out prominently because the mainstream printer of that time was an A3-size dot impact printer. The super compact size was only achievable with Canon's own bubble jet head technology. Thus, the BJ-10v powerfully demonstrated the unique characteristics of the technology. Also, a cartridge head rather than a conventional permanent head brought about the maintenance-free feature that was required in the personal use market. The design that "the head is discarded when ink is finished" was an idea that was inherited from copiers.

Because the BJ-10v (Y74,800) was relatively inexpensive among printers, it was sold faster than it was made. It became the pioneer in "products for personal uses." Ink jet printers established the product concept – "a personal compact printer at a reasonable price." With the wave of the PC boom, ink jet printers adopted a key role in expanding the printer market in the family segment.

The development of ink jet printers prior to the BJ-10v was a part of the development of printing technology for the business market. Because mass quantity and high speed printing capabilities were critical and high reliability and flexibility were required, the body of a printer was large and the price tended to be high. Earlier ink jet printers were positioned as a step-down alternative for laser printers. On the other hand, the design priority of making the BJ-10v compact forced Canon to trim many of the features. There are two prominent examples. First, auto paper feed was omitted; manual paper feed only was available. Second, the complex recovery system and the ink supply pump that adjusted the ink discharge nozzle were omitted, and the revolutionary change happened – the nozzle head and ink tank became one disposable unit.

The change represented a downgrading of the ink jet printer concept from the traditional perspective that was shared by business users. Nonetheless, with the BJ-10v Canon monopolized the ink jet printer market for 3 years from 1991 to 1993.

Epson MJ Series

EP (Electric Printer) SON was the brand name of Seiko Epson's ink jet printers, which were introduced to the market, which was dominated by Canon in 1993. In this year, Epson introduced the MJ-500 and the MJ-1000 model.

Epson countered Canon with introductions of the low-price compact notebook thermoelectric printer AP-300 and the dot impact printer VP-300 in May 1991. Later Epson introduced another thermoelectric printer, the AP-700, which "realized the low running cost and printing speed equivalent to ink jet printers" and the dot impact printer VP-1100 that "realized the quietness equivalent to ink jet printers." However, with the existing technology Epson could not compete against Canon's BJ-10v.

Product development at Epson took a different direction from Canon's super compact ink jet technology. The reference point for Epson was the Hewlett-Packard desktop format ink jet printer, its so called DeskJet series. Having influenced by HP, Epson believed that its personal printers needed to have sufficient functions for desktop use. This position was promising for Epson, because it compensated the weaknesses of piezoelectric technology, large size and high cost, and took advantage of its strengths, the ease of ink control and flexible ink choice.

With this positioning in mind Epson developed a new ink jet head that was installed in the personal compact desktop printers MJ-500 and MJ-1000 in March 1993. Those two personal models were equipped with professional-level functionalities such as high printing speed and large ink capacity, which were superior to those of Canon's BJ-10v. Sales after the introduction went very well. New competitive elements were introduced to the ink jet printer market. Not only compactness but also more features and lower price stimulated the competition in the market.

To counter Epson's move Canon introduced a new series of BJ-desk printers in May 1993. It recognized the market need for mass printing and redesigned the BJ-10v model to be able to be placed vertically and use an auto feeder function. The market was moving toward favoring desktop printers.

MJ-700V2C

The colorization of computer displays and GUI compatible operating systems such as Windows 95 demanded personal printers to support colors. The focal point of printer competition became color. Canon introduced a business color printer BJC-820J (Y398,000) in 1992 and a personal color printer BJC-600J (Y120,000) in February 1994. Epson countered it by introducing its color ink jet printer MJ-700V2C (Y99,800) in June 1994.

With the introduction of the MJ-700V2C, Epson benchmarked against Canon BJC-600J. Its differentiation slogans were: "Our super high resolution is so close to photography," "Environmentally friendly long-lasting permanent head," and "Lower-than-competitor running cost." As a result, MJ-700V2C becomes an overnight success, surpassing BJC-600J. 240,000 units were shipped in 1994. It definitively set the future direction of the ink jet printer market toward achieving high-resolution color images.

The difference in the characteristics of the two ink jet technologies triggered the slogan, "Our super high resolution is so close to photography," with which Epson tried to differentiate its products from Canon products in terms of the resolution of printed image. While Canon's selling point was compactness, the strength of Epson's MJ technology was easy ink control. Since the BJ technology used heat to extract ink, it was tricky to control ink flow. In fact, Canon did not reach the 720 x 720 dpi (dots per inch) level of the MJ-700V2C without a smoothing treatment function[1] until February 1996 with the introduction of the BJC-610W.

Subsequently, Canon continued improving image resolution by using higher density head material and enhancing color ink material. In 1997, ahead of Epson, Canon introduced a high-resolution printer that was capable of 1200 x 600 dpi. This model employed water-resistant reinforcement that allowed the printer to print clear images on plain paper. Epson, on the other hand, introduced the high-resolution Photo Mach Jet (PM) printer with a resolution of 1440 x 720 dpi in February 1997.

---

[1] The smoothing treatment makes the appearance of curved lines smoother at a given resolution level by controlling the timing of ink ejection according to the distance between ink droplets. Although different companies use different names, the basic technology is identical.

Low-Priced Models

Another trend in the ink jet printer market, besides colorization and achievement of higher quality images, was price reduction. When PC sales were growing at a rate of more than 50% and many families began buying PCs during 1994-95, low-price color printer users also grew rapidly. Many of the general users in Japan used printers for their PCs, because they wanted to print New Year's greeting cards. Color printers became replacements for conventional thermoelectric printers for word-processing. To meet the market needs Epson and Canon strove to improve print quality and reduce the product price for both monochrome and color printers.

Epson spearheaded the price reduction of its color printer product line in May 1995 with the MJ-500C (Y49,800). It was a large step in price reduction because none of the previous color printers was sold below Y60,000. In November of the same year Canon followed suit by introducing its BJC-210J at a price of Y29,800, the lowest price in the industry. In 1995, Epson took the first place in market share, however, Canon took it back in 1996. Canon's comeback was believed to be due to the superior cost-performance of its products.

In the above review of the ink jet printer market from the inception to the end of the 1990s based on Miyazaki's study (2002), we have learned about milestone products. In short, during this brief period there were several shifts in competitive dimensions. The first phase was Canon's domination with "portability" being the key competitive dimension. The second phase was characterized by Epson's resurgence with its focus on "functionality". The last phase was the competition of "super high resolution" when Epson insisted on its technical superiority. It is also important to recognize that "price reduction" was an invariable competitive dimension during the entire period.

Comparison of Running Costs

As we mentioned earlier, Canon realized high profitability in its copier business. This strategy is not limited to the copier business. A similar strategy is seen in the ink jet printer business, as well.

Table 1 compares the running cost[2] of ink jet printers of both Canon and Epson during the 1990s. Three pairs of representative models are picked up for the comparison. There are two major observations[3]. First, in the early half of the 1990s the

---

[2]   The publicly available company data, which are used to calculate running costs, are specifically the price of replacement cartridges and the number of pages that one cartridge can print. Each manufacturer can estimate average ink consumption per one A4 sheet because ink jet printers can regulate ink flow as precise as to the quantity of each ink drop. Manufacturers, in order to control running cost to some extent, deliberately design the price and capacity of each cartridge. In other words, running cost is loaded with strategic intents and not simply a passive outcome of technical considerations.

[3]   In the following sections all information, which is used in discussing potential profitability, is obtained mainly from publicly available data on the corporate websites of the

running costs of Canon printers were higher than those of Epson (Row 1 and 2). It is suspected that Canon was aiming for high profitability through consumables as it did in the copier business. Second, Canon's high running costs were adjusted in the latter half of the 1990s, reversing the cost position against Epson (Row 3). This shift is verified in our comprehensive analysis of running cost comparisons with more models and data points (see Appendix 1 for details).

Table 1. Historical running cost comparison of ink jet printers

Year	Canon		Epson	
	Model	Running cost	Model	Running cost
1. Personal use competition in 1993	BJ-10v Lite	Y6.0 (B/W)	MJ-500	Y3.2 (B/W)
2. Early color competition in 1994	BJC-600J	Y18.1 (Color)	MJ-700V2C	Y7.6 (Color)
3. Year-end sales competition in 1998	BJ-F600	Y1.0 (B/W) Y11.2 (6 colors)	PM-770C	Y2.8 (B/W) Y14.0 (Color)

Source: Appendix 1. The cost of paper is excluded.

It is, therefore, premature to conclude that Canon sold the body of its printers at a low price and made all profits from consumables. The facts were not that simple. In the first half of the 1990s Canon's average running cost was clearly high, as was reported correctly in previous studies (Miyazaki 1999, 2002; Fujiwara 2002). There were two main reasons. One was the difference in head design. While Epson printers used a permanent head with consumable ink, the printing head and ink were in one disposable cartridge in Canon printers. Another obvious reason was Canon's strategic intent for profiting from the consumables business.

In the first half of the 1990s at Canon it may have been the intentional emphasis of product development during the design and engineering phase to maximize the strategic focus – the after-sales demand for consumable exchange parts. The difference in head technology mentioned above must not have been a technological issue alone; it must have reflected the business strategy of that time. However, there was a downside – incurring high running costs. Canon started to feel the heat from rival competitors and the threat of third parties who could erode the profitable consumables business. What was the response of Canon to this pressure? As the following time-series analysis indicates, Canon began to tweak added value between the body and cartridge of the printer, to reduce running costs and profitability from consumables, or to add separate attractive features to the product in order to control the ability to gain profits. It was a translation of the change in the competitive dimension of the market into the change in product design.

---

manufacturers. Missing information is supplemented from various sources. The obtained information is summarized in Appendix 1. All the tables and figure in the paper are based on the Appendix.

Product Architecture and Appropriability

In this section the evolution of ink jet printer products in the market is discussed from a product architecture perspective. The architecture of the product is the scheme by which the function of the product is allocated to its physical components (Ulrich 1995; Baldwin and Clark 2000). Our objective is to discover the relationship between product architecture and appropriability of innovations. Although the running cost comparison above is cross sectional at certain points in time, the following analysis is dynamic.

Previous studies about printers indicate that modular architecture cuts lead time, is able to produce diverse products at lower costs, and is suitable for recycling (Davis and Sasser 1995; Ishii 1998; Kiyama 2000). Our study is, instead, interested in how corporations try to control profitability by choosing a specific product architecture in a specific competitive environment.

As mentioned earlier, in the ink jet printer market, competitive dimensions evolved from portability to sufficient functionalities for desktop use, to colorization, and to high print resolution. Also, price reduction was a common competitive dimension throughout the decade. When we discuss appropriability, it is essential to consider the relationship between competitive dimensions in the market and products, as well as the interrelationships among competitive products. In the section that follows, we focus on the analysis of Canon, which we supplement with the analysis of Epson.

Portability

Canon introduced the idea of portability to the market as a competitive dimension with its revolutionary BJ-10v printer. This was path breaking, but the head used in this product was already installed in two of the previous models and was not particularly developed for the BJ-10v. From the business user's perspective, the BJ-10v was a functionally inferior product because several functionalities, such as auto paper feed that handled a large quantity of paper, were eliminated to make it portable. The reason why the BJ-10v was so revolutionary was its product architecture. Its head was "disposable when ink is used up." The architecture realized a maintenance-free printer for personal use and miniaturized it by eliminating the complex structure of a supply pump and recovery system. Furthermore, in terms of appropriability of innovation, the BJ-10v introduced something new.

Prior to the introduction of the BJ-10v in 1990, the BJ-80, a printer for PCs, which used the BJ technology, had been introduced in 1985. The durability problem of the head caused a temporary production stoppage. However, production resumed after the head was improved to be lasting permanently and reliability was assured. In other words, Canon's head technology at that time was able to produce sufficiently durable heads, and it was the same head technology that Canon used for its BJ-10v. However, the company dared to categorize the head of its BJ-10v as consumable in order to realize the revolutionary product concept – a compact notebook printer.

The architecture of the BJ-10v was characterized by expanded replacement modules, which consequently necessitated the high added value of the replacement parts. Thus, the change in product architecture enabled revolutionary portability as well as high value-added replacement parts.

The result was reflected in the running costs of the printer. Table 2 contrasts the BJ-10v against Canon's non-notebook printer BJ-130J, which was introduced prior to the BJ-10v in February 1989. The running cost of Y6 of the BJ-10v was higher than Y3 of the BJ-130J despite the fact that the BJ-10v was introduced after the BJ-130J. As the icons indicate, the architectural change in the replacement cartridge caused the increase.

In sum, by increasing the added value of replacement parts, which users repetitively purchase, Canon was able to expand the post-sales profitability. The focus of profit gaining shifted away from the point of sales to the period when products were in use. It is supposed that the profitability shift positively contributed to the overall profitability of BJ-10v and to the Corporation.

Table 2. Evolution of Canon products: portability

Model name (launching date)	BJ-130J (2/89)	BJ-10v (10/90)
Price, body only (Y)	Y198,000	Y74,800
Resolution (dpi)	360 x 360	360 x 360
Print speed (char/sec)	148(kanji characters)	83
Running cost (Y)	Y3	Y6
Replacement cartridge style	No head, black ink	All-in-one head, black ink

Source: Appendix 1 and 2.

Sufficient Functionalities for Desktop Use

What are sufficient functionalities for desktop use? The pioneer that posed this competitive dimension was Epson's MJ-500, introduced to the market in March 1993. It was equipped with practical business functions, such as the auto sheet feed mechanism and faster printing speed than the BJ-10 series, although the size was larger than the BJ-10 series.

Canon countered Epson with its BJ-desk series, specifically, with the BJ-220JS and the BJ-220JC introduced in June 1993. Printing speed was significantly improved. They were capable of printing 248 characters/second (in the alphanumeric kana mode), which was a major improvement from the 110 characters/second of the notebook printer BJ-10v Lite (February, 1993). However, they compromised portability as they aimed at the desktop market.

As the competitive dimension in the market shifted, the ability to profit changed as well. Table 3 contrasts the BJ-220JS/JC and the BJ-330J/300J business printers introduced in February 1991. It indicates that the printing speed and running cost of the 220JS/JC were downgraded from the earlier business models 330J/300J. In particular, running cost doubled from Y3 to Y6.

Table 3. Evolution of Canon products: functionality

Model name (launching date)	BJ-330J/300J (2/91)	BJ-220JS/JC (6/93)
Price – body only (Y)	330J: Y190,000 300J: Y140,000	JS: Y128,000 JC: Y98,000
Resolution (dpi)	360 x 360	360 x 360
Print speed (char/sec)	300	248
Running cost (Y)	Y3	Y6
Replacement cartridge style	No head, black ink	All-in-one head, black ink

Source: Appendix 1 and 2.

We have learned that by means of altering the product architecture to expand the range of replaceable parts and increasing the added value of replacement parts, Canon was able to extend the post-sales profitability of the BJ-10v. Nevertheless, models BJ-330J and BJ-300J, introduced around the same time, did not have a replaceable cartridge. In fact, all Canon business ink jet printers at that time used the head as a permanent component. On the other hand, the head of the BJ-220JS/JC was an all-in-one consumable, the same as that of the BJ-10v. Similar to the BJ-10v, the architecture of the BJ-220JS/JC supported a wider range of consumables, which ultimately caused high running costs and high added value of consumables. Thus, unlike previous business-purpose printers, the BJ-220JS and the BJ-220JC were designed to earn "exponential" profit from consumables. It was the business model that Canon used when it dominated the market.

The key target of the desktop printers BJ-220JS/JC was supposed to be personal use as that of notebook printers. For this reason, an all-in-one cartridge was employed to cut maintenance requirements. By doing so, profitability was also expected to increase.

Colorization

The pioneer of color in personal ink jet printers was Canon's BJC-600J with a 4-color ink tank introduced in February 1994. It was revolutionary because the BJC-600J made colorization a new competitive dimension in the market in which portability and functionalities for desktop use were two key competitive criteria.

Based on the competition in the market at that time, the introduction of the BJC-600J was contingent upon a steppingstone – Epson's MJ-500. From a financial perspective, the MJ-500 sacrificed profitability. It separated print head and ink cartridge. When the ink was used up, the ink cartridge alone was replaced. The conventional support and maintenance cost of Y7 per A4 page were reduced to Y3.2 (*Nikkei Sangyo Shinbun*, April 9, 1993). The outcome was dramatic. Epson began to regain market share in the ink jet printer market after 1993 in which Canon had dominated before.

Canon responded with its high-speed printers BJ-220JS/JC. In February of the following year Canon introduced the BJC-600J and further differentiated itself from Epson. It kept the printing speed of the BJ-220JS/JC, while it dramatically improved running cost as shown in Table 4. The running cost of Y2.3 in black was less than that of Epson's MJ-500 (Appendix 1).

Table 4. Evolution of Canon products: colorization

Model name (launching date)	BJ-220JS/JC (6/93)	BJC-600J (2/94)
Price - body only (Y)	JS: Y128,000 JC: Y98,000	Y120,000
Resolution (dpi)	360 x 360	360 x 360
Print Speed (char/sec)	248	240 (MAX)
Running Cost (Y)	Y6 (black)	Y2.3 (black) Y18.1 (color)
Replacement cartridge style	All-in-one head, black ink	No head, separate color ink

Source: Appendix 1 and 2.

The product architecture of the replacement parts was the key to this improvement of performance. Unlike the all-in-one cartridge used in the BJ-220JS/JC, the print head of the BJC-600J was permanent and only color ink tanks were replaceable (Refer to the icons in Table 4). This significantly improved running cost; on the other hand, it meant lowering of after-sales profitability.

The traditional Canon BJ Method allowed setting a lower price for the body of the printer because the printer head of the BJ printer could be mass-produced and made disposable. It was the major difference from Epson's MJ method. However, the printer body of the BJC-600J (Y120,000) was more expensive than products of other manufacturers. Colorization as well as the change in product architecture led to this price tag. The added value of the disposable cartridge was shifted to the body of the printer, resulting in lower running cost. However, the profitability from ongoing use of the printer declined, causing the overall profitability to decline.

This move by Canon was a direct response to the market trend at that time or precisely to Epson's strategy of low-running-cost products. This example confirms that Canon followed a clear strategy in knowingly reducing its consumables' profitability by changing product architecture in order to respond to market trends.

High Resolution (1)

Canon was first to develop a cutting edge color printer, the BJC-600J, but Epson made better use of the technology. Fundamentally, the MJ technology that controls the printer head electronically is said to be superior for color output because no heat is involved in manipulating ink output. Epson's personal full-color printer MJ-700V2C was introduced in June 1994. This product became the new benchmark for Canon's BJC-600J and claimed the following differentiation points: "Our super high resolution is so close to photography," "Environmentally friendly long-lasting permanent head" and "Lower-than-competitor running cost." Appendix 1 shows the performance superiority of the MJ-700V2C.

The introduction of the MJ-700V2C marked the threshold to the "super high print resolution era". However, Canon judged that there was no need for such a high resolution and took the strategy of responding to the heated price competition. Canon quickly reduced the price of its BJC-600J to Y98,000 and introduced another low-price model, the BJC-400J, in September 1994. The price of the body of Canon's BJC-400J was Y69,800, which was competitive among competitors' models. To respond to Epson's super high-resolution claim, Canon added a smoothing function to its 400J. This function allowed the 400J to achieve 720 x 360 dpi, compared to 360 x 360 dpi of 600J.

Besides the low price and matching high-resolution, no new elements were added to the BJC-400J. From the new product development perspective it was nothing special. However, it was a noteworthy model in terms of profitability. While the 600J used separate color ink tanks, the late comer 400J used two ink tanks: black and all-in-one color. The head of the 400J was disposable (Refer to the icon change in Table 5). Again, Canon was changing product architecture to increase the running cost as well as the profitability profile of its 400J.

Table 5. Evolution of Canon products: high resolution (1)

Model name (launching date)	BJC-600J (2/94)	BJC-400J (9/94)
Price - body only (Y)	Y120,000	Y69,800
Resolution (dpi)	360 x 360	720 x 360 (black) 360 x 360 (color)
Print speed (char/sec)	240 (MAX)	496 (MAX)
Running cost (Y)	Y2.3 (black) Y18.1 (color)	Y3.7 (black) Y24.6 (color)
Replacement cartridge style	No head, separate color ink	Separate head, all-in-one color

Source: Appendix 1 and 2.

Judging from Canon's emphasis on printing in black, we can suspect that the design of black and color cartridges may have aimed at increasing printing speed in black by increasing the number of nozzles for black ink. Alternatively, Canon may have wanted to effectively use the advantage of existing BJ technology – disposable heads – to counter the price competition. In either case, Canon was able to choose from different types of printer head architectures. In this case, Canon decided to reduce body price and increase value-added contents in exchange parts[4].

High Resolution (2)

The domestic ink jet printer market of the 1990s showed a shift away from Canon's monopoly. Epson gradually gained market share, and Canon lost its market share. The loss of market share has continued annually since 1992 with the exception of 1996. A typical reaction would have been to intend to recapture market share by introducing superior offers, such as better functionalities and lower prices. However, Canon did not abandon the effort to control the profitability profile by changing body prices and running costs, while it improved product performance. To better understand Canon's strategy at that time, let's look at the examples of the BJ-F600 and the subsequent model BJ-F200.

The BJ-F600 (Y54,800), which was introduced in November 1998, was the principal model for the 1998 Year-End Sales. The competing Epson model was

---

[4]   For example, the company catalog shows the retail prices of replacement parts, such as head/ink set (color) Y5,500, black ink tank Y800, color ink tank Y1,500, and all-in-one cartridge (black) Y3,300.

the PM-770C (Y59,800). The BJ-F600 was competitive with regard to the body price, featured lower running costs than the PM-770C, and offered the same resolution of 1440 x 720 dpi as the PM-770C, which was the best in the industry at that time. Despite the superior product attributes, fewer units of the BJ-F600 than of the PM-770C were sold during Year-End Sales of 1998.

In this hardship Canon added its BJ-F200 in March 1999. It was 35% smaller and 32% lighter than the BJC-430Lite and the complement model for the F600. The price was set low at Y34,800. It was most likely intended for "family photo-quality" application (*Nikkei Sangyo Shinbun*, November 8, 1998). The size of the F200 was obviously chosen with the family market in mind. A comparison with the F600 is shown in Table 6. The resolution of the F200 was reduced to 720 x 360 dpi although a new automatic function that analyzed and adjusted the color and the contrast of digital color photo images was added. Its running cost was higher than that of the F600 for both black and color ink.

It is suspected that the reduction of the body price was one of the major objectives during the transition from the F600 to the F200. The separate color ink tanks/heads in the F600 were simplified into all-in-one color and black ink tanks/heads (Refer to the icon change in Table 6).

The change in product architecture suggests that the intent was not only to reduce the price of a printer body but also to make sure that Canon prospered in that tough competitive market. Instead of emphasizing promotional activities to sell the superior quality F-600, Canon changed the product architecture, employing a technological product development solution, to attempt to maintain its profitability.

Table 6. Evolution of Canon products: high resolution (2)

Model name (launching date)	BJ-F600 (11/98)	BJ-F200 (3/99)
Price - body only (Y)	Y54,800	Y34,800
Resolution (dpi)	1,440 x 720	720 x 360
Running cost (Y)	Y1.0 (black) Y7.4 (4 colors) Y11.2 (6 colors)	Y3.7 (black) Y24.6 (color)
Replacement cartridge style	Separate head, separate color ink	Separate head, all-in-one color

Source: Appendix 1 and 2.

The Approach of Epson

We have examined the product architecture of Canon that centered on the exchange cartridge technology. What was the approach taken by Epson?

Epson succeeded to reduce running cost by separating ink tank and printer head for the first time in the MJ-500 model. This product architecture did not change during the 1990s. For this reason, there was nothing to observe in the relationship between the product architecture designed in the product development phase and the ability to control profitability. Recently, when Canon incorporated separate color ink tanks into its printers, Epson also employed this design choice. However, the approach taken by Epson was very different from the one Canon took. This contrast characterized those two manufacturers.

It was the end of 2001 when Epson introduced the top "Colorio" ("Stylus" in the U.S. market) model PM-950C, which was equipped with separate color ink tanks. Six separate color ink tanks were used, which improved the resolution to 2880 x 1440 dpi. This resolution was much better than the one of the previous PM-920C model. The PM-950C became the celebrated top product for photographic quality printing, which appropriately enhanced the reputation of Epson.

Table 7 compares the PM-920C and the PM-970C. Because no running cost information was available for the PM-950C from Epson data sources[5], the PM-970C was used in the comparison instead. The PM-970C was Epson's top product that replaced the PM-950C in 2002. It used the same ink tank modules and the same exchange mechanism as the PM-950C. The body price was the same as for the PM-950C as well. Thus, the PM-970C is an appropriate substitution for the PM-950C in this analysis.

Being able to replace different color ink cartridges separately gave the impression that the running cost of the PM-970C was lower than that of the PM-920C. However, the running cost of the PM-920C per A4 page using the high-quality color mode was Y30.7, and that of the PM-970C was slightly higher: Y32.1 (Table 7). This increase in running cost was even greater, because the figure used for the PM-970C was based on an L-size photo sheet (equivalent to A6), which is smaller than an A4 size sheet. In general, running cost improves when the cartridge becomes exchangeable by individual color. Nevertheless, in Epson's case it was the opposite.

Based on interviews with industry experts, we speculate that a large sum of development cost for improving its ink materials was behind this unusual phenomenon. After the introduction of its 920C Epson took a tremendous step to improve ink materials to achieve dramatic print resolution. It is speculated that, to avoid a rapid increase in running cost due to this development, the company separated each color in a separate cartridge.

---

[5]   Traditionally Seiko Epson had been outspoken about competitive benchmarking of running costs. For its 950C, however, we suspect that the company played it down.

Table 7. Evolution of Epson products (an example)

Model name (launching date)	PM-920C (6/01)	PM-970C (10/02)
Price - body only (Y)	Y64,800	Y59,800
Resolution (dpi)	1,440 x 720	2,880 x 2,880
Running cost (Y)	Y30.7 (color)	Y32.1 (color, L-size photo sheet)
Replacement cartridge style		
	No head, all-in-one color	No head, separate color ink

Source: Appendix 1 and 2.

The approaches of Canon and Epson were fundamentally different. Canon intended to modify product architecture to install added value on consumable exchange cartridges. On the other hand, Epson intended to improve individual technical elements to enhance the attractiveness of its products and to profit from sales volume.

Controlling the Ability to Profit

The above examples illustrate that by understanding the competitive environment and its relationship with competitors Canon introduced products to the market that met consumer needs by skillfully manipulating product architecture. It was an approach that translated competitive dimensions in the market into architectural changes in products. Its approach enabled Canon to flexibly shift added value between the body of the printer and exchange cartridges, so that the company was able to control its ability to profit while it kept its competitiveness in the market.

Canon's decisions whether or not the added value should reside in the body of printer or in its innovative cartridges are summarized in Figure 1, along with a comparison of Epson's evolution[6]. A full explanation of the icons in this figure is given in Appendix 2. The Figure shows that the running cost of Canon does not illustrate a consistent trend, showing irregular ups and downs over time. This is different from the running cost of Epson's printers, which gradually increased. The irregularity in Canon's running cost was the result of the manipulation of product

---

[6]   In order to consistently display the data over a long time span, the vertical axis for Canon represents printing in black and white and for Epson printing in color. Even if the values of Canon's color printers were plotted, the up-and-down movement in Figure 1 would be the same. For clearer illustration the vertical axis is logarithmically transformed.

architecture to control the added value content of cartridges or running cost. The case of Canon shows how the selection of product architecture can determine a company's profitability profile, so that it is able to meet the competitive conditions in its market at a certain point of time.

In contrast to Canon's approach, Epson tried to enhance the product's added value by innovation of technical elements. The two manufacturers' approaches are quite different, and it is impossible to say that one of the two is always superior. It is important, however, to be able to change product architecture based on a given competitive situation and to be able to shift added value within a product because the ability to shift added value could become a key control factor for overall business profitability.

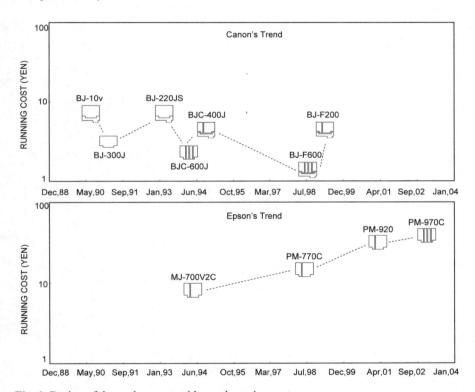

Fig. 1. Design of the exchange cartridge and running cost

Concluding Remarks

This case study of Canon suggests that it is possible to design a company's profitability profile by maneuvering product development. Reaping profits from new products not only involves marketing and sales issues but also engineering and design issues during the development phase. In other words, engineers and designers can control the profitability of each product by designing a specific architecture of the product.

Finally, there are many limitations to this paper. The single case study in the domestic market is just one example. However, this study suggests that Canon's efforts to achieve high appropriability have a historical background and that the resulting cartridge technology of copiers and the flexible change in the product architecture of its ink jet printers both are unique to the company. Designing product architecture for high appropriability is the key to the success.

Appendix 1: The List of Product Specifications

Model	Launching	Body price (Y)		Resolution (dpi)	Print speed (char/sec)	Running cost (Y)[a]
BJ-130J	2/1989	Y198,000	Black	360 x 360[b]	148 (kanji)	Y3.0
BJ-10v	10/1990	Y74,800	Black	360 x 360	83	Y6.0
BJ-330J/ 300J	2/1991	330J: Y190,000 300J: Y140,000	Black	360 x 360	300	Y3.0
BJ-10v Lite	2/1993	Y69,800	Black	NA	110	Y6.0
MJ-500	3/1993	Y74,800	Black	360 x 360	NA	Y3.2
BJ-220JS/JC	6/1993	JS : Y128,000 JC: Y98,000	Black	360 x 360	248	Y6.0
BJC-600J	2/1994	Y120,000	Black Color	360 x 360	240 (max) NA	Y2.3 Y18.1
MJ-700V2C	6/1994	Y99,800	Black Color	720 x 720	NA	Y1.8 Y7.6
BJC-400J	9/1994	Y69,800	Black Color	720 x 360 360 x 360	496 (max) NA	Y3.7 Y24.6
PM-770C	10/1998	Y59,800	Black Color	1440 x 720	NA	Y2.8 Y14.0
BJ-F600	11/1998	Y54,800	Black Color	1440 x 720	NA	Y1.0 4-color: Y7.4 6-color: Y11.2
BJ-F200	3/1999	Y34,800	Black Color	720 x 360	NA	Y3.7 Y24.6
PM-920C	6/2001	Y64,800	Black Color	1440 x 720	NA	NA Y30.7
PM-970C	10/2002	Y59,800	Black Color	2880 x 2880	NA	NA Y32.1 L-size photo sheet

Note: Shaded rows represent Epson, and clear rows represent Canon. Information was compiled using company supplied data supplemented with publicly available information.
[a]   The running cost for the MJ-500 is from *Nikkei Sangyo Shinbun* on April 9, 1993. The running cost for the BJ-220JS/JC is estimated to be Y6 based on other models in the same series that use the same cartridge. All other running cost information is from the corporate website of each company.
[b]   This value is taken from Miyazaki (1999).

Appendix 2: The Icons' List of Exchange Cartridge

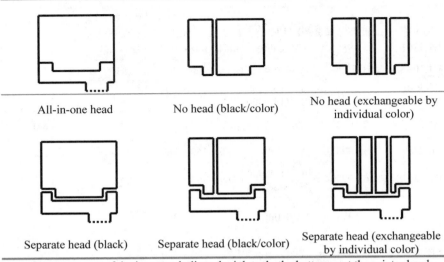

| All-in-one head | No head (black/color) | No head (exchangeable by individual color) |

| Separate head (black) | Separate head (black/color) | Separate head (exchangeable by individual color) |

Note: The upper part of the icon symbolizes the ink tank, the bottom part the printer head. "All-in-one" indicates an exchange module that integrates head and ink tank in one unit. "Separate head" indicates an exchange module where either head or ink tank is sold separately or only the ink tank is sold. "No head" means that the head is not exchangeable. "Color" indicates that all colors are in one replacement cartridge. "Individual color" indicates that individual color cartridges may be replaced independently from each other.

References

Baldwin CY and Clark KB (2000): *Design Rules: the Power of Modularity*, The MIT Press

Cohen WM, Goto A, Nagata A, Nelson RR, and Walsh JP (2002): "R&D spillovers, patents and the incentives to innovate in Japan and the United States," *Research Policy*, Vol. 31, pp. 1349-1367

Davis T and Sasser M (1995): "Postponing product differentiation," *Mechanical Engineering*, Vol. 117 Issue 11, pp. 105-107

Fujiwara M (2002): "Seiko Epson: Printer Jigyo no Gijutsu Senryaku," *Hitotsubashi Business Review,* Vol.50, No. 2, pp. 148-163

Goto A and Nagata A (1997): "Innovation no Senyukanosei to Gijutsukikai," *NISTEP REPORT*, No.48, National Institute of Science and Technology Policy

Ishii K (1998): "Tsukuriyasui Sekkei, Kowashiyasui Sekkei," *Journal of Japan Society of Mechanical Engineers*, Vol. 101, No. 954, pp. 32-34

Kiyama T (2000): "Recycle Jidai no Kigyo Senryaku Ron," *Gekkan Keiei Kanri*, Japan Institute of Management and Administration, No.492, pp. 4-17

Klevorick AK, Levin RC, Nelson RR, and Winter SG (1995): "On the sources and significance of interindustry differences in technological opportunities," *Research Policy*, Vol. 24, pp. 185-205

Levin RC, Klevorick AK, Nelson RR, and Winter SG (1987): "Appropriating the Returns from Industrial Research and Development," *Brookings Papers on Economic Activity*, Vol. 3, pp. 783-831

Miyazaki M (1999): "Canon Kabushiki Gaisha: Ink jet Printer no Kaihatsu," *Keiei Academy Case, Japan Productivity Center for Socio-Economic Development,* Case No. 38

Miyazaki M (2001): "Naiyo Bunseki no Kigyo Kodo Kenkyu eno Oyo," *Soshiki Kagaku*, Vol. 35, No. 2, pp. 114-127

Miyazaki M (2002): "Ink jet Printer Gyokai no Hattenkatei 1977-1997: Canon to Seiko Epson no 20 Nen," *Akamon Management Review*, Vol. 1, No. 2, pp. 159-198

Okubo A (1999): "Kodo Gijutsu no Senryakuteki Kanri (Zoho): Gijutsu wo Ikasu Keiei Senryaku," *Nikkei Business Publications, Inc.*

Takahashi K and Irie M (1999): "Printer Zairyo no Kaihatsu", *CMC*

Teece DJ (1986): "Profiting from Technological Innovation: Implications for Integration, Collaboration, Licensing and Public Policy," *Research Policy*, Vol. 15, pp. 285-306.

Ulrich K (1995): "The Role of Product Architecture in the Manufacturing Firm," *Research Policy*, Vol. 24, pp. 419-440.

von Hippel E (1990): "Task Partitioning: An Innovation Process Variable," *Research Policy*, Vol. 19, pp. 407-418.

Yoneyama S (1996): "Jizokuteki Kyosoyui no Gensen toshiteno Henkaku Noryoku: Canon niokeru Printer Gijutsu Kaihatsu no Jirei Bunseki," *Seinan Gakuin Daigaku Shougakuron Shu*, Vol. 43, No. 1, pp. 105-168.

Case Study Shimano: Market Creation Through Component Integration[*]

Akira Takeishi and Yaichi Aoshima

Clerk:	Hi. How can I help you?
Customer:	My kid wants a mountain bike. Which one is good?
Clerk:	Well, right now I recommend one of these. This one is made in Japan, and this one is made in Taiwan.
Customer:	Made in Taiwan?
Clerk:	Well, it IS a Shimano.

Introduction

We sometimes observe that while an entire industry may be in recession, some companies continue to perform well. Shimano, a bicycle parts manufacturer, is such a company.

The bicycle manufacturing industry has recently been in a structural recession. Imports accounted for 30% of the domestic market in 1997 and 67% in 2001, with over 7 million of the 11 million bicycles sold in Japan being imported (Figure 1). The average price of bicycles commonly seen around town and often called

[*] The main information sources of this case include: Interviews with Masahiro Tsuzaki, Manager of Marketing Department, Engineering Division, Shimano Inc., and Masahiko Jimbo, Manager of the same department (January 25, 2001, October 25, 2001, and March 5, 2001). Interview with Hiroshi Nakamura, Cycle Development Center (January 25, 2001). Speech delivered by Yoshizo Shimano, CEO of Shimano Inc. at a seminar held by the Ministry for Economics, Trade and Industry (June 27, 2001). Shimano Inc. 80-Year -History-Editing Committee, *80 Years of Shimano 1921-2000: Toward a New Future*, March 2001. Shimano Product Catalog. "Shimano Machikoujouteki na Jiyuu ga Katsuryoku, Jitennsha Buhin de Sekaiseiha (Shimano's Active Power like Small Workshops: World Domination in Bicycle Parts)" (In Japanese) *Nikkei Business*, November 2, 1998, pp. 54-56. "Shimano Koukyyuu Jitensha buhin de Toppu, Puro mo Aiyou shi Kouseiseki Renpatsu (Shimano is Top in Quality Bicycle Parts, Continued Success as Professionals become Regular Users)" (in Japanese) *Nikkei Business* February 21, 1998, pp. 39-41. We would particularly like to extend our gratitude to Mr. Tsuzaki and Mr. Jimbo, who cooperated with three interviews and explained everything from the basics, in addition to providing a variety of materials. This case was originally written in Japanese in 2002 and appeared on *Hitotsubashi Business Review*, 50 (1), 2002, pp. 158-177. English translation was financially supported by "The 21st Century COE Program on Knowledge, Corporate System, and Innovation" at Hitotsubashi University. All responsibility for the content of this case lies with the authors.

"granny bikes" is around 20,000 Yen for domestically manufactured models and around 10,000 Yen for imported bikes from South East Asia and China. The difference is clear. Domestic production of bicycles has continued to decline and there has remained no vestige that Japan once shined as the production base for the world bicycle market. Yet, Shimano has managed to maintain an overwhelming share in the world market for bicycle parts, such as derailleurs, shift levers, and brakes. Shimano's brand value is ranked high among Japanese firms. According to the Nihon Keizai Shimbun's brand score, Shimano is ranked 20th in Japan (2001). Companies with the same rank include large firms like Hitachi, Sharp, Denso, Fanuc, and HOYA.[1]

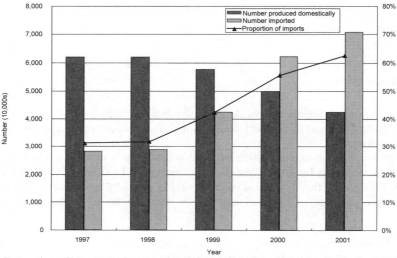

Note: Proportion of imported bicycles (percent) = the number of imported bicycles / (the number of bicycles produced and shipped domestically + the number of imported bicycles). The number of exported bicycles is negligible. Source: Japan Bicycle Association

Fig. 1. Bicycle production and imports in Japan

Bicycle fans proudly say "I have Dura-Ace". Dura-Ace is the brand name of the series of parts Shimano sells for sporting bicycles. As previously mentioned, the use of Shimano parts matters more for customers than who assembled the bicycle. Major bicycle manufacturers cannot even start product development before Shimano announces a new product plan. Intel's former CEO Andrew Grove was reportedly amused to hear that Shimano was called "the Intel of the bicycle industry."

The recent performance of Shimano has suffered somewhat due to setbacks in American and European sales, but its financial performance is far better than oth-

---

[1]   *Nihon Sangyo Shimbun,* February 14, 2001

ers in the industry. How did Shimano reach its present position from its humble start as a small, specialized, pre-World War II bicycle parts manufacturer? What factors separated Shimano from other manufacturers in the bicycle industry?

Outline and History of Shimano Bicycle Component Business

Company Profile

Shimano, with its head office in Sakai, Osaka, manufactures and sells bicycle components, fishing tackle, and cold-forged products. It has approximately 5,500 employees worldwide, with about 1,000 working in Japan. Its sales on a consolidated base in 2001 (Jan. to Dec. 2001) were 125 billion Yen, with profits of 12.7 billion Yen, making it a highly profitable company with operating profit on sales of 10.1%. (Figure 2).

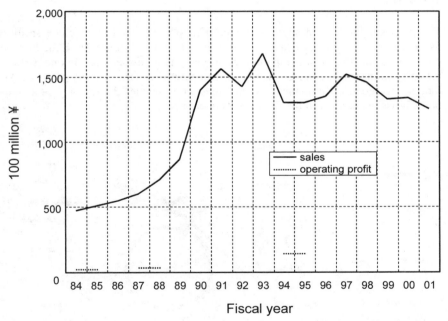

Note: 1983~1999 use November terms (for example, fiscal year 1984 is considered to be December 1983~November 1984). Fiscal year 2000 is the 13 months from December 1999 to December 2000 adjusted (12/13) to 12 months. Fiscal year 2001 is January to December. Source: Shimano Financial Reports

Fig. 2. Shimano's sales and operating profit (consolidated base)

The Bicycle Components Division makes up 68% of sales, and the Fishing Tackle Division accounts for approximately 30%. In addition to these, Shimano produces differential gears for automobiles, snowboards and, more recently, golf clubs. The common theme throughout Shimano's business is to provide leisure equipment used for outdoor activities based on cold-forged technology.

On a consolidated base, overseas sales accounted for 75% and 90% of bicycle parts sales in 2001. The overseas production ratio was 33%. Shimano has a main overseas production base in Singapore, and other factories in Malaysia, Indonesia, China, and Italy. Sales offices are located throughout the world in America, Europe and Asia. Bicycle parts take many paths in their outflow, but the final distribution is 51% in Europe, 26% in North America, 14% in Japan, and the remainder in other areas.

Shimano's Position in Bicycle Parts – "The Intel of the Bicycle Industry"

The parts supplied by Shimano's Bicycle Components Division include shifting (or transmission) systems, brakes, front gears, and hubs. (Figure 3). In the bicycle component industry most companies traditionally tend to specialize in one particular part. Shimano, in contrast, handles a comparatively large variety of parts. Although the scope of Shimano's technologies well matches that of bicycle assemblers, it has never entered the finished product business.

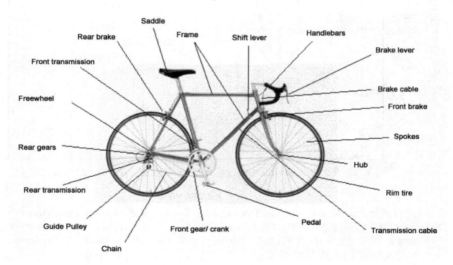

Fig. 3. Major parts of a bicycle (conventional road bike)

In general, the bicycle market consists of four segments.

1. **Road**: Sports bicycles used in professional road races such as the Tour de France. The highest level of performance in gearshift, brake and drive power, and the lightest weight are required in this market.
2. **Mountain Bike (MTB)**: Bicycles for riding off-road through mountains and mud. Toughness and lightweight are required.
3. **Comfort**: A segment centered in Europe. Bicycles for enjoying cycling with the family. Comfort and stable operation are important.
4. **City**: Commuter bicycles used for going to school or work. An inexpensive price is most important; the "granny bike" previously mentioned falls under this segment.

It is estimated that about 95 million bicycles were sold worldwide in 2001. Of this, the road market for racing bicycles was about 1 million and the professional mountain bike market for bicycles such as those used in off-road races was also around 1 million.[2] There is also a market on the fringe of the "serious" mountain bike market for a broader definition of mountain bikes that are used for more general purposes. For example, if we include all the mountain bikes ordered through specialized bicycle shops called IBDs (Individual Bicycle Dealer), the market reaches 6 or 7 million, and if we include all the mountain bike look-alikes that are commonly sold, this figure further increases to 20 million. Bicycles other than these two segments fall under the category of comfort or city.[3] Approximately 40% of the whole market is for bicycles with shifting gears, with 70% of these being external gears and 30% internal gears.[4]

Shimano provides components for all segments from (1) to (4). Shimano is most competitive in the field of bicycles with shifting gears, and has created a strong brand and commanded a high market share in segments (1) and (2).[5] However, Shimano also has maintained a steady income in the high-volume city bicycle market, although the margin is not high. While Japanese companies are having

[2]   The mountain bikes referred to here are racing bikes with at least nine gears.
[3]   Comfort is a segment that does not exist in Japan. It is an important market in Europe, accounting for 25% of the total market in Germany for example. In Europe, the definition of city and comfort is vague, and there is a possibility that the very concept of comfort may change in the future. In America, mountain bikes are used for normal cycling and commuting. The boundaries between the mountain bike market and the comfort/city markets have thus become unclear.
[4]   Internal gears are a type that contains a gearbox on the hub axle. The gearbox stays inside so it is compact and maintenance free, but the number of gears is limited and multiple layering is difficult. The gear ratio cannot be freely changed. External types can be found in (1) to (3) and internal types in (3). (4) does not usually use gears of any kind (single speed), although recently some have gears.
[5]   Accurate data on the market for bicycles and bicycle parts are not available. Shimano's share is also not available. In general terms, it is told that Shimano has an overwhelming share that is substantially higher than the second largest. *Nikkei Business* reported that Shimano "has a 70% share in the shift-gears and brake markets, which require the highest level of technologies." (November 2, 1998)

trouble with overseas competition in this segment, Shimano parts are used in bicycles imported from China.

Campagnolo is a long-standing Italian company that has a strong position in the market for parts for road race bicycles, but Shimano's position is even stronger. For example, in the road race of the 1996 Atlanta Olympics, the bicycles of riders up to the twelfth place all had Shimano gears and brakes. Lance Armstrong, who won the Tour de France for 3 consecutive years, also rode bicycles using Shimano components. Bikes with Shimano components have also swept almost all major mountain bike races including the World Championships. This can be likened to sweeping all the top positions of both the Formula-1 championships and the Paris-Dakar rally.

With its overwhelming share and brand power that surpasses that of bicycle assemblers, Shimano is often called "the Intel of the bicycle industry". This is a good comparison in that the bicycle industry and the personal computer industry have many characteristics in common. Both bicycles and personal computers can be made into finished products from parts bought from a variety of companies. You can see this if you go to a nearby bicycle store. Of course, there are pre-made road race bikes and mountain bikes, but it is also possible to make an original bike that suits your needs and preferences by ordering parts from a catalogue. This is the same as making a PC out of parts bought in Tokyo's Akihabara or from the Internet. This is possible because the function of each part is well defined and interfaces and performance measures are commonly shared by the industry. Systems with these characteristics are said to have "open, modular architecture." This in contrast cannot be done with cars or motorcycles, which have closed, integral architecture.[6]

The reason why many manufacturers specialize in a particular part is that industry standards have been established and it is difficult for final assemblers to take control at their own discretion, while at the same time companies can specialize in a particular part and sell their products worldwide as long as they adhere to the industry standards. We can observe a similar picture in the personal computer industry, where companies are specialized in hard disks, monitors, application software, operating systems, microprocessors, printers and other various peripherals.

Under these circumstances, Shimano has built an overwhelming worldwide share in gears and brakes, which are key parts of a bicycle. This is the reason why

---

[6]   See, for example, Richard. N. Langlois and Paul L. Robertson, "Networks and Innovation in a Modular System: Lessons from the Microcomputer and Stereo Component Industries," *Research Policy* 21 (2001): 297-313; Carliss Y. Baldwin and Kim B. Clark, *Design Rules: The Power of Modularity* (MIT Press 2000); and Takahiro Fujimoto, Akira Takeishi, and Yaichi Aoshima (eds.), *Business Architecture: Strategic Design of Products, Organizations and Processes* (in Japanese) (Yuhikaku 2001). Systems are made up of relatively independent parts and the interaction between these parts has established rules (modular). These rules are shared widely throughout society (open). Bicycles, PCs, and audio systems are examples of open modular systems.

Shimano is being compared with Intel, which has an overwhelming share in the market for microprocessors, which are the heart of a personal computer.

History

Shimano was founded in 1921. The founder, Shozaburo Shimano, who was a craftsman at an ironworks in Sakai, was only 28 years old. At that time, Sakai was the center of Japan's bicycle industry. This town, with a tradition of blacksmiths and known for kitchen knives and guns since the 16th century, shifted its industry to the manufacture of bicycle parts and finished bicycles in the Meiji Period. The first product manufactured by the "Shimano Iron Works" was a single freewheel. Anyone who has ridden a bike knows that the rear wheel turns when you pedal, but the wheel does not stop when you stop pedaling. This function is made possible by the use of a ratchet mechanism attached to the freewheel on the rear wheel. Shimano continues to make freewheels even today.

In its history of more than 89 years, there have been a number of occasions that can be seen as major turning points for Shimano. One of these was around 1960 with the arrival of the boom for light motorbikes and mopeds (motorbikes with pedals). Many bicycle and bicycle component manufacturers entered the moped business, but Shimano remained a bicycle component specialist. The decision was made after some consideration, based on the outlook that the quality bicycle market that was present in Europe at the time would eventually emerge in Japan. The fact that Shimano did not even enter bicycle assembly was a result of a consistent policy that the company had maintained for many years.

The next important event was the expansion overseas. Shimano entered the American market in the 1960s and Europe in the 1970s by establishing local sales companies. This was extremely adventurous for a small local company like Shimano, but this led to global expansion in later years. Furthermore, Shimano started local production in Singapore in 1973. This was an early move toward overseas production among Japanese companies. The Singapore plan has been evolved to become a core base for Shimano's global production system.

Shimano's policy of limiting itself to the bicycle component business, and daringly expanding overseas in this area established the foundation for the later expansion of Shimano. However, the most important factor in building Shimano's present position was the introduction of a series of new products since the 1970s. This includes the introductions of the Dura-Ace Series in 1973, the Shimano Index System in 1984, the New Deore XT Series for mountain bikes in 1986, and the Shimano Total Integration in 1989.

History of Product Innovation

Dura-Ace Series

In 1973, Shimano introduced the Dura-Ace Series for road race bicycles. It took the approach of selling freewheels, derailleurs, brakes, and cranks as a set. This step was taken to respond to the Bikology boom both inside and outside Japan and raise the low recognition in Europe as Shimano expanded into that region after the United States.

They began to provide parts as a "set menu" rather than selling them individually. Products were lined up with sets of parts divided by grade, and their design was unified to make them more attractive. Shimano learned this method from Campagnolo, an Italian parts manufacturer that had established a strong position in the road bike market at the time. Campagnolo devised the original shifting gear system for racing bicycles and was famous for supporting the history of bicycle road racing. The competition was tough for Shimano and its products were not initially well-received. Nevertheless, Shimano slowly penetrated the European market, through intense effort, sponsoring pro teams and gradually building up track records in road racing.

Most critical for the subsequent success of Shimano was that a "system component philosophy" was established in Shimano during 1975 based on the experience of Dura-Ace. It is the philosophy that bicycles are not just a grouping of parts, but represent a collection of inter-functioning components. This is still alive today as Shimano's fundamental development philosophy. Around this time, Shimano expanded its development activities to areas other than shifting systems, such as drive and brake systems, and increasing emphasis was put on functions and performance as a total system that combines these parts, rather than improvement of individual parts. About 10 years later, a great success would bloom from this development philosophy: the Shimano Index System.

Shimano Index System

The Shimano Index System (SIS) was released as part of the Dura-Ace Series in 1984. SIS is a gearshift system comprising of a shift lever, derailleur, and cables.

The conventional shifting system until then was called friction type, using a friction clutch tightened with screws and a shift lever to make fine adjustments, where the lever is shifted in "analogue" fashion. The derailleur, on the other hand, uses a pantograph structure, and guide pulley moves to shift the gear in parallel. On a five-speed bike, for example, the chain moves across five gears layered at approximately 5mm intervals, where gears are changed in "digital" fashion. In other words, this was a shifting system that relied on the rider's skill to use an analog lever to manage digital gears. The rider determines whether the gear has entered the right place after being derailed by listening to the sound it makes and feeling the shock through the pedals. This is like adjusting old camera lenses or double clutches on cars where the user's skill determines the outcome.

In contrast, SIS made the shift lever digital. The shift lever contains a ratchet action indexing unit. One indent movement of the shift lever moves the cable a specified amount and operates the derailleur to shift the chain to the next sprocket (Figure 4).

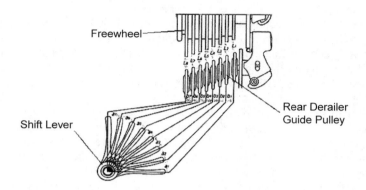

Fig. 4. Shimano Index System

One may feel that this is a concept that anyone could think of. However, this idea had not been established in the bicycle industry before. Normally manufacturers of bicycle parts specialize in derailleurs, gears, or chains, and their interest focuses on the durability or wear of a specific part. A manufacturer of chains may have strong ideas about optimization of the chain as a component of the drive system, but it would be difficult for such a firm to pay attention to the performance for shifting. Gear manufacturers also pay more attention to the durability and wear of gears. Thinking of how to improve gear shifting as an inter-linked system of components was something that went beyond such companies' attention and imagination. Final assemblers, which had traditionally relied upon specialized parts manufacturers, also lacked the ideas required to creatively develop new parts. Shimano could create the idea that others could rarely imagine, because it emphasized the system component philosophy.

However, coming up with a new idea is one thing, realizing the idea is another thing. SIS is a system that combines a variety of parts and only functions well when these are properly matched. If adjustments are not carefully made, operability will be worse than with a conventional system.

The shift lever, gears, inner cable[7] diameter, inner cable attachment points, design and attachment of rear derailleur and gear cogs are all related. The positions of the ratchet on the shift lever are all different for each gear. This is because ca-

---

[7] Of the cables linking the shift lever and the derailleur, in addition to the brake lever and the brake, the curved section near the brake is wrapped in another cable to hold its shape and this is called the outer cable. The parts that are attached to the frame in a straight line do not require an outer cable and only need an inner cable.

bles must be pulled more on the outside than on the inside as the derailing mechanism uses a pantograph structure. Fitness of the chain is also an issue. If adjustments are not made between these, gearshift would actually become problematic.

SIS requires a higher level of precision of each component than the conventional system. In addition, it also demands more precision in the other parts of the bicycle, to which SIS is attached. For example, the rear derailleur is attached to the frame. If the end section of the frame to which the wheel is attached does not have sufficient accuracy, the derailleur would not be installed correctly. The Index System will then not function smoothly. In the friction system, riders could make these adjustments by themselves. In SIS, where the parts related to gearshift are integrated as a system, the manufacture must achieve necessary precision and matching.

Critical to realize this superior total system were other technologies that Shimano had worked on until that time. They included the free hub system that reduced gear shake, the dual servo slant pantograph system that increased shifting performance, and the Uniglide Chain (Table 1). The accumulation of these individual technologies led to the realization of the high precision total system of SIS.

The performance of SIS was superior to the skill of professional riders. SIS can maintain the same level of precision as professional riders in peak condition. Not even professional riders can always be in top condition. For example, there are cases where a race is won or lost in a gear change at the top of a hill after riding for 250 km. Even the best riders cannot shift gears at the same level as SIS under these conditions. "Never miss a shift" was the selling point of SIS.

However, such a claim would also hurt the pride of professionals and in some ways insult them. If anyone could shift gears well regardless of their skill, the techniques that they had so carefully honed would be worthless. This is like the way that professional photographers dislike cameras with auto-focus. Fearing their backlash, initially SIS was designed to also function as friction gears. The traditional method could be used at the flick of a switch, to send the message that Shimano respects conventional shifting skills.

Racers never say that they won thanks to the bike. Indeed, it is difficult to ascertain to what degree the bike made a difference. No one argued that riders started to win once they switched to SIS. At first there was even some opposition to SIS. However, it gradually spread. Professional riders are contracted racers. They move from team to team. If they used Shimano at the previous team, they would say that they want to use Shimano again. As a marketing strategy, Shimano made efforts to increase the number of sponsored teams. Once SIS use reached about 30% of racers, it then grew naturally. The decisive moment was that Campagnolo began to provide an index system afterwards. Until then it was "friction versus index" or "the old versus the new", but when the competition changed to "index vs. index", SIS gained citizenship in the racing community.[8]

---

[8]   Since then SIS's performance has improved cumulatively. A key has been light action. The derailleur is a mechanism that is pulled by a spring. The weaker this spring is, the easier it is for the rider to shift gears. A large amount of fine-tuning has been done over the past 10 years to make the return of gear changes lighter. For example, efficiency

Shimano could not create its overwhelming share with SIS alone. Certainly, the Shimano brand did spread to a degree not seen before. Yet, Campagnolo introduced an index system in the same way, and at home in Japan Shimano's competitor Maeda Industries (SunTour) also introduced a similar system under the name of Accushift. Until then, Maeda Industries had a better reputation in quality bicycles than Shimano. Shimano needed a further innovation to gain its current position.

The New Deore XT Series for Mountain Bikes

The concept of riding bikes through the mountains and off-road began as new recreation among young Californians during the 1970s.[9] In its early days, when other companies showed no interest, Shimano paid attention to the mountain bike market and supported its development. In 1982, Shimano was quick to release the mountain bike component called Deore XT. This was the first time that special parts were provided to endure hard conditions that previous bikes could not handle such as mountain trails, rocks, deserts, rivers and mud tracks. At the time there were virtually no bicycle assemblers that were interested in mountain bikes.

Since the mid 1980s, the mountain bike market began to grow rapidly mainly in the United States. Behind such growth were increasing interests in outdoor activities and the fitness boom. Triathlons also began to spread, and this evoked a desire for serious and yet fashionable bikes. Users with these needs jumped to mountain bikes, which had a lower threshold for riding than road bikes. The handlebars were flat and the saddle position low, making them easier to ride than road bikes. Mountain bikes could be ridden anywhere and symbolized the American culture of pursuing freedom. The collapse of the cold War stricture that brought about renewed interest in American culture also seemed to stimulate the eventual spread of mountain bikes to Europe and Japan from the late 1980s to early 1990s.

In the mid 1980s, around 2.5 million bicycles were sold annually in American bicycle shops (IBDs), but the proportion of mountain bikes was virtually zero at the time. From 1986 to 1988, this rapidly increased to 30%, 50% and finally 70%. By 1992, a global market of around 20 million mountain bikes had been established. Just as this rapid growth started, Shimano released the New Deore XT Series that contained the SIS for mountain bikes in 1986. This was a vital point.

The conditions required to realize an index system for mountain bikes were even harsher than those for road racers. The ups and downs of the riding surface and conditional changes are more pronounced. The demand for shifting performance is much higher. Off-road also implies harsh conditions such as vibration,

---

was improved by attaching the springs between the four parallel sides of the pantograph instead of the four axles. The return efficiency can be improved just by changing the way a spring is attached.

[9] It is said that this began when an American Olympic athlete, Gary Fisher, was having fun riding bicycles on mountains with his friends.

mud, and dust. It is just as the Paris-Dakar Rally cannot be won using Formula One parts.

Index systems for road bikes had a simple cable route as the shift lever was attached to the down-tube of the frame, but the shift lever on mountain bikes had been on the handlebars (called a finger shifter or thumb shifter), making the cable route longer and also making an outer cable necessary.[10] This correspondingly made the application of SIS a complex matter. The inner cable needed only to take into consideration the amount of inner extension. However, the outer cable is required to deal with not only the extension of the inner cable but also the retraction of the outer cable in order to obtain index precision. The outer cable is flexible and made by wrapping resin, nylon, and copper wire, and retracts in response to the expansion of the inner cable. This retraction is a major problem for mountain bikes.

Road racers have two front gears and the difference in the number of teeth is around 10 between the two gears. The difference in the number of teeth in the front gears has a great impact on the positioning of the rear derailleur. On mountain bikes, there are three front gears and the difference in the number of teeth is around 20. The impact is therefore even greater. When the front gear is changed, 20 teeth worth of slack in the chain must be taken up by the rear derailleur. For this reason, the functioning of the guide pulley (a spring for adjusting slack in the chain caused by shifting) also became difficult. Changing gears on a steep slope with a load on the chain was also difficult. To sum up, the development of an index system for mountain bikes was much harder than for road bikes in all respects.

Shimano overcame these difficult conditions by fully mobilizing the technologies that had been accumulated for free hubs, UG gears and UG chains. Maeda Industries and Campagnolo were not competitive in these technologies. Although both companies followed Shimano's lead of making index systems, they were unable to overturn Shimano's predominance that was backed by technologies. As a result the mountain bike market became a place dominated by Shimano. This strength in the mountain bike market has also been beneficial in the road market.

When the mountain bike market was undergoing rapid growth, dealers and finished bicycle manufacturers tended to order parts for road bikes and mountain bikes together. The choice was between SIS and Accushift. It was similar to the choice between a Windows machine and a Macintosh. There was no parts compatibility between the two integrated systems. If an order was placed for both mountain bikes and road bikes, it was easier to use SIS, which covered both road and off-road than placing an order for SunTour, which didn't provide good Accushift for mountain bikes. Even if there had not been a large difference in technologies for road bikes, the difference in the mountain bike field worked in Shimano's favor and spilled over into the road field, with this effect accumulating over time. Shimano's share snowballed and SunTour eventually disappeared.

If there were only the road race market, SunTour might have survived. Campagnolo, which has somehow maintained its strong position in the road race market, still exists. This seems to indicate that Shimano would not have reached its

---

[10]   See footnote 7 for inner and outer cables.

position if the mountain bike market had not emerged and grown so strongly. What made Shimano's overwhelming advantage possible was its lead in SIS for mountain bikes. The final nail in its competitors' coffin was then hammered in: the Shimano Total Integration.

Shimano Total Integration

The Shimano Total Integration (STI) further systematized bicycle components and strengthened Shimano's competitive position. When its competitors were already struggling with index systems, Shimano introduced yet another product on top of its already successful line.

The key was the integration of gear operation and brake operation: the dual control lever for road racers, and the system called "rapid fire" for mountain bikes (Figure 5). Shimano Total Integration was introduced in 1989 by combining SIS[11], Shimano Linear Response, HG gears, and SG gears (Table 1).

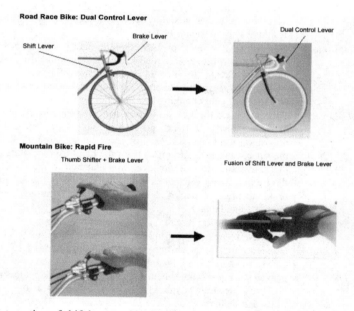

Fig. 5. Integration of shift lever and brake lever in STI (Shimano Total Integration)

---

[11] Just before the introduction of STI, SIS was introduced for the front-shift lever in addition to the rear shift lever. This was called the Dual Index System. The SIS for the front-gear system was not very important on road bikes, since they had only 2 front gears. The SIS for the front-gear system was developed later for mountain bikes, which have 3 front gears.

Table 1. Major parts and component systems developed by Shimano

Shimano Index System (SIS)	This is the system that precisely changes the rear gear one level when the gear lever is shifted one indent. By putting the ratchet used to determine the position of the gear lever to ensure precise gear shifting, anyone can quickly change gears without mistake, as opposed to the friction method, which relied heavily on the rider's skill to move the lever deliberately.
Freehub System	This system integrates the rear wheel hub and the freewheel. Rear wheel balance improves. This system allows faster, easier gear changes and also improved the strength of the rear wheel.
Dual Servo Slant Pantograph System	This system keeps the distance between each gear and the guide pulley (a part that makes adjustments for chain sag during gear changes) below the change gear short and almost constant. The guide pulley's pantograph moves diagonally following a form similar to the path of the gears. It makes gear changes smoother and more accurate.
Uniglide (UG) Gears, Uniglide (UG) Chains	This is the rear change gear and chain for making gear changes smoother. The shape of gear teeth and the shape of chain plates were specially designed for better shifting. Previously they were designed only for better drive.
Shimano Total Integration (STI)	This is a total system for gear changing and braking, consisting of the dual control lever (for road race bikes) or rapid fire system (for mountain bikes), the Shimano Index System, Shimano Linear Response, HG gears and SG gears. It improves ease of use, precision, and speed of gear changing and braking.
Dual Control Lever	This integrates the gearshift lever and the brake lever into one for road race bikes. Vertical move functions as the brake lever and horizontal move as the gearshift lever (index system). Previously, the rider's hands had to move from the handlebars to shift gears, as the conventional gearshift lever was attached to the down tube of the frame. This lever makes it possible for riders to shift gears and brake accurately, quickly, and easily without removing their hands from the handlebars.
Rapid Fire System	This combines the mountain bike gearshift lever (index system) on the brake lever side. Shifting can be conducted with a single thumb. Conventional finger shifters are attached to the front of the upper part of the handlebars, meaning riders had to loosen or change their grip to shift gears, but this makes it possible for riders to shift gears and brake accurately, quickly, and easily without losing one's grip of the handlebars.
SG Gears, HG Gears, HG Chains	These are evolved versions of UG gears and chains. A special shape of gear teeth and chain, designed with computers, fix the path the chain would take to ensure that it moves to the next gear accurately, quickly, and smoothly. By refining the shape of rear change gears (HG), front change gears (SG) and chains, the system improves not only rear gear shift but also front gear shift.

Table 1. (Continued)

Shimano Linear Response	This system reduces the overall friction of the brake system. Previously, springs were only attached to the brake arch (caliper). This system adds a small spring to the brake lever. These two springs reduce the load upon the arch. For cables, this system uses a resin liner and a low-viscosity oil, instead of a coil spring solidified with resin. Overall, friction of lever, arch (caliper), and cable was reduced, and braking performance (braking force, light operation, precision) correspondingly improves.

The dual control lever for road racers works by moving the lever vertically for braking and horizontally for the shift lever. In other words, the shift lever and the brake lever were made into one. In the mid 1980s, Shimano's engineers who were working on faster and more reliable shift levers for road bikes came up with the idea that "the shift lever should be contained within the brake lever," rather than "where the shift lever should be placed". One problem was that for SIS the shift lever remained in place after being moved, but for STI the lever should be returned to its initial position after each gearshift. This made the mechanism quite complex.

The market quickly responded. The decisive benefit of STI was that riders could shift and brake without moving their hand. Being able to shift gears while standing and pedaling up a hill was a great advance. Removing the hand leads to a great setback. Racers could slow down and then quickly speed up at the final corner toward the finish without moving their hands and miss-shift. Racers were also pleased that other riders could no longer see gear changes through the movement of their hands. STI rapidly spread when users quickly realized its value.

The *Rapid Fire* for mountain bikes did not join the shift lever and the brake lever into one as breaking is more important off road than on road. In contrast to road race bikes that conventionally had the shift lever on the downtube of the frame, mountain bikes already had this on top of the handlebars near the hands. This was because the movement of hands must be small as possible off road. This system was called "Thumb Shifter," in which the shift lever was pushed by the thumb and pulled back by the index finger. When this lever was moved closer to the brake lever and placed on the bottom, the rider cannot put enough power of his/her arm when pushing the shift lever. Riders should be able to push the lever only by the thumb and could not use the index finger to pull back (Figure 5). Therefore, in order to move the shift lever closer to the brake lever, the shifting must be made lighter and it must be designed so that gears can be changed without the use of the index finger. Rapid Fire realized this goal.

Off road, it is even more important than on road to change gears and brake precisely, quickly and smoothly. The STI for mountain bikes gained a good reputation and quickly penetrated the market. It was in this manner that Shimano created an unshakeable position through a component system that drastically improved shifting and braking, which are the core functions of a bicycle, for both the road and mountain bike markets. Shimano succeeded in further advancing its competitive base, from mainly in shifting to both shifting and braking.

Shimano's Strategy: Creating Markets Through Component Integration

System Components

Shimano's success was a result of successively introducing innovative new products to pursue ease of use for the rider. Throughout the history of Shimano's successful product innovations, the key was the development philosophy of system components that came out in the mid 1970s.

Dura-Ace, SIS, New Deore XT and STI all commonly share the idea that various parts should be optimized to function and perform as a system. In the bicycle industry, where interfaces are standardized and each part is made by a specialist manufacturer rather independently, most manufacturers viewed the derailleur, gearshift lever and brake as separate components. Shimano, however, viewed these as a single unit, and integrated them as a system achieving new functions and higher performance that could not be reached until then. In other words, Shimano changed the architecture of some of key component systems in bicycles from "open, modular" to "closed, integral".

These "architectural" innovations required a variety of ingenuity and a great deal of effort at Shimano. We have already mentioned many technical problems that had to be overcome in the process of integrating parts. The innovation of a total system was made possible by the accumulation of various improvements and innovations in individual parts technology.[12] The parts technologies newly developed by Shimano include the components that Shimano does not produce such as UG and HG chains. Shimano's attitude is to develop a particular technology if it is required to have the system function and perform as targeted.

Knowledge about a component is not enough for improving the component. An image of the final product must be drawn based on an understanding of the needs of end users. Superior parts cannot be developed without understanding the environment in which they will be used. Therefore, although Shimano has never di-

---

[12] The system component philosophy was realized through the technical development of individual parts, but this system-component philosophy also has an aspect of encouraging technical innovation of individual parts. In the process of improving the functions and performance as a system, it becomes clear that a certain part is holding the system back and there is a mechanism that forces the technical innovation of the part in the bottleneck. Rosenberg found that a particular technical innovation was pursued to overcome an imbalance with other interrelated parts, and this in turn encourages another technical innovation of other related parts. (N. Rosenberg, *Perspectives on Technology*, New York, NY: Cambridge University Press, 1976) For example, for audio systems, increased amplifier performance causes increases in speaker performance, and for automobiles, increased engine performance leads to increases in brake performance. In the case of Shimano, in the process of integrating parts that previously had standardized interfaces, engineers came to be aware of strong interdependence between parts that had not received attention in the past, and this awareness encouraged further technological innovations.

rectly sold bicycles under its own brand, it has a high level of technical expertise with regard to finished bicycles and has attempted to bypass final assemblers and to directly access end users' opinions. Shimano was quick to enter European road racing because it attempted to understand the demands for the bike as a finished product. The "Dealer Caravan", which will be explained later, is another example of such an attempt. Of course, information on end users can be obtained from bicycle assemblers. However, what is important for finished bicycle manufacturers is the customization of bicycles to suit regional characteristics and targeted users. To draw upon universal needs for bicycles, Shimano thinks that it is necessary to maintain close contact with and feel the market directly.

Shimano also needed cooperation from other companies. Shimano is simply a parts manufacturer and is not directly involved in the final assembly. However, the total system that Shimano developed required advanced integration not only in design but also in assembly, which is something that Shimano could not realize alone. The system will not function if the parts are not assembled with the required precision. The rear derailleur is fixed to the frames, and the index system will not function properly if the derailleur is not attached with precision. The management of assembly lines at bicycle manufacturers, the precision of the frame itself, final adjustments to be made at dealerships (retailers) are the areas that are critical to have SIS work effectively but Shimano cannot directly control.

Shimano therefore made frequent visits to manufacturers of finished bicycles when SIS was released and made specific requests regarding assembly processes. Shimano also provided technical notes about how to handle new products. For example, they specified conditions required for the proper functioning of the index system such as the position of the rear derailleur, brake dimensions, and handlebar length to finished product manufacturers, and asked for cooperation to meet with these requirements. In addition to specifying requirements for other components and assembly processes, Shimano provided specialized tools for measurement and adjustment. Similar information was also provided to dealers. Service information is also tied to the shift lever to ensure that end users see the information. SIS requires initial adjustment to determine the base positions, for which dealers and users needed.

In order to realize new functions and performance as a system, Shimano acquired and if necessary advanced technologies that extended beyond its own parts business, and made efforts to obtain the cooperation of outside organizations.

Production Technology and Market Creation

Another issue was increased costs. High quality parts must be made in order to deliver superior functions and performance. For example, in the case of SIS, the cost of the shift lever alone significantly increased[13] since the number of parts was increased because the ratchet was added to the shift lever, and resin parts were changed to sintered parts. Another factor for cost increase was stricter precision requirements. In particular, the precision of the shift lever and gears was increased. Furthermore those parts specially designed for the integrated system have a cost handicap because standardized parts that are generally used for the conventional system have a larger market and enjoy scale of economy. High precision requirements and a limited market mean that integrated parts inevitably cost more. Additional complications in the assembly process and at dealer shops also contribute to increased cost.

How did Shimano overcome this problem? One method was Shimano's superior production technology. Most of Shimano's products utilize cold-forge technology. Precision is higher for cold-forged products than those forged at high temperatures, which allowed efficient production. Cold-forge needs no heat distortion, and the extra cutting process to obtain greater precision after shaping is not required. Shimano established its cold forge technology long before. Shimano has also supplied parts to automobile manufacturers. The aim of this business has been to continue polishing Shimano's cutting edge technology in the automobile market, which has strict demands on quality precision and cost reduction. Shimano actively developed its own automated assembly technologies and the Singapore factory, as mentioned above, is making a great contribution to cost reduction, high quality, and high productivity.

Another important approach in overcoming cost increases was the creation of markets. Although SIS may have been expensive, it was marketed toward professional riders, who are not much concerned about price but will properly evaluate its functions and performance. As described, it took time for Shimano to have them acknowledge the value of SIS, but its value was eventually recognized and SIS spread throughout the market. Shimano's strategy was to make its value be recognized in high-end users, create a market there, and then use the success in this market as leverage to expand into larger (lower end) markets. As the market expanded, the mass production handicap compared to standardized parts got smaller.

Even greater success was gained from the mountain bike market. Shimano noticed the potential of mountain bikes at an early stage, and created a market together with a group of mountain bike fanatics by developing parts specially designed for the market and helping it grow. Not only did Shimano gain fame for being a parts manufacturer that created the market, but it also gained a dominant position by providing SIS and STI for the mountain bike market, which had higher precision requirements and thus appreciated the value of Shimano's systems. The strong brand that Shimano built in this manner made possible pricing that covered the increased cost compared to normal parts.

---

[13]   The shift lever, which was about 2,500 Yen for friction type system, was about 4,000 Yen for the SIS. However, as mentioned above, since SIS initially had the option of using the friction type, a simple comparison cannot be made.

It was not mere luck that Shimano noticed the potential of the mountain bike market much earlier than others. While Shimano is a parts manufacturer, it always monitors end user needs and market trends. One cue for such efforts was the difficult experience that Shimano had more than thirty years ago. Just after Shimano started exports to America, defects were detected in the exported parts. The bicycle manufacturer importing the parts asked Shimano to voluntarily recall the faulty parts. Shimano was forced to dispatch 10 teams of two people to the US to visit all dealers and retailers to replace the defective parts. This voluntary recall journey, however, led to a precious discovery. Shimano learned that a wealth of information could be gained by visiting dealers.

Mishaps can be turned into blessings. After this incident, Shimano devised the so-called "Dealer Caravan", comprising of Japanese and local staff to travel to retailers around the world. It was through the Dealer Caravan that Shimano noticed the potential of mountain bikes. Information regarding rather strange people in California who rode up and down a mountain for recreation was caught by the Dealer Caravan. That mountain became the birthplace of the mountain bike. The Dealer Caravan still continues today.

Shimano sends technicians to professional teams to work as mechanics, and also plans and supports a variety of bike races and events. Shimano is also full of "bike freaks" and "bike geeks." Shimano's employees love the product, which is also the case for Shimano's Fishing Tackle Division. When an employee participates in a bike race, the company covers the travel expenses. There is even a program called "Pedal More," in which employees are given prizes according to the distance they ride to work by bicycle. Although Shimano is a parts manufacturer, its efforts and culture enable it to understand, anticipate, and create markets even more effectively than a finished bicycle manufacturer.

Although integrated systems have high functionality, performance, and quality, their market is rather limited and costs tend to be higher. The ability to lower costs and the ability to find and create markets to maximize product and brand value, were critical to replacing mass-produced standardized parts with an integrated system. These two key abilities are behind Shimano's success.

Conclusion: Searching for New Growth Opportunities

Shimano, which commanded decisive success in mountain bike components, rapidly increased its sales from the mid 1980s to the mid 1990s. The growth was more than threefold, from 51.2 billion Yen in 1985 to 168 billion Yen in 1993, with an average annual growth rate of 16% (Figure 2).

Shimano's growth, however, has leveled off since the mid 1990s. Although Shimano has maintained its top share worldwide with high profitability, sales have stalled. Behind this lie two problems: intensified competition and market maturity.

The competitive environment surrounding Shimano has become harsher than in the past. It is not easy to maintain an overwhelming share. Former competitors like Maeda Industries and Campagnolo competed with Shimano with their own parts, which were not compatible with Shimano systems. However, now that Shimano's products are dominant, new competitors are competing with Shimano-compatible parts. In the United States, there has been an antitrust judgment against Shimano which has made it more difficult for Shimano to sell parts as a total system. A U.S. company, Slam, which makes a product called the Grip Shift that integrates a resin grip and a shift lever, has also become a serious rival. Taiwanese manufacturers with production plants in China are also very competitive and Shimano's ability to dictate prices has been declining over time. As Shimano's parts have become so dominant and widely used, it has become difficult for bicycle manufacturers to differentiate themselves from one another. Some companies have thus begun to intentionally avoid Shimano to make their products unique.

The market has also matured. Shimano's growth through the early 1990s was supported by the market expansion of mountain bikes, to which Shimano made a great contribution. However, once mountain bikes had spread and the growth leveled off, Shimano's growth also leveled off. Shimano's 1993 sales record remains unbroken.

In order to break away from competitors and return to the path of growth, Shimano needs to create another new market based on product innovations. One area that Shimano is currently focusing on is the comfort market. Shimano has introduced comfort category products called the Nexave Series. Shimano is also trying to change the concept of comfort bicycles and create a new market.

With its system component philosophy, Shimano experienced great success riding on the wave of the rapid growth of the mountain bike market. The question still remains whether it can build another foundation to ride the next wave of growth. There is no rest in competition. Shimano's challenges will continue.

Invisible Dimensions of Innovation: Strategy for De-commoditization in the Japanese Electronics Industry

Ken Kusunoki

Digitization, Modularization, and Commoditization

Companies are having increasing difficulty in creating new value. Competition is intensifying and squeezing profit margins. Profit is the difference between revenue and costs; the gap between the cost of providing a good or service and what a customer is willing to pay for that good or service (I shall refer hereafter to the concept of WTP, or Willingness to Pay). There are only two ways to increase profits: Reduce costs or boost customer WTP. Companies have tried various "best practices" to maintain profitability: restructuring with a focus on "core businesses," business process re-engineering, information technology-driven supply chain management (SCM) initiatives, outsourcing, and globalization.

These efforts are fundamentally focused on reducing cost. And while cost reduction is important, it is insufficient to sustain profitability. By its very definition, cost-based competition converges on the physical limits of cost and price and ultimately is a dead-end path. Companies focused exclusively on reducing costs will hang themselves with their own ropes. Firms must increase customer WTP in order to add new value to their products and services.

Competitive environment changes in recent years make it increasingly difficult to boost WTP. One key underlying factor is the threat of commoditization. The essence of strategy is doing things differently from competitors, and it is difficult to create differences once a product or service becomes a commodity; "price" becomes the only differentiator a firm can show customers. Commoditization, therefore, means competition converges on cost. Moreover, the speed at which products and services become commodities has dramatically increased in recent years. We can see many good examples in the electronics industry which has been hit hard by the forces of rapid digitization over the last decade.

Digitization affects natures of product systems in a number of ways. Of these, the most fundamental change is the "modularization" of architectures. Architecture defines how to break a system down into components and how those system components are interrelated in what we call "subsystem interdependencies." It is a concept for understanding system states. Modularization means "breaking down an entire system into multiple groups (modules), each of which consists of a number of highly interdependent subsystems, with predefined rules regarding the interface between modules." Modularization could be defined as a strategy for minimizing system complexity and relational interdependence between components by anticipating and solving beforehand the problems that arise when modules interact. The personal computer is the world's most modularized product-system. The functions a PC must perform – calculation, short-term memory, long-term memory, input, display and so forth – are allocated to the CPU, RAM, hard drive, keyboard, monitor and other physical components. A standardized interface intermediates component interaction.

Modularization has at least three benefits. First, it greatly reduces system complexity by lowering subsystem interdependence. This enables significant reductions in value chain modification and component adjustment costs. Second, modularization enhances system flexibility. Greater modularization makes it possible to localize system changes within individual modules. For example, there's no need to redesign the entire personal computer system simply because rapid growth of the popularity of digital cameras calls for PCs to offer greater image processing capability. Simply developing a faster CPU or installing a speedier graphics board can solve the problem. Third, modularization promotes economies of scale through division of labor. Independent development and manufacture of individual modules spawns new companies dedicated to these particular tasks. This creates horizontal specialization which promotes economies of scale.

For companies, digitization-driven change opens new avenues to achieve efficiency. Thanks to modularization, companies are able to lower costs in ways never before possible. Ironically, though, these trends also work to accelerate commoditization. A completely modularized architecture certainly promotes efficiency at the macroeconomic level. But at the individual corporate level, it inevitably results in price competition between products and services that cannot be differentiated otherwise. And, in fact, this very scenario describes today's personal computer industry.

This paper is about innovations to overcome commoditization and regain customers' WTP. In the modern competitive environment which entraps firms into commoditization, innovation for de-commoditization has been increasingly needed. However, innovation can be a driver of WTP when it creates new values perceived by customers. In other words, if customers do not perceive any new values, innovation cannot result in substantial and sustainable differentiation in the competition, which cannot increase customers' WTP however "new and radical" the innovation is in the eyes of a firm.

Conventional thinking explicitly or implicitly assumes that innovations are dimensional phenomena; in other words, that they progress along clearly defined dimensions of value. PC industry competition in the 1990s, for example, is a typical case whereby firms competed for innovations along clearly visible dimensions. Firms and their customers widely shared specific, objective, and easily comprehensible dimensions: MPU processing speed, memory size, monitor resolution, and other functionality measures. In such circumstances, innovation meant outdistancing rivals in terms of one of these objective dimensions. Efforts for innovation centered on the relative advantages each firm enjoyed along visible dimensions.

Considering whether innovation can create really differentiated value perceived by customers, such conventional assumption of innovation along particular dimensions may have become less effective for creating differentiation and promoting

WTP. Instead, it could do more harm than good for de-commoditization. Firms preoccupied with the "dimensional thinking" of innovation would be entrapped even more into commoditization. In this paper, I explore the logic underlying the dilemma which "innovative" firms may encounter, and try to present a new perspective on innovation, which focuses on visibility of innovation dimensions.

Visibility of Innovation Dimension and Its Dynamics

When thinking about de-commoditization, we must first and foremost understand the logic of commoditization. I propose the concept of "visibility of innovation dimension" as a key to understanding of the commoditization process. The visibility of innovation dimensions means the degree to which both customers and firms can capture innovation's value in terms of a few specific, objectively defined dimensions.

Using this lens, we can recognize different natures of innovations. Some innovations are "visible innovations" of which value can be captured and evaluated along a few objective dimensions. Other innovations are rather "invisible" in terms of dimensions with which customers and firms understand their value. As mentioned above, the PC industry in the 90s experienced many visible innovations along clearly defined functionality dimensions. Inside the PC system, microprocessors, hard disk drives, memory chips, and many other components have also experienced various innovations with visible dimensions.

In contrast, the music, game software, and fashion industries provide classic examples of invisible innovations. Industries like these have also experienced many innovations. Sun Records' release of Elvis Presley's rock-and-roll music, Enix's Dragon Quest role-playing game, and Swatch's fashion watches were all innovations that created new value and produced high WTP. The new music Elvis created certainly had a faster tempo compared to pop music of the time; by timing it we would probably discover a relatively greater number of beats per measure. But the essence of Elvis's innovation was not that he exceeded Frank Sinatra in terms of number of beats per measure. Elvis was definitely new, different, and innovative compared to conventional music, but it is difficult to grasp by *what measure* they were different.

Visibility of innovation dimensions varies depending on the product. But a more critical point is that it is not constant, even when we look at a single industry or product. The visibility of innovation dimensions usually rises and falls as industries and products evolve over time. Although actual dynamics may vary with product or industry, but in most industries it is possible to observe common patterns (see Figure 1).

Let's explain the dynamics of innovation dimension visibility using the PC industry as an example. At the initial stage of an industry's development, before a dominant design has been established, innovations are normally characterized with low visibility of innovation dimensions. When the personal computer industry was in its infancy, the user base was limited to "techies" and "geeks." At this stage, both manufacturers and users lacked a common understanding of exactly what the PC's basic value was and of what functions were critical to defining that value. In other words, at this stage the personal computer's innovations were not so visible in terms of their value dimensions.

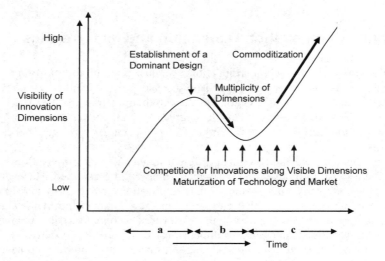

Fig. 1. Dynamics of visibility of innovation dimensions

Manufacturers and users steadily deepened their understanding of what a PC is for, and finally a dominant design was established. The establishment of a dominant design formed a consensus concerning a PC's value. Once IBM and Apple had established dominant designs, PC values could be understood along a limited number of specific dimensions, and firms rushed into visible innovations along those dimensions. In other words, the process of establishing a dominant design is the same as the process of raising visibility of innovation dimensions (phase "a" in Figure 1).

Then, users gradually deepened their product understanding even further, learning ever more sophisticated ways to use their computers. Usage expanded beyond the workplace to consumer homes, and new buyers who were using PCs for a wide variety of applications entered the market. As the industry moved into the 1990s, PC manufacturers sought to enhance their products not merely by processing speed, but along a wide range of distinctive dimensions: body and monitor size, RAM and hard drive capacity, durability, varied functionality, user support, and post-sale services. This phenomenon resulted in a multiplicity of value dimensions. At this stage in the industry's evolution, the number of PC's innovation dimensions had broadened considerably compared to the early IBM-PC days. Such multiplicity of innovation dimensions served to lower specifiability and universality of a PC's value for both users and manufacturers. For instance, one company developed a PC with high-speed processing capability, although it was bulky and consumed more amount of electricity, whereas the other company introduced, a smaller, lighter, more electricity-saving PC which was in turn relatively slow in terms of processing speed. Having many new products of which value of innovation was based on combination of progress in various performance dimensions, it would be more or less difficult to specify the value of a particular new product relative to competitors' products. In addition, some users may prefer a smaller, lighter one, while others may value processing speed, which lowers the universality of innovations' value dimensions. Because of the complexity of multiple innovation dimensions, it became less possible for both users and firms to simply capture the value of innovation at the product-system level. Thus the multiplicity of value dimensions consequently lowered visibility of innovations (see "b" in Figure 1).

However innovation visibility starts to rise again if competition continues along the various innovation dimensions (see "c" in Figure 2). This is because under competition to make better products with higher profit margins for not-yet-satisfied customers, the respective innovation dimensions ultimately achieve levels deemed satisfactory by customers. Manufacturers emulate each other's innovations, and one by one, the innovation dimensions along which competitors can differentiate their products from each other disappear. The pace of technological progress almost always outstrips the ability of customers to utilize or absorb the progress. Once product specifications along each of the dimensions reach levels satisfactory to nearly every customer, further innovation, even if technologically possible, fails to produce new value. This results in "overshooting" of visible innovations[1].

Growth in the personal computer sector, which averaged 15 percent annually throughout the 1990s, slowed starting in 2000 and then suddenly dropped by four percent in 2001. In 2001 only 11 percent of all users considered buying a new PC, the lowest number since 1995. This wasn't because PC demand itself had fallen. It was because the stereotypical industry notion under which "faster new models spur new demand" was simply no longer valid; the PC's various functions had reached levels sufficient to satisfy nearly every user. Customers no longer recognized added value in new products, and hesitated to replace their PCs. This was the most important reason why market growth stopped.[2]

Until the 1990s, the single biggest driving force behind the PC industry was the continuing cycle of innovation between Microsoft and Intel. Intel would develop a faster MPU, and in response, Microsoft would release a new operating system loaded with new functionality. The new OS, in turn, would require an even faster MPU, resulting in a continuous chain of innovation. When there was still plenty of room left for the "processing speed" dimension of innovation, this sort of visible innovation powered PC industry growth and increased corporate revenues and earnings. Processing speed, though, has already reached levels adequate for most

---

[1]   This logic of overshooting provides the basis of the disruptive innovation model by Christensen. See C. Christensen, *The Innovator's Dilemma*, Harvard Business School Press, 1997.

[2]   "The PC's New Tricks," *Fortune*, October 28, 2002

users. With the release of Windows XP, for example, customers feel almost no meaningful difference in processing speed between running applications on 2.4 GHz Intel Pentium 4 and 700 MHz Celeron machines.[3]

It's not just processing speed, though. PC memory and hard drive capacity are already sufficiently large, and monitor performance completely adequate. PC functionality has expanded to the point where it easily exceeds average user requirements; personal computers are loaded to the brim with unused functions. In short, the post-2000 personal computer is already "good" enough; further visible innovations would not create competitive differentiation that boosts WTP.

Under these conditions, price is the only remaining dimension along which companies can attempt to differentiate their offer. This is commoditization. Once commoditization is complete, companies are forced to compete along the single dimension left to them: price. Here the visibility of innovation dimension reaches its peak. It is a condition whereby every innovation effort converges into the cost reduction. For customers, price is an extremely well-specified, easily measurable, and easily comparable dimension. Commoditization drives corporate consolidation, as seen in the Hewlett-Packard-Compaq merger. But there are clear limits to the benefits of cost competition through merger. Maintaining profits amid cost competition in a commoditized product sector is extremely difficult. Most players are bleeding red ink in the post-2000, commoditized PC industry.

The visibility of innovation dimensions is crucial to an understanding of forces of commoditization. The dynamics – whereby technological and market evolution create various innovation dimensions, continuing competition shrinks possibilities for innovating products along visible dimensions, and the visibility of innovation rises as a result – lie behind the phenomenon of commoditization.

Limits of Visible Innovations

What can firms do for innovations that really create differentiation? Christensen's insight on sustaining and disruptive innovations demonstrates three possible approaches to innovations for competitive differentiation[4]. First, firms can pursue sustaining innovations when the market is at a stage where there is still room to differentiate along visible dimensions. A sustaining innovation targets demanding, high-end customers with better performance along visible dimensions than what was previously available. Matsushita Electric scored a remarkable success with its DIGA Series DVD recorder, securing a 45 percent share of the worldwide market in 2003 by being the industry frontrunner in terms of miniaturization and advanced functionality. Matsushita dramatically shrinks printed circuit board size for each new DVD recorder model; its fourth-generation product is one-sixth the size

---

[3]   Ibidem
[4]   See Clayton Christensen (1997) *The Innovator's Dilemma*, Harvard Business School Press, and Clayton Christensen and Michael Raynor (2003) *The Innovator's Solution*, Harvard Business School Press.

of its first release. Meanwhile, models featuring a progressive playback function that displays high-resolution images have been a hit time and again.[5] This is an example of a sustaining innovation which realized improvement along existing visible performance dimensions.

Second, when facing threats of commoditization which makes it difficult to further create substantial differences along existing dimensions, a firm can pursue an alternative strategy of the disruptive innovation to offer less expensive products. This strategy does not attempt to bring better products along existing innovation dimensions. Instead, it targets over served customers in the low end of the existing market. In the PC industry, Dell has successfully implemented this strategy of low-end disruption.[6] Dell succeeded precisely by turning commoditization into a strategic advantage. Leveraging cost leadership based on its direct sales model, Dell aggressively lowered prices starting in 2000. In 2001, while competitors lost market share, Dell managed to boost its U.S. domestic market stake to 30 percent. Components, too, fell subject to vicious price competition as personal computer commoditization progressed. Targeting the low-end customers, Dell perceived commoditization as an opportunity.

Third, a firm can pursue another type of disruptive innovations called new-market disruptions. This strategy does not invade the mainstream market. Rather, it pulls customers out of the mainstream market into the new one by changing competitive dimensions of innovations. Casio's EXILIM Series of digital cameras, released in 2002, was a huge hit in spite of being priced higher than rival products.[7] Casio's first digital camera, the QV-10, was a groundbreaking product that could be considered the dominant design driving the full-scale launch of Japan's "digicam" market. At the time the QV-10 was released, manufacturers featured pixel count as the key innovation dimension. Sony, Canon, Olympus Optical, Fuji Film, and Matsushita Electric jumped into the market one after another to compete for sustaining innovation along the dimension of pixel count. Casio's share quickly diminished as rivals competed along the visible innovation dimension. In response, Casio withdrew from the pixel count competition, adopting a new-market disruption strategy of intense, single-minded focus on product thinness and compact size. The company set a goal of producing a camera the size of a business card and only ten millimeters thick. It held pixel count only to 1.3 million and eliminated the zoom feature on the S Series camera, its mainstay product at the time. This third approach chosen by Casio tried to realize differentiation by finding new innovation dimensions: being smaller, lighter, and thinner.

Although the three approaches have different ways to creating competitive differentiation, there is one thing these innovation strategies have in common: no matter whether the innovation is sustaining or disruptive, it implicitly or explicitly assumes particular innovation dimensions. Sustaining innovations will pursue the

---

[5] "*Kita zo, Digital AV Keiki*" [Good Times are Here for Digital AV] *Nikkei Business*, 7/14/2003

[6] "Dell Does Domination" *Fortune* 1/21/2002

[7] "*Casio no Gyakutenuchi Keiei*" ["Casio's Comeback Management"] *Nikkei Business*, 6/23/2003

existing performance dimensions, whereas low-end disruptions focus on the cost dimension and new-market disruptions on creating new innovation dimensions. All of these strategies are based on the idea that there are some visible dimensions of innovations along which companies and customers can evaluate product offerings.

Each of the three approaches may succeed in profiting from innovation under particular conditions. All approaches, however, may sooner or later encounter threats of commoditization. The success of Matsushita's DIGA is an example of a fruitful sustaining innovation. In the DVD recorder and other growing sectors that still have room for sustaining innovation, clear differentiation along visible dimension may increase WTP. As the model of disruptive innovation shows, however, sustaining innovations will gradually reaches its limits, and are likely to face the threat of commoditization. There are two reasons for this. One is the logic of technological limitations. Although it is good to have a PC with faster processing speed, a DVD recorder with better picture quality, or a digital camera with greater pixel count, there would be physical limits in improving performance along existing innovation dimensions. There is no more accurate watch than the radio-wave watch which is now available at a reasonable price, simply because it makes no error by definition.

The other reason comes from the logic of overshooting. Even if the product's performance can be technologically improved, there is usually a natural limit on the customers' side to absorb or utilize the improved performance. The problem is one of customer perception limits rather than strict technological boundaries. At some point users will stop paying prices that justify the investment needed for further technological innovation, regardless of how compact or high-performance the products have become. As mentioned earlier, most users are totally happy with their PCs' processing speed.

Although disruptive innovations may open up new ways to profiting from innovations for some time, they may become sustaining sooner or later. Casio's EXILIM certainly succeeded in a new-market disruption by finding a new innovation dimension. But others also soon realized the opportunity of the new innovation dimension and rushed into the competition for ever smaller/lighter/thinner models. For instance, Matsushita followed Casio in the direction and released a digital camera that is not only 9.9 mm thick, but features a music playback function. If a disruptive innovation becomes sustaining in a short time, companies will have to face the same threats of commoditization mentioned above in a short time. The more the innovation is visible, the sooner will others follow in the same direction.

Dell has embraced commoditization with its low-end disruption. Nevertheless, the choice to accept commoditization and compete on price and cost is feasible only for few companies. Cost-based competition has a very sustaining nature. In the personal computer industry, Dell is the only company generating significant profits. Under cost-based competition, there can only be one – or at best an extremely limited number – of winners. Accordingly, most companies faced with commoditization must choose another path: de-commoditization.

Commoditization is the phenomenon whereby "product or service value converges along the simple dimension of price, after competing firms are unable to differentiate themselves along existing innovation dimensions due to the limitations of either technology or customer cognition." Once we define commoditization in this way, two basic strategies emerge by which firms may avoid or escape commoditization.

One possible strategy is to consider innovation strictly in a dimensional context, and maintain performance differences that competitors cannot easily catch up with. Increasing WTP is possible if a firm can maintain performance high enough to be unreachable by competitors – even assuming that the innovation is along a visible dimension. I call this *the black-box strategy*, which looks to the internal context of a product system, or "product architecture" as the source of WTP.

As we have seen, progressive modularization in the electronics industry is a major driver of commoditization. Yet even in a commoditized product market, a competitor may be able to maintain differentiation and increase WTP if it can create a difficult-to-imitate innovation in a lower-level subsystem – even if the innovation is visible to competitors. "Black box" means a subsystem incorporating performance competitors cannot easily imitate. Let's return to the PC industry example. As we have seen, it is now difficult to maintain continuous profitability because the industry seems thoroughly commoditized. But if we look down a level from the top of the product-system, we can see Intel successfully maintaining profitability in its MPU business. Intel's Pentium processor holds visible innovations: high-performance and high speed. But at the same time, the Pentium processor is a black box supported by deep product and manufacturing technology; rivals cannot keep up with Intel's performance. Intel's MPU is a classic example of the black-box strategy.

In fact, many Japanese electronics companies try to overcome commoditization through the black-box strategy. Examples include Hirose Electric's connectors, Rohm's custom mobile telephone handset LSIs, Fanuc's numerical controllers, and Nitto Denko's polarized LCD film. Hirose Electric maintains its strong profitability by distancing itself from customers who refuse to recognize values other than price, and focusing its resources on developing high value-added connectors. For example, one of Hirose's mainstay products is a connector that links a mobile telephone's printed circuit board to the handset's internal antenna. With this connector, the width and weight of a single strand of human hair, Hirose commands more than a 50 percent worldwide market share. Hirose Electric's connectors maintain high margins because they outperform rivals' products along the dimensions of compactness, thinness, and weight. The ultra compact mold development technology and multi-model/small lot production expertise that enables Hirose to create its black-box products.

Apart from these components manufacturers, there are other companies profitably using the black-box strategy in the critical subsystems they build for larger product-systems. Canon developed CMOS sensors and controllers at the heart of its digital cameras. Canon's EOS Kiss single lens reflex digital camera uses a unique CMOS sensor to achieve 11-megapixel resolutions, the industry's highest image quality level. Faced with competition from Korean and Taiwanese rivals in the LCD computer monitor sector, Sharp is shifting the focus of its LCD operations to liquid crystal displays for television. Unlike relatively easy-to-manufacture computer LCDs, television LCDs must be two to three times brighter and require dramatically faster refresh rates. Korean television LCDs consume 20 to 50 percent more power than Sharp's products, and offer 40 percent less contrast. Sharp's competitive advantage is made possible by manufacturing technology that can produce large glass substrates with precision levels approaching 1/30th the width of a human hair. The extremely deep manufacturing technology expertise Sharp has built up over many years produces performance along visible dimensions, quality, and yield advantages rivals can not soon surpass – that expertise essentially is a black box.

In the past, Sony profitably executed a black box strategy with charge-coupled devices (CCD). Now it is investing heavily in CELL, a processor for high-speed, high-performance consumer electronics products. The CELL chip will power a wide range of digital products, including next-generation games, digital televisions, and DVD recorders. Matsushita, too, is positioning Black Box components and subsystems as strategic centerpieces. Matsushita's recent hits – its Viera plasma television, DIGA DVD recorder, and LUMIX digital camera – came after the company stopped developing general-purpose semiconductors in 1997, and started specializing in image and audio-processing LSIs. All these are examples of black box strategy implementations.

Invisible Innovations: An Alternative Strategy

An alternative strategy for escaping commoditization is to pursue "invisible innovations" which do not attempt to create differences along visible dimensions. Instead, this strategy attempts to disrupt the very rules of dimensional competition of innovations. The basic idea of underlying this strategy is that *because high visibility of innovation dimensions invokes commoditization, commoditization can be avoided if dimensions of innovations are rendered invisible.*

Conceptually, this is completely different from the black box strategy. The black box strategy treats dimensional nature of innovation as a given, and seeks to prevent commoditization by establishing and maintaining dimensional "differences" competitors cannot easily keep up with. The idea behind invisible innovations, though, is to refuse to compete along visible dimensions. Sooner or later, dimensional competition results in commoditization. In other words, the very source of problems leading to commoditization lies in the fact that innovations have visible dimensions. Firms may be able to escape commoditization by reducing the visibility of value dimensions of innovations, and disrupting the rules of competition for visible innovations.

Invisible innovations seek opportunities to improve WTP, not in the internal context of product architecture, but in the external context in which the customer and the product interact, and the customer benefits from using the product. Invisible innovations often take the form of "concept innovations." I use the word "concept" here as a compressed representation of an essential customer value which defines the external context of the product: what the product or service means to a customer, what they use it for, and why it is valuable.[8] Visible innovations seek to differentiate products and services along specific dimensions such as function or quality. In contrast, while concept innovation encompasses multiple latent values, it doesn't match these one by one with individual dimensions. Rather than boosting existing dimensions one by one, invisible, concept innovation paints an entirely new picture of how, why, and to whom a new product or service should appeal.

Sony's Walkman is a classic example of an invisible innovation which created a new concept of listening to music. Before the Walkman came along, cassette tape recorders were conceived merely as music-playing devices, and consumer interest focused on the dimension of good sound reproduction. But the Walkman freed users to enjoy music in almost any environment. To be sure, the Walkman was dramatically smaller and lighter than other cassette players. But the essence of the Walkman's value lay not in such dimensional measures, but rather in how it enabled consumers to experience new ways of enjoying music. In fact, in terms of sound quality the Walkman was actually inferior to rival cassette tape players. It lacked a high-quality speaker and recording capability. But the essence of invisible innovation lies in *disrupting existing innovation dimensions and rendering rankings along conventional measures meaningless*. Sound quality, speaker quality, and recording capability became non-issues in the context of the Walkman's newly-created concept of "freedom to enjoy music anywhere."

In the electronics industry at large, and in the digital consumer electronics sector in particular, the trend whereby innovations along visible value dimensions grows increasingly difficult – and the focus of competition subsequently shifts to invisible dimensions of innovations – is becoming increasingly conspicuous. On a unit basis, in 2003 Apple sold nearly half as many iPods as it did PCs. Despite being considerably more expensive than rival products, the iPod became a hit, reportedly accounting for a large portion of Apple's $44 million earnings.[9]

The iPod offers a good example of how an invisible innovation can increase customer WTP. Other companies develop and manufacture MPU and operating system for the iPod, so black-box components aren't the source of its superiority. In fact, in terms of visible dimensions such as weight, thinness, continuous playback time, and recording capacity, the iPod is actually inferior to rival products. Yet it sells for a higher price. Featuring a simple design that sharply distinguishes it from conventional digital devices, the iPod lets users compile and continuously update and modify their own "playlists," affording them the ultimate in a personalized music listening experience. Like the Walkman, the iPod differentiated itself not along visible dimensions, but through a revolutionary concept: changing the way consumers enjoy music, just like Walkman did 25 years ago.

---

[8]   The author discusses product concept innovation in detail in "Value Differentiation: Organizing Know-What for Product Concept Innovation" in Takeuchi and Nonaka's *Hitotsubashi on Knowledge Management*, Wiley

[9]   "Shootout in Gadget Land" *Fortune*, 11/10/2003

In the home-use video game industry, Sony's strategy has been to compete primarily with visible innovations. Sony's PlayStation 2 (PS2), the product that dramatically expanded the company's game market share, overwhelmed competitive machines in terms of image quality, complex motion, and video smoothness. Sony's PS2 innovated on visible dimensions such as "polygon count" and "audio quality." Sony is continuing down this path with its next generation game player, which will use the CELL chip described earlier. Sony claims the CELL chip will achieve an image processing capacity 1,000 times that of the PS2.[10] Clearly, Sony intends to boost customer WTP through a black box strategy.

Sony's pursuit of visible innovations required game software makers to invest time and money building ever-more sophisticated computer graphics into their products. Because software scale and complexity has grown so dramatically, only a handful of the biggest houses can afford to invest the necessary development resources. And from a consumer standpoint, the game consoles' increasing sophistication means players must invest considerable effort and practice in learning to play. This situation has driven a growing number of users away from game playing. Japan's home-use game software market peaked in 1997 and has been shrinking. In particular, the portion of elementary school students playing with game machines is dwindling. These consumers' interests are reportedly drifting away from complex, high-priced game software, and toward card games, *beigoma*, and other, easier-to-enjoy toys.[11]

Amid this maturing game market, Nintendo – in stark contrast to Sony – shifted away from feature-centric visible innovations and adopted a strategy of invisible innovations. Judging that consumers were already well satisfied with current game functionality, in 2004 Nintendo decided not to release a successor to its GameCube line.[12] Its strategy was to go back to creating fun through toys with invisible value dimension. It did this by focusing on accessible easy to play, yet absorbing, "laugh out loud" games with mass appeal, such as Mario and Pokemon.

Because it doesn't internally develop or manufacture high-performance semiconductors or other key game player components, Nintendo was constrained in its capabilities to drive game console competition through technological expertise, as Sony does. But even before today's extreme functionality-driven console competition began, Nintendo had a tradition of seeking competitive superiority by developing software such as Pokemon that appeals to a broad and deep customer segment centered on children.

Even Pokemon, the explosive worldwide hit, began life in 1986 as software running on a humble eight-bit GameBoy machine that was already outdated at the time. One of the key factors in Pokemon's success was that Nintendo put the game's "fun" front and center by deliberately selecting a low-priced game console with abbreviated functionality.[13] Nintendo employed an electronic format to en-

---

[10]   "Video Game Planet" *Fortune*, 9/15/2003

[11]   *Asahi Shimbun* [Asahi Newspaper] 2/29/2004

[12]   *Nihon Keizai Shimbun* 2/10/2004

[13]   Author interview with Iwata Satoi, then-Director of Nintendo's Management Planning Group 5/2001

able players to enjoy collecting and trading 151 different types of Pokemon cards with their friends, but that fun didn't depend on imaging processing or sound effect technologies. Amid a maturing game market, Sony's black box strategy and Nintendo's choice to disregard existing game "rules" and innovate along invisible dimensions offer good examples of contrasting strategies.

The crux of the difference between visible innovations and invisible innovations may be easier to understand in terms of the relationship between "function" and "value." "Function" is a value that a corporation can predefine in dimensional terms. Function comprises only a portion of the value a product or service provides, but under the assumption of visible innovations, improving a particular function nearly always translates directly into better value. Consider our PC example: faster speed, bigger memory, and larger storage capacity translates as-is into higher value. In short, in visible innovation, the relationship between function and value is clear and easy to understand by focusing on a particular dimension.

Under invisible innovation of a product concept, however, there's a huge gap between function and value, and the relationship between the two becomes unclear. Let's illustrate this with an example: the *pachinko* machine, used to play a Japanese form pinball. *Pachinko* machine manufacturer Sammy consistently posts strong earnings by developing new-concept products. Needless to say, a *pachinko* machine's value lies in the "leisure time enjoyment" it provides to a *pachinko* player. Yet while a *pachinko* machine's functionality can be described along various dimensions, the cause and effect relationship between particular combinations of functionality – and the enjoyment each produces – is extremely unclear. Functionality explains only a tiny portion of the value produced through an invisible innovation.

Not only is an invisible innovation driven by a new product concept effective for de-commoditization, it is also superior to a visible innovation in terms of sustainability. Once a company succeeds in establishing a new product concept, it is often able to produce powerful loyalty and brand effects that trump dimensional superiority. One of the strengths of invisible innovations is that customers find comparisons difficult. Brands based on visible innovations are rather easily damaged when rivals successfully overtake them along the visible dimensions. But once a company succeeds in creating new customer value at a conceptual level, it becomes difficult for customers to compare the offer with competitive products, precisely because the value dimensions are invisible. That makes it easier to maintain differentiation over the long term. For example, it wouldn't be particularly difficult to replicate the Walkman's hardware functionality or quality. In fact, a number of market latecomers released products that were superior to the Walkman in terms of visible performance dimensions. Even so, Sony has maintained the Walkman brand for a long time, and customers continue to recognize it as "different" from rival products.

Both of the strategies – black box and invisible innovation – seek to escape commoditization through their own respective forms of logic. The two strategic positions can be illustrated as in Figure 2. The black box strategy focuses on product architecture and seeks opportunities to increase customer WTP in the internal context of a product system. The black box strategy means building product subsystems with internal structures that rivals cannot imitate, and countering modularization by aggressively embracing integral architectures at the subsystem level. Integral architectures – those with strong interdependencies between components of the subsystem – require deep knowledge of complex interactions. Subsystems can be made into black boxes because acquiring deep knowledge of interdependencies and interactions is difficult. The black-box strategy looks for highly interdependent components within the subsystem and then intentionally seeks to develop an integral architecture based on those components.

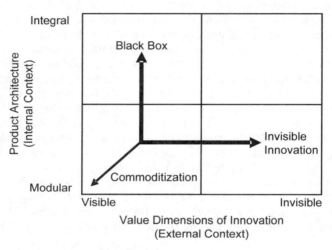

Fig. 2. Innovation strategies for de-commoditization

In contrast, the invisible innovation strategy focuses on the product's value to customers. It seeks opportunities to increase customer WTP in the external context of how customers use the product. It is unconcerned with internal product architecture; it focuses instead on the actual value customers receive. When values are pre-specified in terms of visible dimensions, competition accelerates along those dimensions, driving commoditization. Invisible innovation is a strategy for escaping the threat of commoditization by ignoring the rules of competition for visible innovations and converting customer values into something along invisible dimensions.

Commoditization can be understood as the process whereby product architecture becomes modularized and customer value dimensions grow increasingly visible: movement is toward the lower left quadrant in Figure 2. In contrast, we can hypothesize that customer WTP will be maximized when product architecture is integral and customer value dimensions are invisible, as in the upper right quadrant of the figure. But in the electronics industry, if not other sectors as well, there's a trade-off in the relationship between the two axes, and as a practical matter it is difficult for companies to achieve positions in the upper right quadrant. We've examined the strong trend toward modularization at the level of finished product systems in the electronics industry. Accordingly, companies must compete at lower system component levels in order to maintain integral architectures. At the same time, however, it is relatively feasible to create invisible innovations at the finished product-system level where end-users actually use the device.

In any event, till now most of the arguments on the de-commoditization strategy have focused on the black box, taking a product architecture perspective represented by the vertical "modularization vs. integral" axis in Figure 2. I emphasize that the external-context customer value axis is independent from the internal-context architecture axis, meaning an alternative strategy is available to de-commoditization: invisible innovations.

The Visibility Trap

By rendering visible dimensions of innovations meaningless and changing the rules of competition, invisible innovations make a more complete escape from commoditization possible. Yet it is very difficult for a firm to actually realize invisible innovations, because they are usually invisible also to the firm itself.

Most companies continue to doggedly press ahead with traditional innovation efforts along particular visible dimensions, even after their industry has entered into the commoditization phase. I call this phenomenon the "visibility trap" of innovation in which "innovative" companies may be caught. As I have shown, customer understanding of a product deepens after a dominant industry design is established. As a result, customers seek new, multifaceted dimensions of values. At this point companies discover significant differentiation possibilities, and strive to increase value via visible innovations along various dimensions.

A visible innovation is an easy issue for companies to deal with although it is technologically challenging. It is simple to get customers to understand a clear difference if that difference can be readily measured and expressed. Furthermore, it is easy to justify and make internal decision to invest resources in initiatives for visible innovations. That's because justification criteria are easily understood and achieved; owing to the existence of visible dimensions, companies can readily calculate how much investment will be necessary to make a product faster, more compact, or more lightweight. And when a company succeeds through visible innovations, the experience justifies further investment in dimensional values. Once it enters into this cycle, a company naturally keeps moving forward with visible innovations for competitive differentiation.

But there's no future in that kind of dimensional competition. At some point, visible innovation reaches its technological or cognitive limits and commoditization sets in. Even so, most companies are unable to remove themselves from the vicious cycle of competition for innovating along visible dimensions. This process becomes institutionalized, and most companies are unable to break out of the vicious cycle. Ironically, commoditization looms ever closer to the extent a company strives toward visible innovation. Ultimately, when commoditization is complete, the company finds itself in a position whereby it cannot differentiate along visible dimensions enough to appeal sufficiently to customers, yet it is no longer cost-competitive.

The reason most companies fall into the "visibility trap" and become unable to recast competition in terms of invisible dimensions is that customer perceptions of product value change tremendously under invisible innovations. There are many instances where something that worked under a visible innovation approach becomes a liability under invisible innovations. Likewise, things that should be avoided under a visible innovation approach could be crucial under invisible innovations.

The key point is differences in how customers perceive the innovation's value over time. To use a mathematical metaphor, a visible innovation focuses on *incremental* differences along a specific dimension in comparison to previous products. The greater the incremental change in value, the more effective the visible innovation. The relationship between company and customer is fundamentally a one-time "transaction" whose value does not extend across time. In contrast, an invisible innovation creates certain values that only materialize gradually over time as the customer uses the product over and over again. It's therefore important to think of invisible innovation's value as *cumulative* and extending over time. The visible innovation model of incrementally maximizing value and attempting to communicate this to customers in one-time transactions only leads companies into the trap.

Let's return to our game example. It's reasonable to say that visible innovations around game consoles have until now been effective in creating value; note how Sony attracted customers to the PS2 with unprecedented audiovisual advances. But rivals may release machines with identical functionality and performance. Or as time passes, consumers may gradually take for granted once-extraordinary audiovideo quality. The value users recognize today along the dimension of "visual and auditory beauty" is likely to shrink steadily over time.

Meanwhile, game software value can actually *grow* over time as users accumulate experience through repeated play. I believe this tendency is strong to the extent the company pursues invisible innovations, as Nintendo does with Pokemon. The more Pokemon users play, the more deeply they understand the game's characters and peculiarities. The more they learn the Pokemon strategies, the more fun they have collecting and exchanging Pokemon cards. Ultimately each user "gets hooked" on the world of Pokemon in his own way. At this stage, the value of the Pokemon game software to a user is dramatically greater than it was when he first bought it. This is how value of an invisible innovation extends across time.

As we saw with the Walkman, "inferior" values – when measured by conventional performance yardsticks – often go hand-in-hand with invisible innovations. A company must break the stranglehold of convention to achieve invisible innovations. Companies bound to the paradigm of incremental value see the value of their new offerings as mere "bundles of visible dimensions," and compare them both with rival products and their own previous models only in terms of dimensional superiority or inferiority. As a consequence, they neglect the approach of integrating user experience over time. A successful invisible innovation requires a mindset that enthusiastically allows existing dimensional values to grow marginally "inferior."

The approach to maximizing cumulative value requires companies to reconsider the timing of new product releases. Under the paradigm of visible innovation, the key competitive issue is which company can boost value fastest along a specified dimension. Incremental value increases should be achieved as quickly as possible. But under invisible innovations, this conventional wisdom doesn't necessarily apply.

When a dominant product or service design is not yet established within an industry, a company could conceivably succeed by introducing a completely new product concept and establishing a dominant design in one fell swoop. But after the dominant design is established and while the industry still has room for visible innovations along specified performance and quality measures, invisible innovations – even if executed ahead of rivals – carries the risk of failure. That's because the visible value with large increment draws user attention to products with visible innovations.

Sony's Cocoon provides an example of this phenomenon. The Cocoon is a product that can digitally record television programs on a hard disk drive. But Sony positioned the Cocoon as a "next generation TV" that would supplant conventional television, rather than as a replacement for conventional video tape recorders. The Cocoon has a function whereby it learns customer preferences during the process of repeated use. Once it understands the user's preferences, it automatically starts recording different kinds of programs. By using Cocoon, customers can reduce lost opportunities to see programs they might have enjoyed watching. The Cocoon was based on Sony's insight that, amid too many content choices, customers faced the problem of selecting programs matching their interests. It presented consumers with a new concept innovation: taking program editing out of the exclusive domain of television stations and making it available to individual users.

Unlike rivals Matsushita Electric and Toshiba, who put high screen resolution, hard drive capacity, DVD recording functionality, and other visible dimensions front and center when developing their new digital video recorders, Sony emphasized the Cocoon's new concept as "a television with a brain," and didn't even bother to equip it with DVD recording capability.[14] And in fact the Cocoon sold well and was enthusiastically received: early adopters gave it extremely high marks.

But immediately following the Cocoon's release, other new DVD-equipped digital television recorders started diffusing to the general home-user market at a furious pace. What's more, digital recorder performance and functionality quickly improved. When customer interest shifted to the recorders' visible value dimensions, Sony was forced him to respond. It changed strategies, releasing a new DVD recorder called SugoRoku that emphasized visible dimensions.

---

[14] Author interview with Tsujino Koichiro, President of Network Terminal Solution Company, Sony Corporation (2/2003)

Cocoon appears a good example of seeking to create a new concept through an invisible innovation, in this case "an entirely new way of enjoying television." Like the Walkman, it made possible a fundamentally different "television experience." But in terms of timing, the Cocoon was too far ahead of the market. The Cocoon's case suggests that invisible innovations are likely to have greater impact on customers when markets are more mature and innovations along visible dimensions are already approaching its limits.

Seeing and Showing Invisible Dimensions

The two innovation strategies for de-commoditization – the black-box strategy and invisible innovation strategy – need certain types of knowledge as organizational capability for successful implementation. We can derive two implications for creating and managing knowledge for realizing innovations for de-commoditization out of our discussion. First, knowledge of complex interdependencies and interactions becomes ever more critical regardless of the strategy adopted. Such knowledge does not allow a single interpretation, nor can it be formulated in a universal way. Rather, it is produced within specific contexts and is built upon longstanding accumulations of tacit knowledge. The role of tacit knowledge in de-commoditization strategy is more critical than ever before.

Second, while tacit knowledge lie at the heart of both de-commoditization strategies, the black-box and invisible innovation strategies require different types of tacit knowledge, and the methodology for creating such knowledge under each strategy is therefore different. Let us look at each of these two implications in more detail.

The black-box strategy from a knowledge management perspective lies in the paradox of product architecture whereby "modularization drives integration."[15] Conceptually, the relationship between modularization and integration is mutually exclusive. In other words, a trend toward modularization – whereby subsystem interface rules become increasingly predefined – is simultaneously a trend away from integration. But assuming there are limits to a system's ability to handle complexity, modularization at the product-system level triggers integration at the subsystem/component level. Thus modularization and integration progress in parallel.

This produces the phenomena whereby the burden of boosting overall product-system performance falls disproportionately on subsystems, as customer demands for ever-higher performance progressively "roll downhill." Let's consider the case of the hard disk drive, a modular PC subsystem. As PCs become increasingly sophisticated, they place greater loads on subsystems. The hard disk drive is no exception; it must read and write data at extremely high speeds, yet perform within a

---

[15]   See Aoshima and Takeishi's *The Perspective of Architecture* in Fujimoto/Takeishi/Aoshima's *Business Architecture* (Yuhikaku, 2001) for a discussion of how modularization and integration proceed in parallel.

limited physical space. The internal structure of a hard disk drive product-system is quite modularized: components include heads, media, firmware, and so forth. Under tough operating conditions, demands for high speed and compact size fall on subsystem components such as heads and media. In order to meet stringent demands for functional improvement, subsystems must solve complex interdependency and interaction problems. As a consequence, subsystem components such as heads must have extremely integral architectures. In other words, as higher level systems such as PCs and hard disk drives become more modular, lower-level subsystems become increasingly integral. In light of this phenomenon, we can understand why many companies strive to develop CCDs and CMOS sensors for digital cameras or other key image processing subsystem for audiovisual products.

Modularization increasingly breaks the overall system down into separate modules and reduces subsystem interdependency. Yet within each module, internal interdependencies become more complex than ever. Modularization can be understood as the codification of architecture knowledge related to pre-defined interface rules. Yet such knowledge is never exhausted. Codification of higher-level system knowledge, in fact, has the effect of increasing tacit knowledge at the subsystem level. Thus knowledge of the most modularized subsystem is, in one sense, knowledge of the most integral type. This extremely context-dependent tacit knowledge of complex interdependencies and interactions is what makes it possible for a company to make subsystems into black boxes not easily duplicated by rivals. Creating and storing this kind of tacit knowledge is the key to succeeding with a black box strategy.

The tendency for context-dependent tacit knowledge to become increasingly important is equally true with invisible innovations. As we have seen, invisible innovations focus on the context in which customers derive value from products. Under visible innovations, customer-product interaction is a relatively minor issue, because value of a particular innovation can be expressed in the form of specific improved functionality along visible dimensions. Value can be context-independently defined and perceived. Under invisible innovations, though, the product-customer interaction process is crucial. Here, too, the key is creating tacit knowledge – but in the context of product-customer interactions.

According to the SECI (Socializing, Expressing, Combining, Internalizing) model of organizational knowledge production, knowledge is created through four recurring processes[16]. "Expressing" means codifying tacit knowledge; "Combining" means assembling codified chunks to put in SECI order; and "Internalizing" means making explicit knowledge tacit. "Socializing" means adopting others' tacit knowledge as one's own. Of these four processes, internalization and socialization are particularly important for the creation of tacit knowledge, and the key issue becomes the context (place or *ba*) in which knowledge interactions take place.

"Know-how" forms the bulk of tacit knowledge at the core of back-box strategies. Know-how means expertise in the interdependencies that enable multiple subsystems with integral architectures to function flawlessly as a single, higher

---

[16]   See Ikujiro Nonaka and Hirotaka Takeuchi (1995) *The Knowledge-Creating Company*, Oxford University Press

level system. To acquire and store this type of know-how, a company must develop within its internal organization ways to promote interactions that encourage internalization and socialization.

In contrast, the tacit knowledge at the core of the invisible innovation strategy is not know-how, but rather "know-what." Know-what views value from the customer's perspective, and involves knowledge of what the product should be like, which customers will use, and what benefits they will seek. Successful invisible innovations depend on the depth and breadth of the company's know-what.

The decisive difference between the black-box and non-dimensional differentiation strategies lies in the difference between creating tacit knowledge in the context of the internal organization and producing it in the context of the external environment, which extends to and encompasses customers. In the black-box strategy, a company produces know-how in the internal context of interactions between individuals or groups within the organization. In contrast, in order to achieve invisible innovations, a company must produce know-what in the external context of interactions with customers. Here, the central issue becomes how to build and maintain an external context in which to interact with customers.

Under the paradigm of visible innovations, it may be sufficient for the company to simply secure a channel through which it can interact with customers to obtain understandings of what customers are looking for and what dimensions and levels of innovation they require. Under the non-dimensional differentiation approach, however, "listening to what customers want" is by definition no simple matter. This sort of reactive, "market-in" approach may not work effectively, because value innovation dimensions are originally invisible. After all, customers usually don't have a clear, prior understanding of innovations they need. Asking customers what they need when they themselves do not know is unlikely to be productive.

The "ask customers what they want" paradigm is not merely ineffective, it can actually impede invisible innovations.

When speaking about their "needs" customers express the dissatisfactions and hopes they've had for products up till that point. But their comments are generally predicated along specific value dimensions. For example, most large-scale customer research studies present lists of multiple value dimensions deemed important to customers. Researchers then investigate how participants rank each dimension and the extent to which current customer status deviates from expressed priority for each dimension. Even assuming there are latent opportunities to create new product concepts, efforts to "listen to customers" inevitably – and ironically – wind up focusing company attention on an innovation along visible dimensions.

In short, for realizing invisible innovations, needed are seeing invisible dimensions of customer value, and then showing customers invisible dimensions of an innovation. This requirement of seeing and showing invisible dimensions presents challenging new issues to organizational knowledge creation. Compared to creating an internal organizational context that encourages internalization and socialization, it is far more difficult to create a comparable external environment – especially one that encompasses customers over whom one exerts no direct influence. Companies intending to create invisible innovations must build bridges to their customers – I call this creating "context" for interactions – that allow knowledge to be internalized and socialized more consciously and proactively than is possible during the usual in-house accumulation and dissemination of tacit know-how. Greater depth of customer interaction, both direct and indirect, is indispensable to seeing and showing invisible dimensions.

Software development team leaders at Nintendo who have many hit games to their credit don't "listen" to customers, nor do they spend much time playing games themselves. Instead, their approach is to peer over the shoulders of users who are actually playing games, observing such play closely and in great detail to discover what customers truly seek in games. They analyze through single-minded observation; the over-the-shoulder perspective allows them to see what users find fun, surprising, emotionally compelling, or boring, and how they move controllers in response to their feelings. Developers say that frequently moving between the developer and player perspectives in this way is indispensable to creating interesting new games.[17] For example, while developing the Super Mario 64 game, the Nintendo team believed that camera motion would be the key to fun and comfortable three-dimensional play. Until then, three-dimensional games didn't place the camera in any special position or otherwise use it in novel ways; the camera simply tracked the hero. As a result, depending on how the hero moved, he would often end up hidden behind an object, invisible to the player. Patiently observing users at play and accumulating insight after insight concerning user experience enabled Nintendo's developers to create "fun game software." Here, too, "seeing the invisible dimension" through internalization and socialization with customers played a crucial role in creating a new product concept.

It is relatively easy to demonstrate to customers the value of specific differentiated functionality. But it is no trivial matter to get customers to understand the value of product concept innovations, precisely because the value dimensions are invisible. Another key to concept innovation is making customers understand the invisible dimensions of concept innovation. However, "showing the invisible dimension" is the most important, yet most difficult, task. A one-time product or service "transaction" alone cannot correctly communicate concept values to users. Companies need continuous interactions with users. Moreover, "ongoing customer relationships" in the form of conventional after-service and post-sale support are inadequate. Follow-up services and post-sales support usually assume the existence of visible dimensions such as functionality, performance, and quality, and try to respond to customers' complaints or problems along those dimensions; they don't necessarily promote understanding or reinforce invisible dimensions of concept innovations. In order to get customers to fully understand value of concept innovation, companies must deliberately build and provide a context for internalization and socialization with customers.

We previously saw how Apple's iPod succeeded with its concept innovation. Apple's promotions didn't simply emphasize the iPod's design and functionality; the company worked continuously to spotlight post-purchase user experiences and how the iPod concept matched a new type of lifestyle. Next, by releasing iTunes

---

[17] Author interview with Iwata Satoi, then-Director of Nintendo's Management Planning Group 5/2001

music editing software and launching its iTunes Music Store in 2003, Apple furnished a context for users to continuously extract and reinforce the iPod's value through repeated use. iTunes lists more than 30 million songs, and by 2004 it had won 70 percent of the fee-based Internet music market. But because of the low $0.99 per-song price, iTunes itself is not especially profitable. The key source of Apple's music business earnings is the high-priced yet popular iPod, which enjoys a 30 percent market share. Connecting an iPod to a computer lets users immediately copy downloaded tunes onto the device so they can easily carry their favorite music with them wherever they go. iTunes is thus a powerful tool for encouraging customers to use the iPod in ways consistent with Apple's new concept.[18]

Spontaneous interactions between customers are the most effective way to communicate invisible dimensions embodied in a new product concept. When it began selling its Pokemon game, Nintendo simultaneously released two versions featuring different character ratios. For example, the A-Bok character appears frequently in the "Red" version of the game, while the Persian character is almost entirely absent. In the "Green" version of the game, the ratio at which these two characters appear is reversed.[19] The purpose is to create a mechanism for promoting the new concept of Pokemon as a fun game, whereby players collect cards, "battle" with friends, and exchange characters. In this case, the "context" for customer interaction is built into the product itself. In a sense, the Pokemon game has already begun when potential users look around to see which Pokemon software their friends have, then agonize over whether to buy "Red" or "Green" versions of the game. Nintendo's unique insight into how it could spark interactions between customers drove the company to develop two different versions of Pokemon.

In 2004 Nintendo released a new Pokemon series for the Game Boy Advance (GBA), a portable game player. This new software is bundled with a "wireless adapter" peripheral device. The adapter allows GBA owners to transmit data wirelessly between them without incurring communications charges. Previously GBA owners had to connect their players to cable Internet or other online services in order to exchange cards or battle friends. With the wireless adapter, they can readily battle or exchange cards without fussing with wire connections. The software also has a "Union Room" feature that provides a virtual space in which wireless adapter-equipped GBA users can assemble. Once a player enters the Union Room, his wireless adapter automatically searches for other comparably-equipped players in the area, and starts transmitting when it finds one.[20] These tactics can be understood as Nintendo's way of promoting customer understanding of the value inherent in the product concept by furnishing a context for spontaneous user interactions.

---

[18]   Nihon Keizai Shimbun 3/1/2004
[19]   Nihara Shigero, *Nihon no Yushu Kigyou Kenkyu* [*Inquiries into Outstanding Japanese Companies*], Nihon Keizai Shimbunsha 2003
[20]   www.pokemon.co.jp (3/2004)

Conclusions

Amid growing commoditization, companies must devise innovation strategies for regaining customer WTP. There are two basic ways: building a specialized subsystem black box which competitors are unable to imitate, or innovating a product concept along invisible dimensions. Literature on strategic management of innovation has paid much attention to the black box strategy. Our perspective of the visibility of innovation dimensions sheds new light on issues often overlooked under conventional innovation theories that tacitly or explicitly assume the existence of visible dimensions. Escaping commoditization through invisible innovations requires a firm to re-conceptualize innovation and competition under a completely different paradigm. That is the key message of this paper.

The concept of invisible innovation is not completely new. Companies in the fashion and entertainment industries have long been acutely aware of these ideas. Strategy, marketing, and innovation scholars, too, have discussed related issues, if only in bits and pieces, using terms such as value proposition, experience economy, emotional benefits, brand, CRM, design management, and so forth. But at a time when many companies and industries suffer from falling profitability due to commoditization, it can be tremendously beneficial to reconceptualize strategy from the standpoint of visibility of innovation dimensions. I believe one key benefit lies in the potential of this perspective to provide a common language of discourse for the many arguments and experiences expounded in different industries.

What's important now is to transcend disparate industry- and company-specific practice to a more universal view of how firms can create "differences" between themselves and rivals through innovations. The concept of invisible innovation proposes logic to achieving that aim.

The Customer System and New Product Development: The Material Supplier's Strategy in Japan

Junichi Tomita and Takahiro Fujimoto

Introduction

Who is the real customer and what does he need? Recently, as customer needs have become increasingly sophisticated and diversified, new product development competition has also intensified in many industries. In order to offer the customer new value, it is one of the most important tasks for firms to understand their relationships with their customers.

In general, customer relationships have become more complex for suppliers than their relationships with final products manufacturers. For instance, for polymer manufacturers for coatings direct customers are coatings manufacturers, though it is more important to understand their buyers' needs. These customers include wholesalers, general contractors, and owners of buildings. Moreover, design offices, general contractors, and painters etc. often influence the coatings specifications that the owners finally decide upon.

In short, for polymer manufacturers for coatings customers form a hierarchical structure and these broadly defined "customers" are often dependent on each other and have diverse needs. Therefore, it is not only necessary to consider the intermediate user (final products manufacturer), but also the end user (consumer)[1]. This paper defines the downstream of the value chain as a "customer system," and argues what an effective development pattern in a "customer system" oriented manner should be through a case study. It is important to understand the information flow in the customer system in the product development process.

We seek to answer what impact the product development process in a "customer system" oriented manner has, and in what conditions the process is most effective. This paper examines these questions by means of a case study.

---

[1] Our previous research revealed that material suppliers who corresponded to the intermediate user needs adequately tended to fail in sales, but the suppliers that anticipated in advance the potential needs of consumers tended to success in sales (in 35 materials development projects) (Kuwashima and Fujimoto 2001; Tomita 2003a). This result implies that even material suppliers are required to understand the end user needs.

Customer System

It is not a new idea at all that customers form a hierarchical structure. It has already been discussed in research on distribution channels, relationship marketing, supply chain management, and value networks, etc.

For instance, in channel selection theory, channel selection is treated as a structural problem including two or more players at multiple stages (Takashima 1994). In research related to relationship marketing, it is suggested that it is not only necessary to pay attention to dyad relationships such as seller-buyer (customer) relationship, but also to hierarchical relationships including suppliers, firms (final products manufacturer), distributors, and the end user in the value chain (Day and Montgomery 1999).

The value network describes how all products are nested into a product hierarchy structure (Christensen 1997). Research on supply chain management shows that a firm cannot achieve competitive advantages without supply chain management and that it should understand strengths and weaknesses by analyzing three levels of the supply chain: organizational structure level, technological level, and business process capability level (Fine 1998).

However, such a hierarchy of customers has hardly been discussed in the context of the new product development process. This is due to the fact that in research on product development management, a simple dichotomy is assumed with regard to the firm-customer relationship: one vis-à-vis many (final products manufacturer vis-à-vis many end user) in the final products case, and one vis-à-vis one (one supplier vis-à-vis one final products manufacturer) in the components/raw materials case (Clark and Fujimoto 1991; von Hippel 1988).

Exceptions are Kuwashima (2003) and Fujita and Ikuine (2005). Kuwashima (2003) researches industrial product development in the chemical industry, and discusses that a direct approach to the end users called "customer of customer" strategy is needed in cases, such as when the direct customer cannot appropriately translate end users' needs into suppliers' specifications. Fujita and Ikuine (2005) research non-packaged software development, and argue that acquiring information by "organizing users" is an effective pattern in rapid prototyping. Although they comment that organizing customers beyond the boundaries of firms is effective in product development, they hardly discuss interdependent relationships of multiple customers.

On the other hand, a lot of research on supplier systems is related to hierarchical structures between firms. But these studies mostly focus on the final products manufacturer's view and only a few proceed from the supplier's point of view. Exceptions are Nobeoka (1996) and Konnnou (2003). They address the scope of customers and observe that broader a scope of customers allows for more profitable and continuous transactions. However, they don't comment extensively on the hierarchy of customers.

This paper focuses on the hierarchy of customers and examines it's linkage to the new product development process. Specifically, like in the components/raw materials case, this paper assumes the situation that customers form a hierarchy including two or more interdependent economic players labeled "Customer System" (Figure 1). In the customer system, customers are often dependent on each other and have different needs and negotiation power.

In this case, it is not only necessary to consider the intermediate user, but also the end user (consumer). The final products may not appeal to the end user (consumer) if components or raw materials are developed exclusively according to the needs of the intermediate user (final products manufacturer). Therefore, it is necessary to understand the flow of information and the interdependent relationships between customers within the entire customer system.

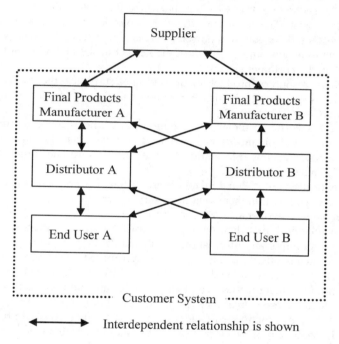

Fig. 1. Conceptual map of the customer system

Why is it important to understand the customer system? To answer this question, we first discuss the flow of information in the system. In distribution theory, distribution flows are investigated from three points of view: transaction flow, money flow, and information flow (Yahagi 1996).

Glazer (1989) focused on information flows and defined the distribution channel including supplier, final products manufacturer, distributor, and end user as an information processing system with many players in the channel trying to create, acquire, and use valuable information. Like Glazer, this paper also considers the "customer system" as an information processing system.

In this case, important information for suppliers developing new products might be needs information and seeds information. The former is the information that the suppliers mainly receive from their customers, and the latter is the information that they mainly provide their customers with. They can also develop new products more effectively by appropriately understanding the flows of their information, and acquiring, using, as well as offering necessary information.

However, for suppliers, it isn't necessary to acquire the information for product development, even if the flow of information can be understood. And therefore, such information is cut off by several factors.

Thus, the second point is whether and where the factors that cut off the information flow exist. The main cut-off factors considered are "lack of resources", "diverse customers' negotiation power", "channel conflicts", "weakness of the mutual trust between customers", "limit of the needs translation ability of the specific customer" in the customer system.

If financial resources, product lineup, and sales staff lack, then it is difficult for manufacturers to promote to distributors and end users or to collect information from them (Corey et al. 1989).

When the specific customer's negotiation power, i.e., economic power, information power, and organizational power, is stronger than the other customers' ones, only advantageous information for the specific customer might flow (Ishihara 1982; Takashima 1994).

If goals or needs of channel members are different from each other, then channel conflicts occur within them, and necessary information is likely to be transmitted inadequately (Stern et al. 1989; Uehara 1999).

In trust relationships, when the mutual trust between customers weakens, they might not offer important information (Sheth and Parvatiyar 2000).

End user needs might not be adequately transmitted to the supplier, when the intermediate user needs and end user needs are different from each other, or when the final products manufacturer can't exactly translate end user needs into components/raw materials specification (Kuwashima and Fujimoto 2001).

Moreover, above-mentioned factors often exist simultaneously in the customer system. If some cut-off factors exist, they should be removed, weakened or avoided. It is the first step of a customer-oriented strategy to understanding the information flow in the customer system

To examine how the customer system orientation has been applied in new product development by a supplier, this paper focuses on the case of LUMIFLON, a fluoropolymer developed by Asahi Glass Company, Limited (AGC).

Case Study – Development of LUMIFLON at AGC[2]

Product Feature

In 1982, AGC developed and commercialized the first soluble fluoropolymer for coatings called LUMIFLON[3]. In general, coatings are composed of four basic elements: polymer, pigments, solvent, and additive. Especially the polymer has a strong impact on the specifications of coatings (weather resistance, gloss retention, adhesiveness, flexibility, transparency, etc.).

LUMIFLON offers some excellent features such as a superior weather resistance and durability compared to existing coatings' polymers such as acrylic silicon, and has been applied in wide markets, i.e., large-scale buildings, bridges, cars, airplanes, and plants since it was introduced to the market.

LUMIFLON is now used in about 80% of all cases as fluoropolymer for coatings except for those, which need to be applied at high temperatures in factories for example. And it recorded 15000 usages for about 20years since entering the market.

Development of LUMIFLON

In 1975, the development of LUMIFLON began. At that time the buildings in Japan, were planned to be built ever higher, and concerns about the long-term maintenance of these building rose. But the existing coatings for the exterior of these buildings needed frequent repainting because of low durability. AGC expected high potential demand for durable coatings, and started to develop a soluble fluoropolymer for coatings.

At AGC's Yokohama Laboratory, the synthetic research team consisting of 3 or 4 members was formed, and research of fluoropolymers for coatings started. At that time, another fluoropolymer for coatings already existed, but it wasn't soluble well and needed to be applied in factories at high temperatures. Therefore, the goal was set to develop a highly durable coating that could also be applied to large-scale buildings.

After five years of experimentation, a prototype of this polymer was developed. The new fluoropolymer obtained was named LUMIFLON (LF). As a result of having promoted LUMIFLON, AGC had come to develop a new coating jointly with three coating manufacturers. At AGC, the LF-team consisting of 15 members from the synthetic research team, the applied research team, and the process development team cooperated with the other coating manufacturers in the joint de-

---

[2]   Details of the case are discussed by Tomita (2003b).

[3]   LUMIFLON is the brand name, and the formal chemical name of this polymer is Fluoroethylene-Alkyl Vinyl Ether (FEVE). At that time, another fluoropolymer for coatings already existed, but it wasn't soluble in a solvent well and needed to be applied in factories at high temperatures. Therefore, a highly durable coating that could also be used for large-scale buildings didn't exist.

velopment project. Thus, the new coating was developed by close cooperation between four firms.

Sales Failure and Cause Analysis

In 1982, the new fluoropolymer coating was offered in the construction market at first, but was hardly sold. Analyses revealed that there were several problems: First, the price of the new coating was higher than the price of existing ones. Second, evidence of LUMIFLON's durability was insufficient because it could only be acquired after a period of several years (Matsushita 1991). Third, painters, LUMIFLON's customers' customers, wouldn't accept the new coating, as they argued that "if high durable coatings were adopted, then painters' work would decrease." Fourth, wholesalers and general contractors also tended to avoid buying a new coating because of the high sales risk. Rather, they aimed for large transactions involving existing coatings to obtain higher margins. Fifth, sales promotions by coating manufacturers were insufficient. Coating manufactures also tried to obtain the orders of big customer (for existing coatings) in order to gain market share efficiently. Therefore, they didn't focus on sales of the new coating.

As mentioned above, the advantages of LUMIFLON such as high durability weren't transmitted adequately to the end user (owners of buildings). Another problem was that coating manufactures couldn't understand the needs of owners of buildings adequately, because they tended to focus on close customers like wholesalers and general contractors (Figure 2(a)). The following comment expresses the problems of the coatings industry well:

"In the coating industry a firm in the distribution channel tends to meet with direct customers, i.e., general contractors and design offices meet with owners' needs and wholesalers meet with needs of general contractors and design offices. Therefore, only superficial needs like cheaper price are transmitted to the material supplier, instead of potential needs like quality (durability)" (Kagaya 2002).

Towards a Market Oriented Organization: Introduction of Backsell

Based on the results of these analyses, AGC built a market-oriented organization. In 1984 a "Project Group" was established in the chemical division to understand end users' needs and in 1985 a special team was set up when LUMIFLON was relocated to "Star Products"[4]. This was a cross-functional team consisting of sales, R&D, and production and was managed independently from other teams under the direction of the Star Products Leader.

In addition, in 1985 AGC aimed at market development by using an approach called "Backsell" in cooperation with selected coatings manufacturers. Backsell meant that polymer manufacturers like AGC promoted their products from downstream to upstream in the distribution channel. For example, first AGC's promo-

---

[4]   Star Products was an in-house venture system at AGC.

tion of LUMIFLON based coatings was directed at end users (the owners of build-ings) and only in a second step was it also geared towards general contractors. (Matsushita 1991) (Figure 2(b)).

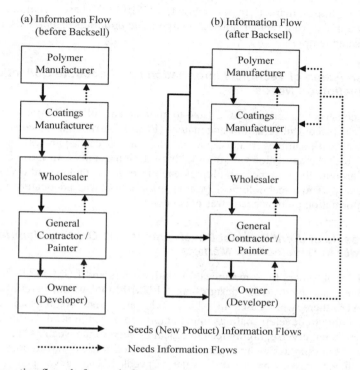

Fig. 2. Information flows before and after Backsell

Market Development

Based on the market oriented organization described above, coating manufacturers such as AGC tried to promote LUMIFLON based coatings to end users by their Backsell approach. Target markets were buildings, construction, and cars. Goals were set to develop these markets. As mentioned above, the definition of the Backsell was an approach for end users, but its practical goal was a broader range of activities as follows.

1. Transmission of technical information and adequate collection of information on needs
2. Proposals of joint product development with coating manufacturers in order to develop new markets

3. Provisions of incentives to each level of customers by offering new orders from end users

We now explain how AGC behaved to achieve its goals by analyzing the case of the buildings market. In the market, LUMIFLON based coatings are now widely applied from regular houses to large-scale buildings, event halls, as well as shrines and temples.

Transmission of Technical Information and Adequate Collection of Information on Needs

In the construction market, AGC tried to approach as follows to transmit the technological (seeds) information adequately (Figure 2(b)). That is, sales promotion was done with samples, panels, photos, test data by catch phrases, i.e., "maintenance free", "many color variations", "high design quality". In those cases, AGC asked around about owners' buildings each in order to understand owners' needs adequately. Thus, technological (seeds) information was adequately transmitted and information on new needs was collected.

Proposals of Joint Product Development with Coating Manufacturers in Order to Develop New Markets

If AGC took orders by communication with owners and LUMIFLON based coatings were accepted at the design stage, LUMIFLON would certainly be used. However, there were cases in which AGC and other coatings manufacturers weren't able to develop coatings immediately, because the needs of building owners were often diverse, highly technological or very vague, such as "remove stains easily", "building design arrangement with rows of houses" and so on.

In those cases, based on owner's needs AGC developed (improved) LUMIFLON based coatings jointly with coating manufacturers and presented new coatings to the owner. This development cycle was repeated until the owners of buildings gave his approval.

Provision of Incentives to Each Level of Customers by Offering New Orders from End Users

As mentioned above, general contractors and painters saw little merit in adopting LUMIFLON based coatings. Then, AGC tried to increase sales by giving incentives to its customers. For instance, AGC not only promoted LUMIFLON to general contractors and painters but also offered them new orders for LUMIFLON based coatings from end users (owners of buildings). As a result, they had incentives of using the coatings.

Moreover, if coatings manufacturers were able to increase new orders from building owners, they sold large quantities of LUMIFLON based coatings. As a result, AGC offered to build long-term cooperative relationship with them.

Consequently, by introducing the "Backsell" approach, AGC linked market development with product development (improvement) effectively, and also has applied the coating to other markets, i.e., bridges, cars, airplanes, and plants, etc.

Management of Customer System

Based on the LUMIFLON case, this section discusses how a customer system approach like Backsell influences the product development process and in what kind of situation this approach is effective.

Influence of Customer System Oriented Manner

In the last section, we described how AGC used an approach called Backsell in order to increase sales of LUMIFLON based coatings. This system discusses what impact the product development process in a "customer system" oriented manner has, and in what conditions the process is most effective

In LUMIFLON's case, there were the following two problems from a customer system point of view. First, AGC couldn't understand the needs of buildings' owners adequately. Second AGC encountered the problem that it couldn't transmit new product information (seeds information) to the owners adequately. Factors underlying these problems such as channel conflicts, limits of the needs translation abilities of specific customers, and diverse customers' negotiation power were identified, which influenced the distribution channel for construction coatings including coating manufacturers, wholesalers, general contractors, painters, and owners (developer) of the buildings (Figure 2(a)).

With regard to the first problem, AGC depended on coating manufacturers to promote LUMIFLON based coatings. However, owing to the limited number of sales people, the coating manufacturers couldn't promote enough. They rather focused on bulk orders for existing coatings by big customers (wholesaler and general contractor) in order to get market share efficiently.

In sum, the goals of AGC and coating manufacturers were different from each other. And the power of big coating customers strongly influenced sales decisions of coating manufactures. As a result, it seemed that coating manufacturers couldn't acquire enough information on owners' needs and translate it into polymer specifications adequately.

In addition, the latter problem also resulted from channel conflicts. The wholesalers and general contractors also tended to avoid buying a new coating because of the high sales risk. Rather, they aimed for large sales of existing coatings to obtain more favorable margins.

Furthermore, the painters tended to avoid using the durable coatings because using them might lead to decrease the coating order for the long term.

That is, the goals of AGC, wholesalers, general contractors, and painters were different from each other. As a result, AGC and the coating manufacturers couldn't transmit technological information to the owners adequately.

Due to these goal differences between AGC and its customers, AGC couldn't transmit new product information (seeds information) to the owners adequately.

Based on these results of its analyses, AGC built a market-oriented organization. In 1985, it tried to develop its markets by using an approach called "Back-sell" in cooperation with a few coating manufacturers. This approach helped to weaken, remove, or avoid the factors that cut off the flow of information in the customer system. First, action 1. and 2. described in the last section allowed AGC to avoid the cut-off factors (channel conflicts) and transmit new technological (seeds) information and to collect information on needs by contacting owners directly. Second, action 3. in the last section enabled AGC to weaken the cut-off factors (channel conflicts) further by giving incentives to wholesalers, general contractors, painters.

As a result of its analysis, AGC implemented a customer system called Back-sell, and achieved a high market share by feeding back needs information to the product development process and by promoting new technological (seeds) information to the end users.

Effectiveness of Customer System Approach

Next, we investigate in which situation the customer system approach is most effective. Generally speaking, this approach isn't always critical to the new product development of a supplier. For instance, when a new product is a commodity that is difficult to differentiate, or when the intermediate user translates end user needs into component/raw material specifications adequately, the supplier only has to correspond to the intermediate customer needs accurately (Tamura 2001; Akase 2000).

On the other hand, when the supplier doesn't understand the needs information adequately, or when it doesn't transmit the new product (seeds) information adequately owing to above-mentioned factors, i.e., "channel conflict", and "diverse customers' negotiation power", etc., the customer system approach should be effective.

In addition, it is important to discuss in which stage of the product development process a customer system approach should be started. In this case study, this approach was employed as an emergency measure – so to speak – after the commercialization of the polymer for coatings. Yet, sales-opportunity losses after commercialization could possibly have been avoided if this approach had been taken before commercialization. Based on this case study, we thus argue that executing s customer system approach during the early stages of new product development is also effective.

Knowledge Accumulation of Customer System

This chapter suggested the "customer system" and argued how an effective development pattern in a "customer system" oriented manner should be executed by means of a case study. It is implied that suppliers not only need to consider the intermediate user, but also the end user or their customers' customers in their new product development process. It also implies that knowledge accumulation through a customer system may be an important aspect of new product development for suppliers.

Knowledge about the customer system consists of knowledge about each customer's needs in the customer system and knowledge related to interdependencies between customers. Ogawa (2000) stated that "background knowledge of needs" is needed to translate needs information into necessary functions for customers and this type of information can only be obtained by participating in the activity that generates the information. Knowledge of the customer system in this chapter is also closely related to "background knowledge of needs" because suppliers can only get information by contacting the customer system directly.

However, for knowledge accumulation the opposite may be true. For instance, in a piece of research on supplier management, Takeishi (2003) mentioned that having organizational capabilities in-house which evaluate suppliers from multiple angles is a critical point in order to effectively outsource for car manufacturers. It implies that knowledge accumulation about the supplier system is also important for final products manufacturers.

Of course, this research and our findings are subject to several limitations: We focus on a single case study. More sophisticated conceptualization and systematic analyses are needed in the future.

References

Akase H (2000): Gousei jushi no seihin kaihatsu. [The polymer development] In Fujimoto T and Yasumoto M (Eds.), *Seikou suru seihin kaihatsu* [The effective pattern of product development] pp.129-150, Tokyo: Yuuhikaku (in Japanese)

Clark KB and Fujimoto T (1991): *Product development performance.* Boston, MA: Harvard Business School Press

Corey RE, Cespedes FV, and Rangan KV (1989): Going to market: Distribution sysmetes for industrial products. Boston, MA: Harvard Business School Press

Christensen CM (1997): *The innovator's dilemma.* Boston, MA: Harvard Business School Press

Day GS and Montgomery DB (1999): Charting new directions for marketing. *Journal of Marketing*, 63, 3-13

Fine CH (1998): *Clockspeed: Winning Industry Control in the Age of Temporary Advantage.* Reading, MA: Perseus Books

Fujita H and Ikuine F (2005): Datsu package-ka shita software no kaihatsu. [Non-packaged software development] *Akamon Management Review*, 4(2), 51-70 (in Japanese)

Glazer R (1989): *Marketing and the changing information environment.* Cambridge, MA: Marketing Science Institute

Ishihara T (1982): *Marketing kyousou no kouzou.* [The structure of marketing competition.] Tokyo: Chikura Shobo (in Japanese)

Kagaya K (2002): Sozai maker no brand sennryaku ni manabe. [Learn from brand strategy of material suppliers] *THE21*, 209, 45-47

Konnou Y (2003): Suppliers' performance and parts transactions with customers. *Annals of Business Administrative Science*, 2(1), 1-10

Kuwashima K (2003): Shin seihin kaihatsu ni okeru "kokyaku no kokyaku" senryaku. ["Customers of customers" strategy in new product development] *Kenkyuu gijutsu keikaku* [The Journal of Science Policy and research management], 18(3/4), 165-175 (in Japanese)

Kuwashima K and Fujimoto T (2001): Kagaku sangyou ni okeru koukateki na seihin kaihatsu process no kenkyu. [The effective product development pattern in chemical industry] *Keizaigaku ronshu* [Journal of Economics], 67(1), 91-127 (in Japanese)

Matsushita K (1991): Joushiki no kabe ni idomu shanai venture seido [Corporate venture system challenging the common sense]. In Senryaku keiei kyoukai (Eds.), *Sinki jigyou kaihatsu ha kosureba seikou suru* (pp.104-115). [Success factors of new business development], Tokyo: Toyo Keizai (in Japanese)

Nobeoka K (1996): Kokyaku hani no keizai. [Customer scope of economy] *Kokumin keizai zasshi* [Journal of National Economics], 173(6), 83-97 (in Japanese)

Ogawa S (2000): Innovation no hassei ronnri. [The emergent logic of innovation] Tokyo: Tikura Shobo (in Japanese)

Sheth JN and Parvatiyar A (2000): *Handbook of relationship marketing*. Thousand Oaks: Sage Publications

Stern LW, El-Ansary AI, and Brown JR (1989): *Management in marketing channels*. Prentice Hall

Takashima K (1994): *Marketing channel soshikiron*. [The organization theory of marketing channel] Tokyo: Chikura Shobo (in Japanese)

Takeishi A (2003): *Bungyo to kyouso*. [Division of labor and competition] Tokyo: Yuuhikaku (in Japanese)

Tamura M (2001): *Ryutsu genri*. [The principle of distribution] Tokyo: Chikura Shobo (in Japanese)

Tomita J (2003a): Kagaku sangyo ni okeru koukateki na seihin kaihatsu pattern [The effective product development pattern in chemical industry]. *Keizaigaku Kenkyu* [The research of Economics], 45, 25-34 (in Japanese)

Tomita J (2003b): Sozai sangyo ni miru shinki jigyou kaihatsu [New business development in material industry]. *Akamon Management Review*, 2(1), 7-38 (in Japanese)

Uehara Y (1999): *Marketing Senryakuron*. [The theory of marketing strategy] Tokyo: Yuuhikaku (in Japanese)

von Hippel E (1988): *The sources of innovation*. New York: Oxford University Press

Yahagi T (1996): *Gendai yyuutsuu*. [Modern distribution] Tokyo: Yuuhikaku Aruma (in Japanese)

Part II: Process Aspects

The Japanese Know-Who Based Model of Innovation Management – Reducing Risk at High Speed

Sigvald J. Harryson

From Time-Based Competition to Time-Based Innovation

Introduction

Global competition and risk in innovation call for unique approaches and processes to win on time with outstanding projects. Time-based competition in innovation received particular attention in Japan in the 1980s and the early 90s (Abegglen and Stalk 1985; Harryson 1998; Stalk and Hout 1990). This is also where our research started with more than 150 interviews conducted during the mid-90s and follow-up interviews in early 2000 to explore and better understand how Canon, Sony and Toyota manage to reduce time in their innovation processes. The interviews were conducted across all functions performing and supervising innovation, including some top executives, such as Akio Morita in June 1993, who strongly inspired the development of the know-who based concept through the following statement:

> The driving force of our rapid innovation is the conviction that if we lose money we can always recover, but if we lose time we can't. Therefore, time has always been a critical issue at Sony. The best way to gain time is to communicate a lot and establish as many personal relationships as possible... The more people you know, the better it is.

Whereas know-how is the ability to solve problems efficiently based primarily on internally accumulated knowledge, experience, and skills, know-who is the ability to acquire, transform, and apply that know-how through personal relationships. The 'who' in know-who based companies knows who has the know-how, has the active empathy to rapidly establish the trustful relationship required to acquire that know-how, and has the multiple competencies required to transform and apply it in a new context so that innovation can occur. Increasingly, it seems that to know who has the know-how gives new opportunities for corporate entrepreneurship and disruptive innovation through proactive exploration and creation of new knowledge and invention, while simultaneously using know-who to transform the results into target-driven and resource-efficient R&D processes for global exploitation of innovation.

An important suggestion of our research on all three Japanese companies is that external sourcing of technologies and skills does not have to result in a hollowing out of internal R&D capabilities. In contrast, it seems to energize and create powerful synergies in know-who based companies' capability to network tacit knowledge into innovation. Neither these networking synergies have been revealed so far in the current literature on the topic – nor how to combine exploration and exploitation of disruptive technologies by leveraging such networking synergies across individual, corporate and extra-corporate levels.

Reviewing Current Literature on the Topic

As witnessed by numerous authors, the Japanese approach to managing innovation processes – especially in the automotive and consumer electronics industries – provided a role-model for many other industries and companies across the globe during the 1980s and early 1990s (Ayas 1996; Clark and Fujimoto 1990, 1991, 1992; Jones 1990; Nonaka and Kenney 1991; Pinto and Kharbanda 1996; Womack et al. 1990). National and corporate networks are often provided as rationales for the high innovation performance of Japanese companies during this period (Laage-Hellman 1997; Imai 1989a, 1989b). Assimakopoulos (2003, p.103) even holds that:

> The very existence of Japanese innovation is enough to confirm the responsibility of the country's networks; no further evidence is required.

Reviewing further key elements of this Japanese approach, another important factor is that project managers usually rank as high as division managers and exercise strong informal leadership. They coordinate entire projects, including production and marketing, and have direct influence on working engineers. Through their strong power and status, they can mobilize all the resources necessary to design, develop, and commercialize a new product or service.

Very challenging targets are either induced by top management or emerge within the team. They usually begin as overall visions that involve contradictions in terms of opposing views or technological limitations, which make them hard to reach (Itami 1987, p. 92; Nonaka 1988a, p. 15, 1988b, pp. 66–67). The initial visions are often equivocal and gradually disintegrated into more tangible tasks and goals[1]. The teams are quite self-organizing, autonomous and ensure overlapping development phases in a 'rugby approach' (Imai et al. 1985; Kenney and Florida 1993, p. 61; Parsons 1991, p. 16; Smothers 1990, p. 523; Takeuchi and Nonaka 1986, pp. 137–41; Walker 1991) where engineers follow the project across its overlapping phases, thus ensuring that generated knowledge is incorporated into

---

[1]   The development of the Toyota Lexus (Harryson, 1995a; 1998) illustrates how visions are used in practice. See also Bartlett and Ghoshal (1989, p. 204); Clark and Fujimoto (1990, p. 110, p. 118); Schütte (1991, p. 266). Kusunoki (1992, pp. 69–70) and Nonaka (1988b, p. 10) provide good examples of disintegration.

the project until it turns into a manufactured product. A tradition of frequent interaction between divisions and, perhaps more important still, across corporate borders promotes parallel development for optimal speed (Aoki 1988, p. 216; Hamel 1991, pp. 96–99; Imai et al. 1985, p. 543; Nonaka 1990, pp. 28–32; Schütte 1991, p. 267).

Sharing of information through open communication is well reported (Ealey and Soderberg 1990; Hatvany and Pucik 1982; Karlsson 1989; Kennard 1991; Kenney and Florida 1993; Kobayashi 1990; Lu 1987). This lays the ground for a greater degree of overlap. It is usually argued that information-sharing activities take place in an environment of creative chaos with few managerial hierarchies or formalism (Nonaka 1988a, pp. 61–62, 1990, pp. 28–33, 1991, pp. 96–104, 1994; Ealey and Soderberg 1990, p. 8; Hedlund and Nonaka 1991, p. 34; Itami 1987, p. 92); Nonaka and Yamanouchi 1989, pp. 306–309).

Proposing a New Synergy Between Internal and External Networking

An emerging question in this context is: what is new with the know-who based approach to knowledge and innovation (K&I) management? Many of the mechanisms above are applied in companies today and external networking is clearly recognized as an essential instrument to gain speed and flexibility. However, this is rarely combined with the development of internal know-who, multicompetency, or the use of human knowledge carriers. This is where the unique networking synergy emerges as the external networking for acquisition of specialized technologies and skills can enhance a company's ability to develop internal know-who and networking capabilities. Know-who based companies develop outward-oriented entrepreneurs and multiple K&I networks, not only for R&D and innovation, but also for the overall management of technologies and skills within and beyond the company. In a highly holistic manner, these networks both explore and exploit external sources of creativity and technology to commercialize the knowledge acquired thereby through a synergistic combination of external and internal networking. Here, 'External networking' refers to the process of linking a firm with extracorporate sources of technology. 'Internal networking' refers to the integration of the research, development, production, and marketing functions that make up the innovation process. The 'synergistic' combination of external and internal networking is a process by which the acquisition of technology from external sources enhances a company's ability to commercialize that technology through integrative mechanisms inherent in the know-who based approach.

A second aspect that has not been highlighted in literature so far is the paradoxical coexistence of hierarchy and its opposite, 'heterarchy' as introduced by Hedlund (1986), which is a cornerstone of the know-who based approach. Most literature emphasizes the self-organizing and organic aspects of Japanese innovation management, but does not describe the role of hierarchy to move from exploration to exploitation, so as to navigate around two dilemmas of innovation that will be introduced in the theoretical framework.

Introducing a Know-Who Based Approach to Networking

The new economics of information and knowledge, coupled with accelerating technological complexity and shrinking product live cycles[2], create intractable dilemmas for companies that rely on internal technological development to meet their K&I needs. Such know-how based companies often seem to be 'stuck' and unable to respond quickly enough to time-paced (Eisenhardt and Brown 1998; Tabrizi and Walleigh 1997) market shifts, because they have concentrated on making their pool of knowledge and technology more and more specialized. Instead of preserving their competitive edge, this has actually left many people in marketing, R&D, and production short of the cross-functional skills they need to perform rapid and radical innovation[3]. Exploiting given advantages does not seem to be sufficient in a competitive environment that increasingly calls for creation of novelty – geared towards clearly identified or successfully created market needs. Due to the decomposition[4] of the industrial system and its value-chains, many firms increase their knowledge intensity through deeper specialization. Paradoxical as it may seem, this seems to make them less well equipped to handle the equally increasing knowledge extensity, i.e., the geographical and organizational dispersion of knowledge important to competitiveness (Hedlund 1994, 1995). As a consequence of these two seemingly opposite dynamic forces, it appears that the real challenge is not simply to advance technological know-how, but to get the balance right between technology depth (knowledge intensity) on the one hand, and customer-driven speed of delivery through concrete market applications with global reach (knowledge extensity) on the other hand.

The know-who based approach's synergistic combination of external and internal networking anchors on two theoretical dilemmas of innovation, which seem to limit the efficacy of pure internal technological development:

- The dilemma of technological leadership is that its successful pursuit tends to focus firms on intracorporate activities. This decreases their sensitivity and responsiveness to external technological and market factors that ought to guide product development. Moreover, the rigidity of typical technology problem-

---

[2]   The importance of time is well captured by Nelson and Winter (1982, p. 279), who, in turn, refer to Schumpeter's thinking, as they contend that 'the payoff to an innovator may depend largely on his ability to exploit that innovation over a relatively short period of time'. See also Stalk et al. (1990, 1992) for more recent findings on time-based competition.

[3]   Hedlund (1992, p. 16) states that 'it is by now well-known that inter-functional collaboration problems are at the root of difficulties to develop new products'.

[4]   Hedlund (1994, p. 19) rolled out pioneering thoughts on decomposition through a scenario in which 'strong intensification and extension of knowledge would lead to the decomposition of the industrial system, entailing a global dispersion of specialized activities, in many cases eschewing existing firm boundaries'. That scenario is absolute reality today, and these thoughts on decomposition are being published widely by leading consulting firms such as *Blown to Bits* by Evans and Wurster (1999).

solving processes impedes cross-departmental collaboration and knowledge transfer across units, which are vital enablers for radical innovation. The technology development process becomes increasingly self-driven and irreversible[5].

The decreasing networking capability also makes it more difficult for the organization to unlearn and to create new knowledge. Finally, the knowledge transfer that needs to take place between R&D, design and manufacturing (D&M), and marketing and sales (M&S) decreases as well. The resulting functional isolation and loss of networking capabilities thus make it highly unlikely that knowledge will transform into innovation. The tacit knowledge-base might increase at the level of specific individuals, but without systematically transforming it into organizational knowledge that creates any real business impact. This dilemma provides an initial rationale for external sourcing of specialized technologies and skills, which is further strengthened by the second dilemma:

- The organizational dilemma of innovation is that the creation and exploration of inventive technologies and knowledge appear to require small and organic organizational structures, whereas rapid innovation through effective exploitation of that knowledge, in contrast, calls for large and rigid organizations (Burns and Stalker 1961; Nonaka and Konno 1998; Nonaka et al. 1994; Martins and Terblanche 2003; Stern 2004). Companies trying to achieve entrepreneurship by pursuing both creative invention and rapid innovation are most likely to be caught in this dilemma.

As suggested by Figure 1, the organizational dilemma of innovation can be described along the two critical dimensions that seem to influence an organization's capability to explore and exploit knowledge, i.e., size of the organization and the degree of managerial hierarchy.

While the lower left-hand square seems to be most adequate for organic knowledge flows that stimulate creative invention, the upper right-hand square depicts the ideal conditions for well-structured and efficient processes. Accordingly, for innovation to happen, both small organic organizations and a large hierarchic unit are typically required.

He and Wong (2004) make a significant contribution to our knowledge about ambidextrous organizations' pursuit of both exploration and exploitation and how this combination impacts the overall innovation performance and sales growth rate. Their extensive empirical study of 206 innovating firms provides support for the two alternative interpretations of the ambidexterity hypothesis, namely that:

1. The interaction between explorative and exploitative innovation is positively related to sales growth rate; and
2. The relative imbalance between explorative and exploitative innovation strategies is negatively related to sales growth rate.

---

[5] In this context, O'Connor *et al.* (2002) note that companies that dominate one generation often fail to maintain their leadership in the next, as a result of self-confidence and perhaps also of focusing too much on incremental innovation. See also Kusunoki (1992) and Harryson (2002).

Their data also shows that for highly ambidextrous firms that consider both exploration and exploitation as 'very important' the relationship between ambidexterity and sales growth rate becomes insignificant. Accordingly, He and Wong (2004, p. 492) conclude that 'the organizational tension inherent between exploration and exploitation may become unmanageable when both are pursued to extreme limits'.

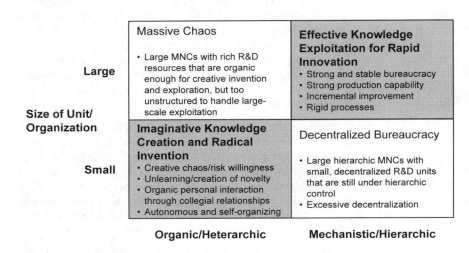

Fig. 1. The paradoxical organizational needs of radical innovation

So, then, how can companies bring disruptive technologies to market and achieve both speed and revolution in innovation? In practice, this would call for a management approach that interlinks the two (shaded) opposite ideal positions without moving into the undesired positions of massive (exaggerated) chaos or decentralized bureaucracy. These two (white) fields are organizational disequilibriums that seem to work against innovation. The main challenge for most companies is to be innovative and exploit the results globally, while avoiding these two dilemmas of innovation – which brings us back to the know-who based approach – this time explored in a network perspective outlined in further detail below.

Proposing a Network Perspective to Enhance Our Understanding of Growth Through Innovation Performance

As an overall reflection on both theory and practice, it seems that relationship-building for multilateral knowledge-sharing is critical both in creating and exploiting innovation. Numerous authors have adopted a network perspective in which relationships and linkage patterns constitute the core element of analysis (Aldrich and Whetten 1981; Bartlett and Ghoshal 1989; Easton 1992; Håkansson and Ford 2002; Håkansson and Henders 1992; Håkansson and Laage-Hellman 1984; Laage-Hellman 1997; Jansson et al. 1990, 1995; Harryson 1995; Johansson and Elg 2002). Some general elements of such a network perspective are:

- Networks typically emerge because no organization is self-sufficient, but rather dependent on extra-organizational resources for its sustained competitiveness.
- A network perspective aims at understanding the totality of relationships and how they jointly accomplish the result.
- Networks are often divided into different (sub-) levels so as to better concentrate the level of analysis to a specific phenomenon where the main-activities happen at that specific level of the network.
- Organizations and large corporations can be regarded and analyzed as integrated networks of complex communication linkages, interdependent actors and activities, and cross-organizational/corporate flows of resources.

As argued by Andersson (1998, p. 64),"the main message in the network view is that cooperation is more efficient than competition for the firm's development." If companies trust each other and develop bonds and communication channels between the different actors in the network, the resources and activities in the network can be organized in a more efficient way. Trust, in particular, is a conditional resource that can be better understood and leveraged to lubricate knowledge transfers across islands of knowledge. We certainly know that no business is an island in today's business context (Håkansson and Snehota 1989; Håkansson and Johanson 2001). Sophisticated networks support the creation and application of knowledge all the way through from key-suppliers to the factory complex where social interaction between individuals, groups and organizations is fundamental to the corporate knowledge creation process. The combination of actors and resources in multiple networks renders possible activities of tremendous breadth, notwithstanding sharply focused individual efforts. As each individual product development activity can be seen as part of a total knowledge creation process, which in turn may be an integral feature of a specific network, it follows that a network perspective will help us to more fully understand corporate technology development and innovation processes.

According to Pfeffer and Salancik (1978), organizations are rarely able to internally generate all the resources and functions required to maintain themselves. Håkansson (1987, 1989, 1990) considers how companies handle their technological development in relation to external clients and organizations, particularly in terms of collaborative projects, claiming that the question is not how the company manages its technological development per se, but 'how it manages to relate its technological development to what is happening inside and between other organizations' (Håkansson 1990, p. 371). In line with the essence of holism, the right combination of technologies and skills often yields a whole that is greater than the sum of its parts. Accordingly, it is essential to know where these parts are and, more essential still, to know who can best contribute to their transfer and transformation, and integrate the parts into a greater whole. As opposed to the atomic view of transaction cost approaches, which take transactions as given instead of considering their creation, a systemic view is required to understand how information transactions happen, including the actors and their relationships (their know-who).

Companies that move from know-how to know-who make extraordinarily effective[6] and efficient[7] use of external networking to acquire both, tacit and explicit knowledge with and from extracorporate centers of excellence. The most important synergistic effect is that these external knowledge links free up key-employees in the company to participate in sophisticated processes of internal networking with three critical objectives:

1. Enhancing the return on R&D through more effective transfer, transformation, and application of knowledge across divisions and business units.
2. Enhancing innovation performance by ensuring that all R&D activities are clearly attuned to market needs through the interlinking of creativity- and process networks.
3. Enhancing the speed of innovation by securing an earlier and more intensive knowledge transfer between R&D, design and manufacturing (D&M), suppliers, and marketing and sales (M&S) networks.

Proposing a Know-Who Based Approach to Interlink Organic Flows of Exploration and Structured Processes of Exploitation

Taking a know-who based approach to K&I management aims at identifying the essential parts that contribute to the K&I management process as a whole. We need to start already at the individual level and combine it with the organizational and the extra-organizational levels. Finally, we need to better understand how these different networks are interlinked into a whole so as to combine exploration and exploitation – for both speed and revolution in innovation. To start with, two different networks with different foci and key-objectives can be outlined:

1. *Extracorporate creativity networks* linked to the research center to internalize external scientific knowledge of explicit and tacit nature;
2. *Intracorporate process networks* for more effective transformation of invention into innovation – thus improving R&D efficiency by:
   - Enabling corporate-wide diffusion and fusion of strategic technologies and skills

---

6   Effective in the sense that any networking activities are explicitly targeted towards the type of knowledge needed for business purposes, e.g., a specific project, or a special skill needed for a process.

7   Efficient in the sense that the cost and efforts of their networking activities to acquire, transform and apply knowledge are comparably low, thanks partly to their know-who, which supports rapid identification of both those who have the knowledge as well as of those who need it, and partly to their multicompetent skills, which support rapid acquisition and transformation of both tacit and explicit knowledge.

- Aligning R&D with market and customer needs through linkages to product management and marketing networks
- Securing fast and efficient transfer of technologies and skills between R&D, D&M, and supplier networks.

These two network levels correspond to the two organizational extremes outlined in Figure 1. A critical question that remains is how to manage for both, creative exploration and rapid market exploitation, i.e., how to capture the advantages of small and big at the same time. As will be illustrated throughout the case-study, the know-who based approach to K&I management centers around the creation and management of organic project networks, which interlink and create complementarities between the creativity networks and process networks. Figure 2 outlines the two types of networks that need to be interlinked to form a know-who based K&I system.

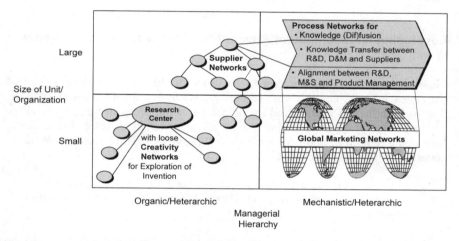

Fig. 2. Core networks of the know-who based K&I system

As suggested by the model, the organizational gap between creativity networks and process networks needs to be bridged so as to accomplish both exploration and exploitation. In this context, Canon's development of the ferroelectric liquid crystal display (FLCD) illustrates how such bridges were built in practice for creative exploration and effective exploitation of a disruptive display technology.

Canon's Know-Who Based Approach to Commercializing a Disruptive Display Technology

As a detailed case study, we will now investigate how Canon deployed a know-who based approach to commercialize a disruptive technology that was invented but never produced in the West, where most companies claimed this would be impossible. A brief complementary example of a know-who based innovation processes from Sony will follow to further illustrate and complete our understanding of effective goal-completion and efficient knowledge transfer through a network system. Many of the factors mentioned above will appear in this case study, but in addition to these well-documented factors the case study will also stress the importance of networking synergies through know-who and multicompetent engineers, and speed and efficiency in knowledge transfer through the use of human knowledge carriers.

Before describing the entire innovation process, from initial acquisition of the technology to development and production of FLCDs, the multicompetent profiles of the initial project leader, Dr. Kanbe, and of the second project manager and design and manufacturing centre manager, Mr. Hirokuni Kawashima will be introduced.

Developing Multicompetent Project Managers with Extensive Know-Who

Chief engineer Kawashima majored in physics and, before joining Canon, carried out research in physics at a state laboratory. When he joined Canon in 1970, he first went through a manufacturing and sales rotation program that is typical for any researcher or engineer joining Canon, and then started his career in the Canon Research Centre to develop photo sensors. Three years later, he started to work on materials for copying machines:

> My official location was at the Research Centre, but in fact I was serving rather as a link between our laboratory and the development centre of a Copying Machine Business Group.

When trial and final production started in 1980, Kawashima was moved to the production plant in question, where he stayed for two years until production was stable, and was then moved to a development centre of silicon drums, where he spent a few years in the chemical division. After this period, he was put in charge of a magnetic optical discs project. In 1988, Kawashima assumed responsibility for the design and manufacturing centre of the Component Business Operation Headquarters that hosted four development projects, one of which was the FLCD project. It was at this point that he took over the formal responsibility for the FLCD project, as this was transferred to the design and manufacturing centre. The equally multicompetent initial project leader, Dr. Kanbe, will be described below.

Know-How and Know-Who in Production as a Critical Prerequisite to Enter the R&D Lab

Although Dr. Kanbe joined Canon Inc. with a PhD in solid state physics, his first two years of job assignments were to gain know-how and, above all, know-who in production. To begin with, he worked in a calculator production line and then in the inspection line of a camera production line. He then gained three months of (compulsory) on-the-job sales experience in a Canon shop before he arrived at his desired destination – the Research Centre, where he supported research on thermal printing technology.

This rich production experience supported Dr. Kanbe's first formal project assignment, which was to develop a toner production process for copiers. After having finished this project and having successfully accomplished another three-year research project, his closest chief, Mr. Toru Takahashi, charged him with a new mission: to find the future key technology of Canon. As will be described in more detail throughout this case study, both the multicompetency and the expanded know-who in production proved to be critical assets in handling the challenges of Dr. Kanbe's new mission.

Specialized Know-How from Knowledge Satellites

Three overall visions were given to the task force by Mr. Toru Takahashi, the division manager, indicating important fields of the future:

- High definition;
- High image quality;
- High density of information.

With the three visionary directives in mind, the task force decided to concentrate on future display technologies. Dr. Kanbe was made aware of the FLCD discovery through an Applied Physics Letter that reported on the technology in 1980, written by the inventors Dr. Lagerwall from Chalmers University of Technology in Sweden and Dr. Clark from the University of Colorado in the USA[8]. In 1983, Dr. Kanbe suggested to his chief, division manager Mr. Toru Takahashi, that he go and see the inventors. The reason for this suggestion was that their discovery of a new bistable liquid crystal technology could possibly be used in panel displays. Neither division manager Mr. Toru Takahashi nor Dr. Kanbe were familiar with liquid crystal technology at that time, but the initial meeting in the USA was successful and a cooperative relationship was established between Canon and the two scientists. At this stage, the task force of Dr. Kanbe was put to work on FLCD technology.

---

[8] The invention was partly based on previous research that had been conducted at Harvard University and at Université Paris-Sud in France. The discovery of Clark and Lagerwall at Chalmers University of Technology enabled very fast switching speed and bistability in ferroelectric liquid crystals, which had major implications for FLCDs. The main obstacles were in manufacturing techniques.

Know-Who in Production Made Convincing Prototypes Possible

Dr. Kanbe had samples of the ferroelectric liquid crystal compound prepared by engineers in the Central Research Laboratory, but it was through his know-who of former production engineer colleagues in the Component Development Centre that critical glass plate prototypes could be successfully prepared. A lot of trial and error of the resulting components followed and a small FLCD prototype was eventually presented to division manager Mr. Toru Takahashi, who encouraged and supported a presentation to upper management. After some hesitation, the task force was allowed to pursue the technology. Later that year (1984) negotiations were started with Chalmers University of Technology and, in 1985, an agreement was reached by which Canon was granted the right to use two fundamental patents held by the scientists.

Local Focus on Manufacturing While Leveraging Global Scientific Skills

Attempts had been made by the researchers to sell the technology to companies like Ericsson, ABB, Philips and other giants, but it had proved impossible to find any buyers in either Europe or in the US as all potential commercialization candidates claimed it would be impossible to bring the FLCDs to production. Canon also hesitated at first, but pursued the purchase of the technology, as it became clear that Seiko was already working on an FLCD prototype. To catch up as soon as possible, Canon immediately sent some people to the two universities in which the invention was made – Chalmers University and the University of Colorado – for support in the science of physics. The two inventors were also requested to make frequent visits to Canon so as to bring additional scientific progress into the project. Alongside the FLCD team, Canon had a task force working on a competing display technology, thin film transistor (TFT). Both task forces succeeded in developing functioning prototypes, but the yield in trial manufacturing fell short of requirements for real manufacturing. Thus far, the limited R&D activities of the task forces had mainly taken place within the development centre or in small trial production plants in the near vicinity. However, larger facilities would be required to go from trial to real manufacturing. Having two competing task forces going to this stage would have required too much money and too many people. The question was which technology to stop? To decide this, the two task forces presented their prototypes to a committee consisting of the CTO and several SBU managers. During two intensive days, the two task forces had to convince this committee that their embryos would be manufacturable in final production and that they would face a strong market need when commercialized. The criterion of manufacturability was demonstrated by presenting working prototypes and predicted plans and resource needs in real manufacturing. In order to provide evidence of market needs, the FLCD team presented market studies and trend analyses that were conducted in parallel. It also reported on the progress made by Seiko and other competitors in the field of displays so as to raise a sense of urgency to take the lead.

After those two days, the manager of the Office Imaging Products Operation said he would sponsor the display project if FLCD were to be the selected technology. As the TFT task force did not find an equally convinced sponsor, the CEO of the time, Dr. Keizo Yamaji, announced the choice of FLCD, which then passed the critical milestone of becoming a development project. The core of this project's activities and key-people were immediately transferred to a production plant in Hiratsuka, some 10 miles away from the research centre. Key-researchers from the discontinued TFT project were also transferred to the FLCD team at this plant. An additional research agreement was signed with the inventors, in order to provide the necessary competencies in material design and other related research activities. Some FLCD technology also seems to have been sourced from Bell Laboratories. For further support in the development of liquid crystal material, Canon established joint development with a supplier and maintained cooperation contracts with three professors at two domestic universities: Tokyo Institute of Technology and Saitama University. In this context, Dr. Kanbe stated that

> We can go freely to these universities to have free discussions with the professors and researchers there. We also conduct joint experiments.

Human Know-How Shuttles Supported the Knowledge Creation Process

A Senior researcher, Dr. Miyata, joined the material analysis division of the Canon Research Centre in 1989, but was soon dispatched to Tokyo University, to rejoin his initial creativity network, where he acquired new specialized skills in material evaluation and fine-precision measurement. On his return to the Canon Research Centre, he was assigned to the new-generation FLCD task force, for which he worked three days a week, commuting between the Research Centre and the production site. He still continued to work with the research team at the university to secure further creation and acquisition of scientific knowledge. This interactive knowledge creation and application process is illustrated in Figure 3.

Fig. 3. Production know-how as a necessary entry-ticket to R&D

Leveraging Intracorporate Process-Oriented Skills

After a few years, the FLCD project expanded to a Display Business Operations Centre with three FLCD projects focusing on:

- Materials: in particular, alignment of ferroelectric crystals.
- Production technologies: panel manufacturing and high-precision mounting techniques.
- Interface: the connection of computers to the FLCDs, mainly software engineering.

As the display project progressed towards trial manufacturing, engineers from three units, which were tied to operations management (i.e., Cost Engineering, Quality Management and Production Management), were transferred into the project. In early 1993, the Display Business Operations Centre consisted, of some 100 engineers who were involved in one or several of the materials, production and interface technology projects. The Display Business Operations Centre manager stated:

Knowledge from external divisions is brought in, whenever necessary, by moving in members from these divisions. As a result, a project team is not in a rigid form but rather transitory and flexible through the continuous moving in and out of members.

Considerable synergies were exploited by migrating and cross-fertilizing technologies and skills within the Component Business Operations HQ, partly between flat panel displays and solar cell panels, and also with semiconductor production technology, in particular aligners and steppers. The Project sponsor, Mr. Toru Takahashi, stated that:

Canon's experience in development of aligners and steppers has been of great use to us when developing production equipment for FLCD. Also, a lot of the work that our material engineers in the Canon Research Centre have done on toners and on optical products has greatly benefited our development of FLCD materials.

As FLCDs had never before been mass produced, some additional manufacturing know-how as well as new equipment were necessary. Key suppliers were therefore involved as soon as the pilot production line began to develop. A senior researcher stated:

We studied the technology together, which was advantageous for all of us. The key suppliers could acquire more knowledge on our FLCD technology and its development and we could build know-how within specialized production technology.

Close contacts were maintained with several competing suppliers to remain up to date on all state-of-the-art production technologies and to increase the competitive pressure on the suppliers. Some ten suppliers, labeled 'co-developers' were closely involved in the development activities of all the aforementioned core technologies. Equipment was not purchased until it had been confirmed for full-scale manufacturing, which left Canon with the flexibility to try different production technologies throughout the project.

Leveraging a Global R&D Network for Creativity in Software Engineering

Some of the interface software engineering activities were pursued in Canon's software lab in Shin-Kawasaki, but the larger part took place in the Canon Information System Research Laboratory in Sydney, Australia, supported by research centers in Cambridge, UK as well as Stanford and Costa Mesa in the USA. The interaction with these labs was very intense, as stated by chief engineer Dr. Kanbe:

> Some of our engineers go to Australia five–six times a year. This lab strongly supports our development of software simulation programs and interface electronics. Our R&D labs in the US and in the UK also give us some support in these fields.

These labs also served the purpose of extensive local networking to tap into the resources and creativity that was available at these nodes of software development excellence. Again, rotation of researchers was employed to secure an effective know-how transfer from the external labs to the Display Business Operations Centre. Japanese engineers were acting as human know-how shuttles between Japan and the different overseas teams. They could align external research activities with the application-oriented needs of the display centre, as well as learn from the overseas experience and bring the results directly back to the team in Japan.

Transferring R&D Staff into a Marketing Network to Perform Market Intelligence and Product Planning

As soon as the trial production line started to yield non-defective prototype displays in 1990, a Planning and Marketing group of approximately five engineers was formed and dispatched to the Planning and Marketing HQ in Shinjuku, where they were joined by a few marketing experts – usually with R&D background as exemplified by Mrs. Akiko Tanaka. When she joined Canon in 1986, her first two years consisted of testing and measuring the results of extensive trial-and-error activities of liquid crystal materials. In 1988, she changed field and started to develop software for the display–computer interface. Then, in 1990, she was dispatched to the Planning and Marketing HQ in Shinjuku to undertake market intelligence activities. These activities, which related to her previous development of interface software, mainly consisted of observing what competing display companies offered and identifying what computer companies and other potential customers needed and wanted. In addition, Mrs. Akiko Tanaka monitored those associations and societies that relate to display technology. Observing the competition was possible in several ways. Mrs. Akiko Tanaka used computer manufacturers as a source of information regarding flat panel display competitors. Mrs. Akiko Tanaka stated that "as the computer company is the potential customer of newly developed displays, it will know of any improvement or problem that a manufacturer like Sharp and Matsushita may have." Mrs. Akiko Tanaka also mentioned the importance of scanning patent-applications, research reports and press releases and going to fairs. As an example, Canon takes part in the Ferroelectric Liquid Crystal Symposium of Chalmers University of Technology.

Transferring Critical Knowledge to the Manufacturing Floor Through Increasingly Empowered Project Leaders

In the early 1990s, as the project progressed towards production, the formal project leadership role was handed over from Dr. Kanbe to Mr. Hirokuni Kawashima. He also headed the Display Business Operations Centre in which the FLCD project was hosted. A large part of the R&D activities also took place outside the centre. Research on liquid crystal materials was pursued in the Canon Research Centre in Atsugi, initially involving approximately ten researchers. As the project advanced, most of these researchers were transferred into the Display Business Operations Centre, where more applied and strongly production-oriented development activities were required.

Figure 4 depicts the most important units that contributed to the project. In 1993, as the project advanced further towards final production, Mr. Toru Takahashi, the former head of Component Business Operations, took over the formal project responsibility – in addition to his function as head of one of Canon's six business areas, Office Imaging Operations.

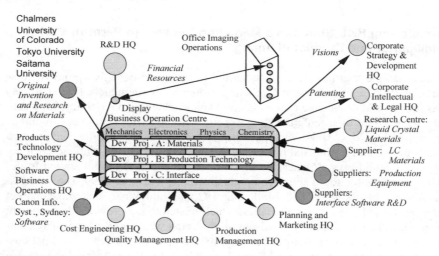

Fig. 4. Main contributors to Canon's development of FLCDs

Using Organizational Hierarchy to Transfer Further R&D Brainpower to Production

As of late 1994, the FLCD group had grown to a 200-person operation. Ninety per cent of all members were located directly in the Display Business Operation Centre. Eight per cent of the engineers were still located in the R&D HQ, where they did some interface development and coordinated these software development activities that took place overseas. The remaining two per cent were researchers with the Canon Research Centre, working on next-generation FLCD materials in collaboration with external university-based creativity networks. Mr. Toru Takahashi's powerful position at Canon further accelerated the transfer of relevant skills to the project and supported the transfer of most people in the increasingly large project directly to the factory floor.

Paying More Attention to Group-Wide Results than Individual Project Performance

Although commercial production has been running for several years now, and the size of the displays has kept increasing, Canon does still not enjoy any significant sales volumes on FLC displays. The most significant barrier is the high sales price. Still, this price may not cover even half of the actual costs, given the significant investments that the project sponsor Mr. Toru Takahashi pushed through the board to make commercial production possible.

With respect to the extraordinarily high costs of this project and the relatively limited revenues from commercialized FLCDs, most Western organizations would probably have fired the project sponsor, or 'punished' him or her with a lateral move – as often practiced in many Western companies. At Canon, Mr. Toru Takahashi was rewarded with a promotion to CTO not long after completion of this project. Why? The answer seems to reside in the holistic network approach taken both to K&I management and to performance evaluation. Although the FLCD project investments may never be covered purely through sales of FLCDs, the unique production technologies and skills that were acquired and created throughout the project have already been networked and propagated across the company.

These skills and technologies also encouraged Canon to revitalize the TFT display project that was put on ice as it competed against the FLCD project for resources to proceed towards production. As a consequence, Canon is today the worldwide leader in TFT display manufacturing equipment (i.e., of a competing product). The patents[9] (now over 200) that were awarded during the project also

---

[9]   The President at the time, Dr. Keizo Yamaij, pursued a very powerful patenting strategy requiring each engineer to submit twelve patent applications per year (Harryson, 2000). In 1992, when I started my empirical research in Japan, Canon ranked first in patent registrations in the US – with IBM ranking sixth that same year. Taking a time-perspective of the decade from 1990 to 2000, Canon has had consecutive annual revenues of approximately 10 billion yen from their patents, which is ten times their patent

protect Canon's position as unchallenged master of ultrafine precision in both crystal displays and in additional related manufacturing equipment. Much of this ultrafine precision has also found its way into Canon's steppers and aligners – another field in which Canon can boast world leadership today. Companies that commit the mistake of focusing on individual profit and loss (P&L) accounts and isolated project performance would not have sponsored this project, although it resulted in a significant competitive advantage for the company as a whole.

Analyzing the Canon Case with Further Illustrations of Know-Who Based K&I Management

Prior Know-How and Know-Who in Production as Critical Catalysts for Linking Exploration to Exploitation

It seems clear that the vital transfer of both explicit and tacit knowledge from inventive concept ideas to innovative production processes was enabled through the migration of engineers from creativity networks to a rather organic project network with a clear application focus. Then, by transferring the larger part (90 per cent) of this team directly to the manufacturing floor, Canon ensured that all necessary competencies were effectively integrated into a production process instead of remaining isolated in upstream research labs. Such a transfer was facilitated by the fact that most of these internal researchers and engineers had prior experience from, personal know-who within, and respect for production. Through the frequent changes a sense of belonging towards the company as a whole, rather than to a specific function or location, had emerged. Hence, the transfer was not resented but instead seen as a necessity to make innovation happen. I see this as the most important reason why Canon succeeded in commercializing a disruptive technology that was invented, but never produced, in the West. Internal multicompetency and know-who also allowed for the migration of ultrafine precision technologies and skills into other business areas and product applications so as to enhance the return on the FLCD investment and strengthen the overall innovation performance and net sales growth of Canon. The principles and benefits of transferring technologies and skills within Canon are also reflected in the holistic performance evaluation practiced by this company – as illustrated by Mr. Toru Takahashi's promotion to CTO.

Accordingly, we can add a know-who based project network to the initial model in Figure 2 so as to interlink the creativity network and the process network – including its underlying supplier and marketing networks – as outlined in Figure 5.

cost over this period. In my last meeting with Dr. Yamaji (March, 2002), he stated that "we have to leave some proof that we have lived." In this sense, patents are monuments in the career of any engineer.

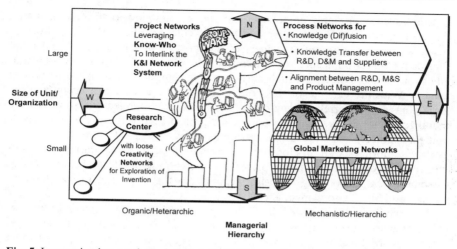

Fig. 5. Leveraging know-who to interlink the K&I network system

Accordingly, the dilemmas of innovation can be circumvented by interlinking creativity networks and process networks through a combination of latitudinal and longitudinal navigation along the dimensions of organizational size and managerial hierarchy. Such strategic navigation builds networks across small specialized units geared towards creative invention and large process-oriented units geared towards efficient product management and production for global commercialization.

Deploying a Know-Who Based Innovation Process to Commercialize the Sony Mini Disc Walkman

Sony's development of the Mini Disc (MD) Walkman was quite different from Canon's FLCD development. The actual MD project network never exceeded 30 formal full-time members. Hence, most activities were performed by researchers and engineers who were not formal members of the actual project team, but core members in other creativity or process networks. These supporting engineers were not transferred to a growing project team, but remained instead in their original locations. The chief engineer and his deputy coordinated the entire process by continually meeting with the managers of the different interrelated divisions, centers and business groups.

The management structure of the project appeared to be even more powerful than that of the FLCD project. Because of a strict 18-month deadline set by President Ohga for the development as a whole, the development project received the status of 'corporate project', thereby enabling a more effective mobilization of resources. This has only happened to three other projects during Sony's history: the Betamax, the 8 mm video camera and the compact disc (CD) player.

Consequently, a highly empowered steering committee was formed, including the development centre manager and overall chief engineer Mr. Kenichi Tsurushima, the senior general managers of the most involved business groups and President Ohga, who headed the committee. Mr. Kenichi Tsurushima was eventually promoted to Director, which may reflect the importance attached to project leaders. With the backing of this committee, it became easier to encourage the large number of interrelated engineers to cooperate and monetary resources were mobilized more easily. At some points, the project involved close to 300 development engineers and 20 researchers from the Sony Research Centre.

Patent attorneys were in close interaction with the MD group during the entire innovation process, thus offering protection of emerging intellectual property and, to some extent, supporting licensing negotiations that were run in parallel with competitors like Sharp, Sanyo, and Matsushita.

A marketing network called the MD Promotion Department pursued an aggressive licensing process that was run immediately after Sony's official announcement of the MD technology in May 1991. Two people were appointed to establish links with music software producers overseas, one in New York and one in London. Both of them were in daily communication with the MD Promotion Department in Japan. A new market research study was prepared in May 1992 by a private market research company in the USA. Early customer feedback was interlinked through the establishment of a monitor program, and through focused group discussions with specially selected Sony customers.

For the modularized technology development of the next-generation MD, a lot of interaction with foreign and domestic universities took place. This extracorporate interaction was mainly with the Research Centre, but a large number of Sony's design and manufacturing process networks in different business groups were also involved in miniaturization activities related to the MD.

Similarities Between Different Companies and Projects

It seems reasonable to conclude that even though Canon and Sony are in quite similar businesses, their approaches to project management differ mainly in terms of formal resource allocation to one project within Canon, versus temporary use of brainpower within Sony. However, even though Canon pursued an integral development and Sony a modular development, the two innovation cases showed several similarities:

- The project leaders were highly experienced across several functions (multicompetent) and had strong networks (know-who) within their companies.
- Through different means of networking, both projects made extensive use of, and created significant diffusion of, knowledge and technologies across functional and divisional boundaries.
- All projects had a mid-term change in project leadership, starting with less senior but highly multicompetent leaders, and ending with senior leaders from hierarchically strong and empowered positions – representing a longitudinal

move in Figure 5 from heterarchy to hierarchy, or from exploration to exploitation.

- The stronger and more hierarchical leadership style was introduced at a stage where the projects grew in size and shifted from creation to application of knowledge through physical transfer from R&D to production.

Human know-how carriers integrate the different networks. Referring to the know-who based model introduced in Figure 2 and expanded in Figure 5, Senior researcher Dr. Miyata served as a human know-how shuttle between Tokyo University in the creativity network linked to the Canon Research Centre and the design and manufacturing process network at the Display Business Operation Centre. The whole innovation process started as a small creativity network of only three people with strong ties into external centers of excellence like Chalmers University and the University of Colorado. The team gradually grew into a project network, which still maintained strong ties to external sources of specialized skills and creative invention, while also building increasingly strong ties to the Design and Manufacturing process networks of the Display Business Operation Centre. Finally, 90 per cent of the 200 members of this project network were permanently transferred into this process network to secure full application of the knowledge, strong ties to the marketing network, and tight control of the supplier network. To enhance the return on knowledge, some key-FLCD people also migrated into the (competing) TFT team, as well as into completely different divisions working on steppers and aligners where Canon's unique know-how in fine-precision mechanics created a new competitive advantage for the company as a whole.

Accordingly, by applying an innovation process that was born in Japan, Canon was not only first in commercializing a disruptive technology that was born in the West, but also first in applying this knowledge to other applications for further growth through innovation.

Similarly, Sony has deployed a highly know-who based approach to K&I so as to acquire and build a sustainable leadership position in several segments and categories of consumer electronics.

Know-who based networking patterns – as illustrated by Canon and Sony – may be particularly relevant for companies in which the step between invention and innovation is large and requires a lot of cross-functional teamwork to happen. More process oriented companies like those in chemical and pharmaceutical industries may be able to bridge the innovation gap also with less networking and perhaps even without multicompetent engineers. This may be one reason why the Western and, perhaps more static, know-how based approach still seems to secure leadership positions in many process-based industries, whereas the dynamic know-who based approach to innovation continues to build leadership positions throughout Asia in many industries related to ICT and consumer electronics.[10]

---

[10] For further reference on how Canon reached its leadership position and on the key-characteristics of Japanese leadership for growth through innovation, see Yamai (1997).

References

Abegglen J and Stalk G (1985): Kaisha: The Japanese Corporation, Tokyo, Tuttle Company

Aldrich H and Whetten DA (1981): *Organization-Sets, Action-Sets, and Networks: Making the most of simplicity*, In Nystrom PC and Starbuck WH (eds.), *Handbook of Organizational Design*, Oxford: Oxford University Press

Andersson S (1998): 'The Network Perspective – Its Origin and Differences to the Marketing Management Approach', *ESBRI*

Aoki M (1988): *Information, Incentives, and Bargaining in the Japanese Economy*, New York, Cambridge University Press

Assimakopoulos D and Macdonald S (2003): 'A dual approach to understanding information networks', *Int. J. Technology Management*, Vol. 25, Nos. ½, pp. 96-112

Ayas K (1996): 'Professional project management: A Shift Towards Learning and a Knowledge Creating Structure', *International Journal of Project Management*, vol. 14, no. 3, pp. 131–136

Bartlett C and Ghoshal S (1989): *Managing Across Borders: The Transnational Solution*, US, Harvard Business School Press

Burns T and Stalker G (1961): *The Management of Innovation*, London, Tavistock

Clark K and Fujimoto T (1990): 'The Power of Product Integrity', *Harvard Business Review*, November–December, pp. 107–18

Clark K and Fujimoto T (1991): *Product Development Performance: Strategy, Organization and Management in the World Auto Industry*, US, Harvard Business School Press

Clark K and Fujimoto T (1992): 'Product Development and Competitiveness', *Journal of the Japanese and International Economies*, no. 6, pp. 101–43

Ealey L and Soderberg L (1990): 'How Honda Cures Design Amnesia', *McKinsey Quarterly*, Spring, pp. 3–14

Easton G (1992): 'Industrial Networks: A Review', in Axelsson and Easton (Eds), *Industrial Networks. A New View of Reality*, London, Routledge, pp. 3–27

Eisenhardt K and Brown S (1998): 'Time Pacing: Competing in Markets that won't Stand Still', *Harvard Business Review*, March–April

Evans P and Wurster T (1999): *Blown to Bits: How the New Economics of Information Transforms Strategy*, Boston, MA: Harvard Business School Press

Håkansson H (ed.) (1987): Industrial Technological Development: A Network Approach, Beckenham, Croom Helm Ltd.

Håkansson H (1989): Corporate Technological Behaviour: Co-operation and Networks, London, Routledge

Håkansson H (1990): 'Technological Collaboration in Industrial Networks', *European Management Journal*, vol. 8, no. 3, September, pp. 371–9

Håkansson H and Ford D (2002): 'How should companies interact', *Journal of Business Research*, Vol. 55, pp. 133-139

Håkansson H and Henders B (1992): 'International Co-operative Relationships in Technological Development', in Forsgren M and Johanson J (eds), *Managing Networks in International Business*, Philadelphia, Gordon and Breach, pp. 32–46

Håkansson H and Johanson J (Eds) (2001): *Business Network Learning*, Amsterdam: Pergamon

Håkansson H and Laage-Hellman J (1984): Developing a network R&D strategy, *The Journal of Product Innovation Management 1*, No 4, pp 224-37

Håkansson H and Snehota I (1989): 'No Business is an Island: The Network Concept of Business Strategy', *Scandinavian Journal of Management*, vol. 5, no. 3, pp. 187–200

Hamel G (1991): 'Competition for Competence and Inter-Partner Learning within International Strategic Alliances', *Strategic Management Journal*, vol. 12, pp. 83–103

Harryson S (1995a): *Japanese R&D Management: A Holistic Network Approach*, PhD thesis submitted at the University of St. Gallen in Switzerland, Research Institute of International Management

Harryson S (1995b): 'The Japanese Approach to Innovation – Research for D&M', *PRISM*, First Quarter

Harryson S (1997): 'From Experience: How Canon and Sony Drive Product Innovation through Networking and Application-Focused R&D', *Journal of Product Innovation Management*, July, vol. 14, no. 4

Harryson S (1998): Japanese Technology and Innovation Management: From Know-How to Know-Who, Cheltenham, Edward Elgar Publishing

Harryson S (2002): *Managing Know-Who Based Companies: A Multinetworked Approach to Knowledge and Innovation Management,* Second fully revised and updated edition, published by Edward Elgar Publishing, Cheltenham, UK

Harryson S (2005): *Know-Who Based Entrepreneurship: From Knowledge Creation to Business Implementation,* Cheltenham, Edward Elgar Publishing (forthcoming 2005)

Hatvany N and Pucik V (1982):'Japanese Management: Practices and Productivity', in Tushman M and Moore W (Eds), *Readings in the Management of Innovation*, London, Pitman Books Ltd, pp. 520–34

He ZL and Wong PK (2004): 'Exploration vs. Exploitation: An Empirical Test of the Ambidexterity Hypothesis', *Organization Science,* Vol. 15, No. 4, pp. 481 – 94

Hedlund G (1986): 'The Hypermodern MNC – A Heterarchy?', *Human Resource Management*, Spring, vol. 25, no. 1, pp. 9–35

Hedlund G (1992): *A Model of Knowledge Management and the Global N-Form Corporation*, Research Paper RP 92/10, Stockholm School of Economics

Hedlund G (1994): *The Future of the Global Firm*, Research Paper RP 94/8, Stockholm School of Economics

Hedlund G (1995): The Intensity and Extensity of Knowledge: Implications for Possible Futures of the Global Firm, Research Paper RP 95/6, Stockholm School of Economics

Hedlund G and Nonaka I (1991): *Models of Knowledge Management in the West and Japan*, Research Paper RP 91/9, Stockholm School of Economics

Imai K (1989a): 'Evolution of Japan's Corporate and Industrial Networks', in Carlsson B (ed.), *Industrial Dynamics. Technological, Organizational and Structural Changes in Industries and Firms*, Boston, Kluwer Academic Publishers, pp. 123–55

Imai K (1989b): *The Japanese Pattern of Innovation and its Evolution*, Tokyo, Hitotsubashi University, Institute of Business Research, Discussion Paper no. 136

Imai K, Nonaka I, and Takeuchi H (1985): 'Managing the New Product Development Process: How Japanese Companies Learn and Unlearn', in Clark K, Hayes R, and Lorenz C (eds), *The Uneasy Alliance: Managing the Productivity–Technology Dilemma*, Boston, Harvard Business School Press, pp. 533–61

Itami H (1987): *Mobilizing Invisible Assets*, Cambridge, MA, Harvard University Press

Jansson H, Saqib M, and Sharma D (1990): *'A Methodology for the Study of Transorganizational Networks',* Lund University Working Paper Series

Jansson H, Saqib M, and Sharma DD (1995): The State and Transnational Corporations. A Network Approach to Industrial Policy in India. Aldershot: Edward Elgar

Johansson U and Elg U (2002): *'Relationships as Entry Barriers: a Network Perspective'*, Scandinavian Journal of Management, No. 18, pp. 393-419

Jones D (1990): 'Beyond the Toyota Production System: The Era of Lean Production', Paper for the 5th International Operations Management Association Conference on Manufacturing Strategy, Warwick, 26–27 June

Karlsson C (1989): 'High Rates of Innovation: The Japanese Culture Shock to Europe', *European Management Journal*, vol. 7, no. 1, pp. 31–9

Kennard R (1991): 'From Experience: Japanese Product Development Process', *Journal of Product Innovation Management*, vol. 8, pp. 184–8

Kenney M and Florida R (1993): *Beyond Mass Production: The Japanese System and its Transfer to the US*, New York, Oxford University Press

Kobayashi H (1990): 'Organization Development Efforts by "Self-Confirming" Task Groups: A Japanese Case', in Massarik F (ed.), *Advances in Organization Development*, US, Ablex Publishing Corporation

Kusunoki T (1992): 'The Dilemma of Technological Leadership: A Conceptual Framework', *Hitotsubashi Journal of Commerce and Management*, vol. 27, no. 1, November, pp. 63–79

Laage-Hellman J (1997): Business Networks in Japan: Supplier–Customer Interaction in Product Development, London, Routledge

Lu D (1987): *Inside Corporate Japan: The Art of Fumble-Free Management*, Tokyo, Charles E. Tuttle Company

Martins E and Terblanche F (2003): 'Building Organizational Culture that Stimulates Creativity and Innovation', *European Journal of Innovation Management*, 2003, vol. 6, no. 1; pp. 64-75, MCB University Press

Nelson R and Winter S (1982): An Evolutionary Theory of Economic Change, Cambridge, MA, Harvard University Press

Nonaka I (1988a): 'Creating Organizational Order Out Of Chaos: Self Renewal in Japanese Firms', *California Management Review*, no. 3, pp. 57–3

Nonaka I (1988b): 'Toward Middle-Up-Down Management: Accelerating Information Creation', *Sloan Management Review*, pp. 9–18

Nonaka I (1990): 'Redundant, Overlapping Organization: A Japanese Approach to Managing the Innovation Process', *California Management Review*, Spring, pp. 27–38

Nonaka I (1991): 'The Knowledge-Creating Company', *Harvard Business Review*, November–December, pp. 96–104

Nonaka I (1994): 'A Dynamic Theory of Organizational Knowledge Creation', *Organization Science*, vol. 5, no. 1, February, pp. 14–37

Nonaka I and Kenney M (1991): 'Towards a New Theory of Innovation Management: A Case Study Comparing Canon and Apple Computer', *Journal of Engineering and Technology Management*, no. 8, pp. 67–83

Nonaka I and Konno N (1998): 'The Concept of "Ba": Building a Foundation for Knowledge Creation', *California Management Review*, Spring, vol. 40, no. 3, pp. 40–54

Nonaka I and Yamanouchi T (1989): 'Managing Innovation as a Self-Renewing Process', *Journal of Business Venturing*, no. 4, pp. 299–315

Nonaka I, Byosiere P, and Konno N (1994): 'Organizational Knowledge Creation Theory: A First Comprehensive Test', *International Business Review*, vol. 3, no. 4, pp. 337–51

O'Connor GC, Hendricks R, and Rice MP (2002): 'Assessing Transition Readiness for Radical Innovation', *Research Technology Management*, vol. 45 Issue 6

Parsons A (1991): 'Building Innovativeness in Large US Corporations', *The Journal of Services Marketing*, vol. 8, no. 1, Winter, pp. 5-20

Pfeffer J and Salancik G (1978): *The External Control of Organizations*, New York, Harper and Row

Pinto J and Kharbanda K (1996): 'How to Fail in Project Management Without Really Trying', *Business Horizons*, vol. 39, no. 4

Schütte H (1991): 'Strategische Allianzen mit Japanischen Firmen', in Schneidewind D and Töpfer A (Hrsg.) *Der Asiatisch-pazifische Raum*, Lech, Schweiz, Verlag Moderne Industrie AG and Co., pp. 251-75

Smothers N (1990): 'Patterns of Japanese Strategy: Strategic Combinations of Strategies', *Strategic Management Journal*, vol. 11, pp. 521–33

Stalk G and Hout T (1990): Competing Against Time: How Time-Based Competition is Reshaping Global Markets, New York, The Free Press

Stalk G, Evans P, and Shulman L (1992): 'Competing on Capabilities: The New Rules of Corporate Strategy', *Harvard Business Review*, March–April, pp. 57–69

Stern S (2004): 'How to Make Creativity Contagious', *Management Today,* March 2004, pp. 52-56

Tabrizi B and Walleigh R (1997): 'Defining Next-Generation Products: An Inside Look', *Harvard Business Review*, November–December

Takeuchi H and Nonaka I (1986): 'The New New Product Development Game', *Harvard Business Review*, January–February, pp. 137–46

Walker D (1991): 'Creative Empowerment at Rover', in: Henry J and Walker D (Eds), *Managing Innovation*, London, Sage Publications Ltd, pp. 277–86

Womack J, Jones D, and Roos D (1990): *The Machine that Changed the World*, New York, Macmillan Publishing Company

Yamai K (1997): *One Proposes, God Disposes – My Curriculum Vitae*, Tokyo, Nihon Keizai Shimbun, Inc

The Domestic Shaping of Japanese Innovations

Marian Beise

Introduction

Every salesman who travels to Japan experiences differences of the Japanese market to the markets in Europe and the US. A unique culture, language, the traditional way of living have created a very special preference system. How can the sometimes overwhelming export success of Japanese companies and their dominance in particular innovations be explained? The rise of Japanese electronics, optics, and automobile industries and the decline of some of these industries in Europe and the US have been analyzed and discussed extensively. A commonly held conviction is that the Japanese have sidestepped their own home market and copied western technology and products for export. The competitive strength of Japanese companies has been credited – among others – to general management techniques, a hyper investment climate, long-term orientation of companies and institutions, and strong relationships to suppliers. The success of Japanese innovations has hardly ever been put down to originality but to new production techniques that increased operational effectiveness at companies like Toyota, Canon, and Matsushita to unprecedented levels. The ability to learn from western countries and the capacity to assess new scientific knowledge and quickly transfer new technology from western laboratories to the shop floor have long been both admired and decried in the west. High risk-taking and long-term commitment of Japanese mammoth conglomerates such as Toshiba, Hitachi, and Nissan would have ensured an investment driven growth backed up by governmental guaranties for survival (Johnson 1982). The remarkable entrepreneurship and vision of the CEOs of companies like Sharp, Yamaha, Honda, Kyocera, and Sony (e.g. Johnstone 1999), although often underestimated by western scholars, are important ingredients of the tremendous efforts of Japan to make new technology beneficial and affordable for a mass population. Yet, Porter (1990) and more specifically Porter, Takeuchi, and Sakakibara (2000) have pointed to another important factor of competitiveness: that the seemingly disadvantageous distinction of the Japanese market created a home market advantage in certain industries. In this chapter the effect of the characteristics of the Japanese market on innovations and on the international competitiveness of Japan shall be discussed.

Innovation theories from Vernon's international product life cycle theory to induced innovation and local user-producer interaction theory have suggested that innovations emerge in response to local market dynamics. These market-based innovation theories have been confirmed by numerous empirical studies and – in a luminously stimulating way – by v. Hippel's observation of lead-users. As a result of significant differences from country to country most innovations remain popular only regionally. In fact, most brands worldwide are local brands accustomed to a country-specific context. Some locally induced innovations, however, become internationally successful. Export success may stem from specific advantages of a company. But if a country becomes specialized in international trade in a particular product or industry, then, there must be a country-specific advantage (Porter 1990).

The common hypothesis suggests that local interaction theories are not applicable to the case of Japan. Instead, Japanese companies would have started in somehow the 1960s to develop innovations for foreign markets, primarily the US market. Only later were they introduced in Japan. The export-led growth hypothesis states that Japan achieved high growth throughout the 1950s and 60s, because it copied and produced goods demanded in the west and could export them based on low labor costs and an undervalued exchange rate (Shinohara 1975, 1982). The growth of exports stimulates investments in turn. The export success led to wage increases and therefore domestic market growth. The implication of this hypothesis for innovation management is striking, because it would imply that the Japanese found a way to overcome the inefficiency of regional and cultural distance in innovation development and to surpass foreign competitors in their own home markets.

Yet, it will be argued in this chapter that they have not. Instead, the traditional local-interaction-based theories of innovation development management are applicable to Japan as well. Japanese innovations are shaped by the Japanese market and the global success of those very innovations has been enabled – besides innovation management techniques that are described in the other chapters in this book – by certain characteristics of the Japanese market.

Furthermore it will be argued that even some important Japanese innovation strategies are shaped by the distinct market characteristics in Japan. The role of the Japanese market demonstrates that the relationship between Japanese innovation management and its innovation success is embedded in a market context. Western managers as well as politicians were often frustrated by the ability of Japanese companies to utilize western technologies and inventions and turn them into billion dollar mass market products. Technology management, innovations and the worldwide success of innovations, however, are not independent from the local market context.

Why would the relationship between market context and innovation be of any importance for technology management studies? The domestic shaping of innovation and innovation management leads to a contingency theory of innovation management. The contingency theory in business strategy suggests that companies must select a strategy that fits with its environment (Hofer 1975, Venkatraman and Prescott 1990). If countries have different environmental characteristics, different strategies might be advantageous. Strategies and innovation management approaches that work well in one country can fail in other countries, because they do not "fit" into the foreign market context. For example Beechler and Yang (1994) report that several Japanese companies were unable to transfer their human resources management practices to the USA, because of differences in the environmental contexts of both countries such as labor market conditions, alternative job opportunities, and regulatory conditions and were forced to adapt to the US style of HRM. Nigel Holden explains the ongoing deterioration of the market position of General Motors in spite of the introduction of Toyota techniques in a similar fashion (Glisby and Holden 2003). The embeddedness of Japanese management techniques also changes the view on what western companies can learn from Japanese innovation management and production processes. It puts a question mark behind the virtue of Japanese innovation management techniques for western companies. A more obvious example is the tremendous product variety at Toyota. This approach is certainly not imperative for all automotive companies even if it is tremendously successful for Toyota. But the reason given here is that the product variety approach of Japanese companies is induced by the Japanese market in the first place.

It is therefore important to identify the market context that induces an innovation approach in order to assess its true value. We need to carefully evaluate, what conclusions western companies can draw from the local success of these techniques. Even if the Japanese innovation strategy leads to exports, the same strategy does not have to be successful in other countries as well. Yet, western companies in turn might be able to make use of the Japanese advantage not only by adopting Japanese innovation techniques but by focusing their development activities on the Japanese market.

The questions of why localized strategies in Japan lead to export success and why these mechanisms do not need to succeed in other countries are discussed at the end of this chapter. We start with the hypothesis that Japanese companies respond predominantly to their local market and not to export markets.

The Local Embeddedness of Japanese Innovations

It was the American consumer who was recurrently perceived as the major trend leader for innovations. The Japanese consumer, in contrast, has been portrayed as a follower but a leader who willingly embraces western technology (Tsurumi 1973). Ozawa (1974), for instance, argues that "the consumption pattern of the American people played a particularly important role as a standard for the Japanese to emulate." The post war history of Japan is purportedly characterized by the "Americanization of consumer tastes" (Ozawa 1974, p. 33). Along the line is a common misunderstanding that Japanese innovation development lacks creativity and is merely based on copying and refinement of western product design.

This perception, however, rests merely on the fact that basic scientific knowledge for Japanese innovations was often discovered in the West. The traditional view of the Japan as a follower ignores important historical technological breakthroughs that occurred in Japan. It is oblivious to characteristics of market demand in Japan for products in which Japanese companies ultimately became leaders. It has been noticed before, most prominently by Michael Porter (1990), that demanding users, the sophistication and quality of demand in Japan, play a decisive role in shaping the innovations of Japanese companies.

National fondness for particular products is often a cause of national competitive advantage. The world consumes French luxuries, Italian clothes, German automobiles, American fashion and fast food. Japanese products might lack an overly national flavor. Yet, it will be argued here that there is the same home market advantage for Japanese home electronics, cameras and office equipment.

For this purpose, the history of twelve innovations in which Japanese companies have succeeded in the world market was reviewed under the hypothesis that the domestic market played a role in shaping the innovation and facilitated the international success of Japanese companies. The products are electronic calculators, television sets with cathode ray tube (CRT), television sets with flat panel displays, traditional silver halide cameras, digital cameras, game consoles, hydraulic excavators, audio and video tape recorders, facsimile machines, copy machines, and semiconductors. In all these innovations Japanese companies have achieved a high world market share or even global dominance. First, it can be shown that these innovations are somehow related to the Japanese market. The reasons for their global success will be discussed in the final sections below.

Demand in Japan is idiosyncratic in many respects which creates disadvantages for export oriented firms but also unique innovation opportunities. Cultural, linguistic, traditional factors, values, and motivations make the preferences of the Japanese market different from those in other countries. A closer look reveals how the Japanese culture has shaped globally successful Japanese products as much as the American way of life has shaped global fast food. Besides culture, the Japanese market context as a whole, the strategy the domestic market evokes and the interaction between the market and innovators determine the design and the technology of Japanese innovations.

Japanese innovations are domestically shaped by three factors which are described in the next section. First of all, the structure of demand in Japan is different in details compared to Western countries. The complementariness between technologies and between technologies and infrastructure as well as price disparities and varying national budget preferences ensue different demand structures from country to country. Second, the cultural context of Japan gives rise to specific innovations or increases the preference for certain designs varying from high density displays to super-hygienic fresh food. At first glance, these innovations are not considered as cultural-specific; nevertheless the Japanese are more inclined to them than consumers in any other country. Third, significant market structure conditions in Japan in a number of industries channel the attention of users, producers, and human resources and bring about particular product designs as well as production techniques. The strategic-fit theory suggests that successful companies follow strategies and management techniques in order to match the requirements of the home market (Venkatraman and Prescott 1990). New management techniques may well have been introduced because of the unique market context in Japan.

The government is another factor that has been believed to be influential in shaping the domestic industrial structure. Yet, the industrial policy and the support that Japanese firms have received from the government, albeit influential as initiator and driver of the rapid growth of the heavy and chemical industry in post-war

Japan, have had surprisingly little impact on the trade *specialization* of Japan. While en vogue in the 1980s as an explanation for Japan's success, it is commonly agreed today that in the latter stage of Japan's economy industrial policy had a more preserving effect on the less successful part of the Japanese economy but was hardly accountable for the internationally very successful part. The officials in the Ministry of Industry and Trade which has been given overly high credit for Japanese innovation successes in the past (e.g. Johnson 1982, Ozawa 1974, Shinohara 1982) was much more conservative and uninspiring in its views regarding what technologies and products were promising and should be pursued by Japanese companies. In the 1950s, MITI set up a list of the most "desired technologies" which were to receive preferential treatment in the resource allocation process (Ozawa 1974, p. 21). It listed – among others – artificial fibers, chemicals, petrochemicals, pharmaceuticals, aircraft, steel and medical equipment but not a single consumer good. All these industries have eventually been set up in Japan. Yet, Japan did not gain a sustainable competitive advantage in most of the listed industries compared to consumer electronics, automobiles, and optics that did not receive the same official attention.

Instead, the role of entrepreneurs and visionary CEOs, who perceived market opportunities in the domestic consumer market, is apparent throughout the history of technology in Japan since Sony's founders Masaru Ibuka and Akio Morita were convinced that the transistor radio, the tape recorder, and television sets were the most promising products to pursue. While becoming most visibly successful they were not alone in their perception. Sharp, Kyocera, Canon, Matsushita, Yamaha and many others experienced a clear preference in the Japanese market for specific consumer goods and office equipment that were in line with the Japanese context. Stereotypes about Japanese needs and skills, however, don't travel far, when studied more thoroughly than in an anecdotal way. For instance, miniaturization and integration are attributes often named as the foundation of Japanese competitive advantage (Albach 1993, p. 81). But these terms are too general to explain the pattern of success and failure in Japan. Japan is not the overall master of miniaturization, automation and integration. For instance, Japan has been constantly successful in semiconductors related to consumer goods, but its ambitious goals in the computer industry have never been achieved. Nor are Japanese companies always leaders in electronic gadgets in general. While Japanese manufacturers did succeed in commercializing VCRs for a mass market by transforming the large video recorder for the professional segment into a version suitable for the private home (Rosenbloom and Cusumano 1987; Prahalad and Doz 1987), the markets for pocket computers (PDA) and MP3 players are dominated by US firms (because of the specific market conditions in the USA). Japan did not become the main exporter of cellular mobile phones, a masterpiece of miniaturization and integration. Instead, two Scandinavian companies and one American company are the world leaders. These are countries hardly notorious for their miniaturization skills (Economist 1995, p. 60).

Innovation and Market Interaction in Japan

It was often acknowledged that Japanese companies have developed a strong customer orientation and cross-functional integration that facilitate the diffusion of market knowledge within the whole firm and R&D-customer contacts all stages of the new product development process (Song and Parry 1997). Japanese companies would follow the market closely without attempting to educate the market to buy what their engineers think are useful product designs. Quality improvements are focused on customer needs and customer acceptability (Cole 1999). Since this user-producer-interaction is most efficient or convenient in cultural and geographic proximity, Japanese innovations would be shaped by the Japanese market as a result.

There is some evidence that the Japanese market played a major role in the innovation activities of Japanese firms. For once, the export-led-growth hypothesis cited above, which suggests that Japanese companies have initially aimed at exports and responded predominantly to foreign demand, can easily be refuted. While for some countries in Asia such as Korea and Malaysia the causality between exports and growth might be true, empirical studies on Japan suggest that the local market played a much bigger role for innovation and growth than exports.[1] For all the products I have studied, there is a considerable lag of several years between the start of production and first exports. Figure 1 shows examples of the typical pattern of domestic production and exports of innovations. This pattern is also visible in the scarce data on new technologies such as flat panel television sets, digital cameras and game consoles. For some products such as automobiles it took even decades until high export shares were reached. In industries, in which Japan eventually reached high export shares and which are marked by large economies of scale, domestic sales were much larger than exports over a long period until exports took off. For instance, since the 1950s the Japanese automobile industry built large production capacities overturning Germany in 1970 with an annual production of 5 m Motor vehicles, while exports remained low. In 1980 the

---

[1]   There is ample statistical evidence that the Japanese growth was not export-led. Chen (1979), Afxentious and Serletis (1991), Krause and Sekiguchi (1976) and Boltho (1996), using several different statistical tests, conclude that while exports improved the current account balance and economies of scale, "the stimulus to growth was mainly domestic in origin" (Krause and Sekiguchi 1976, p. 402). Kanamori (1968) finds that among 55 manufacturing industries, an increase of exports by 15 % annually between the mid 1950s and the mid 1960s occurred only for those products for which domestic demand increased more than 15 % as well (but not for all of those). Sluggish domestic demand was always followed by sluggish exports. With the temporary exception of footwear, which is still the most mobile industry most sensitive to labor costs, Japan has never reached an export success in products for which there is no or only a small market in Japan itself. In addition, since 1952 prices of export goods from Japan fell while export quantities increased: This is contrary to a positive correlation between prices and quantities that the export-led hypothesis predicts (Boltho 1996).

export share was just above 20 %. In the 1980s however, the export share increased dramatically and surpassed 50 % in 1990.

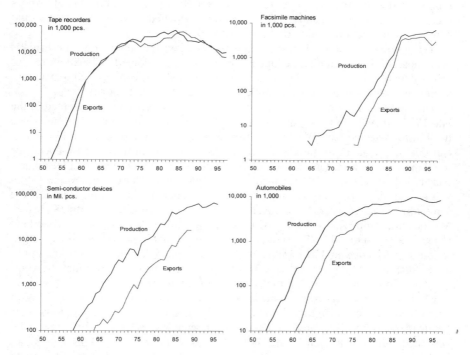

Source: Japan Trade Association, METI

Fig. 1. Production and exports of selected innovations in Japan 1950-1997

Statistics, however, do not reveal how applications of new technologies were induced by the domestic market. Gomory (1989) argues that Japanese firms do not bother to do a lot of market research but quickly develop a variety of products in order to find out what matches user preferences best based on the feedback receive from the market. High horizontal product differentiation is indeed a characteristic of Japanese companies and it is often stated by firms active in Japan that the Japanese market is unpredictable about what will find appreciation. Kodama (1995) on the other side argues that local demand already appeared before and during the development of successful Japanese innovations or was intentionally created by governmental institutions through a variety of policy instruments. Kodama asserts that Japanese manufacturers were aware of needs for sophisticated displays, home VCRs, and other electronic consumer goods and that the government had a strong influence on demand in setting regulation in favor of the use of new technology. The facsimile machine, for example, was indeed given a boost at the beginnings of the 1980s by allowing subscribers of fixed lines to connect to the heavily regulated public telephone network and declaring facsimiled documents legally valid (Scherer 1992). Yet, the pictorial Japanese language and a cumbersome process of typing a letter in a typewriter or word processor clearly signified the benefit of fax machines and copiers in Japan. The government opened up regulation that would hamper the market but it did not *create* the market.

Yet, among the innovations studied active market development by the firms is also apparent. For example, the tape recorder has been adopted in Japan more vigorously than in other countries because of the firms' dedication to convince consumers to use products formerly confined to the professional market.

The first tape recorder with a sufficient sound reproduction was invented in the late 1930s at AEG in Germany and regularly used at German radio stations since the 1940s. After the 2nd World War, this tape recorder was discovered by American GIs and brought to the US where it was copied, improved and produced for the American market. One recorder was employed at the Occupations Headquarters in Tokyo where in 1949 it inspired the founders of Sony Corporation to develop a similar tape recorder aimed at the consumer market (Sony 2004. At the same time, tape recorders were developed by several companies in the US (Brush, Magnecord, Ampex), Germany (AEG, Grundig, Studer Revox), and Switzerland (Naga) based on the old AEG model. The company that later became Sony Corporation was founded in 1945 and started to sell typical Japanese electronic appliances such as rice cookers and electric blankets. The tape recorder that the company developed in 1950 was initially solely aimed at the domestic market as well. A whole sale dealer tried to persuade potential users to buy it. While in the West tape recorders were being used mainly by stenographers and news reporters, new applications were discovered in Japan. After relentless efforts, the tape recorder was successfully marketed for use in schools as audio visual teaching aid as part of the Occupation forces education program. As the tape recorder steadily gained popularity in schools, mass production was subsequently set up. Competitors entered the market attracted by the emerging opportunity and competition further enhanced market growth. As a result, tape recorders were more widely adopted in Japan than in any other country. In the mid 1950s, the US company Superscope imported and distributed the Sony tape recorder in the US and by 1960 Sony set up an own distribution network in the US. Years after the first Japanese tape recorder was developed exports increased dramatically and only from them on did exports dominate the Japanese tape recorder industry.

Similar stories can be told for the electronic calculator, the video recorder, and the digital camera, all of which were still perceived as professional instruments in the West at a time when the Japanese consumer market was pursued, persuaded and won over. In the cases studied, Japanese firms responded to innovation opportunities in Japan by the absorption and refinement of recent technological inventions that were discovered around the world. In an interactive process between innovator and market, a specific technological trajectory was followed, guided by the preferences of domestic users. Innovations are therefore shaped by the market but are not totally determined. International differences in the market penetration of new products have an effect on the consumption pattern of a country. A cross-country comparison of the structure of demand demonstrates that the consumption pattern varies internationally. In the next chapter the distinctive consumption pattern of the Japanese market is discussed further.

The Structure and Size of Demand in Japan

On a very basic level consumption patterns are determined by the income of a household. Vernon's international product life cycle is based on the observation that in countries where the per-capita-income of a growing middle class increases (that is, where wealth is not totally concentrated in just a few hands), the consumption pattern follows the course of the US, the country with the highest per-capita income at that time. Because of this leading role of the domestic market American firms were able to commercialize their products abroad a couple of year after they were introduced in the US market. Yet, there are distinct differences in national consumption patterns even if income levels are equal. And these structural differences could be responsible for the cultivation of specific innovation in other counties than the US. For instance, the early fondness of the Japanese market for consumer electronics probably results from a lack of alternatives that are more prominent in the US such as a house, a private college education, international travel or investments in a start-up company. Structural differences result from differences in the cultural, geophysical, infrastructural, and institutional context of a country as well as from different prices of non-tradable goods such as energy or the existence of certain infrastructure.

The composition of the local market can have an important effect on innovation and innovation management. This is clearly apparent in the case studies of successful consumer innovations. For instance, US electronics companies did not pursue consumer innovations as aggressively as the Japanese. The consumer market in the US was relatively less attractive a market segment compared to other segments (although the US consumer market was bigger than that in any other country). It was often reported that the top management of large electronics companies like RCA, AT&T, and Westinghouse and semiconductor manufacturers didn't provide enough backing for innovation projects focusing on consumer goods. The military and the computer industry were more profitable and less risky customers. They were easier to persuade to use new technologies and it was therefore more attractive to assign the best R&D resources to their projects. Because profits were close to zero in the consumer sector, many US companies exited the market and concentrated on highly profitable industrial markets and defense programs. Semiconductor manufacturers focused on military applications and shunned consumer applications, which even made it difficult for Japanese electronics companies to procure ICs in the US for their innovation projects (Johnstone 1999). The largest TV producer in the world, RCA, neglected research at the TV set division for the sake of the computer business unit, which eventually failed (Scherer 1992). In Japan there was no such choice. The Japanese defense budget is much lower even on a per-capita basis and arms exports are prohibited. Japanese companies had to focus on private consumption and the domestic consumer market was clearly willing to endorse new products. Another example for the early consumption orientation of the Japanese market besides the tape recorder is television. The demand for TVs grew tremendously – even compared to Europe – since the 1950s. The abrupt take-off in the diffusion of TV sets was launched with the broadcasting of the royal wedding in 1959 and the Olympic Games in 1964. Color TV broadcasting was introduced in 1960, seven years earlier than in Europe.

Within private consumption, the more consumers spend on particular items the more attractive these products are for companies in terms investments in mass production and R&D. If a country spends relatively more on a particular product, local companies are more likely to spend more talent, R&D, and marketing efforts in those products (Porter 1990). The market signals that the consumers consider these products more important than other products. The demand structure can shape the awareness of the whole country, including the effort of consumers to evaluate new products the attention of the media and the decisions of the smartest brains what to study and where to apply for a job.

Table 1. Specialization index of consumption expenditure in selected goods in 1998

Product	Japan	USA	Germany	France	UK	Italy
Food	37	-38	10	29	-5	59
Clothing	15	-16	11	-21	3	67
Footwear	-18	-17	5	21	-5	110
Housing	19	-15	16	15	-12	20
Furniture	-135	-7	60	-3	17	102
Household appliances	28	-40	19	21	15	66
Dishwasher	-131	-15	110	12	-38	46
Microwave oven	33	-9	-35	35	5	-85
Electric toaster	-87	28	-26	-44	37	-91
Hardware, DIY	-8	-9	19	-10	27	44
Health goods	-113	50	-93	-106	-190	-88
Purchases of cars	-16	-4	31	-16	26	18
Rail travel	70	-278	-167	92	125	37
Air travel	-95	6	-50	-2	112	-91
Communications equip.	32	9	-43	-47	-249	-2
Communications services	10	-7	0	-18	-8	41
Video recorder	69	-50	-4	-44	39	-29
Video cameras	113	-76	-49	-9	-58	-58
Audio equipment	48	-55	34	38	36	-4
Home computers	-96	49	-30	-188	-188	-181
Television sets	48	-32	28	-30	-2	20
Cameras	58	-25	-9	34	-10	-90
Gardening tools	-87	16	37	-188	40	16
Writing instruments	29	-60	51	44	-46	-92

Source: Euromonitor, own calculations

An analysis of Japanese consumption expenditures for a selected set of products in Table 1 reveals distinct differences to the US, Germany, France, the UK, and Italy. To highlight these differences, a consumption specialization measure is used. The consumption specialization index is calculated as the share of a particular good within total private consumption of a country divided by the average share of that good among the six industrialized countries examined. In the table the logarithm of this ratio multiplied by 100 is shown in order to shift the average to zero and make it a more intuitive figure. A negative sign means therefore below average expenditure and a positive sign above average expenditures of a country for a specific good.

The analysis shows that the Japanese spend relatively more on food, rail travel, and consumer electronics, optics, and pens, and less on health care and some household products. Remarkable is the low willingness to spend on computers (and software), much in contrast to the Americans, who spend more on computers and computer related equipment than on audio and video equipment. Japanese buyers purchased about one fifth to one sixth the number of PCs compared to Americans during the 1990s (OECD 2000). This pattern is also observable in related product fields such as semiconductors. Japan is more specialized in chips for consumer electronics (OECD 2000). In contrast, US companies hold a sustainable competitive position in computer related ICs.[2] Consequently, the market for MP3 players and pocket computers (PDAs) which are complementary goods to computers are dominated by US companies. In the 1990s digital cameras were widely expected to be a computer accessory as well, in order to take photos that could be stored and altered in computers and viewed on a computer screen. This led computer companies such as HP and Apple to enter this new market at an early stage. But the digital camera took a different road that started in Japan. The traditional fondness of the Japanese for cameras poured over to digital ones. Instead of being used solely for computers digital cameras were used independently and ultimately substituted the traditional film cameras[3] As a result cameras had to be optimized for print outs. For instance, the numbers of pixels had to be increased (computer screens require a much lesser number of pixels). The Japanese market went on to significantly shaping advanced digital cameras. In contrast, in the computer industry, the proprietary designs of Japanese computer manufacturers could not set standard, which corresponds (and is probable due) to the low share of computer expenditures in Japan.

Local consumption patterns matter for other countries as well. Germans spend more on cars and Italians more on clothing and footwear. This corresponds to each countries trade specialization as Linder (1961) originally postulated. Yet, only a few studies, for instance Anderson et al. (1981), Fagerberg (1992) and Porter (1990) have looked into this causality. We will discuss the relationship between demand structure and export performance of a country in the following section.

---

2   The dominance of the Japanese in memory chips, so called DRAMs was only temporary. The demise of the Japanese manufacturers of DRAMs in the 1990s demonstrates that Japan has no genuine competitive advantage in computer related electronics.

3   One of the reasons for the early adoption of digital cameras in Japan that was mentioned during an interview with the Japanese camera association was the significant higher price of print outs in Japan.

In the early stage of a new technology, a large share of consumption is often synonymous for a large market size relative to other countries even if the country itself is small. For instance, Finland and Sweden were the largest markets for mobile telephony in the late 1970s and early 1980s. Japan has less than half the population of the US but sometimes was the largest market during the introduction phase of a new innovation, which eventually became a worldwide success. And it was already mentioned that Japan was at one time the largest market for tape recorders because of the discovery of new market segments. Estimates derived from trade organizations, newspaper reports, and interviews suggest that Japan was also the largest market for copiers in the 1960s, facsimile machines in the 1980s, and for digital cameras in the late 1990s. After these products became world standards in their categories the US and Europe overtook Japan in market size, usually in this order. And still more years later, China and India would become even larger markets. When this occurred, Japan's companies had already secured their leading competitive position through mass production and accumulation of technical expertise. The next section explores the cultural reasons for the distinct consumption pattern of Japan.

The Cultural Shaping of Japanese Innovation and Management

The reasons for Japan's inclination towards specific technologies or particular innovation designs are often based on cultural factors. Cultural factors of the demand for innovations have recently attracted a range of studies.[4] The adoption of innovations is suggested to be affected by cultural factors such as norms, religion, and general education (Rogers 1995). For instance, Mansfield (1989) concludes that the reason why Japanese firms adopted robots more widely than firms in the United States (where the robot was invented) was the long-term orientation of Japanese firms and not economic profitability factors such as scale economies, factor prices etc. Terpstra and David (1991) define culture as the problem-solving mode of nations and therefore relate innovation activities of countries directly to culture. Different cultures would therefore generate *different* solutions or innovation designs to the same problems. Cultural shaping of technology occurs when the societal norms and behaviors favor specific technologies and technical specifications. This is most obvious when different cultures choose different technologies for the same function. For instance, it has been suggested that personal computers, having no real technological advantage over mainframe computers,

---

[4]   Such as Albach (1993), Albach et al. (1989), Steenkamp et al. (1999), Herbig and Palumbo (1994). Most authors, however, study the relationship between culture and new product development, see e.g. Nakata and Sivakumar (1996) for a review. Cross-national diffusion research in marketing evaluated the impact of Hofstede's cultural dimensions on national attitudes towards adopting innovation (innovativeness) (e.g. Gatignon et al. 1989; Lynn and Gelb 1996). In these studies cosmopolitanism, mobility, individualism, and low uncertainty avoidance have a positive effect on the early diffusion of innovation, all dimensions on which Japan scores low.

invaded large companies in the US in the 1980s through the back door because engineers were most individualistic (Freiberger and Swaine 1984, Ceruzzi 1996) while the Japanese happily share a large computer among their colleagues.

Yet, factual characterizations of Japanese consumers are sparse. Lazer et al. (1985) for example list four main characteristics of the Japanese consumer that shape Japanese products: 1. demanding and "choosy", 2. fond of new and diverse features, 3. hold a preference for compactness and 4. sensitive to the effects on the quality of life. Our case studies indeed imply that some major cultural factors shape innovations in Japan besides early mass-market appeal for electronic consumer goods. Especially the Japanese language seemed to have an important effect on Japanese innovation design. Copiers and fax machines proofed to be most successful in Japan, because they were more beneficial for a country were most documents were hand written. In the history of flat panel displays, it is sometimes mentioned that the complex structure of Japanese characters made it necessary to follow a matrix design for LCD displays, whereas the roman letters used in the western world were less technically demanding to type, transfer and screen (Kawamoto 2002). This could explain the massive effort of Japanese firms to develop copiers, faxes and displays.

Not only can we relate product innovations demand conditions to a country' market characteristics but also process innovations. Mishina (1989) suggests that as much as Taylorism is related to the mass of low educated workers in the US at that time, Toyotaism is rooted in the post war social conditions in Japan. The sophistication of Japanese consumers affected their motivation at the work place, which brought Toyota's chief production planner Taiichi Ohno to think how he could involve the employees in the process of increasing quality and lowering waste. This leads us to the contingency theory of management practices.

The Quest for Quality

A characteristic feature of Japanese products is quality. In the old paradigm, the demand for quality came initially from the export markets. However, the quality level of products also reflects the local demand conditions of a country. Brouthers et al. (2000) reason that strategies of multinational firms are derived from demand conditions and the competitive structure of their home markets. They suggest that regional differences in the consumer market context led to the development of typical nation-specific combinations of price and quality. While the US market would set the incentives in a way that makes it most profitable for a local firms to sacrifice quality for a lower price, the European market is said to be most advantageous for a premium price strategy and high quality. The basic epitomes of Japanese management strategy, high quality and low cost, are also suggested to reflect the domestic market context. There is some anecdotal evidence that the lower price higher quality combination in Japan results from the unique demand conditions in Japan. Quality requirements in Japan are commonly described as high (Deshpande, Farley, and Webster 1993, Lazer, Murata, and Kosaka 1985). Of course, US consumers also demand high quality. However, for the US consumer market, it is reasoned that the quality became less important for middle class consumers *compared* to other product characteristics. Schonberger (1982) refers to shorter fashion trends in the post war years that made products obsolete earlier resulting in a "throw-away" attitude within the increasing consumerism in the US. Statistical evidence for international different relative quality levels of demand compared to other product features is rare. [5]

Another reason for the Japanese quest for quality at low prices is that quality improvements and cost cutting techniques are complements rather than substitutes (Wheelwright 1981, Schonberger 1982). Cost-reduction efforts can lead to increases in quality and vice versa. For instance, the introduction of just-in-time was motivated by the desire to reduce inventory, yet it required a more reliable manufacturing process with less defects. Successes to reach near perfection were ultimately reducing costs instead of increasing costs.

The strong effort for cost-cutting in the Japanese manufacturing sector described by management literature is more obscure though (for instance, Ohmae 1988, p. 151 talks about an "instinct to built market share"). Yet, given that the consumer market was predominantly targeted by Japanese corporations even for new technology as explained above, the only way to establish this mass market is to lower the price considerably.

At first glance it seems that a specific quality-price strategy applies to all industries equally and thus lacks the power to explain the specialization pattern of Japan. Yet, it cannot be applied to all industries to the same degree. First, the high-quality/low-price strategy only fits the consumer sector and not always to the business sector, and not to military and space applications. These early adopters played a major role for new technologies in the US but not in Japan. High quality was required of those applications while the price was not a major concern. And the US companies were not unable to match the quality requirements for these applications. Second, while the Japanese market on average demands high quality for low prices, in some industries this combination is less pronounced. For instance, food is required to be of extremely high quality but is rather expensive compared to other countries and home appliances are cheaper but lack the quality levels common in Europe.

Third, in many industries the unique mix of low price and high quality was feasible in all industries. Substantial price reductions were not possible in all industries because either economies-of-scale were low or there is a trade-off between quality and cost. This means that the cost of production necessarily increases with

---

[5]   Empirical evidence of the attitudes of buyers towards quality is difficult to collect, since consumers in most countries regard quality as important if asked (e.g. Barksdale et al. 1982). The success of Japanese products in the US market shows that demand in the US prefers quality as well. Robert Cole of Haas Business School at Berkeley pointed out, that the Japanese have educated the US market that quality is available for the same or even a lower price (private conversation). It can therefore be reasoned that quality levels in the US dropped below those of other countries because US manager perceived other product characteristics as relatively more important than companies in Japan and Europe.

quality. Regulation and traditional market structure can also limit cost reductions as is the case in the Japanese agricultural sector, in which small scale farms prevailed backed by political lobbying and protectionism. Another reason for low exports is that quality requirements in Japan become too high for international standards. For instance, freshness requirements for food actually hamper exports. Third, the term quality of a product might cover a characteristic of a product that makes it difficult to adapt to other countries' environments. For example, NTT has a record of stringent quality requirements that rendered telecommunications equipment made in Japan incompatible to the telecommunications infrastructure in other countries (Grupp 1991, Cole 2004). It was therefore suggested that the Japanese succeeded internationally only in those industries in which the Japanese strategy mix (low price, high quality) was most feasible, for instance in the semiconductor and automobile industry.

Coping with Variety

While mostly discussed for the automobile industry, large or 'excessive' variety is apparent in many Japanese industries and in most industries in which Japan became very competitive internationally. This is clearly in contrast to the US competitiveness that that is often associated with dominant company (Microsoft, Boeing) or specific product designs (IBM-compatible PC). Many management techniques such as just-in-time were in fact introduced not only to lower cost but also to manage variety. Japanese companies have a market-based incentive to produce variety. NC machines diffused earlier and wider in Japan than in other countries because they were used for a different purpose: to facilitate variety. Kodama (1995) notes that in western companies, NC machines were mostly employed in mass production lines to increase quality whereas Japanese manufacturers used NC machines to reduce the time needed to switch to a different model on the assembly line in order to increase the flexibility of the production process.

The demand for variety, however, is not a unique characteristic of the Japanese consumer market. The Japanese market has been characterized by higher homogeneity compared to other western countries which contradicts the standard argument for variety based on customer heterogeneity. Empirical observations find indeed that Japan does not have an exceptional demand for variety. Despite a variety of models of each manufacturer, demand is concentrated on few models. Bélis-Bergouignan and Lung (1999) find that in 1993 the top two models of each of the Japanese car manufacturers comprise between 37 % (Nissan) and 68 % (Honda) of total sales. This share has decreased since, but in 2003, Toyota's three top models still comprise 30 % of the number of all cars sold despite offering an almost absurd variety of 63 models in the Japanese market. A comprehensive comparison of Japan with Germany, the USA and Britain confirms that there is no higher demand for variety in Japan than in other countries. The concentration ratio of automobile models sold in 2003 is actually higher in Japan than in all other countries.[6]

Companies with a wide product variety exist in all industrialized countries but the evolution of variety in Japan was quite different. In the west, a specific pattern of the evolution of a new industry has often been observed. When a new technology emerges, many new firms enter the market and offer distinct product variants (Utterback 1994). Product variety is generated by the large number of firms in the market. When the growth rate of adoption decreases, the industry enters a consolidation phase, in which the number of competitors declines steeply. Unsuccessful companies exit the market, companies merge and larger companies acquire smaller competitors. As a result of this M&A activity the remaining companies have a higher product variety. The US carmaker General Motors, for example, increased model variety mainly by taking over competitors. Its famous platform strategy was the result of a consolidation of several similar models of the acquired firms (Chandler 1962). Variety in Europe is automatically caused by the free intra-European trade. Yet, Volkswagen of Germany, which was a one-product-company for years, followed a similar path than GM after acquiring competitors in other European countries. With the acquired firms came additional factories, which avoided the pressure for flexible production like in Japan, where a variety of model had to be produced in the same plant.

The increasing affluence of the Japanese consumer required the Japanese manufacturers to increase variety at a time when the Japanese market was still protected from imports and new local entrants were barred by high R&D costs and other market entry barriers. Due to a low import share of the Japanese market model variety has to be provided by the Japanese manufacturers. For instance, while 30 % of the cars sold in Germany in 2003 were imported from foreign manufacturers, Japan' import share was as little as 7.7 %. Assuming that the general demand for variety is equal in Japan and Europe, the Japanese companies, in the automobile industry basically only three large companies, would have to create in-house the same variety that emergence from all the European countries combined so that no market segment is left vacant for imports.

The advantage of increasing model variety was challenged by lower product volumes per model. This was tackled by increasing the flexibility of the production system for small lot production. Higher variety also means higher fluctuation in the production process, precisely for each particular model, even if the total number of cars sold stays the same. Toyota's lean production which made labor a truly variable cost factor was an answer to this fluctuation problem in production. And while the degree of platform variety equalized between US and Japanese car manufacturers in the late 1970s, the Japanese – because of the lower number of plants – had to achieve a higher platform variety on the plant level. Thus, production lines had to be more flexible in Japan than in the US. The ability to produce a

---

[6] The share of the three top models (CR3) is 17 % in Japan, 13 % in Germany and Britain and 12 % in the USA, while the CR5 is 25 % in Japan, 19 % in Germany and 17 % in the USA.

product mix with frequent retooling is one the core production principles of Toyotaism, refined by smaller Japanese manufacturers.

Another economic reason for a firm to offer a variety of products is uncertainty in the market. Variety can be induced by preference uncertainty even if customers are homogenous (Carlton and Dana 2004). One reason for market uncertainty could be that Japanese consumers are influenced by their peers' choices, which creates externalities. A market with strong externalities converges to single standards or at least to a low degree of variety over time. Yet, it is highly unpredictable what product variant becomes a standard (Arthur 1989). The Japanese market is often associated with larger uncertainty. In an oligopoly, an increase of product variety can increase market share if there is some degree of market uncertainty or heterogeneity (segment fragmentation) in the market. Toyota's growing product variety was first clearly aimed at offering distinct models for separate consumer segments. But it is characteristic for the later phases of variety augmentation, that several models for the same segments were introduced to the market (Cusumano and Nobeoka 1998, p. 28).

What about the applicability of the Japanese approaches to flexibility in Western countries? While many Japanese companies successfully run transplants around the world applying almost the same management techniques, they have carefully adapted their production strategy in foreign markets. For instance, Toyota follows an almost excessive variety strategy in Japan offering 63 models, but only 27 in the US and 20 in Europe. Overall, the manufacturing strategy of managing a worldwide model variety makes perfect sense; the same does not apply to a car manufacturer like BMW that concentrates on five standardized models for the world market. In addition, Toyota only reached a high market penetration abroad when it designed car models for large overseas markets. The breakthrough in the US market came after Toyota developed cars for the US market. In Europe, the market share remained low, partly because of import restrictions but partly because the preferences in the European market are different. Toyota started to develop its own European models as well which are selling better than the Japanese models. Design and technical centers in the US and Europe helped to implement the adaptations to the local market, a strategy that European manufacturers only recently began to follow.

Toyota's practices are justified by its dominant market share in the Japanese market (Mishina 1989). However, while its production and innovation strategies match the Japanese market requirements, the success of Toyota does not imply that all of them will be successful in other countries as well. In general, assessing the value of the principles of Japanese manufacturing systems for US and European manufacturers requires a detailed analysis of the local market situation in Japan.

Domestic Competition

The high degree of competition in the market is in itself a factor that shapes local innovations. Fierce competition is a main characteristic of the Japanese market in many industries (Abegglen and Stalk 1985; Kotabe 1985). Probably the most important function of competition is that it reveals the preferences of users and the benefits of numerous product variants. The more competitors and the higher the degree of competition the more product variants are introduced in the market. As a result in a highly competitive market different products are used than in a country with a dominant manufacturer. A beverage company that dominates a market has less incentive to innovate and focuses marketing activities on its established set of brands.

An example for this innovation process is the soft drink industry. In Japan a high number of new soft drinks are introduced into the market every year (Markides 1997). The Japanese are fond of soft drinks and like to test new formulas. The market is highly competitive; many beverage companies are active in the market. While the brands of the American soft drink mammoth Coca-Cola dominate the market in most countries, in Japan they hold an unusually small market share. Market entry barriers are low compared to Western countries because of differences in the distribution system. Soft drinks in Japan are mainly distributed through street vending machines, which are easier to set up for new entrants. In such a national context new flavors are discovered and some of them survive the market introduction phase. The Coca-Cola drink emerged in a situation similar to that in Japan today. Many soft drinks originate from the southern States of the US caused by the south's hot climate as well as its strong religious culture, which frowned upon harder beverages (Economist 1999, p. 81). Drink bars offered a variety of carbonated mixes in order to identify consumer's preferences. As Riley (1958) notes, the variety of flavors added made it a typical American industry. In the South of the United States a strongly increasing demand initiated fierce competition, which spurred the search for and market tests of new flavors by local bottlers. A very large variety of flavored carbonated beverages was tested in the local market. Most of these did not appeal for long or they were demanded locally only. But some like Coca-Cola became an international success. In the next section, the relationship between local market conditions and international success of a local innovation is discussed.

Domestic Shaping and Export Success

Japan's economic success is accompanied by a tremendous export performance that started in the 1960s and dramatically sky rocketed in the 1970s and 1980s. In several industries, Japanese companies as a whole have virtually monopolized the world market. During the in 1960s exports included steel, ships, and basic chemicals. Since the 1980s exports are mainly based on innovation-intensive industries such as automobiles, electronics, optics and machinery. If Japanese innovations are domestically shaped, as has been argued in this essay, why did Japanese innovations become so successful internationally? The Japanese's fondness for seaweed and miso paste has not generated any exports, why did it work for fax machines and LCD displays? To begin with, a look at Japanese historical export statistics shows that Japan never was an export intensive country as Germany or

Sweden. In 2000, Japan's export share of GDP stood at around 16 % which was as low as the export share of the USA, but much lower than Germany's share of 44 % and Sweden's share of 56 % (Schumacher et al. 2003, p. 23). Looking at the historical evolution of the Japanese companies, exports never came easy. A tremendous effort and motivation to export was needed in order to overcome the cultural hurdles between Japan and other countries (Lazer et al. 1985). Japanese companies often started as OEM suppliers for foreign corporations and distributors. They had to learn extensively in foreign countries before they could successfully adapt their products to foreign market conditions. Not all industries were successful. Japan has gained world market dominance only in a few industries or products such as copiers, facsimile machines, television sets, motorcycles, video game consoles and audio and video equipment. On the other hand, although being early in the game, Japan did not gain a sustainable large world market share in many related high-tech products such as personal computers, cellular phones, microprocessors, aircraft, medical equipment, pharmaceuticals and petrochemical. Western industrialized countries generate high revenues and profits in many low-tech industries, in which Japan is not successful at all such as fashion clothing, sports goods, furniture, oil extraction and refinery and food. The distinction between export success and failure is not easily put down to distinct innovation management strategies. Japans trade specialization is partly determined by Japan's market and demand conditions.

Japan's Trade Specialization

Central to our argument is the observation that the export specialization of Japan is not initially determined by technology and innovation. Initial technology gaps do not explain Japan's export success. In contrast, Japan is successful in many non-R&D-intensive industries such as pens, musical instruments, rubber, and magnetic tapes. Another simple test reveals that the competitiveness of Japan in particular industries is not determined by R&D intensity. Within most R&D-intensive industries there are R&D-intensive products and non-R&D-intensive products. If the competitiveness of a country is base on R&D inputs then the country must be more competitive in the R&D-intensive parts than in the non-R&D intensive parts of each industry. To test this proposition, the revealed comparative advantage or RCA was calculated for the R&D-intensive and the non-R&D-intensive parts of 20 industries that include R&D-intensive and non-R&D-intensive products.[7] A comparison between the RCA's of the R&D- and the non-R&D-intensive parts of each industry shows that in 11 of the 20 industries Japan is more competitive in the non-R&D-intensive than in the R&D-intensive industries.

---

[7]   The RCA is a widely used measure for international competitiveness. This analysis has been conducted on the basis of the product list of R&D intensive industries that is used in the report on the technological performance of Germany. This report is annually prepared by five research institutions and published by the German Ministry of Education and Research, see BMBF (2003).

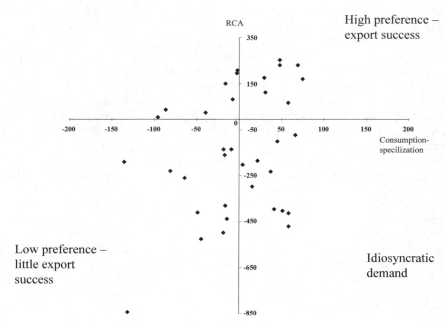

Source: OECD, Euromonitor, own calculations

Fig. 2. The relationship between consumption and trade specialization in Japan in 1998

The industrial specialization of countries reflects not only the capacity to innovate but also the structure of local demand. Since demand for goods of R&D-intensive industries increases with income, high-income industrialized countries are naturally somehow specialized in R&D industries. In order to test the relationship between demand structure and trade performance, trade and domestic consumption specialization patterns have to be aligned and compared. For 37 product categories the structure of consumption expenditure was matched and compared to their RCA measure of trade specialization (Fig. 2). There is a significant but weak correlation between specialization of trade and consumption. Observations are basically in three quadrants. The most common observations are products in which Japan either has a high trade and a high consumption specialization or products in which is has a low trade and low consumption specialization. These two combinations are in line with the argumentation that consumption specialization determines trade specialization. An important observation is that there are virtually no products in the sample in which Japan has a low consumption but a high trade specialization. This suggests that it rarely happens that Japan extensively exports a good for which there demand in Japan is relatively low. There are, however, some product categories, in which Japan has a low export performance in spite of domestic demand that is above average. In these industries local demand does not lead to high trade performance. These industries are for example food, alcoholic drinks, and washing machines. The cultural context of Japan is such different that the local products cannot be adapted to the global market. The limitations of the Japanese to export certain white goods such as dishwasher and washing machines underline their dependence on the domestic market. For example, the Japanese traditionally wash with cold water which has a fundamental effect of the design of washing machines while dishwashers are rare in Japanese households (see Table 1). All in all, we can say that Japan successfully exports only those products in which the Japanese are on average spending relatively more money than other industrialized countries and in which the domestic market context is close to the international market context. In the next section we will discuss the export success factors of Japan for those products for which the Japanese market context is more favorable.

Factors of Export Success

It is argued here that Japanese companies are most successful in international trade in those industries in which the domestic market led the word market. International competitiveness of a country is sustainable if the domestic market produces a continuous stream of knowledge or information along an application trajectory that keeps it ahead of competitors. The Japanese market gave Japanese companies a home-market advantage for many specific innovations, which the Japanese now dominate.[8] Domestic firms are more effective to react to changes in local demand and thereby get faster and better feedback from the first applications of their innovations. This interactive learning process refines innovations for widespread application. By analysis the characteristics of the Japanese market for 12 products in which Japanese companies have enjoyed a strong world market performance over a long period we have learned that for these products

- Japan offered the largest domestic market at an early stage of the technology life cycle[9], or
- the penetration rate was highest in the growth phase of the diffusion, and

---

[8] The home market theory was introduced by Linder (1961). It suggests that domestic companies perceive national demand more efficiently than foreign companies. There are two general arguments, which are especially true in the case of Japan. First of all, firms have better information on local customer needs and consumer preferences. These information asymmetries regarding local demand conditions are explained in innovation theory by the need for close contacts between producers, customers, suppliers, and industrial services in the introduction phase of innovations and, thus, regional proximity and low cultural distance such as language or societal rules (e.g., Anderson et al. 1981, Fagerberg 1992).

[9] The Japanese bought more tape recorders, electronic calculators, digital cameras, and flat panel TV sets than the US or the European market. For instance, according to market estimations by DisplaySearch the Japanese Market represented around 75 % of the worldwide market for LCD TV sets in 2001, above 50 % in 2002 and around 40 % in 2003.

- product designs or technological trajectories were favored in Japan, that became economically advantageous worldwide, and
- the degree of competition in the Japanese market exceeded those in other countries

These characteristics gave Japanese companies a home market advantage that could be exploited internationally in the form of lower manufacturing costs or market knowledge. The most obvious Japanese advantage is low costs through mass production. This cost advantage has been achieved through the early mass market in Japan for many of the analyzed innovations. As a result, Japanese companies had incentives to build up mass production facilities and to drive down costs with a refined production organization. They were successful in foreign market with innovation designs that were originally fitted to the Japanese market because of a lower price or a higher quality than foreign manufacturers. If price differences are large, even substantial preference differences between the Japanese and the western markets can be compensated. In the words of Theodore Levitt, the customers succumb to the attraction of lower prices and abandon their previously held preferences (Levitt 1983). Especially for innovations that included electronics, the cost reduction potential of mass production was large enough to overcome the differences between the unique market contexts of the Japanese and overseas markets. For example, western markets initially preferred the teletypewriter for the facsimile machine because of the roman letters were easier to type in and more economical to transfer via the typewriter. The fax machine was better suited for the Japanese writing system than the teletypewriter. The large price decline in the Japanese mass market gave the fax machine an advantageous price-benefit-ratio compared to the typewriter. For this reason it was adopted world wide.

Within this framework, we can characterize three groups of industries. First, if markets are almost similar, such as in the steel industry, the electronic calculator or the DRAM industry, small cost advantages can lead to high exports. But the competitive advantage can be lost quickly when foreign competitors compensate for the productivity difference. This happened in all three examples, in which US and European companies (and Korean in the case of DRAMs) could come back and regain market share. Second, although there are substantial and persistent differences between the Japanese market and overseas markets, the Japanese market has a persistent lead so that the cost advantage can compensate for the differences in preference. This was the case with the facsimile machine, the robot, and the camera industry. The third group comprises those industries, in which the differences are too large or the cost reduction potential too small so that there is no global standardization. The large size of the Japanese market ensures that in most industries there is an innovation design available so that the Japanese market does not have to adopt a foreign innovation design (exception are the aircraft and the pharmaceutical industry). This means that companies can fully concentrate on identifying and matching the preferences of the market they know best. The following hypothesis can be derived: the relationship between the similarity of the preferences in the Japanese and overseas markets and the export success of Japanese companies is an inverted u-function.

Besides the market size, the penetration rate in Japan was higher for most of the analyzed innovations for much of the diffusion cycle. A penetration rate that is higher than in any other country gives local companies an advantage with regard to market knowledge. Higher penetration rates mean that a broader range of users give feedback about what they like and what they do not like about the specific design. Some market segments demand new features and applications. A wider circulation in the whole market creates new benefits for users. The wider usage of tape recorders, video recorders, electronic calculators, and digital cameras in Japan, for instance, have suggested that portability and compactness are more essential than professional features like programmability in the case of calculators. A mass market normally has lower requirements than professional applications. Fax machines were used more and more for normal business communications and private households.

The Japanese market has demonstrated that was a trend leader in several industries. A trend leader selects technologies or innovation designs that later turn out to be beneficial in other countries as well. In the camera industry, Japan traditionally leads in the adoption of many innovations, some of them invented in western countries. The Japanese market was not only the largest market for digital cameras in the early years, but it switched several years earlier from more traditional silver halide to digital cameras than the US and the European market. In 2001 digital cameras represented already more than half of the total camera market, whereas this threshold was reached in the US market only in 2003. In the flat panel industry, the Japanese market has always preferred liquid crystal displays, while in the US plasma was the preferred choice mainly based on military applications but also for home TV sets. Yet, it became recently clear that LCD-displays will gain market share in the TV segment worldwide with technical improvements that make large LCD panels possible, a domain that was previously dominated by plasma.

Last but not least, a higher degree of local competition (compared to other countries) is not only leading to innovation designs that harmonize with the domestic context but is also to exports. The argument here is that hidden preferences are discovered in competitive markets since more innovations are tested. There are regularly tradeoffs between features of a product, one innovation design offers more of A but less of B and with another design it is vice versa. Manufacturers often don't know beforehand what features users prefer. In using various alternative product designs users discover whether A or B is more important. In the digital camera industry, for instance, Japanese consumers were able to constantly select from a large number of different models signaling those manufacturers that were active in the market (Kodak and HP were not) what features were valued more and, therefore, more profitable to concentrate scarce R&D resources to. Although the resulting improved designs are still somehow culture-specific, they might be even better than the corresponding designs available in overseas markets with low competition.

Contrary to the above argument runs the common claim that the Ministry of trade and industry (MITI) established cartels in order to strengthen the industry by preventing "excessive competition", competition that would lead to market exits and burden companies with losses. Before the war, the large Japanese conglomerates indeed monopolized industries under the provision of the commerce ministry. After the Second World War, the successor of the commerce ministry, the MITI, continued an intervening approach to industrial policy. However, the situation changed in an important detail. Virtually all of the new zaibatsus could now enter each new industry. Johnson (1982) suggests that, overall MITI's policies even increased competition. MITI's announcements of desired technologies reduced the risk, because it was clear that the government would help those companies that invested in the desired technologies, in case the venture failed. Competition was even more enhanced, because all companies tried to gain market share, since this was the criterion according to which subsidies would be allocated in case of a crisis of the industry. An analysis by Sakakibara and Porter (2001) should be able to end the controversy. They found statistical evidence that domestic competition is an essential factor for the international competitiveness of Japan. Industries with a high degree of competition, measured by market share fluctuations, accomplish a higher export performance than industries with a low degree of domestic competition.

Yet, the Japanese government did increase the export success of innovations in a few cases. By recreating market conditions in Japan that are similar to those in foreign countries, Japanese companies would face a market context at home that would allow them to develop innovations for the domestic market that could later be exported. For instance, in the late 1970s the US standards on exhaust gases of automobiles were introduced in Japan – due to a delay in the US legislation process – even one year before they came into effect in the US (Beise et al. 2003). Since this specific regulation could only be matched with a catalytic converter, Japan was the first country that adopted this innovation that would later become an international standard. As a result, Japanese manufacturers of catalytic converters are international leaders.

Yet, contrary to the examples discussed above, our analyses suggest that the competitiveness of Japan's auto industry is not directly based on domestic innovativeness. Japan is not really successful with indigenous Japanese auto designs but mainly with derivates of western models. For example, the new 'tall wagon' genre in the small car segment became highly successful in Japan but not in other countries; neither do boxy cars like the Nissan Cube (Fig. 3) which became the second best selling car in Japan in 2004. The market potential abroad is limited because these models do not fit into foreign market conditions (too small, underpowered, the aerodynamics are unfavorable) and other advantages (low price, high quality) are not big enough to compensation for that. The successes in foreign countries are based on adaptations to or even separate models for overseas markets. After 1985 Japanese companies dramatically increased their direct investments and set up manufacturing capabilities to serve foreign markets with country-specific models. Since the automobile industry in the triad countries remained quite different, Japanese auto manufacturers were able to increase their overseas market share by developing exclusive models, first for South-East-Asian countries, than for the US market and - since in the beginning of the 1990s – for the European market. The same strategy was chosen by American companies already before the Second World War.

Fig. 3. Japanese creativity with low exports

Up to the end of the 1990s (before the introduction of the hybrid cars), the Japanese competitive advantage in the automobile industry appears to be mainly derived from a better price-quality ration based on the superior organization of production and not from pioneering product innovation. As has been described above the production techniques are induced by the unique market situation in Japan, the increase in model variety and the need to cope with this in production for a smaller market when compared to the US.

Conclusions

In this essay, it is suggested that the Japanese market has to take into account in order to explain the characteristics of Japanese innovations and the export success of Japan. Innovation management techniques or the technology gap theory often cannot explain why Japan has succeeded to export vigorously and even dominate the world market in various industries and why it failed in others. Of course, technological knowledge gaps and superior management formulas strengthened the world market role of Japanese companies. Yet, it is argued here that these factors are acquired or learned in the specific context of the Japanese market. The R&D efforts of companies were guided or encouraged by the unique signals from the Japanese market. Japanese companies are pushed towards mass-market-excellence in particular industries competitive climate of the Japanese market. This mass-market-excellence enabled the Japanese at the same time to overcome the substantial differences between the domestic and the overseas markets, which are often frustrating for western companies that were initially determined to thrive in the Japanese market (Czinkota, Kotabe 2000).

Japanese business behavior is often embedded in the market context of Japan. Culture pays an import role here but that is not the only emanating factor of the Japanese market. Other factors are the demand specialization in Japan, extreme competition, the corporate structure and a low import share. The consequences of this framework for western firms are twofold. First, Japanese management techniques have to be related to the specific Japanese context in order to reveal the contingencies of their functioning. Successful application of Japanese approaches to innovation might require similar contexts in the countries where they are to be implemented. This means either that companies in non-Japanese countries have to recreate the Japanese context along with the one they already have adopted or that the applicability is confined to the Japanese market. Second, western companies can directly learn from the Japanese market in those industries, in which it has assumed a leading role by being present in Japan. Although Kodak had established an R&D center in Japan in the 1990s it exited the Japanese market and therefore missed a decisive learning opportunity. With the take over of the Japanese cameras manufacturer Chinon in 2003 and the presence in the Japanese market Kodak can fully benefit from the leading position of Japan in the digital camera industry. P&G and Coca Cola have realized similar advantages by setting up market intelligence and R&D capabilities in Japan in the baby care and soft drink market respectively. Although Japan is not a profitable market in many industries in which Japan leads the world market, a company's presence in the Japanese market is a kind of investment a firm has to make in order to gain a knowledge advantage that can be leveraged in other markets.

References

Abegglen JC and Stalk G (1985): Kaisha, the Japanese corporation. Basic Books, New York

Afxentious PC and Serletis A (1991): Export and GNP Causality in the Industrial Countries 1950-1985. Kyklos 44:167-179

Albach H (1993): *Culture and Technical Innovation: a Cross-Cultural Analysis and Policy Recommendations*. Akad. d. Wiss. zu Berlin Working Group Culture and Technical Innovation, de Gruyter, Berlin

Albach H, de Pay D, and Rojas R (1989): Der Innovationsprozeß bei kulturspezifisch unterschiedlich innovationsfreudigen Konsumenten. *Zeitschrift für Betriebswirtschaft*, Ergänzungsheft Nr. 1:109-129

Anderson ES, Dalum B, and Villumsen G (1981): International Specialisation and the Home Market - An empirical analysis. Industrial Development Research Series No. 19, Research Report, Aalborg University Press, Aalborg

Arthur B (1989): Competing Technologies Increasing Returns and Lock-in by Historical Events, Economic Journal 99, 116-131

Barksdale HC, Perreault WD, Arndt J, Barnhill JA, French WA, Halliday M, and Zif J (1982): A cross-national survey of consumer attitudes toward marketing practices, consumerism and governmental regulations, Columbia Journal of World Business 17 (2):71-86

Beechler S and Yang ZJ (1994): The transfer of Japanese-style Management to American subsidiaries: Contingencies, Constraints and Competencies. Journal of International Business Studies 25:467-491

Beise M, Blazejczak J, Edler D, Jacob K, Jänicke M, Loew T, Petschow U, and Rennings K (2003): The Emergence of Lead Markets for Environmental Innovations. In: Horbach J, Huber J, Schulz T (Eds) Nachhaltigkeit und Innovation: Rahmenbedingungen für Umweltinnovationen. München, pp 11-53

Beise M and Rennings K (2004): National Environmental Policy and the Global Success of Next-Generation Automobiles, International Journal of Energy Technology Policy (IJETP), Special Issue "Energy Conservation", Vol. 2, No. 3: 272-283

Bélis-Bergouignan MC and Lung Y (1999): The Progressive Emergence of Product Variety in the Japanese Automobile Industry, in: Lung Y, Chanaron JJ, Fujimoto T, and Raff D (Eds) Coping with variety: flexible productive systems for product variety in the auto industry, Aldershot, pp. 81-110

BMBF (2003): Zur Technologischen Leistungsfähigkeit Deutschlands, Bonn

Boltho A. (1996): Was Japanese Growth Export-Led? Oxford Economic Papers 48:415-432

Brouthers LE, Werner S, and Matulich E (2000): The Influence of Triad Nations' Environments on Price-quality Product Strategies and MNC Performance, Journal of International Business Studies 31 (1), 39-62

Carlton D and Dana J (2004): Product variety and demand uncertainty, NBER working paper 10594, Washington

Ceruzzi P (1996): From scientific instrument to everyday application: the emergence of personal computers, 1970–77. History and Technology 13:1–31

Chandler A (1962): Strategy and Structure, Cambridge, Mass: MIT Press

Chen EKY (1979): Hyper Growth in Asian Economies Macmillan: London

Cole R (1999): Managing Quality Fads, New York, Oxford: Oxford University Press

Cole R (2004): Telecom Competition in World Markets: Understanding Japan's Decline and Possible Renewal, mimeo

Cusumano MA and Nobeoka K (1998): Thinking beyond Lean: How Multi-project Management is transforming product development at Toyota and Other Companies, New York

Czinkota MR and Kotabe M (2000): Entering the Japanese Market: A Reassessment of Foreign Forms' Entry and Distribution Strategies, Industrial Marketing Management 29 (6): 483-491

Deshpande R, Farley JU, and Webster FE (1993): Corporate Culture, Customer Orientation, and Innovativeness in Japanese Firms: A Quadrad Analysis." Journal of Marketing 57 (January): 23-27

Economist (1995): Hello Japan? Are you there?, August 12th, European Edition, p 60

Economist (1999): America is Going Soft, April 3rd, Europäische Ausgabe:81-82

Fagerberg J (1992): The Home Market Hypothesis Re-examined: The Impact of Domestic User-Producer Interaction on Export Specialisation. In: Lundvall BA (ed) National Systems of Innovation, London, New York: Pinter, pp 226-239

Freiberger P and Swaine M (1984): Fire in the Valley: The Making of the Personal Computer. Osborne/McGraw-Hill, Berkeley

Gatignon H, Eliashberg J, Robertson TS (1989): Modeling Multinational Diffusion Patterns: An Efficient Methodology, Marketing Science 8 (3): 231-247

Glisby M and Holden N (2003): Contextual Constraints in Knowledge Management Theory: the Cultural Embeddedness of Nonaka's Knowledge-creating Company, Knowledge and Process Management 10 (1): 29-36

Gomory R (1989): From the Ladder of Science to the Product Development Cycle, Harvard Business Review (November-December):99-105

Grupp H (1990): Japan, in: Grupp H and Schnöring T (Eds) Forschung und Entwicklung für die Telekommunikation – Internationaler Vergleich mit zehn Ländern, Band I, Berlin, pp. 141-240

Grossman GM and Helpman E (1990): Innovation and Growth in the Global Economy, Cambridge, MA

Herbig PA and Palumbo F (1994): The Effect of Culture on the Adoption Process: a Comparison of Japanese and American Behavior, Technical Forecasting and Social Change 46, 71-101

Hofer CW (1975): Towards a Contingency Theory of Business Strategy, Academy of Management Journal 18: 784-810

Johnson Ch (1982): *MITI and the Japanese miracle: the growth of industrial policy, 1925-1975*, Stanford, CA

Johnstone B (1999): *We were burning: Japanese Entrepreneurs and the Forging of the Electronic Age*, New York

Kanamori H (1968): Economic Growth and Exports. In: Klein L, Ohkawa K (Eds) Economic Growth: The Japanese Experience since the Meiji Era, Illinois, pp. 303-325

Kawamoto H (2002): The History of Liquid-Crystal Displays, *Proceedings of the IEEE*, Vol. 90, 4:460-500

Kodama F (1995): *Emerging Patterns of Innovation. Sources of Japan's Technological Edge*, Boston

Kotabe M (1985): The Roles of Japanese Industrial Policy for Export Success: A Theoretical Perspective, *Columbia Journal of World Business* 20 (Fall): 59-64

Krause LB and Sekiguchi S (1976): Japan and the World Economy, in: Patrick H and Rosovsky H (Eds) Asia's New Giant – How the Japanese Economy Works, the Brookings Institution, Washington, DC

Lazer W, Murata S, and Kosaka H (1985): Japanese Marketing: Towards a better Understanding, Journal of Marketing 49 (Spring):69-81

Levitt T (1983): The Globalization of Markets, Harvard Business Review 61 (3):92-102

Linder SB (1961): *An Essay on Trade and Transformation*, Almqvist & Wiksells Uppsala

Lundvall BA (1988): Innovation as an Interactive Process – From User-Producer Interaction to the National System of Innovation, in: Dosi G (ed.) technical Change and Economic Theory, London, pp. 349-369

Lynn M and Gelb B (1996): Identifying Innovative National Markets for Technical Consumer Goods, International Marketing Review 13 (6):43-57

Mansfield E (1989): The Diffusion of Industrial Robots in Japan and the United States, Research Policy 18:183-192

Markides CC (1997): Strategic Innovation. Sloan Management Review 38(3) Spring, 9-23

Mishina K (1989): Essays on technological evolution, Boston

Nakata C and Sivakumar K (1996): National Culture and New Product Development: An integrative Review, Journal of Marketing 60 (1): 61-72

OECD (2000): OECD Information Technology Outlook 2000. Paris

Ohmae K (1988): Getting back to Strategy, Harvard Business Review, November-December: 149-156

Ozawa T (1974): Japan's Technological Challenge to the West, 1950-1974: Motivation and Accomplishment, The MIT Press: Cambridge, Mass., London

Perlmutter HV (1969): The Tortuous Evolution of the Multinational Corporation, Columbia Journal of World Business 4:9-18

Porter ME (1990): The Competitive Advantage of Nations, New York

Porter ME, Takeuchi H, and Sakakibara M (2000): Can Japan Compete? Macmillan Basingstoke

Prahalad CK and Doz YL (1987): *The multinational mission: balancing local demands and global vision*, New York

Riley JJ (1958): A History of the American Soft Drink Industry: Bottled Carbonated Beverages, Washington, D.C.: American Bottlers of Carbonated Beverages

Rogers EM (1995): Diffusion of Innovation, 4th Ed., New York.

Rosenbloom RS and Cusumano MA (1987): Technological Pioneering and Competitive Advantage: The Birth of the VCR Industry, *California Management Review* 29 (1): 51-76

Sakakibara M and Porter ME (2001): Competing at Home to Win Abroad: Evidence from Japanese Industry, Review of Economics and Statistics 83 (2):310-322

Scherer FM (1992): International High-Technology Competition, Cambridge: Harvard University Press

Schonberger RJ (1982): Japanese Manufacturing Techniques: Nine Hidden Lessons in Simplicity, New York

Schumacher D, Legler H, and Gehrke B (2003): Marktergebnisse bei forschungsintensiven Waren und wissensintensiven Dienstleistungen: Aussenhandel, Produktion und Beschäftigung, Studien zum deutschen Innovationssystem No. 18-2003, Berlin, Hannover

Shinohara M (1975): On the evaluation of the 360 Yen Exchange Rate, Japanese Economic Studies 4:3-22

Shinohara M (1982): Industrial Growth, Trade, and Dynamic Patterns in the Japanese Economy, University of Tokyo Press

Song XM and Parry ME (1997): A Cross-National Comparative Study of New Product Development Processes. Japan and the United States, Journal of Marketing 61 (2): 1-18

Sony Corporation (2004): Sony History, downloaded on 21.05.2004 from http://www.sony.net/Fun/SH/index.html

Steenkamp JB, ter Hofstede F, and Wedel M (1999): A Cross-National Investigation into the Individual and National Cultural Antecedents of Consumer Innovativeness, Journal of Marketing 63 (2), 55-69

Terpstra V and David KH (1991): The Cultural Environment of International Business, 3rd Ed. Cincinnati, OH

Tsurumi Y (1973): Japanese Multinational Firms, Journal of World Trade Law, Vol. 7, No. 1 (January-February):74-90

Utterback JM (1994): *Mastering the Dynamics of Innovation*, Boston

Venkatraman N and Prescott J (1990): Environment-strategy coalignment. Its performance implications, Strategic Management Journal 11 (1), 1-23

Wheelwright S (1981): Japan – where operations really are strategic, Harvard Business Review, July-August, 67-76

Exploiting "Interface Capabilities" in Overseas Markets: Lessons from Japanese Mobile Phone Handset Manufacturers in the US

Masanori Yasumoto and Takahiro Fujimoto

Introduction

It has been asserted that close interfirm relationships enhance relation-specific knowledge, and thus contribute to product development performances (Clark and Fujimoto 1991; Dyer 1996; Ogawa 2000; von Hippel 1994). Particularly drawing on the case of the manufacturer-supplier relationship in Japan, antecedents have asserted that close relationships between firms enhance interfirm collaborative relationships for product/technology development. These studies shed light on the advantage of the close manufacturer-supplier relationships in Japan, and suggest the criticality of relation-specific knowledge (Asanuma 1989; Dyer and Singh 1998; Nishiguchi 1994).

The close interfirm relationships may not allow Japanese firms to collaborate with other firms outside the relationship in Japan. A firm embedded in an interfirm network could be vulnerable outside the incumbent network that the firm commits to (Uzzi 1997). The idiosyncratic interfirm relationship between specific firms in Japan could hinder the Japanese firms from sufficiently exploiting the technologies and product development capabilities according to expected customer/partner firms in oversea markets.

However, the case of a Japanese mobile handset manufacturer in the US casts doubt on the concept of "relation-specific knowledge" in relation to close interfirm relationships. As embedded in the close local manufacturer-provider relationship, Japanese mobile phone handset manufacturers are not necessarily successful in the global market. However, some of the Japanese manufacturers have recently built close relationships with US providers, and thereby enjoyed a high evaluation of their products in the US market.

The case makes us infer that Japanese firms could be adept at coping with expected customer/partner firms in oversea markets even outside the local interfirm relationships in Japan. Drawing on the case of a Japanese handset manufacturer in the US, the study attempts to explore how a Japanese firm adherent to specific local customer/partner firms can make use of accumulated technologies and product development capabilities beyond the local interfirm network.

At first, the article overviews the characteristics, benefits, and problems of a close interfirm relationship between manufacturers and customer/partner firms drawing on the findings from the Japanese automobile industry. The article proposes the concept of "*interface capabilities*" following the overview. At the following section, the article attempts to outline the characteristics of the manufacturer-provider relationship and associated handset development capabilities in Japan, and envisages the case of a Japanese handset manufacturer in the US. At last, the article discusses how Japanese manufacturers make use of the technologies and product development capabilities across boarders.

Background

Many studies emphasizing interfirm collaborative relationships have focused on the manufacturer-supplier relationship in the Japanese automobile industry. These studies have identified the effectiveness of interfirm collaborative relationships in automobile development (Clark 1989; Clark and Fujimoto 1991; Dyer 1996; Helper and Sako 1995; Nishiguchi 1994; Wasti and Liker 1999).

A close interfirm relationship helps an automobile parts supplier assimilate the customer automobile manufacturer's specific knowledge and customize the component design in accordance with the customer's requirements. The collaborative relationship enhances the design-in activities. The interfirm relationship in the Japanese automobile industry encourages the supplier firms to elaborate technologies and product designs, so that the product development performances of Japanese automobile manufacturers are enhanced (Clark and Fujimoto 1991). Also it is suggested that close communication helps firms assimilate intangible customer/partner firms' knowledge, such as "sticky information", which is regarded as the critical source of product innovations (von Hippel 1994; Ogawa 2000).

However, a strong interfirm relationship may hinder a firm from adapting to new environments beyond the incumbent relationship. An interfirm relationship is based on social contexts (Eisenhardt and Shonhoven 1996; Gulati 1995; Uzzi 1997). Reflecting the emphasis on the influences of social contexts, studies have examined the country-specificity of interfirm relationships (Chesbrough 1999a; Gulati 1995; Shan and Hamilton 1991; Helper and Sako 1995; Wasti and Liker 1999). If the technologies and capabilities of a firm are bound to a country-specific interfirm network, the firm would have difficulties in coping with overseas customers/partners because of its local relationships with specific customer/partner firms in its country.

A close interfirm relationship could impose relation-specific costs on a firm (Chesbrough 1999b; Eisenhardt and Schonhoven 1996). A firm is likely to develop technologies and product development capabilities in accordance with the requirements of existing major customer firms (Christensen 1997). Developing customized products/components for a customer/partner firm requires a firm to make customer/partner-specific investments in design/manufacturing knowledge. As a result, the technologies and product development capabilities could be bound to the customer/partner specific knowledge. Thus, the investments specific to an existing interfirm relationship may cause the firm to have difficulties in effectively exploiting the accumulated technologies and product development capabilities outside the incumbent relationship.

Outside the local relationship, a firm would need to make extra-investments to build new relationships with expected customer/partner firms. Otherwise, the firm may be resigned to relinquish the technologies and product development capabilities, which the firm has accumulated in the incumbent interfirm relationship. Thus, a Japanese firm that adheres to specific local customer/partner firms is likely to have difficulties in coping with expected customer/partner firms in oversea markets, where the firm can hardly expect benefits from the local interfirm relationship with specific Japanese customer/partner firms.

Distinction Between Interface Capabilities and Relational Knowledge

The role of shared knowledge between customer/partner firms is critical for successful product development (Clark and Fujimoto 1991; Dyer 1996; Dyer and Singh 1999; Ogawa 2000; von Hippel 1994). In order to enhance knowledge interaction with a customer/partner firm and thereby nurture shared knowledge, a firm is presumed to have absorptive capacity, which helps the firm assimilate the knowledge of the specific customer/partner firm (Dyer and Singh 1998).

In the argument, the absorptive capacity seems to be mingled with relation-specific knowledge for the customer/partner firm. If the absorptive capacity as well as the relation-specific knowledge is idiosyncratic to the interfirm relationships with a specific customer/partner, a firm could not employ the absorptive capacity for any other customers/partners. The emphasis on the interfirm relational specificity would obscure the specific capabilities of the firm.

The specific capabilities of a firm, which could complement partner firms' capabilities, could attract the partner firms. The firm-specificity of the capabilities encourages the partner firms to build close relationships with the firm (Eisenhardt and Shonhoven 1996). As the critical sources of the firm's attractiveness for the partner firms, the firm-specific capabilities should be explicitly distinguished from the relational knowledge between the firms.

Meanwhile, the determinants of interfirm relationships include external determinants, such as social contexts, technological interdependencies, and so on, as well as firm's internal resources (Eisenhardt and Shonhoven 1996). Interfirm relationships are particularly associated with architectural interdependencies between the components of a product system (Brusoni and Principe 2001; Chesbrough 1999b; Fujimoto 2004; Takeishi and Fujimoto 2001).

Scholars have focused on product architectures in order to consider related effective product development capabilities (Ulrich 1995). In the line of studies, firms are presumed to benefit either of two alternative types of interfirm relationships, "closed" or "open", according to the interdependencies between the sub-systems of the products concerned: integral/modular architecture.

Particularly a close interfirm relationship related to the interdependencies between sub-systems would encourage firms to develop relation-specific knowledge for a specific customer/partner firm. An automobile is a complex integral product, in which the components are mutually interdependent. The interdependencies between components require relation-specific knowledge exchanges between manufacturers and suppliers, and thus engender the close manufacturer-supplier relationship (Clark and Fujimoto 1991; Dyer and Singh 1998). The Japanese close interfirm relationship particularly in the automobile industry has drawn the attention for being adept at nurturing the relation-specific knowledge in the closed interfirm relationship.

However, the necessity of specific knowledge exchanges between firms does not necessarily result in "closed" interfirm relationships. As reported on several Japanese electronic firms (*e.g.*, Denso, ROHM, Keyence), firms may successfully customize the products to various customers'/partners' specific requirements (Fujimoto 2004)[1]. These cases of the Japanese electronic manufactures make us infer that a firm's interface (*i.e.*, interface architecture), which defines the specificity of customer/partner firms, should be distinguished from the knowledge specificity (Figure 1).

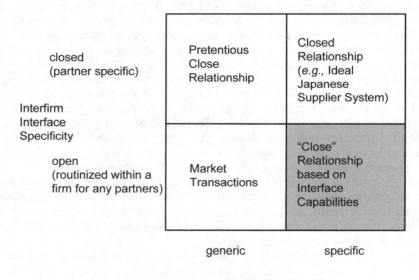

Fig. 1. Interfirm interface specificity and knowledge specificity

In many of past studies, which emphasize the criticality of close interfirm relationships, it is implicitly presumed that a firm could exchange or share specific knowledge with intimate customers/partners in closed interfirm relationships. Open interfirm relationships are assumed to be related to generic knowledge exchanges between firms. Nevertheless, even though the relationship is "open" to

---

[1]   Regardless of the internal design architecture of the product concerned, a firm can either choose closed or open interfirm relationships (Fujimoto 2004). Also see the cases of US manufacturers, such as Cisco, Intel, and Microsoft (Gawer and Cusumano 2003).

any customers/partners, a firm would assimilate the customer/partner-specific knowledge, and thereby could customize the products for the customers/partners.

If the interface activities which enhance specific knowledge exchanges with customer/partner firms are routinized within a firm, the interface activities would be applicable to any customer/partner firms. The interfirm interface of the firm could be open to any of customer/partner firms even though specific knowledge is exchanged with the firm and customer/partner firms. Thus, the open interfirm interface allows the firms to exchange both of "specific" and "generic" knowledge.

The routinized interface activities of a firm could be applied to any customer/partner firms. Focusing on the interface between firms, the study posits that a firm could have "interface capabilities", which are nurtured in the close interaction with incumbent customer/partner firms. As are specific to the firm, the interface capabilities are distinguished from the specific knowledge of customer/partner firms (Figure 2). Irrelevant to customer/partner firms, the interface capabilities could help a Japanese firm assimilate the specific knowledge of the requirements of customer/partner firms and reflect the knowledge on the products.

• Assimilated Relational Specificity

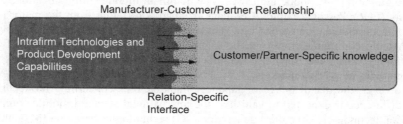

• Relational Specificity Mediated by Interface Capabilities

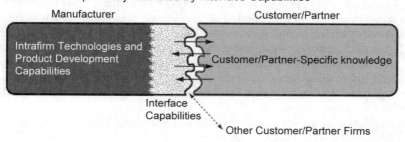

Fig. 2. Decomposability of interface capabilities and specific knowledge

Furthermore, the interface capabilities may help a firm insulate and secure the internal technologies and associated product development capabilities from the idiosyncratic knowledge of each of specific customer/partner firms. As is the case in the automobile industry, Japanese suppliers may be frequently required to customize the component designs for the customer manufacturers. However, even in the automobile industry, the interfirm relationship does not necessarily compel the suppliers to fully optimize the internal technologies and product development capabilities for the customer manufacturers (Takeishi 2002; Takeishi and Fujimoto 2001).

As is suggested in the cases of the above Japanese electronic firms, a firm can customize its products according to its customers/partners without optimizing the accumulated technologies and product development capabilities for each of customer/partner firms (Fujimoto 2004). If properly mediated by the interface capabilities, the technologies and product development capabilities, which have been accumulated in the close relationships with specific Japanese customer/partner firms, could be also available for prospective customer/partner firms in oversea markets.

Overview of Japanese Mobile Phone Manufacturers

Whereas commercializing the most advanced technologies in the world, Japanese mobile phone handset manufacturers' performances are not necessarily prominent in the global mobile phone industries. The dominant mobile communication technology (PDC: Personal Digital Cellular) in Japan is different from the major mobile telecommunication technology standards, particularly GSM (Global Service for Mobile communications), in the international market. Partly because of the technology difference, Japanese manufacturers could not sufficiently exploit the technologies in oversea markets.

However, the disadvantage of Japanese manufactures concerning the technology difference is expected to vanish as the international standard mobile communication technologies, the third generation (3G) technologies based on IMT-2000[2], CDMA (Code Division Multiple Access) technology (including cdma One, cdma One 1x and cdma One 1x EV-DO) and W-CDMA (Wideband Code Division Multiple Access), diffuse in the world. The 3D technologies enable much faster network speeds than the second generation technologies[3].

High-speed networks reduce the costs and time of downloading data, contents, and programs, and thus enrich mobile telecommunication services such as more advanced information services, faster entertainment content/program download, faster graphic and video data exchange, interactive video communication, smoother browsing, and so on.

The diffusion of the 3G mobile network and associated handsets depends on the collaboration between manufacturers and providers[4]. As the 3G services increase

---

[2]   IMT-2000 is the global mobile telecommunication technology guideline by the ITU (International Telecommunication Union).

[3]   For instance, NTT DoCoMo's PDC, the second generation technology, is capable of exchanging data at a speed of 29.8K bit per seconds. On the other hand, one of the 3G technologies, CDMA, is capable of exchanging data at 64K-2.4M bits per second. The W-CDMA standard's network speed is 384K bits per second.

[4]   "Tokusyu: Keitai-taikoku ga kawaru!!", *Syukan Daiyamond,* Jan, 24, 2004. Also see Funk (2004).

the interdependencies between handsets and mobile network services, the interdependencies between manufacturers and providers have also increased. Manufacturers would need to develop customized high-specification handsets, which are equipped with sufficiently high-speed processors and large memory and battery capacities, for specific providers since the advanced mobile services are not sufficiently materialized.

In one of the leading markets in the world[5], Japanese manufacturers have elaborated technologies/handsets in the close interfirm relationship with Japanese mobile service providers. The following case attempts to delineate how Japanese manufacturers could successfully cope with oversea customer providers exploiting the accumulated technologies and product development capabilities.

Relationship Between Mobile Phone Manufactures and Service Providers in Japan

In the Japanese market, most of handsets have been developed and manufactured for specific Japanese providers: NTT DoCoMo, KDDI (the brand name of the mobile business is "au"), Vodafone (former J-Phone), and Tu-Ka. The manufacturers are OEM (original equipment manufacturing) manufacturers for the providers. Japanese providers as the OEM customers of the manufacturers plan the handset lineup, and thus have strong influences on the production quantity and life cycle of each handset.

The providers require novel and/or distinguished handsets in order to enrich mobile telecommunication services and attract new subscribers. Japanese providers subsidize the handset sales so that the OEM manufacturers could be emancipated from the rigid constraint of the development and production costs. The sales subsidies enable manufacturers to develop and manufacture novel/distinguished handsets, which are specific to the providers.

In the Japanese market, a new handset model is usually manufactured no longer than 12 months. The handset models of a product line are renewed every 10 to 12 months. The manufacturers can neither pursue the scale-merit of handset production nor cover the development cost with the handset sales *per se* (Funk 2002). But, as at least the half of the shipment price of the handset is compensated with the sales subsidy from the customer provider, the manufacturers could continue to develop new handsets regardless of the development and production costs[6].

---

[5]   Most of the handsets are classified into the high-end or the middle-range product categories in the Japanese market while, as Strategy Analytics reports, about 70% of the handsets in the US market are low-end/entry products. Also see *Wireless Week*, Oct, 15, 2004. The average monthly payment of users to providers (APRU) in Japan, about $75, is the highest in the world compared to about $49 in the US. Press releases, JD Power (2003) and CTIA (2003).

[6]   *Syukan Daiyamond, op., cit.* Moreover, the providers provide manufacturers with technology development costs for novel handset development. As for FOMA (W-CDMA)

Meanwhile, the competition between more than 10 manufacturers is harsh in the Japanese market. As is the case of the suppliers in Japanese automobile industry (Nobeoka 1996), the manufacturers compete for the orders of the handsets from the providers[7], and thus need to impress the handset model development projects on the providers. As a result, Japanese manufacturers provide new handset models for the customer providers every 6 to 8 months in Japan – except other minor model changes. The manufacturers have pursued product novelty and distinguished features for each of customer providers, so that the manufacturers build close relationships with the customer providers.

Also there are relatively stable interfirm relationships in the US (*e.g.*, AT&T Wireless and Motorola). Mobile service providers in the US also provide sales subsidies[8]. There are several large vendors, AT&T Wireless & Cingular Wireless, Verizon Wireless, Sprint PCS and Nextel, Voice Stream (T-Mobile), and more small vendors. As the competition between the providers is harsh, the providers are also encouraged to provide new handsets with reasonable prices in order to attract subscribers.

However, the basic designs of handsets are usually not customized for each of the providers in the US. Major manufacturers in the US market have their own handset development policies, product lineups, and development cycles (Funk 2002). The local providers are not involved in the planning of handset models and platforms[9].

Different from the case in Japan, the interfirm relationship is not expected to include the collaborative product/technology planning between manufacturers and providers. The sales subsidy in the US is not intended to cover the development costs for customizing handsets/technologies for specific providers, but to make up for the handset manufacturing costs in order to simply lower the sales prices.

---

handset development, NTT DoCoMo had provided six manufacturers 650 million dollars for 4 years.

[7]   In the handset selection process of Japanese providers, manufacturers, as OEM manufacturers, usually need to compete against each other. NEC and Panasonic have competed for the top position of NTT DoCoMo handset vendors. Sharp, a new entrant has drastically increased the handset share for NTT DoCoMo in the early 2000s.

[8]   *Chicago Tribune*, Dec, 4, 2002. Providers have provided about $100 per handset on average. For instance, AT&T Wireless has subsidized more than $100 for each of the handsets of Motorola, which is one of the AT&T Wireless's largest handset vendors.

[9]   The platform of handsets is defined as a set of units of base band and RF (radio frequency) band, which consist of integrated circuits and discrete components mounted on printed on circuit boards (Funk, 2002). However, a basic platform is not necessarily defined by Japanese manufacturers, and it may vary according to who manufactures it. Several manufacturers also include digital signal processing chips /units in their platforms.

Handset Development Strategy of Japanese Manufacturers

Major European and US manufacturers build a platform for each of the product lines, which defines a standardized product design and core components common across handset models over several years (Funk 2002). Even though developing several handset models in a product line for the years, a platform/basic product design is shared among handset models within a product line.

Taking advantage of a standardized basic product design and a set of common parts, particularly a platform, enhances the cost reduction, and enables the manufacturers to provide the handset models for various providers within a mobile telecommunication technology in the world[10]. Based on the basic product design/platform, the manufacturers modify the exterior designs, specifications, and software for each of the customer providers. This strategy helps these manufacturers gain large market shares in the global market.

On the other hand, the functions and structures of the relationship between mobile service providers and manufacturers in Japan are similar to the manufacturer-supplier relationship in the Japanese automobile industry (Funk 2002). The product development strategy of Japanese handset manufacturers is largely influenced by the close manufacturer-provider relationship, which is characterized by the collaborative product and technology planning and OEM vender contract based on the subsidy system. In the close relationship with specific domestic providers, Japanese manufacturers have developed most of the handset models "customized" for each of the customer providers.

The harsh competition between manufacturers as well as the sales subsidy system has encouraged the manufactures to pursue product novelty and/or product integrity rather than development and manufacturing costs. As a result, the basic product design (architecture, circuit design, and mechanical design) and components are almost entirely furbished in a new handset model even if succeeding a preceding model of a product line.

In contrast to the case of international major manufacturers, Japanese manufacturers have not developed sufficient consideration of product lineup strategies and platform management (Funk 2002). However, in recent years, several Japanese firms also attempt to have the handsets in a product line mutually share common parts[11]. The handsets which are developed in a season mutually share 70-80 % of

---

10   In one year, Motorola develops more than 50 models, and Samsung develops more than 200-300 models. However, most of the models would not be platform models, but derivative models according to various providers and markets in the world.

11   Based on a questionnaire sheet on product development, the clinical data was collected from manufacturers in the US and Japan from 1999 to 2004. The responding manufacturers for the Japanese market include Kyocera (Oct 18, 2000; Dec 2, 2003), Mitsubishi Electronics (Oct 20, 2000), NEC (Jun 16, 2004), Panasonic (Aug 19, 1999; Nov 9, 2000; Oct 26, 2004), Sanyo (Dec 26, 2002; Jun 25, 2003), Sharp (Jul 7, 2004, e-mail response), Sony-Ericsson Mobile Communications (Oct 17, 2002), and Toshiba (May 19, 2004, e-mail response). For the US market, the responding manufacturers are Kyo-

common parts (cost-base) in several major manufacturers. The parts may include the base band unit, digital signal processor, and RF unit, which are regarded as platform units in the definition of international major manufacturers.

The manufacturers also take advantage of the technologies and software, which have been accumulated in past development projects. Nevertheless, the ratio of common parts between models over more than a year (*i.e.*, carried-over parts) is still small, at most 10-15 %. Accordingly, the basic product design, particularly circuit and mechanics, is designed afresh in most of the cases. Japanese firms have not developed sufficiently standardized basic product designs/platforms, which could be applicable to several models over several years.

The lack of standardized product designs/platforms over several years requires Japanese manufacturers to develop new product designs and parts, which are customized for each of the models. In other word, Japanese manufacturers are liable to develop "model-specific" design and components in each of handset development projects.

Japanese Mobile Phone Manufacturers in the US

The saturation of the Japanese market and the international standardization of mobile telecommunication technologies have encouraged Japanese manufacturers to advance to oversea markets since the end of the 1990s. Several Japanese manufacturers, including Panasonic and NEC, realize or aim at more handset sales in oversea markets than the sales in Japan.

Whereas frequently fluctuating, the market share of handset shipment demonstrates that top handset manufacturers in the US and the world have been Nokia, Samsung, Motorola, Siemens, LG, and Sony-Ericsson in recent years[12]. However, the total handset shipment volume includes the shipment volume of low-end handsets for matured mobile telecommunication technologies.

On the other hand, the 3G technologies, CDMA and W-CDMA[13], are expected to realize more innovative services based on the network speeds. As an international standard, one of the 3G technologies, CDMA has been already diffused to a certain extent in several areas including the US and Japan[14]. Thus, the article focuses on CDMA manufacturers.

---

cera (Sept 24, 2004, Kyocera Wireless, US), Panasonic (Aug 26, 2002, Panasonic America, US), Sanyo (Dec 26, 2002, Sanyo Telecommunications, Japan), and Sony-Ericsson (Dec 3, 2002, Sony-Ericsson Mobile Communications USA, US). Additional data was supplemented by e-mail correspondences.

[12] Press release, IDC (2004).

[13] Major Japanese manufacturers, such as Panasonic, NEC, Mitsubishi, and so on, adopt W-CDMA in close relation to NTT DoCoMo whose is one of its major developers.

[14] CDMA subscribers account for 46 % (70.5 M) of the total subscribers in the US (EMC World Cellular Data Base, Apr, 2004) and for 21 % (17.25 M) in Japan (TCA, Apr, 2004). In both of the markets, CDMA subscribers have grown by more than 15-20 % annually. Whereas GSM network subscribers represent more than 70 % of the world's

LG, Samsung, Motorola, Kyocera, and Sanyo are leading CDMA handset manufacturers in the US. In 2001, Motorola enjoyed the top-notch position, and other manufactures, Nokia, Audiovox, and so on followed. However, in recent years, Korean and Japanese manufacturers have dramatically gained the market shares by the high-specification handset models. The total market share of Korean and Japanese manufacturers amounted to 40% in 2004, and is expected to exceed 60% within several years[15].

Whereas the market shares of manufacturers could be largely influenced by the amount of investments in target markets, using customer satisfaction indexes would help us eliminate the effect of the investment scale, and thus approximate the product development capabilities of manufacturers[16]. A customer satisfaction index has ranked Sanyo, LG, and Samsung as top three manufacturers in recent years[17]. The ranking is explicated by the high-end features of the manufacturers' handsets. Kyocera is not ranked as the top manufactures, but is evaluated higher than several major manufacturers.

In the ranking, the manufacturers continuously excel major manufactures from 2001 to 2004 (*e.g.*, Nokia and Motorola). These manufacturers fall behind Korean and Japanese manufacturers in developing high-specification models in terms of the features: color display, digital camera, MPEG player, shell style design, and so on[18]. These features are closely related to advanced mobile telecommunication services such as contents download, graphical data transmission, and user-friendly graphical interfaces.

It is reported that Korean and Japanese manufactures flourish as the handsets are in accordance with the demand for high-specification models, particularly CDMA handsets, in the US[19]. The demand for high-specification handsets, which have been already diffused in the Japanese market[20], has grown even in the US market.

---

subscribers and still are growing in number, their ratio is 20% in the US (EMC World Cellular Data Base, Sept, 2004). Of the total subscribers in Japan, W-CDMA subscribers, though increasing, account for up to 5 %, and PDC subscribers still represent about 75 % (TCA, Apr, 2004).

[15] Press Release, Strategy Analytics (2004). Also see *Wireless Week, opus cited*

[16] The Customer satisfaction index also helps researchers elucidate the product development capabilities in the world automobile industries. See Clark and Fujimoto (1991).

[17] "U.S. Wireless Mobile Phone Evaluation Study", JD Power press releases from 2002 to 2004. The handset performance rank is evaluated by features, durability, physical design, battery function, and operation.

[18] *Wireless Week, opus cited*

[19] "Quest for handset dominance", *Wireless Week*, June 15, 2004. For instance, the APU of the handsets of Samsung, which has gained market share with high-specification handsets, is reported to amount to $190 while that of Motorola amounts to less than $150. Also see *Competitive Intelligence*, March 9, 2004.

[20] Soumu-syou (The Ministry of Internal Affairs and Communications, Japanese Government), 2004, *Jouhou Tushin Hakusyo (Information and Communications in Japan 2004)*.

Japanese manufacturers are experienced in developing high-specification handsets in accordance with advancing providers' mobile telecommunication services. Particularly after the introductions of cdma One by KDDI in 1998 and i-mode by NTT DoCoMo in 1999, Japanese manufacturers have preceded European and US manufacturers in the experiences of the handset development for the advanced mobile telecommunication services. In recent years, several Japanese manufacturers have showed that the manufacturers could also make use of the advanced technologies and handset development capabilities even in the international market.

Sanyo[21]

Sanyo would demonstrate a new handset development strategy of Japanese mobile handset manufacturers. Sanyo as well as Kyocera is not the vendors of NTT DoCoMo, which has been the largest provider in Japan and led Japanese advanced mobile technologies and services. As a CDMA handset vendor, Sanyo and Kyocera have attempted to build the position not only in the Japanese market but also in oversea markets, particularly in the US market.

In particular, Sanyo have enjoyed the high evaluation on the handsets and increased the handset sales in the US market. Thus, we here focus on Sanyo partly considering the case of Kyocera (Kyocera Wireless)[22].

Background in Japan

Sanyo Electronics is one of the largest consumer and industrial electronics manufacturers in Japan. In 2004, the annual sales of the group amount to more than 20 billion dollars in the world[23]. The handset business is under the control of the Personal Electronics Group, which also includes the digital camera business. Sanyo Wireless Telecommunications and Tottori Sanyo take charge of the handset business. Sanyo Wireless Telecommunications, once the personal communication

---

[21] The information on the strategy, handset development, and manufacturing as well as relationships with providers both in the US and Japan was provided by the senior director of planning and engineering and the Planning Section manager, Sanyo Telecommunications (Dec 26, 2002) and Plant General Manager, Sanyo Seimitsu (Jun 25, 2003). Additional data was supplemented by e-mail correspondences.

[22] The information on the strategy, handset development, and relationships with providers in Japan was provided by the Corporate Development Group Manager, Head Office (Oct 18, 2000) and the Marketing Department manager, Corporate Mobile Communication Equipment Division (Dec 2, 2003). The information on the US was provided by the product manager, Kyocera Wireless (Sept 24, 2004). Additional data was supplemented from both manufacturers by e-mail correspondences.

[23] See *Sanyo Electronics Co., Ltd. Corporate File* for the following general information on the firm

business division of Sanyo Electronics, was established as a group company of Sanyo Electronics in 2002.

Sanyo Wireless Telecommunications develop technologies and handsets for both Japanese and oversea markets[24]. Tottori Sanyo is a manufacturing company of Sanyo group, and develops and manufactures handsets mainly for the Japanese market. As for the handset business, Sanyo group also has the factories in Hiroshima and Osaka and a manufacturing company in Nagano in Japan. Hereafter, the article examines the case of Sanyo Telecommunications.

Sanyo's handset business as well as other major Japanese handset manufacturers, such as Mitsubishi, NEC, Panasonic, Sharp, and so on, not only procures most of the handset components from the outside of the group, but could also take advantage of the group companies' resources. For instance, Sanyo group has the battery and device business sectors.

Sanyo Electronics, the Power Group, is the leading battery firm for lithium-ion and lithium-polymer batteries, which are critical particularly for high-specification phones. The device business sectors are organized under the Device Group, which includes the Electronic Device (capacitor, SAW filter, micro speaker/receiver etc.) and Semiconductor (CCD camera module, LED driver, power control, MP3/WMA decoder, multi-media processor LSI etc.) companies and the Display Business Unit. Sanyo also set out other product areas related to handset products, such as audio and visual products and digital camera.

In Japan, most of NTT DoCoMo's vendors mainly committed to the PDC standard, which has been the dominant mobile communication technology in Japan, until the manufacturers started providing W-CDMA handsets for NTT DoCoMo in 2003. Different from these NTT DoCoMo's top vendors, Sanyo, as a non-NTT DoCoMo vendor, entered the mobile handset market late in the mid 1990s.

While mainly focusing on CDMA, Sanyo has provided the handsets for both of CDMA and PDC providers: KDDI, Vodafone, and Tu-Ka[25]. In the Japanese market (sales volume), Sanyo ranks 6th in market share (8.1%), and is the top manufacturer in the CDMA handset market (26% in Japan, 2004) and the top vendor of KDDI, which is the only CDMA provider and second largest provider in Japan[26]. Sanyo has increased its market share from 5% to more than 7% since 1999[27].

The sales shares of manufactures for each of the providers fluctuate as Japanese manufacturers compete for gaining larger amount of handset order from the providers. Sanyo has developed the handset business in a close relationship with KDDI. Whereas KDDI procures about 20% of the handsets from Sanyo, KDDI is also the top customer of Sanyo. Sanyo ships about 80% of the handsets to KDDI.

---

[24] The handsets for the Japanese market are manufactured at the group manufacturing companies.

[25] For the following data on Sanyo and KDDI, see Yano Research Institute (2004), *2004-2005 Mobile Communication Sou-Shijo*.

[26] Press release, MM Research Institute (2004). Toshiba and Sony-Ericsson are other CDMA handset manufactures in Japan.

[27] Press release, MM Research Institute (2004).

The relationship between KDDI and Sanyo would be close and mutual as is the case of the relationship between NTT DoCoMo and the vendors.

Competing with other KDDI vendors, Kyocera, Sony-Ericsson, and Toshiba, Sanyo has built the position of the leading manufactures for KDDI in the early 2000s[28]. In 2000, Sanyo introduced shell style browsing phones, which were equipped with 256 color display, in advance of other vendors of KDDI. In accordance with KDDI's handset lineup strategy, the high-specification handsets supported KDDI's mobile service progress. The high-specification handsets have helped Sanyo gain the market share.

In the US Market

The business of Sanyo in the US is under the control of Sanyo North America[29]. Under the management of Sanyo North America, Sanyo Fisher Company takes charge of the mobile phone handset business. However, Sanyo does not have the local group company to develop and manufacture the handsets for the US. The handsets for the US are developed in Japan and manufactured in China.

In 1998, Sanyo started to provide handsets for Sprint PCS. Sprint PCS is one of the largest US providers (4th position in 2004) and the second largest CDMA provider in the US. As several mobile communication technologies, including GSM and CDMA, have been used in the late 1990s in the world, Japanese manufacturers, such as Panasonic, NEC, and Mitsubishi, could not decide to commit to any of the global mobile communication technologies. Thus, many of major Japanese manufacturers have lost the opportunities to nurture close relationships with providers in oversea markets. On the contrary, from the beginning of the diffusion of the CDMA technology, Sanyo has focused on the standard and built the relationship with a CDMA provider in the US.

Sprint PCS also procures handsets from Samsung, Nokia, LG, Motorola, and Toshiba. Sanyo has provided its handsets only to Sprint PCS in the US. In recent years, Sanyo competed with Samsung for the position of the top vendor of Sprint PCS. As one of the top vendors of Sprint PCS, Sanyo achieved an annual sales growth of 40%.[30]

It should be noted that two major handset manufacturers, Samsung and LG, also focused on CDMA handsets, accelerated investments in the oversea business based on CDMA technology in the late 1990s, and became leading vendors of Sprint PCS and Verizon Wireless. Samsung and LG have also made large investments in GSM handset business. As a result, in contrast to many of Japanese handset manufacturers, the Korean manufacturers built the position in the global market.

---

[28] Yano Research Institute, *opus cit*ed

[29] See http://www.sanyo.com/home.cfm for the following general information on Sanyo's wireless business and history in the US.

[30] Strategy Analytics also reports that the growth of CDMA sales, 26%, has boosted the CDMA sales of LG (mostly for Verizon) to 63% in North America market in 2003.

Product Development Strategy in the US

At the product engineering stage, both of the CDMA handsets for the US and Japan are developed in a product development group of Sanyo Wireless in Japan. Sanyo's handsets for the US market are roughly divided into two types: the handsets designed specifically for the US market and the applied handsets of the Japanese models to the US market. Kyocera also employ both of the types.

In the project for the former type model, both of the hardware and software are designed for a specific model for Sprint PCS. Nevertheless, the components (including base band chip, digital signal processor, and RF unit) and the software platform/common software (including BREW/JAVA application platform and wireless interface software) are often shared among the Japanese and US models.

The project for the latter type model reuses the basic hardware design, components, and related software of the past handset model for the Japanese market. Considering the specifications to the US customer provider and subscribers, the project modifies the portions of the preceding model: exterior design, devices (*e.g.,* display unit), and provider/model specific software and data (*e.g.,* related to handset system control, device applications and controls, user interfaces, wireless interface data).

As the projects for the Japanese market is more advanced and complex than for the US market, both the project types for the US market attempt to exploit the technologies and product development capabilities based on the projects for the Japanese market. The basic product development process of the handsets for the Japanese market is almost same as the process for the US market. The lead-time of the product development process in the projects for the US market, 10-12 months, is as long as the lead-time for the Japanese market[31].

However, the model change cycle in a product line, 8-12 months, in Japan is faster than in the US. Moreover, the handsets and services are more advanced in Japan than in the US. The advanced handsets in Japan need to be equipped with advanced displays (65536 colors, TFT, after 2002), processors (133 MHz in 2003), memory (1 MB in 2003), and batteries, according to the complex product function (more than 1 million step software in 2003) for the high-end handset features and services[32].

In addition to the hardware, control software and drivers for user/wireless interface devices (*e.g.,* control unit, display, keypad, power management chip) and related applications are required to be optimized for each of models. Thus, Sanyo as well as other Japanese manufacturers almost entirely furbish both of the hardware and software (except common applications, device driver programs and software platform) in the projects for the Japanese market. The projects for Japanese market need to integrate the renewed design, components, and software.

---

[31] Based on data collected from manufacturers in the US and Japan from 1999 to 2004.

[32] See Funk (2004). The processor speed would be 500 MHz in 2005. The memory size would be 5 MB, which may allow 100 BREW/JAVA programs, in 2005. Also, support for external memory, such as SD memory cards, was added in recent years.

As a result, the handset and development activities for the Japanese market are far more complex than for the US market. The required resource for a typical handset development project for the Japanese market, several hundred thousand engineering-hours, is sometimes ten times as large as the typical project for the US market. Compared to the process for the US market, the handset development process for the Japanese market is characterized with overlapping between stages, particularly between design, prototyping, test, software stabilization, and manufacturing, due to trial and error iterations.

The ratio of software engineering for advanced handset features have increased, particularly in Japan, as the mobile services and consumer needs are elaborated. As for the project for the Japanese market, more than 70% of human resources are assigned to software engineering[33]. The ratio of software engineering is estimated at least as large as the ratio of hardware engineering (more than 50%) even in the projects for the US market.

Sanyo uses common software platforms and programs for both the US and Japanese markets. Basic software related to wireless interfaces (*e.g.,* base band and radio frequency) and OS are common across providers within a technology standard. Application platform and software (*e.g.,* BREW/JAVA) could be also usable across providers.

Based on the platform and common programs, Sanyo develops/modifies the software and related data in accordance with the services and specification requirements of the customer provider. These software and data are related to the provider-specific applications, user interfaces, and detail wireless interface specifications. Also, model-specific software such as system control software and device-related applications/drivers (*e.g.,* digital camera, display, and keyboard) can be developed/modified.

On the other hand, as for the hardware, Sanyo has developed product-specific designs and components without definite hardware basic designs, platforms, and other common parts of the handsets for both the Japanese and US market. Sanyo sometimes furbishes the basic designs and components of the handsets even for the US market. Nevertheless, the handset models for the US market owe the designs and technologies to the handsets for the Japanese market.

In most of cases, the basic design of a product line, such as architecture and circuit design, is inherited from a former model to a new model both in the US and in Japan. Even the base band chip, RF unit, and related digital signal processor, which are defined as platform in European and US major manufacturers, are liable to be common between the former and new models. These designs and components are not only shared among the models for the Japanese markets but also carried over from the preceding handset models for the Japanese market to the following models for the US market. The accumulated technologies, sometimes specific designs and components, as well as software platforms and common programs are carried over from advanced Japanese models to following US models.

---

[33]   Based on data collected from manufacturers in the US and Japan from 1999 to 2004.

Managing Close Relationships in the US and Japan

The product development strategy of Sanyo is different from both the international major manufacturers' and other Japanese manufactures' strategies. Sanyo basically develops model-specific designs, components, and software customized for each of the US and Japanese providers. As other Japanese manufacturers, Sanyo does not define specific hardware platforms. Nevertheless, Sanyo successfully exploits the technologies and product development capabilities for the handsets for a US provider outside the Japanese local manufacturer-provider relationship.

a) Customization (e.g., Sanyo)

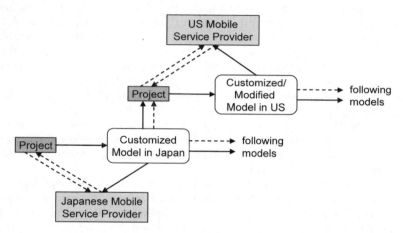

b) Modification (e.g., Major International Manufacturers)

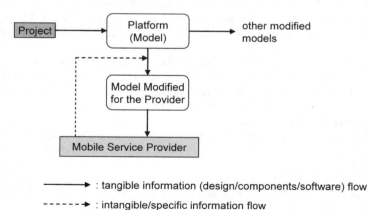

⟶ : tangible information (design/components/software) flow

- - - ▸ : intangible/specific information flow

Fig. 3. Difference in customer-interface process

The product development strategy largely rests on how Sanyo can manage the relationships with the customer providers. As is the case of the relationship between Sanyo and KDDI in Japan, Sanyo has built a close relationship with Sprint PCS in the US. In the relationship with the US provider, Sanyo enrolls the provider in the handset planning process as Japanese manufacturers including Sanyo do in Japan (Figure 3).

In contrast to the case of major European and US manufacturers, Sanyo exchanges specific knowledge with the customer providers from the product planning stage. In the stage, the provider's requirements are assimilated and reflected on the handset features, specifications, and even designs/components.

In Japanese firms including Sanyo, the planning process takes on average 2 to 3 months of the total handset development lead-time (about 10 months) whiles the product design starts 1 month before the formal approval of a handset development project. The planning lead-time is as long as the average planning lead-time in Japan, but is shorter than the average planning lead-time, 4 to 5 months, of the projects for the US market. During the planning process, the product planners communicate with the customer provider once in a week on average.

In the process, the product planning group and product design group collaborate to develop the basic product concept and features, product design, exterior design, and specification. Sanyo as well as Japanese manufacturers offers the plan to the customer provider. Based on the handset lineup plan, the provider exchanges the information on the requirements for the handset with Sanyo, and reviews the proposed handset development plan.

The exchanged information does not only include materialized requirements but also intangible request information. The information could include the information of basic design, battery, digital camera, display, memory, processor, and other detail functional specifications, related devices/software, and basic wireless technology specifications, which are closely related to provider-specific services and user interfaces. Particularly at the early stage of the planning, the customer provider also provides the intangible request information on the exterior design, handset features, and user interface (*e.g.,* application features, body color, and so on).

Reflecting the provider's review, the product planning group decides the detail specification, cost, and schedule, and offer the revised product plan and exterior design to providers. When the providers accept the proposal, the handset development project is formally approved. The information exchange-proposal-review cycle may be repeated several times.

In the collaborative process with the providers, Sanyo attempts to assimilate the specific requirements from the customer providers, propose the handset model plan, and reflect the requirements on the handsets both in the projects for both the US and Japan. Sanyo applies the same product planning process to the handset development project for the US market though the product planning section for the US market is separated from the section for the Japanese market.

It should be noted that Sanyo does not simply reflect the customer provider's materialized requirements on the handsets. Assimilating the requests from the provider, Sanyo is active in proposing high-specification handsets for Sprint PCS based on the advanced technologies accumulated in the Japanese market. Sanyo has a similarly close relationship with providers in both the US and Japan, which enhance customized handset designs and specifications according to specific requirements from the providers.

The handset development strategy would not rely on any specific providers, but would be facilitated by the routinized interface activities to collaborate with providers. In the close relationship with the customer providers in the Japanese market, Sanyo as well as other Japanese manufacturers has experienced in assimilating provider-specific requirements, proposing distinguished/novel handsets in accordance with the requirements, and developing the requirements into the handset specifications, designs, and software.

We could suggest that Sanyo takes advantage of the experiences in the Japanese market for a US provider. Beyond the specific manufacturer-provider relationship in Japan, Sanyo have exploited the interface activities reflecting the specific knowledge from the offshore provider on the handset models.

Discussion

In contrast to major international manufacturers, Sanyo as well as other Japanese manufacturers have developed customized handsets for specific customer providers without well-defined hardware designs and platforms. The technologies and product development capabilities have been nurtured in the local provider-manufacturer relationship in Japan.

As described in the cases of the automobile and computer/electronic device industries (*e.g.*, Chesbrough 1999a; Nishiguchi 1994), the technologies and product development capabilities of the firms in a local interfirm relationship may be idiosyncratic. Nevertheless, Sanyo has successfully made use of accumulated technologies and product development capabilities even for the handset development projects for the US market.

The case of Sanyo witnesses that the interface capabilities should be distinguished from customer/partner specific knowledge even though nurtured in the close relationship with specific local providers in Japan. The interface capabilities would not rely on specific customer/partner firms, but would be routinized as the firm-specific capabilities of a manufacture so that the manufacturer could cope with prospective customers/partners.

Due to the interdependencies between handsets and mobile telecommunication systems, high-specification handset development depends upon the collaboration between manufacturers and providers. The case would demonstrate that, in spite of the increasing necessity of closer collaborative manufacturer-provider relationship, the internal technologies and capabilities of a firm could be distinguished from the knowledge on specific customer/partner firms. With the interface capabilities, a firm could cope with customer/partner firms' requirements without adapting internal technologies and capabilities to each of the customer/partner firms.

The case suggests that the interface capabilities could help Japanese firms assimilate tangible/intangible specific requirements even from offshore customer/partner firms. Japanese firms could propose and develop advanced handsets in accordance with even the offshore customer providers' expectations. The interface capabilities would enable a firm to take advantage of the accumulated technologies and product development capabilities in accordance with the requirements from customer/partner firms in oversea markets.

It is emphasized that a firm needs to standardize technologies and product/component designs, particularly platforms, within the firm to accelerate the effective product development processes (Baldwin and Clark 1997). Furthermore, a firm could lead interfirm networks as well as customer/partner firms based on the standardized technologies and product/component designs (Brusoni and Prencipe 2001; Gawer and Cusumano 2002; Sturgeon 2002).

However, a firm may also need to cope with each of customer/partner firms. The knowledge of a specific customer/partner firm is a critical factor for product success (Ogawa 2000; von Hippel 1994). The criticality of customer/partner-specific knowledge does not impel a firm to fully integrate the internal technologies and capabilities according to the customer/partner firm's requirements. The case here demonstrates that interface capabilities could mediate the relevance between the internal technologies and product development capabilities of a firm and customer/partner-specific knowledge.

It is expected that Japanese manufacturers could successfully enter oversea markets with Japanese providers, particularly NTT DoCoMo and Vodafone. However, as the case showed, Japanese manufacturers may pursue an alternative strategy. The case reveals that Japanese firms may take advantage of their accumulated technologies and product development capabilities even in international interfirm relationships when exploiting the interface capabilities. The alternative strategy based on the interface capabilities may allow Japanese manufacturers to cope with various customers/partners in the global market.

Conclusion

Drawing on the case of Japanese mobile phone manufacturers in the US, this study explores how a Japanese firm in the close local relationship successfully copes with prospective customers/partners in an oversea market. The case demonstrated that firms in a close local interfirm network may make use of the interface capabilities, which have been nurtured in the interfirm relationships with specific customers/partners.

The interface capabilities of a firm allow the firm to exploit the technologies and product development capabilities encouraging the firm to assimilate customer/partner firms' expected requirements into products. Thus, the interface capabilities are expected to play a critical role in building close, not necessarily closed, relationships with customers/partners even in oversea markets.

The interface capabilities enable manufactures to create opportunities for cooperation with new customer/partner firms, and thus to choose product development strategies other than the traditional strategy based on the close provider-manufacture relationship. The Japanese interfirm relationship may require customized and model-specific product/component designs, which enhance product integrity for specific customer/ partner firms. Thus, firms are liable to pursue distinguished/novel product in each of product development projects (Clark and Fujimoto 1991; Yasumoto and Fujimoto 2005).

In contrast to this, the interface capabilities may help a firm devise a coherent product strategy, such as a platform/multi-project strategy, beyond single product development projects. Without the product strategy, a firm may face problems of over-specifications and high costs (Cusumano and Nobeoka 1998). In related interfirm networks, the firm also may have difficulties to build a position if the firm could not successfully exploit the core technologies and capabilities based on the product strategy (Brusoni and Prencipe 2001; Gawer and Cusumano 2002). We need to not only further examine the process of interface capabilities but also explore how interface capabilities could be employed in relation to platform/multi-project strategies and contribute to elaborate these strategies.

We are also required to understand the impacts of the technological bases of the interface capabilities. An interfirm relationship would heavily rely on technological interfaces, such as network protocols and technology standards, which define interdependencies between the sub-systems of a product/service system (Brusoni and Prencipe 2001; Sturgeon 2002). Thus, the relevance of an interfirm relationship and its dependence on technological attributes of the interface should be explored hereafter.

Acknowledgement

The research was supported by the "Grant-in-Aide for Young Scientists (B) for Scientific Research (No. 14710127)" from 2002 to 2005, the Ministry of Education, Culture, Sports, Science and Technology, Japanese Government. I wish to thank my gratitude to the directors, project managers, and staffs for the assistances to my research.

References

Asanuma B (1989): 'Manufacturer-supplier relationships in Japan and the concept of relation-specific skill', *Journal of the Japanese International Economies*, Vol.31, No.2, 19-30

Baldwin CY and Clark KB (1997): 'Managing in an age of modularity', *Harvard Business Review*, Sept-Oct, 84-93

Brusoni A and Prencipe A (2001): 'Managing knowledge in loosely coupled networks: exploring the links between product and knowledge dynamics', *Journal of Management Studies*, Vol.38, No. 7, 1019-1035

Chesbrough HW (1999a)::The organizational impact of technological change: a comparative theory of national institutional factors', *Industrial and Corporate Change*, Vo. 8, No. 3, 447-485

Chesbrough HW (1999b): 'Toward a more contingent view of 'Japanese' supplier relations: an empirical study of disk drive sourcing decision in Japanese notebook computers', *Working Papers—Harvard Business School Division of Research*, 1-48

Christensen C (1997): *The Innovator's Dilemma: When New Technology Cause Great Firms to Fail* , Harvard University Press, Cambridge, MA

Cusumano MA and Nobeoka K (1998): *Thinking Beyond Lean: How Multi-Project Management Is Transforming Product Development at Toyota and Other Companies*, The Free Press, New York, NY

Clark KB and Fujimoto T (1991): *Product Development Performance: Strategy, Organization, and Management in the World Automobile Industry*, Harvard Business School Press, Boston. MA

Dyer JH (1996): 'Specialized supplier networks as a source of competitive advantage: evidence from the auto industry', *Strategic Management Journal*, Vol. 17, Issue 4, 271-291

Dyer JH and Singh H (1998): 'The relational view: cooperative strategy and sources of interorganizational competitive advantage', *Academy of Management Review*, Vol. 23, No. 4, 660-679

Eisenhardt KM and Schonhoven CB (1996): 'Resource-based view of strategic alliance formation: strategic and social effects in entrepreneurial firms', *Organization Science*, Vol. 7, No. 2, 136-150

Funk JL (2002): *Global Competition between and within Standards: the Case of Mobile Phones*, Palgrave, New York

Funk JL (2004): *Mobile Disruption: the Technologies and Applications Driving the Mobile Internet*, Wiley & Sons, Hoboken, NJ

Fujimoto T (2004): *Nihon no Mono-Zukuri Tetsugaku*, Yuhikaku, Tokyo

Gawer A and Cusumano MA (2002): *Platform Leadership: How Intel, Microsoft, and Cisco Drive Industry Innovation*, Harvard Business School Press, Boston

Gulati R (1995): 'Social structure and alliance formation pattern: a longitudinal analysis', *Administrative Science Quarterly*, Vol. 40, 619-652

Helper SR and Sako M (1995): 'Supplier relationship in Japan and the United States: Are they converging?', *Sloan Management Review*, spring, 77-84

Nishiguchi T (1994): *Strategic Industrial Sourcing*, Oxford University Press, New York, NY

Nobeoka K (1996): 'Alternative component sourcing strategies within the manufacturer-supplier network: benefits of quasi-market strategy in the Japanese automobile industry', *Kobe Economic and Business Review*, Vol. 10, Issue 41, 69-99

Ogawa S (2000): *Innovation no Hassei-Ronri*, Tikura-Syobou, Tokyo

Shan W and Hamilton W (1991): 'Country-specific advantage and international cooperation', *Strategic Management Journal*, Vol. 12, Issue 6, 419-433

Sturgeon TJ (2002): 'Modular production networks: a new American model of industrial organization', *Industrial & Corporate Change*, Vol. 11, Issue 3, 451-496

Takeishi A (2002): *Bungyo to Kyouso*, Yuhikaku, Tokyo

Takeishi A and Fujimoto T (2001): 'Modularization in the auto industry: interlinked multiple hierarchies of product, production, and supplier systems', *Discussion Paper F-Series*, Center for International Research on the Japanese Economy, Faculty of Economics, The University of Tokyo

Ulrich K (1995): 'The role of product architecture in the manufacturing firm', *Research Policy*, Vol. 24, 419-440

von Hippel E (1994): '"Sticky information" and the locus of problem solving: Implications for innovation', *Management Science*, Vol. 40, No. 4, 429-439

Wasti SN and Liker JK (1999): 'Collaborating with suppliers in product development: A U.S. and Japan comparative study', *IEEE Transactions on Engineering Management*, Vol. 46, Issue 4, 444-461

Yasumoto M and Fujimoto T (2005): 'Does cross-functional integration lead to adaptive capabilities? Lessons from 188 Japanese product development projects', *International Journal of Technology Management*, Vol.30, Nos.3/4, 265-298

"Fuzzy Front End" Practices in Innovating Japanese Companies

Cornelius Herstatt, Birgit Verworn, Christoph Stockstrom, Akio Nagahira, and Osamu Takahashi

Introduction

In a comparison of 14 German and 14 Japanese NPD projects, Herstatt et al. (2004: 20) report on front-end related activities in these countries. They found Japanese companies to rely on a comparatively formal approach with strong methodological support to reduce uncertainty. With this paper we try to extend and test their propositions in order to develop a deeper understanding of Japanese front end activities in the context of a large scale study. We will report on findings about typical activities such as idea generation and assessment, and the reduction of market and technological uncertainty. In addition, we will show differences in the practices between successful and unsuccessful companies with regard to the execution of several front end activities.

For this purpose, the paper is organized as follows: Part 2 provides an overview of our study describing our sample and addressing methodological issues. We present our findings concerning typical front-end-related activities in part 3. Next, we report on the differences between successful and unsuccessful companies. This paper ends with a discussion of our results and suggestions for further research.

Study

Aim of the Study

Empirical work by Cooper and Kleinschmidt showed that "the greatest differences between winners and losers were found in the quality of execution of pre-development activities" (Cooper and Kleinschmidt 1994, p. 26). Two factors were identified as playing a major role in product success: the quality of executing the pre-development activities, and a well defined product and project prior to the development phase (Cooper and Kleinschmidt 1990, p. 27).

A study of 788 new product launches in Japan confirmed that Japanese new product professionals view the importance of pre-development proficiency in much the same way as their American and European counterparts (Song and Parry 1996, pp. 422, 433).

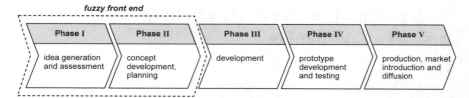

Fig. 1. The new product development process

Beside this acknowledged relevance of the fuzzy front end, most of existing studies do not look in any greater detail into the various distinct activities within the frame of the fuzzy front end and present them collectively under the heading "pre-development activities". This study tries to develop a deeper understanding of fuzzy front end practices in Japanese companies as well as innovation projects. Which methods, tools, and approaches are used? Which techniques support the important task to reduce project uncertainties, e. g. related to market or technology? How do successful companies approach the fuzzy front end of innovation compared to less successful or unsuccessful companies? These are the questions we will take a closer look at.

Methodology

We reviewed literature about front-end activities (e.g., Khurana and Rosenthal 1998; Koen, Ajamian and Burkart 2001; Kim and Wilemon 2002; Rubinstein 1994; Verganti 1997; Zhang and Doll 2001) and developed a standardized questionnaire to assess front end related activities in Japanese companies. Figure 1 shows our frame of the fuzzy front end phase within a model of the new product development process.

In Japan, the interpretation of the questions was verified during exploratory interviews and a mailed pre-test. For the large-scale study, we identified a total of 2000 mechanical and electrical engineering companies. MOST (Management of Science and Technology Department) at the Tohoku University in Sendai send the questionnaire to the R&D directors of these companies. 553 companies finally answered the questionnaires (response rate = 28%).

Sample

The Sample contains companies ranging in size from below 50 employees to large corporations, one of which has more than 100,000 employees. The structure of our sample is further reflected in annual sales which vary between 5 million and 31.1 trillion Yen. Therefore the majority of the sample consists of medium to large companies employing with 100 to 10,000 employees and annual sales between 1 billion and 1 trillion Yen.

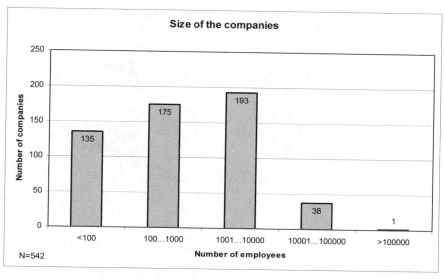

Fig. 2. Size of the companies

Company Success

Company success was measured by two items: The achievement of corporate profitability and growth goals during the last five years. In doing so, we follow the notion of evaluating success by comparing the actual outcome of the companies' activities with the organizations' planned objectives (Zhang and Doll 2001, p. 102). While this approach may be criticized for not generating standardized measures of success and failure across firms, this rather reflects an artifact of real-world differences between firms, industries, economic conditions, accounting rules, temporal situations, and decision criteria rather than a criticism of these scales (Song and Parry 1997, p. 7).

Reflecting Japan's difficult economic state (Yoshida 2002, p. 2), it was not surprising that 47% of the companies stated that they did not meet expected profitability goals during the last five years. In addition, 50% of the companies stated that corporate growth remained below expectations during the same time.

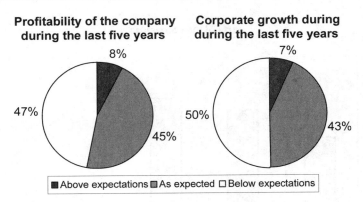

Fig. 3. Corporate success

In order to be categorized as successful, companies had to meet or exceed their corporate goals on both of the aforementioned items, while companies which did not meet either goal were considered to be unsuccessful for the purpose of our analysis. Companies which achieved one of these goals but failed concerning the other were not included into the analysis in part 5. Overall, 238 companies were labeled successful, while 225 companies were unsuccessful.

Results

This section summarizes our key findings about fuzzy front end practices in the Japanese companies. Firstly, we will describe how ideas were typically generated, assessed, and selected. Secondly, we will summarize how market and technological uncertainty were reduced prior to project execution. Finally, we will describe typical project planning activities as a further opportunity to reduce project related uncertainties and as a basis of controlling during the following steps of the product development process.

Idea Generation

27% of the companies engage in a systematic search for new product ideas. When this is the case, ideas are primarily sought internally. Only a small minority of companies additionally looks for ideas outside of the firm. None of the respondents searched for new product ideas exclusively outside of his company. Clear responsibilities are standard: almost every firm assigns the search for new product ideas to an individual or a group. However, only about a third of the respondents use databases to store and process new product ideas.

Our present study corresponds with former findings about the frequent use of brainstorming in Japan (Harryson 1996, p. 26): Close to 60% of the companies regularly apply brainstorming to develop new products. Only the use of kaizen, which is also employed by 60% of the companies, is equally widespread. While value analysis is still applied by 44% of the participants, only 11% of the companies report the use of other creativity techniques, which therefore seem to play a minor role. While answers showed a wide variety of different practices, a frequently mentioned instrument is an employee proposal system usually connected to a reward scheme.

Idea Assessment

54% of the companies have their ideas assessed by individuals as well as by groups. The minority of the companies employs only one of these two possibilities: 26% only let groups assess their ideas, while 20% rely on assessments by individuals.

In 99% of the companies, upper management is at least sometimes involved in the idea assessment, for 78% of the companies, this is a typical procedure.

Following the aforementioned notion of reducing as much uncertainty as possible by employing interdisciplinary teams for idea assessment, 46% of the companies frequently use multifunctional groups. Another 34% at least sometimes do so. However, 20% of the companies do not consider this to be necessary. Out of the 440 companies which at least sometimes use interdisciplinary teams to assess new product ideas more than 60% involve the R&D department in this process. The marketing department is employed by more than half of the companies. 20% have the after sales or customer service department participate in the assessment, while 12% include other functions.

28% of the participants stated that they generally use technical criteria to assess new product ideas. Another 32% sometimes include technical criteria in their consideration. The remaining 40% do not bear these in mind during their evaluation process. Regarding the nature of these technical criteria, the 329 firms which at least sometimes employ them mainly consider technical feasibility (78%). The availability of the required technology inside the firm is a criterion used by 48% of these 329 respondents.

45% of all companies frequently assign weights to economic and technical criteria in accordance with their importance. Another 29% sometimes resort to scoring the various criteria.

Reduction of Market Uncertainty Prior to Development

We found that 53% of the participating firms contact their customers very often. Another 41% at least sometimes contact their users to develop or evaluate new product ideas. Despite the important role of customers in the new product development process, especially with regard to the reduction of market uncertainty, 6% of the companies only very seldom contact their customers for this purpose.

When customers are contacted, this is most often done by the marketing department (48%) and/or the R&D department (47%). Other functions such as application engineering (14%) and after sales/customer service (13%) play a minor role.

Customers can be selected according to different criteria and motivations. Depending on which criteria the selection process is based on, the integration of users may be more or less beneficial. Figure 4 summarizes our results:

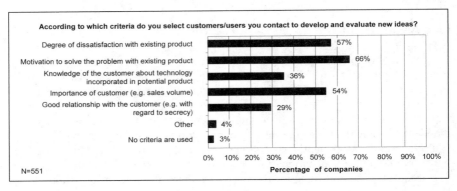

Fig. 4. Criteria for customer selection

The factors representing drivers for participation in the NPD process on behalf of the customer seem to be most important: The motivation of the customer to solve his problem he has with the existing technology is the most important criterion and is applied by 66% of the companies. In addition, the degree of dissatisfaction with the existing product plays an important role, as this criterion is used by 56% of the respondents. In contrast to this, the following criteria rather consider benefits on behalf of the companies: For 54% of the firms, the importance – in terms of e.g. sales volume – of the customer is a criterion for asking him to participate in the NPD process. 36% hope to benefit from the customer's knowledge about the technology incorporated in the new product and select them accordingly. A good relationship with the customer is a selection criterion for 29% of the respondents. Among the diverse other criteria for selecting users to develop and evaluate new product ideas, two themes stick out: Some companies randomly select their users to participate – thereby employing no criteria. Besides, some companies ask users of a current product to participate – regardless of whether they are their own or customers of a competitor. In only one case the company specifically searched for competitors' customers to advice them in the development and evaluation of new product ideas.

Direct customer contact represents the most often used market-related source of information. For other means to acquire knowledge about the target market see Figure 5. As has been described by Harryson (1996, p. 61), Japanese companies put a strong emphasis on analyzing competitive products. We find support for these findings, as 78% of the companies acquire information this way. Customer complaints also play an important role. They are analyzed by 72% of the firms. In contrast to this, only half of the respondents conduct customer surveys and 46% rely on studies and market research carried out by third parties. Other market-related sources of information only play a minor role.

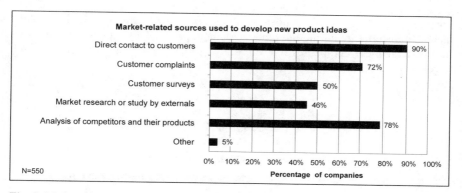

Fig. 5. Market-related sources used to develop new product ideas

Considering the importance of the customer as a source of information, it is surprising to see that only 27% of the companies very often systematically integrate customer requirements into the definition of their new product concepts. This may be due to the fact that it is sometimes hard for users to specifically articulate their needs and functional fixedness may hinder them to imagine the requirements they want future products to meet (Herstatt 2002, p. 71; Mullins and Sutherland 1998, p. 228). Consequently, 53% of the firms just sometimes integrate customer requirements and 20% even only very seldom.

Systematically translating the customer requirements into technical specifications allows the companies to incorporate the information into their product concepts. This step is at least sometimes carried out by 85% of the firms. While 15% refrain from any translation of customer requirements into technical specifications, 39% systematically do so. A well-known tool for this translation is QFD (Quality Function Deployment). For an overview of this technique see Griffin and Hauser (1993).

Reduction of Technical Uncertainty Prior to Development

There is a variety of different tools and methods which allow for the reduction of technical uncertainty during the pre-development phase. One way to reduce technical uncertainty is to evaluate technical feasibility with early prototypes. This could be either based on virtual prototypes, rapid prototypes or early, rough physical prototypes. In addition to showing technical feasibility, such early prototypes can be used for improving the communication within the development team, with customers or with top management. It enables an early assessment of customers' needs and enhances top management support e.g. for the commitment of resources (Clayton et al. 1996, p. 449; Watts et al. 1998, p. 48).

In our study, almost 90% of the companies make use of early physical proto-types, 15% apply rapid prototyping and 11% use virtual prototyping (see Figure 6). Almost half of the companies use simulation to reduce technical uncertainty. Overall, only 5% of the respondents do not apply any methods or tool to reduce technical uncertainty during the predevelopment phase. This supports the proposition that Japanese companies rely on a strong methodological support to reduce uncertainty (Herstatt et al. 2004).

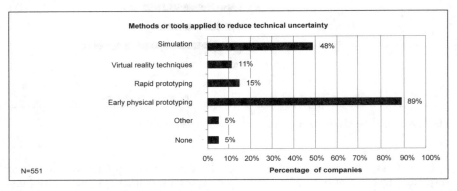

Fig. 6. Methods or tools applied to reduce technical uncertainty

Front End Project Planning

For 40% of the respondents, a systematic initial planning is a standard procedure. 49% at least sometimes plan their projects systematically. 11% do not engage in systematic initial planning at all. In the next section, we evaluate the effect of systematic initial planning on success. In this section, we look at the different planning activities and support of these activities by methods and tools in more detail.

In our study, almost half of the companies define milestones with deliverables (see Figure 7). Terms like work packages are not widespread in Japan. Instead, projects are broken down into "teams". Cost plans are assigned to these teams. This is the case in 64% of the companies we looked at. In addition, more than half of the companies determine the required staff for the project already during the initial planning. With regard to tools, bar charts, network diagrams and project management software are not often used (18%, 3%, and 14% of the companies). This is in line with former results (Herstatt et al. 2004).

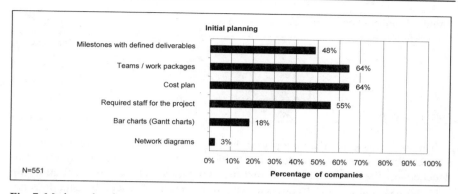

Fig. 7. Market-related sources used to develop new product ideas

In sum, the descriptive results about fuzzy front end practices in the Japanese companies we looked at confirm a rather systematic approach to the front end with strong methodological support. In the next section, we will look at the effect that different front end practices have on companies´ success.

Comparing Successful and Unsuccessful Companies

In this section, we compare successful and unsuccessful companies with regard to different front-end-related activities that we argue to be influential on NPD success. We do so with the help of contingency tables which classify the companies by the achievement of their corporate growth and profitability goals on the one hand and by the execution of the respective activity on the other.

The product development process starts with an idea originating from basic research, customer based techniques, or creativity techniques (Cooper and Kleinschmidt 1990, p. 45). Not only may ideas stem from a variety of sources, also their generation often is a complex and creative task associated with considerable uncertainty. While researchers argue about whether to have individuals generate ideas (Rochford 1991, p. 289) or to leave this task to – preferably multidisciplinary – teams (Baker et al. 1985, p. 40; Geschka 1992, p. 284, 294–296; Rubinstein 1994, p. 656; Rochford 1991, p. 289; Song and Parry 1997, p. 9), a systematic approach to this endeavor is likely to contribute to the reduction of uncertainty and thereby positively influences success. Hence, we conjecture that

P1: Companies engaging in a systematic search for new product ideas are more successful than companies which do not search systematically for new product ideas.

Table 1. Number of companies by success and search strategy

Systematic search	Success		Total frequency
	Yes	no	
yes	73	61	134
no	165	164	329
Total frequency	238	225	463

Table 1 reveals that the majority of the respondents do not engage in a systematic search for new product ideas. In addition, performing a chi-square test of independence, the results also show that the hypothesis that there is no relationship between row and column frequencies cannot be refuted. Hence, the data does not support our proposition.

One possible explanation for this is that a systematic search for new product ideas is only the beginning of a NPD project. Many uncertainties still remain at this point, such as the question whether the ideas generated will pass the assessment step or be terminated there. Consequently, a systematic approach to searching for new product ideas may in itself not be influential enough to already have an effect on corporate success at such an early phase of the NPD process.

After generating a number of ideas, the next step, idea assessment, is necessary to decide on the execution of an idea or to select the most promising idea from alternatives. The importance of this step within the product development process is empirically supported by studies in Western countries as well as in Japan and other countries (Cooper and Kleinschmidt 1986, p. 82, 1994, p. 25; Johne and Snelson 1988, p. 119; Mishra et al. 1996, p. 540; Song and Parry 1996, p. 431).

The risk in this step is twofold: On the one hand, the decision to continue with a project based on a bad idea entails further cost which leaves less available resources to other more promising projects. On the other hand, good ideas may not be recognized as such and promising ideas may be terminated with the consequence that the company may forgo a profitable business case.

Upper management support has frequently been found to contribute to successful NPD (Brown and Eisenhardt 1995, p. 352). The involvement of upper management in the assessment of new product ideas may prove supportive to success inasmuch as upper management is likely to be more involved and offer greater support for ideas of which they approved during assessment in order to insure their success. Therefore, involvement of upper management in the assessment of new product ideas may result in support and championing for a project which has repeatedly been identified as contributing to new product success (Kim and Wilemon 2002). Consequently, we propose that

P2: Upper management involvement in the assessment of new product ideas contributes positively to success.

Table 2. Number of companies by success and upper management involvement in the assessment of new product ideas

Involvement of upper management	Success		Total frequency
	yes	no	
Yes	189	169	368
Sometimes	47	52	99
No	2	3	5
Total frequency	238	224	462

Table 2 reveals that the majority of the companies involve upper management in the process of assessing new product ideas. However, performing a chi-square test of independence, we do not find support for our proposition in the data. This can be explained by the evidence, that almost every company in our sample involved upper management. Therefore, we can only compare companies which most of the time involve upper management to companies which sometimes involve upper management and not test our proposition.

Given that decisions frequently have to be made without having all of the relevant information at hand, idea assessment is accompanied by a high degree of uncertainty. The more radical the innovation project, the more difficult an early assessment of an idea becomes. In this context, interdisciplinary teams may be of value in order to account for as many facets and perspectives on a problem as possible.

Interfunctional integration has long been identified as a success factor for NPD (Cooper and Kleinschmidt 1987 p. 171; Salomo et al. 2003, p. 167). Especially, cooperation between R&D and marketing is regarded as vital to new product success (Souder 1990, p. 15). Some authors suggest that the assessment of new product ideas provides a greater reduction of uncertainty if various corporate functions can contribute their specific knowledge and thereby allows for more successful products (Aggteleky and Bajina 1992, pp. 154–156; Song and Parry 1997, p. 9). Hence, we suggest that

P3: New product idea assessment by interdisciplinary teams contributes positively to success.

Table 3. Number of companies by success and interdisciplinary teams in the assessment of new product ideas

Involvement of interdisciplinary teams	Success		Total frequency
	yes	no	
yes	121	93	214
sometimes	74	83	157
No	43	49	92
Total frequency	238	225	462

From Table 3 the calculated $\chi^2 = 4.209$, which has less than a 15% probability of occurring if the classifications were independent. Our suggestion that the assessment of new product ideas by interdisciplinary teams contributes to success therefore cannot be supported by the data.

After the assessment and selection of an idea, the concept has to be worked out in more detail. This includes the reduction of market uncertainty in order to arrive at a deeper understanding of the external environment. The target market has to be defined and customer requirements have to be integrated into the product concept, prior to development (Balbontin et al. 1999, p. 274; Cooper and Kleinschmidt, 1990, p. 26, 1994, p. 26; Khurana and Rosenthal 1997, p. 113; Maidique and Zirger 1984, p. 198; Song and Parry 1996, p. 427).

One possible way is to extensively use customer or user information for developing the new product concept. This type of information can either be gathered by direct contact with customers or by relying on functions operating closely with client organizations such as after sales/customer service. Consequently, companies should maintain close and direct relationships with their customers. While it is frequently argued that it is more difficult to reduce market uncertainty in new markets as potential customers are often unable to articulate their needs or may not even be aware of them (Mullins and Sutherland 1998, p. 228). Callahan and Lasry (2004, p. 116) argue that customer input is always important but for the case of very new products. Following this notion we suggest that

P4: Successful companies contact their customers more often to develop and evaluate new product ideas than unsuccessful companies.

Table 4. Number of companies by success and frequency of customer contact

Customer contact	Success		Total frequency
	yes	no	
very often	144	105	249
Sometimes	84	102	186
very seldom	9	18	27
Total frequency	237	225	462

Table 4 reveals that the majority of the respondents contact their customers very often. In addition, the chi-square test of independence ($\chi^2 = 10.546$) shows that there is only a less than 1% probability that the frequencies are independent. Hence, we find strong support for our proposition in the data.

Within the process of NPD, each corporate function should contribute according to its special strengths and abilities. The marketing department has been repeatedly identified as a source of valuable knowledge for the project team (Benkenstein 1987; Griffin and Hauser 1996; Cooper and Kleinschmidt 1987). It is in close contact with a company's customers, and is more knowledgeable about their problems and needs than any other corporate function. It understands the "voice of the customer" and thereby allows for the development of products that correspond to market needs. Therefore, we suggest that

P5: Contact between marketing and customers positively contributes to success.

Analogous to the description of the results in the former section, we perform this analysis only for the 435 companies which contact their customers at least sometimes to develop and evaluate new product ideas.

Table 5. Number of companies by success and department contacting customers

Marketing contacts customers	Success		Total frequency
	yes	no	
Yes	126	87	213
No	102	120	222
Total frequency	228	207	435

From Table 5 the calculated $\chi^2 = 7.604$, which has less than a 1% probability of occurring if the classifications were independent. These data reveal strong support for our notion that the frequency of marketing contacting customers is higher for successful firms than for unsuccessful companies.

However, listening to one's customers and gathering information from them is not sufficient. In order to develop products which will be successful in the market place, the companies have to derive customer requirements from the information gathered and integrate these into the definition of their new product concepts. We therefore propose that

P6: Systematic integration of customer requirements into the definition of new product concepts contributes positively to success.

Table 6. Number of companies by success and systematic integration of customer requirements into new product concepts

Systematic integration of customer requirements	Success		Total frequency
	yes	no	
yes	89	46	135
sometimes	109	122	231
no	39	57	96
Total frequency	237	225	462

From Table 6, the calculated $\chi^2 = 17.503$, which has less than a 0.1% probability of occurring if the classifications were independent. Hence, we find strong support for our proposition in the data.

The final step then is to translate the customer requirements into technical specifications, which can be done using QFD, as was described above. The customer information is rephrased in a way that allows for the engineering of the product concept. Hence

P7: Companies systematically translating customer requirements into technical specifications are more successful than companies not doing so.

Table 7. Number of companies by success and translation of customer requirements into technical specifications

Translation of cus-tomer requirements	Success		Total frequency
	yes	no	
yes	107	77	184
sometimes	99	107	206
no	31	40	71
Total frequency	237	224	461

Table 7 reveals that the majority of the respondents at least sometimes translate customer requirements into technical specifications. In addition, the chi-square test of independence ($\chi^2 = 5.981$) shows that there is a 5% probability that the frequencies are independent. Hence, we find support for our proposition in the data.

According to the "rational plan" research stream in NPD, "a project that is well planned, implemented, and appropriately supported will be a success" (Brown and Eisenhardt 1995, p. 348). As has been stated above, planning of NPD projects has been repeatedly identified as a significant determinant of new product success in Western countries as well as in Japan (Thieme et al. 2003; Song and Parry 1996, p. 432; Balachandra and Friar 1997, p. 279; Pinto and Slevin 1988, p. 67; Maidique and Zirger 1984, p. 198). On the other hand, it is argued that planning might not be beneficial under all circumstances, such as in a rapidly changing environment for example, and that NPD success in those cases rather depends on the company's ability to improvise (Benkenstein 1987). However, as this second view only addresses more specific circumstances, we follow the first argument and propose:

P8: Companies systematically planning a project prior to its start are more successful as companies which do not systematically plan innovation projects.

Table 8. Number of companies by success and systematic initial planning

Systematic planning prior to start	Success		Total frequency
	yes	no	
Yes	109	82	191
Sometimes	101	122	223
No	28	21	49
Total frequency	238	225	463

As is evident from Table 8, there exists a relationship between the two frequencies. The chi-square test of independence shows that there is a less than 5% probability that the frequencies are independent. We therefore find support for our proposition in the data.

Conclusions

The companies in our sample engage in a variety of activities to generate new product ideas. In accordance with prior research (Herstatt et al. 2004, p. 20; Harryson 1996, p. 26) we find that Japanese companies employ a number of different creativity techniques of which brainstorming is the most important.

As advocated by previous research (Cooper and Kleinschmidt 1987, p. 171; Souder 1990, p. 15; Aggteleky and Bajina 1992, pp. 154–156; Song and Parry, 1997, p. 9; Salomo et al. 2003, p. 167), the majority of the companies involve interdisciplinary teams and upper management in the assessment of new product ideas. However, our analysis cannot link these practices to corporate success.

The respondents use various sources of information to reduce uncertainties inherent in NPD. Customers represent the most prominent source of information for the companies followed by competitor analysis. Information from customers is not only gathered via direct contact. The companies also evaluate customer complaints and conduct surveys. It shows to be most beneficial, if marketing contacted customers.

We found strong support for our suggestion that frequent contact with customers is important to company success. However, this is not sufficient in itself: The gathered information and customer requirements need to be integrated into the product concept. This requires them to be translated into technical specifications. Both of these activities are more often carried out by successful companies than their unsuccessful competitors.

Finally a systematic approach to planning NPD projects is found to be positively related to corporate success.

Overall, we were able to support and extend the findings of Herstatt et al. (2004) with regard to Japanese management practices during the fuzzy front end of the innovation process.

References

Aggteleky B and Bajina N (1992) *Projektplanung: ein Handbuch für Führungskräfte*, München and Wien: Hanser

Baker NR, Green SG, and Bean AS (1985) How management can influence the generation of ideas, *Research Management*, **28**, 6, 35-42

Balachandra R and Friar JH (1997) Factors for success in R&D projects and new product innovation: A contextual framework, *IEEE Transactions on Engineering Management*, **44**, 3, 276-287

Balbontin A, Yazdani B, Cooper RG, and Souder WE (1999) New product development success factors in American and British firms, *International Journal of Technology Management*, **17**, 3, 259-280

Benkenstein M (1987) *F&E und Marketing: eine Untersuchung zur Leistungsfähigkeit von Koordinationskonzeptionen bei Innovationsentscheidungen*, Wiesbaden: Gabler

Brown SL and Eisenhardt KM (1995) Product Development: Past Research, Present Findings, and Future Directions, *Academy of Management Review*, **20**, 2, 343-378

Callahan J and Lasry E (2004) The importance of customer input in the development of very new products, *R&D Management*, **34**, 2, 107-120

Clayton MJ, Kunz JC, and Fischer MA (1996) Rapid conceptual design evaluation using a virtual product model, *Engineering Applications of Artificial Intelligence*, **9**, 4, 439-451

Cooper RG and Kleinschmidt EJ (1986) An investigation into the new product process – steps, deficiencies, and impact, *Journal of Product Innovation Management*, **3**, 3, 71-85

Cooper RG and Kleinschmidt EJ (1987) New Products: What Separates Winners from Losers?, *Journal of Product Innovation Management*, **4**, 3, 169-184

Cooper RG and Kleinschmidt EJ (1990) *New products: The key factors in success*, American Marketing Association, United States 1990

Cooper RG and Kleinschmidt EJ (1994) Screening new products for potential winners, *Institute of Electrical and Electronics Engineers IEEE engineering management review*, **22**, 4, 24-30

Geschka H (1992) Creativity techniques in product planning and development: a view from West Germany. In Parnes SJ (ed.), *Source book of creative problem-solving*, Buffalo: Creative Education Foundation Press, pp. 282-298

Griffin A and Hauser JR (1993) The voice of the customer, *Marketing Science*, **12**, 1 1-27

Griffin A and Hauser JR (1996) Integrating R&D and marketing: a review and analysis of the literature, *Journal of Product Innovation Management*, **13**, 3, 191-215

Harryson S (1996) Improving R&D performance through networking – lessons from Canon and Sony, *Arthur D. Little – Prism*, Fourth Quarter 1996

Herstatt C (2002): Search fields for radical innovations, *International Journal of Entrepreneurship and Innovation Management*, **2**, 1, 71-95

Herstatt C and Verworn B (2004) The Fuzzy Front End of Innovation. In: EITIM (ed.) *Bringing Technology and Innovation into the Boardroom*, Houndmills and New York: Palgrave MacMillan, pp. 347-373

Herstatt C, Verworn B, and Nagahira A (2004) Reducing project related uncertainty in the "fuzzy front end" of innovation – A comparison of German and Japanese product innovation projects, *International Journal of Product Development*, **1**, 1

Johne FA and Snelson PA (1988) Success factors in product innovation – a selective review of the literature, *Journal of Product Innovation Management*, **5**, 2, 114-128

Khurana A and Rosenthal SR (1997) Integrating the fuzzy front end of new product development, *Sloan Management Review*, **38**, 2, 103-120

Khurana A and Rosenthal SR (1998) Towards holistic "front ends" in new product development, *Journal of Product Innovation Management*, **15**, 1, 57-74

Kim J and Wilemon D (2002) Focusing the fuzzy front-end in new product development, *R&D Management*, **32**, 4, 269-279

Koen P, Ajamian G, Burkart R, Clamen A et al. (2001) Providing clarity and a common language to the "fuzzy front end", *Research Technology Management*, **44**, 2, 46-55

Maidique MA and Zirger BJ (1984) A study of success and failure in product innovation, *IEEE Transactions on Engineering Management*, **EM-31**, 4, 192-203

Mishra S, Kim D, and Lee DH (1996) Factors affecting new product success: cross-country comparison, *Journal of Product Innovation Management*, **13**, 6, 530-550

Mullins JW and Sutherland DJ (1998) New product development in rapidly changing markets: an exploratory study, *Journal of Product Innovation Management,* **15**, 3, 224–236

Pinto JK and Slevin DP (1988) Critical success factors across the project life cycle, *Project Management Journal*, **19**, 3, 67-75

Rochford L (1991) Generating and screening new product ideas, *Industrial Marketing Management*, **20**, 4, 287-296

Rubinstein AH (1994) At the front end of the R&D/innovation process – idea development and entrepreneurship, *International Journal of Technology Management*, **9**, 5, 6, 7, 652-677

Salomo S, Gemünden HG, and Billing F (2003) Dynamisches Schnittstellenmanagement radikaler Innvoationsvorhaben. In: Herstatt C and Verworn B (Eds), *Management der frühen Innovationsphasen: Grundlagen, Methoden, Neue Ansätze*, Wiesbaden: Gabler, pp. 161-194

Song XM and Parry ME (1996) What separates Japanese new product winners from losers, *Journal of Product Innovation Management,* **13**, 5, 422-439

Song XM and Parry ME (1997) A cross-national comparative study on new product development processes: Japan and the United States, *Journal of Marketing*, **61**, 2, 1-18

Souder WE (1990) Managing the Interface between R&D and Marketing, *Advances in Telecommunications Management*, Volume 1, pp. 15-33

Thieme JR, Song XM, and Shin GC (2003) Project Management Characteristics and New Product Survival, *Journal of Product Innovation Management*, **20**, 2, 104-119

Verganti R (1997) Leveraging on systematic learning to manage the early phases of product innovation projects, *R&D Management,* **27**, 4, 377-392

Watts T, Swann PGM, and Pandit NR (1998) Virtual reality and innovation potential, *Business Strategy Review*, **9**, 3, 45-54

Yoshida PG (2002) Japan's R&D remains strong as economy struggles to turn corner, *Research Technology Management*, **45**, 6, 2-4

Zhang Q and Doll WJ (2001) The fuzzy front end and success of new product development: a causal model, *European Journal of Innovation Management*, **4**, 2, 95-112

Implementing Process Innovation – The Case of the Toyota Production System

René Haak

Introduction

For more than twenty years now, the Toyota production system has been the subject of lively interest and debate in the West. Particularly the 1980s and early 1990s saw a real boom in the publication of scientific writings and works of popular science which tried to get to discover the secret of Toyota success. One of the best known papers is the study carried out by Massachusetts Institute of Technology (MIT) researchers Womack, Jones and Ross in 1990, which intrigued whole legions of production scientists, management researchers and industry practitioners and had a key impact on subsequent research and on the Western view of the Toyota production system and also on the self-image of Japanese production management itself.

In the course of the International Motor Vehicle Program (IMVP) the MIT researchers highlighted the differences between the factories in the automobile industry world-wide. They derived from the data for this study the basic hallmarks of the production system that became known globally as Lean Production.

The MIT researchers posited the theory that Lean Production would change the world in the same way as Fordist mass production had in the past, so that sooner or later all the important automobile manufacturers would be forced to adopt the Japanese system. However, the existence of 'one best way' revealed itself as a myth during the 1990s. A number of Japanese automobile manufacturers, once paradigms of Japanese production management, were forced to enter into partnerships with foreign counterparts; in some cases, the management of the company was also handed over to ensure continued competitiveness. Others, however, such as Toyota and Honda, were able to maintain their world-wide leadership and continued to develop their specific forms of production system. Toyota's profits increase with each year and it now occupies second place in the world ranking behind General Motors and ahead of Ford.

In order to examine the Toyota production system one must first of all ask what is meant by production system, the development and nature of which will be analyzed on the following pages. In this contribution, the production system is meant as the management system of manufacturing companies. This interpretation is based on the integrative approach to production management where production management includes the running of production processes, quality management, logistics, maintenance, industrial engineering and procurement.

The Toyota production system can be seen as a technology-based, comprehensive production management system with the primary goals of increasing productivity and reducing costs (Monden 1983). This is achieved by reducing cycle time, increasing flexibility, reducing stock levels and shortening machine changeover times. According to Ohno the basis of the Toyota production system is "the absolute elimination of waste. The two pillars needed to support the system are:

- just-in-time
- autonomation or autonomation with human touch.

Just-in-time means that, in a flow process, the right parts needed in assembly reach the assembly line at the time they are needed. A company establishing this flow throughout can approach zero inventory. The other pillar of the Toyota production system is called autonomation – not to be confused with simple automation. It is also know as automation with a human touch. At Toyota, a machine automated with a human touch is one that is attached to an automatic stopping device. In all Toyota plans, most machine, new or old, are equipped with such devices as well as various safety devices, fixed-position stopping, the full-work system, and *baka-yoke* foolproofing systems to prevent defective products. In this way, human intelligence, or human touch, is given to the machines." (Ohno 1988, pp. 4-6)

The difference between the concepts of Lean Production and the Toyota production system is that Lean Production (Jürgens 1994) was coined by the MIT researchers Womack, Jones and Ross and is used for any company in any branch of industry, whereas the term Toyota production system refers to the production management system at Toyota, but includes basically the same elements. In his latest book "The Toyota Way" (2004) Liker give us an impression of what exactly a lean enterprise is. "You could say it's the end result of applying the Toyota production system to all areas of your business. In their excellent book, Lean Thinking, James Womack and Daniel Jones define lean manufacturing as a five-step process: defining customer value, defining the value stream, making it "flow", "pulling" from the customer back, and striving for excellence. To be a lean manufacturer requires a way of thinking that focuses on making the product flow through value-adding processes without interruption (one-piece flow), a "pull" system that cascades back from customer demand by replenishing only what the next operation takes away a short intervals, and a culture in which everyone is striving continuously to improve." (Liker 2004, p. 7)

This contribution cannot discuss all the aspects of Toyota production system mentioned here in high detail. It is more important to highlight key developments, identify changes and challenges in the Toyota production system and to illustrate the particular characteristics of this worldwide famous production management system.

The Toyota production system is unique, or in other words it is Toyota's unique approach to manufacturing, and the result is unique in the world of manufacturing. Toyotas specific production system is the basis for much of the "Lean Production" movement that has dominated manufacturing trend for the last 15 years. It is clear, that Toyota's performance is a direct result of operational excellence. This excellence is based in part on tools and quality improvement methods made famous by Toyota – with roots in the United States – in the manufacturing world, such as kaizen, jidoka, just-in-time, and heijunka. Tools and techniques are one part of Toyota's approach to be better than the competitors. But the success at implementing these tools stems from a deeper business philosophy based on its understanding of people and human motivation. According to Liker (2004, p. 6) the "success is ultimately based on its ability to cultivate leadership, teams, and culture, to devise strategy, to build supplier relationships, and maintain a learning organization." So, in this contribution special attention will be paid to the tools and also to the philosophy of the Toyota production system.

Two central issues for discussion in this chapter arise from these preliminary observations. On the one hand, we examine the question of which central factors have influenced the development of the key features of the Toyota production system; in other words, where were its roots, where were the important factors shaping the tools and the philosophy. On the other hand, we look at the issue of whether the strength of Toyota production system, derives from its nature as a dynamic rather than as a static system, from the fact that constant change is inherent in the Toyota production system, forming the basis for a flexibility which ensures that the system can survive in the face of rapidly changing competition and market constellations. In other words, can the Toyota production system be understood as a key factor in the corporate processes of learning, adaptation and improvement, as the key factor in a learning organization? Are change and continuity the main characteristics of the Toyota production system and which challenges is Toyota facing in the future?

Technology and Knowledge Transfer

A look back at the development of Toyota production system reveals that the global successes of Toyota over recent decades can be linked in no small part to technology and knowledge transfer and the associated advances in organizational learning. One of the areas in which the success of Toyota production system crystallized was automation technology and, following on from that, the development of the autonomation system (*jidoka*) at Toyota and the just-in-time system which will be examined in greater detail later. Successful transfer and further development of advanced technologies from the USA and Western Europe were important prerequisites for the emergence of a specifically Toyota production system and also therefore for the unstoppable business and technological advance of Toyota following World War II.

Adopting and improving technology from the United States and Western Europe, increasing productivity with new forms of work organization, management and staff development together with autonomation technology, a nation-wide program to improve quality based on the thinking of the Americans Deming and Juran coupled with a high degree of flexibility were the key elements that enabled also Toyota to catch up quickly with advances in organizational learning. Ohno

(1988, p. 3) pointed out: "We have learned a lot from the U.S. Automobile empire. America has generated wonderful production management techniques, business management techniques such as quality control (QC) and total quality control (TQC), and industrial engineering (IE) methods. Japan imported these ideas and put them into practice. The Japanese should never forget that these techniques were born in America and generated by American efforts."

On an individual level, it was the commitment and willingness to learn on the part of Japanese technicians, engineers and managers, particularly those in companies engaged in electrotechnology, mechanical engineering and machine tool building, and in laboratories undertaking research into manufacturing science which made the advances in production management possible. Toyota played a key role in this process. Improving the existing situation and implementing the findings in practical applications characterize the development of the Toyota production system.

Along with the transfer of technology and knowledge, it was the industrial integration of innovative technology and new forms of work organization and company leadership which characterized the Toyota production system.

The Company: A Whole System

The Toyota production system has made its mark on industrial practice and on manufacturing science research in places other than in Japan. It embodies in Lean Production a corporate approach and a basic company strategy that view the factory as a whole system, as a work system overlaying the single work station and the workshop. Essentially, Toyotaism concerns the developmental mainstays of production management: manufacturing technology and work organization. It tries, whilst avoiding any form of waste, to combine the benefits of manual production – Taylor's central interest in rationalization – with the advantages of mass production (Fordism).

As Toyotaism became more widespread, internal and external production logistics (just-in-time) took up a key position for corporate success along with work organization and manufacturing technology (autonomation, *jidoka* in Japanese). Toyota people usually explain just-in-time and *jidoka* as the twin pillars of the Toyota Production System (Ohno 1988; Nihon Noritsu Kyokai 1978; Monden 1983) and do not highlight the work organization system specifically, although it plays a large part in the success of the Toyota Production System.

The term *jidoka* can be translated as autonomation. This term includes on the one hand the concept of automation and on the other that of autonomous monitoring for defects and elimination of their causes. In automated work processes, a defect or poor quality can cause the machines to come to an immediate standstill. Work can only continue when the cause of the problem has been removed. If one work stage is interrupted, the whole production system can come to a stop, as the constraints of kanban only allow minimum interim stocks. In some cases there are no interim or buffer stocks.

Therefore the production workers have to be in a position to find the defect as soon as possible and take the appropriate steps towards fixing it to minimize production down time. For example, all the work places are supplied with light indicators called *andon* which call the workers allocated to that particular production section to help. The potential for disruption to the production system resulting from autonomation, quality assurance and cost reduction has also earned Toyotaism the name 'Management by Stress' (Parker and Slaughter 1988). Furthermore, social pressure on less productive employees in the group can cause problems for the productivity and motivation of the group members. From the point of view of the learning organization that is looking at autonomation from the aspect of learning theory, stress within a certain context (taking into account intensity, time period, the constitution of the individual, social norms) can however promote learning.

Toyota production system was developed for the manufacture of passenger cars in the Toyota Motor Company's factories and is used primarily in the automobile and the automobile supply industry. It did not remain limited to Japan: it has proved an effective structure for production in other economies and achieved considerable productivity and quality effects (Schmitt 1998; Yui 1999).

The Toyota production system approach originated with Eiji Toyoda and Taiichi Ohno. In a well-known study by the Massachusetts Institute of Technology, which was published in 1990 under the title 'The Machine that Changed the World', Toyota's factors for success are named as technology leadership, cost leadership and time leadership.

In their comparative study, the authors find the main factor for success in Japanese companies is a different system of production from that practiced in European and American companies: lean production. In their view, lean production combines the advantages of manual production with those of mass production, whilst avoiding the high costs of the former and the inflexibility of the latter. On the one hand, many multi-skilled workers work in groups, as is the case in manual production; on the other hand, large volumes of standardized parts are produced with the aid of flexible automated machinery – similarly to mass production (Womack, Jones and Ross 1990).

The findings of the international comparison made in this study between mass and Toyota production system are summarized in the following list of "lean production" features:

- fewer defects in automobile manufacture;
- the manufacturing process is much faster;
- the repair area in the company is smaller;
- the stocks held by the company are smaller;
- the majority of employees work in teams;
- the workers frequently change their job within the company in the production area;
- the workers offer more suggestions and are trained for longer;
- the organizational structures are flatter.

Essentially, the key factor is organizational learning, which manifests itself as the result of the advances in manufacturing technology and in work organization, improved product quality and careful use of resources. Other features of this organizational learning system are low warehouse stocks, shorter product development times and low staffing levels and, especially at Toyota, involving assembly workers in the permanent quality control system and the continuous process of improvement (kaizen) (Shimizu 1988). As a result, production errors fell dramatically and costly post-processing was minimized.

Kaizen

Kaizen can be interpreted as the Toyota management philosophy which involves every employee in achieving the goal of continuous improvement of structures and systems (Hayashi 1991, Jürgens 1991), and stand behind the successful implementation of tools and techniques of the Toyota production system. The starting point for this philosophy is the knowledge that each business is confronted with many problems which can be solved by establishing a company culture with two main features: each employee can with impunity point out errors and identify problems, and solutions for the weaknesses identified are found by the employees of the organization working together (Yamashiro 1997; Imai 1993).

Continuous improvement of structures and systems uses a systematic procedure based on Deming's PDCA cycle (**P**lan, **D**o, **C**heck, **A**ct). The PDCA cycle is used in Japanese companies to initiate, track and review improvements. Approaching the matter systematically, the cycle begins with the **p**lanning phase (Liker 2004, p. 24). For example, the area earmarked for improvement is discussed in the work group and the most important findings and the biggest obstacles are identified. Then the current situation is analyzed. In order to proceed efficiently, the problem under investigation is defined and described precisely. To identify causes, relevant data is collected from the production workers. A quantitative base of data is indispensable for identifying clearly the potential for improvement and defining appropriate interim goals and actions. This is also a requirement for making the targeted improvements unmistakably visible to all the employees in the course of the improvement process.

In the **d**o phase of the improvement cycle, the actions selected are carried out. This does not mean however that it is impossible to return to the plan phase if necessary, in order to gather more information and review the actions. Defining the actions is only the first step on the way to achieving the improvement of the production systems and structures.

In the **c**heck phase that follows, the effects of the planned actions are analyzed. An investigation is carried out into whether and how the goals defined in the planning phase can be achieved. The results are monitored, documented and illustrated in the activity catalogue. Regular monitoring reveals whether the goals have been achieved. If this is not the case, then investigations are carried out into why the undesirable deviations occurred. Even failures hold important information for shaping the improvement process.

The last phase of the cycle – **act** – serves to review the previous phases and to record the experiences made during the process, by standardizing successful factors and making them obligatory for other employees in the company, and to initiate follow-up activities, from which targets for subsequent improvements can be set up. If the cycle is carried out sequentially as it is intended to be, the problems under consideration are increasingly limited as knowledge and experiences from the previous cycles can be applied.

The newly created standards or rules set up by the *kacho* or *bucho* (in some Japanese companies by the *kakaricho* or *kumicho*) as results are not set in stone. The aim of the standard is to create a basis for further improvement, but also to encourage confidence in consistent quality, to create a solid basis for worker education and training and to remove product liability problems (Suzuki 1994). The old standard is only replaced when a new one is defined in the course of the improvement process. The role of the *kakaricho* or the *kumicho*, the immediate supervisor, who does not work in production with the other employees, is to find new templates for standards on the basis of the daily production data and to push through improvement measures together with expert kaizen teams, who are assembled specifically for the problem situations, or with work groups.

The PDCA cycles running on the different levels of the company can be integrated both upwards and downwards in the hierarchy. This creates multifunctional project teams primarily in the area of product development or in production process innovation. Problems which cannot be dealt with on one level of the company or in a functional area are referred to the next highest level or to a level with the specific subject knowledge, as are faults in the production process, so that precisely the knowledge required for solving the problem can be applied. In this context, the integrated PDCA cycle can also be understood as a process of organizational learning, in which subject knowledge and experience can be gathered on an individual basis and made available through the improved standards to be worked with throughout the company.

Avoiding Waste

A central concern of kaizen is to eliminate or avoid waste of all kinds in the company. Frequently, waste in a company is not perceived because it is associated with processes that have developed historically and new, simpler options are not even considered. Seven areas with the potential for waste have been identified in the production area.

The most important area is overproduction (1) where a larger volume is manufactured than is required by the internal or the external customer. Unnecessary process stages are created with this kind of waste with serious consequences, as overproduction in its turn can cause a number of different types of waste. The just-in-time system developed by Toyota and product control with the kanban system have provided a remedy in this situation.

Overproduction leads to more work-in-progress (2). This represents waste as it requires space, incurs storage costs, requires to be searched, makes additional movement of materials necessary and, above all, conceals problems in the production process (e.g. machine downtime) or unstable processes.

Also, any form of transport (3) is classified as waste in the Toyota production system, as material transport does not in itself add value. Work stations placed at distance from each other result in additional costs for the transport of work-in-progress. The turnaround time of the product or the workpiece is longer, thus increasing the job time calculated for the manufacturing process.

One outcome of big buffer inventories and lengthy transport are waiting and idle periods (4). This form of waste results in an unbalanced utilization of workers and machines.

Waste in the manufacturing process (5) is frequently a result of the previously listed types of waste. However, there is also waste in the manufacturing process if there is a simpler or faster way to carry out a certain production task. This waste is caused by ambiguous instructions, lack of ability, skill or knowledge on the part of the employees or by too many unnecessary inspections.

One of the basic premises of kaizen, that the manufacturing process can always be improved, is that unnecessary motion (6) should be avoided, by reducing the number of movements in the work flow by changing the work systems (e.g. avoiding long distances, repeated refamiliarization due to too many unnecessary interruptions).

Defects (7), the seventh waste area, arise frequently due to inattention or lack of concentration. Defects in their turn also cause other kinds of waste, such as the same work having to be carried out twice or more, or long idle or waiting times.

Employees – The Secret of Toyota's Success

One of the basic convictions of kaizen is that nobody knows a work station as well as the employee who works there in the production process day in, day out. For this reason, the aims of kaizen and hence the lean production philosophy as embodied by the Toyota production system are to increase productivity and employee motivation by eliminating waste within the framework of a systematic and consistent operation.

How should waste be eliminated from the work environment? This is one of the central issues of kaizen and therefore one of the fundamental issues of the Toyota production system and its philosophy. In other words, how can the knowledge, the experience, the skills and the expertise of the workers be used to create the most effective work system? The 5 S process can be applied to the whole company or focus on just one work station. The core of the 5 S process to combat waste can be understood as follows:

- S (*seiri*): The employee needs to decide which tools and accessories are required at the work station.
- S (*seiton*): The employee needs to put the tools and accessories he thinks he requires in order so that they are at hand in the right place at the right time when he needs them for his work.

- S (*seiso*): The employee needs to keep the workstation clean; that is, clean and take care of the orderly workstation and the tools and accessories.
- S (*seiketsu*): The employee must observe standards, rules, and regulations; he must turn instructions into rules.
- S (*shitsuke*) The employee must observe all the points listed and improve on them continuously.

The 5 S process is not a fashionable trend in management science. One can posit the theory that the 5 S process forms part of the self-image of a Japanese production manager at Toyota. The central question from a business management point of view is: what are the benefits of continuously maintaining and improving the work environment? The answer is quite easy: it creates more time for the value added process or time can be better utilized.

Tools for Solving Problems

Through kaizen, tools have been developed for solving problems which are intended to enable continuous improvement in the interests of the customer. Quality assurance, just-in-time, automation, extensive product monitoring, kanban, suggestion schemes, and much more are linked together under the kaizen 'umbrella' (Nonaka and Takeuchi 1997; Sebestyén 1994).

First and foremost, kaizen encourages process-oriented thinking, as it is mainly corporate processes that are to be improved to allow goals to be reached more efficiently (Matzky 1994). Following Argyris and Schön (1999), this process-oriented thinking is equivalent to organizational learning. Implementation of the kaizen philosophy and its tools places the organization in a problematic situation. For example, the employees in a multifunctional project group (Hyodo 1987) find after systematic investigation that there is a discrepancy between the results they expect from their actions and the actual outcome of the actions. The employees examine the matter and try to rearrange their activities so that their actions and results are again congruent (Nonaka and Takeuchi 1997). Following Argyris and Schön's concept of the learning organization, the organization members' theory-in-use is modified if the discoveries leading to the solution of the problem are fixed in company-specific artifacts such as a change in the manufacturing organization and in new work programs. The result of these modifications is that the organization has learnt (Argyris and Schön 1999).

A key element of this problem solving process specified in the kaizen philosophy which can find negative deviations (performance gaps) is repeated analysis of an existing set of facts (Nonaka and Takeuchi 1997). Looking at the company to find the causes of problems and the reasons for performance gaps and identifying solutions is the core thinking behind kaizen. Continuous improvement of the processes means that all the members of the company are constantly learning so that they can on the one hand react flexibly to permanently changing challenges and on the other improve on the existing situation more and more. Kaizen is quite different from traditional methods of business rationalization as it is not a matter of large-scale innovation but of small, but continuous improvement.

Group Work

In order to diffuse the philosophy of continuous improvement further throughout the company, product teams on the level of work organization and personnel management were put together under the leadership of Taiichi Ohno. In these product teams, each member was able to carry out all the stages in production. The group members were supposed to distribute the work in the group themselves and discuss and agree with each other on the ways to optimize the production process (Hyodo 1987; Nonaka and Takeuchi 1997; Ernst 1999).

Group work organization was seen above all as communication and dialogue to improve the group members' performance. Rotation within the jobs allocated to the group played a key role in employee training. The rotation plans were compiled on a daily basis by the supervisor and planned to allow weaker group members to improve their skills and to make provision for more effective employees to be kept on standby for when production was disrupted.

This form of work organization has cost cutting (avoidance of waste) and productivity increase as its foremost goals; employee training is seen as the tool that will achieve the goals. Training group members is important in planning for and working with a work force that is as flexible as possible. However, note here that there are groups of employees (such as short-term workers, new recruits, or employees from other areas) who are not considered for participation in these job rotation schemes. It also takes some time before work experience is sufficient to allow group members to be included in the rotation scheme.

The existing training and problem solving potential of employees deployed in the context of wide-ranging improvement activities also form a key source of information for creating adaptable work systems. The structural integration and harnessing of individual knowledge gained through experience is a comprehensive program which runs on all levels of the company. For production, these are quality circles, suggestion schemes and improvement measures at the individual worker level. All these activities are supported by work groups, teams of experts or individuals.

Just-in-Time

On a concrete level – the flow of parts in the production process – Ohno developed the well-known just-in-time system, which is represented in the literature in many different and occasionally contradictory ways. The determining features are group technology, the kanban system, short set-up times, harmonization of the production process and quality assurance (Görgens 1994, p. 15).

This astonishingly simple and economically so promising idea was that in each stage of the process only as many parts are produced as necessary to cover the immediate requirements of the next manufacturing stage. Empty containers are returned to the previous processing stage which is the automatic signal to produce more parts (Ohno 1988). Essentially, this just-in-time system is oriented towards intracompany and intercompany processes. A just-in-time system would not be thinkable without the conscious implementation of collective strategies in the organization. Toyota undertook to guarantee its suppliers a certain volume of orders over a certain period and furthermore, was prepared to share with them the profits achieved with the cost savings if the partner adopted the Toyota production system – in this particular case the just-in-time principle of pulled material flow.

Teams

Another modification to work organization which affected the whole production process at Toyota was the grouping together of design and manufacturing engineers in teams and the encouragement given to group-based success. Learning and knowledge boundaries within the organization were abandoned and the knowledge available on different hierarchical levels and the associated methods for solving problems were put on a broader plane. As a result of this change to work organization, development time for new car models fell dramatically and product quality again improved. This structural change also represented a considerable advantage from the marketing policy point of view. It was possible to respond more quickly to changes in customer requirements and penetrate a number of niche markets intensively and at a low cost.

Organizing a team as an independent and accountable business unit initiates learning where performance gaps are identified and makes knowledge available so that team members can carry out their work. Each team member has the ability to carry out many, in some cases different, types of work within the group and the resulting redundancy creates a very flexible company (Hyodo 1987).

With shared knowledge bases, organization as a team forms the basis and is a catalyst for organizational learning in Japanese companies (Ducan and Weiss 1979).

Quality Management

At Toyota, quality is at the centre of the product and process-oriented efforts towards improvement and innovation integrated in the kaizen company philosophy. Economic success only comes when the customer is convinced of the quality of the product. The high quality of Toyota products and the quality management systems in his production system are considered exemplary today.

Originally the development of production-oriented quality procedures derives from American ideas and industrial applications (Deming circle and quality control). The process of continuous improvement is based on the PDCA cycle which was developed in the 1950s by W. Edwards Deming, an American. Following World War II, these American 'achievements' were methodically developed into

Total Quality Control (TQC) in Japan and then developed further to the Total Quality Management (TQM) of today. Quality circles are a central core element of the total quality management system (Goetsch and Davis 2003). These quality circles, which are held regularly and are supported by engineers, can also be seen as a central element of the learning organization as they identify performance gaps and lead to a review of the way the organization works.

Before World War II, the emphasis in Japan was on (final) inspection, which in line with Taylorism, was carried out by a dedicated quality control department. American influence after World War II brought the introduction of statistical quality control (1946). The modern Japanese concept of quality circles therefore has its roots in the period shortly after World War II. 1946 saw the foundation of the Union of Japanese Scientists and Engineers (JUSE) which promoted the development of quality control in Japanese manufacturing businesses considerably. In the 1950s, on the initiative of the Japanese Union of Scientists and Engineers the idea of systematic quality assurance was brought to Japan.

It was American quality experts who shaped the eventually independent quality system in Japan. In the years 1950-52 Deming held a series of lectures on the subject of 'Statistical quality control' (inspection during production). Joseph M. Juran emphasized in his seminars (1954) the role that top and middle management should play in quality control. Armand V. Feigenbaum, who invented the term TQC (Total Quality Control), extended responsibility for quality to all areas of the company. Quality no longer meant the elimination of defective products but that they were avoided from the beginning by monitoring the process. These methods were developed further in Japan. One of the most important representatives of the Japanese movement was Kaoru Ishikawa, who extended quality management to include social aspects. Another step forward was taken by Masaaki Imai, who postulated that continuous improvement of processes to raise the standard of all output would be a recipe for success in Japanese quality management.

These efforts resulted in 1962 in the first official registration of a quality circle. At the beginning of its development, the quality circle was originally a learning group which then gradually addressed itself to solving problems with practical application of techniques it had learnt. Toyota production management moved further and further away from traditional inspection-oriented quality control and developed quality procedures for use within the production process and within product development.

Today, this idea is also applied to suppliers and other business partners from Toyota who play their part in the value added process. Whilst quality control originally focused on production and other technical areas in the company, efforts are made far beyond that nowadays.

The core idea of the quality circle is that problems are most likely to be identified and eliminated where they occur. Using this approach, production employees are supposed to identify the weak points in their day-to-day work and find the solution themselves. The primary goal of the quality circle is to improve the quality of the product and the process.

Quality circles have two main aims:

To optimize manufacturing processes and work flow using the employees' knowledge and experience.

To improve job satisfaction and motivation with regular group meetings which also improve company-internal communications (knowledge transfer, exchange of experience, transparency).

Kaizen – Core of Toyota Production System and Embodiment of Organizational Learning

Organizational learning processes have been made possible by the transfer of knowledge and technology (for example, automation technology and the autonomation system at Toyota) and frequently form the basis for the development of systems (NC and CNC-technology and manufacturing applications), which in their turn enable organizational learning by modifying the knowledge base (knowledge linked to the technology, for example, manufacturing processes) in the organization of Toyota.

Organizational learning in production through the company-wide and cross-company process of continuous improvement (kaizen) is one of the main characteristics of Toyota production system, a key hallmark of the success of Toyota. The endeavor to achieve a zero-fault strategy in Toyota plants as part of the total quality management system, which means that a defective part is not only rejected but that the cause of the error is also removed, is an expression of kaizen and as such an expression of the fundamental thinking by Toyota managers and workers.

In response to the technical problems with products and production which arose in the interplay between American, Western European and the Japanese' own methods and applications, the continuous improvement system today concentrates on production, but as a management concept includes all the activities and employees throughout the whole company. This means that Toyota production management can be considered the management of the process of continuous improvement which forms the basis of the "Toyota Way" (Liker 2004).

For instance, Toyota production workers, marketing experts and design engineers actively co-operate in groups to identify problems, find solutions and develop better technology in order to eliminate performance gaps they have identified. The improvements they work out apply not only to their particular working group but also become valid for other working groups via a central integration and co-ordination mechanism; works management for example.

The improvement becomes obligatory for all the members of the organization, becomes a new standard and a long-term theory-in-use also for employees new to the company. The search for improvements to products, processes and systems applies not only to the company itself, but as part of a collective strategy creates a bridge to intercompany co-operation (for example, involving supplier companies).

The high degree of standardization in the formal management systems of Toyota brings about successful learning in groups which benefits the whole organization, that is, it enables organizational learning. This knowledge is also passed on to or shared with other companies via the collective strategies (collaborating companies, value added partnerships, alliances, supplier networks). New knowledge circulates through companies in the same networks very quickly. The highly-regarded kaizen concept, the manufacturing leadership philosophy which still remains valid even under the currently prevailing low growth conditions, has proven to be an effective method for learning particularly in the area of production and enables progress in a combination of individual, organizational and interorganizational learning.

Toyota production system and his philosophy is associated with specific forms of work organization (for example, group work, team organization), of logistics and quality (for example, just-in-time, kanban, quality circles), of manufacturing processes (high-tech manufacturing systems, NC and CNC systems, autonomation), of personnel deployment (for example, job rotation) and of education. Its main characteristic overall is that it has been strongly molded by step by step learning and is expressed in the philosophy of continuous improvement. The challenge for Toyota in the frame of rapid internationalization is to continue this successful way of doing business worldwide. The manager and the worker in various Toyota plants and numerous nation and different cultures have to understand the "Toyota Way", which based on the main principle "kaizen".

References

Abegglen JC and Stalk G (1985) *Kaisha: The Japanese Corporation.* New York: Basic Books.

Adler PS (1988) 'Managing Flexible Automation', *California Management Review*, 30, 3, Spring, p. 34-56.

Argyris C and Schön DA (1978) *Organizational Learning. A Theory of Action Perspective.* Reading, Massachuchetts: Addison-Wesley.

Argyris and Schön DA (1999) *Die lernende Organisation*, Stuttgart: Klett-Cotta.

Asanuma B (1989) 'Manufacturer-supplier Relationships in Japan and the Concept of Relation-specific Skills', *Journal of the Japanese and International Economies* (3), pp. 1-30.

Asanuma B and Kikutani T (1992) Risk Absorption in Japanese Subcontraction. A Microeconomic Study of the Automobile Industry, *Journal of the Japanese and International Economies* (6), pp. 1-29.

Beason R and Weinstein DE (1994) 'Growth, Economies of Scale, and Industrial Targeting in Japan (1955-1990)', *Harvard Institute of Economic Research Discussion Paper 1644*, Boston, June 10.

Behrendt WK (1982) 'Die frühen Jahre der NC-Technologie: 1954 bis 1963', *Technische Rundschau* 19, pp. 19-21.

Boesenberg D and Metzen H (Eds) (1993) *Lean Management. Vorsprung durch schlanke Konzepte*, Landsberg: Verlag Moderne Industrie.

Brödner P (1991) 'Maschinenbau in Japan – Nippons Erfolgskonzept: so einfach wie möglich', *Technische Rundschau*, 37, 1991, pp. 54-62.

Chalmers J (1986) *MITI and the Japanese Miracle. The Growth of the Industrial Policy, 1925-1975.* Stanford: Stanford University Press.

Champy J and Hammer M (1994) *Business Reengineering - Die Radikalkur für das Unternehmen*, Frankfurt and New York: Campus.

Chokki T (1986) 'A History of the Machine Tool Insutry in Japan', in Fransman M (ed.) *Machinery and Economic Development*. New York: St. Martin's Press, pp. 124-52.

Clark KB, Fujimoto T, and Stotko EC (Eds) (1992) *Automobilentwicklung mit System. Strategie, Organisation und Management in Europa, Japan und USA,* Frankfurt am Main: Campus-Verlag.

Collis DJ (1988) 'The Machine Tool Industry and Industrial Policy 1955-1988', in Spence ME and Hazard HA (Eds) *International Competitiveness*, Center of Business and Government at the John F. Kennedy School of Government, Harvard University, New York, pp. 75-114.

Ducan RB and Weiss A (1979) 'Organizational Learning: Implications for Organizational Design', in Staw BW (ed.) *Research in Organizational Behavior 1*, pp. 75-123.

Durand J-P; Stewart P and Castillo JJ (Eds) (1999) *Teamwork in the Automobile Industry. Radical Change or Passing Fashion?* Houndsmill: Palgrave Macmillan.

Ernst A (1999) 'Personnel Management of Japanese Firms and Information Flows', in Albach H, Görtzen U, and Zobel R (Eds) *Information Processing as a Competitive Advantage of Japanese Firms*, Berlin: Edition Sigma, pp. 239-53.

Fischer W (1979) *Die Weltwirtschaft im 20. Jahrhundert.* Göttingen: Vahlen.

Ford H (1922) *My Life and Work.* New York: Doubleday & Page.

Freedman D (1988): *The Misunderstood Miracle – Industrial Development and Political Change in Japan*, London, Ithaca: Cornell University Press.

Freyssenet M, Mair A, Shimizu K, and Volpato G (Eds) (1998) *One Best Way? Trajectories and Industrial Models of the World's Automobile Producers*, Oxford, New York: Oxford University Press.

Fujimoto T (1994) 'Buhin Torihiki Kankei to Suparaiyâ Shisutemu' (Parts Transaction Relationships and the Supplier System), *Discussion Paper Series 94-J-19, Research Institute for the Japanese Economy*, Tokyo: The University of Tokyo Press.

Fujimoto T (1996) 'An Evolutionary Process of Toyota's Final Assembly Operations. The Role of Ex-post Dynamic Capabilities', *Discussion Paper Series 96-F-2, Research Insitute for the Japanese Economy*, Tokyo: The University of Tokyo Press.

Fujimoto T and Takeishi A (1994) *Jidôsha Sangyô 21 Seiki e no Shinario* (Scenario for the Car Industry in the 21st Century), Tokyo: Seisansei Shuppan.

Fujimoto T, Sei S, and Takeishi A (1994) Nihon Jidôsha Sangyô no Supuraiyā Shisutemu no Zentaizô to sono Tamensei (The Whole Picture of the Supplier System of the Japanese Car Industry and its Diversity), *Kikai Keizai Kenkyû 24*, pp. 11-36.

Fujimoto T (1999) *The Evolution of a Manufacturing System at Toyota*, Oxford and New York; Oxford University Press.

Furin WE and Nishiguchi T (1990) The Toyota Production System. Its Organizational Definition in Japan, *Keizai Kenkyû 42* (1), pp. 42-55.

Garratt B (1990) *Creating a Learning Organisation. A Guide to Leadership, Learning and Development*, Cambridge: Director Books.

Geißler H (1996) 'Vom Lernen in der Organisation zum Lernen der Organisation', in Sattelberger T (ed.) *Die lernende Organisation: Konzepte für eine neue Qualität der Unternehmensentwicklung*, Wiesbaden: Gabler, pp. 79-95.

Görgens J (1994) *Just in time Fertigung. Konzept und modellgestützte Analyse*, Stuttgart: Schäffer-Poeschel.

Goetsch DL and Davis SB (2003) *Quality Management; Introduction to Total Quality Management for Production, Processing, and Services*, Upper Saddle River, NJ: Prentice Hall.

Griffin GC (1955) 'Maschinensteuerung – die Grundlage der Automatisierung, *Mach. shop. Mag.* 16, pp. 46-50.

Haak R (2001a) 'Innovationen im Werkzeugmaschinenbau – Ein Überblick über die Frühphase der japanischen und deutschen Fertigungsautomatisierung', *Japan Analysen und Prognosen*, 175. Japan-Zentrum der Ludwig-Maximilians-Universität. Munich.

Haak R (2001b) 'Technologie und Management in Fernost- Ein Blick auf die Frühphase der japanischen Automatisierungstechnologie', *Zeitschrift für wirtschaftlichen Fabrikbetrieb* (ZWF), 96 (2001) 5, pp. 274-80.

Haak R (2002) 'Japanische Zuliefernetzwerke in der Globalisierung', *Zeitschrift für wirtschaftlichen Fabrikbetrieb* (ZWF), 97 (2002) 3, pp. 133-36.

Haak R (2003a) 'A new theoretical approach to internationalisation strategies: First thoughts about a metastrategy', *Innovation: management, policy & practice*, Volume 5, (1), September/October 2003, pp. 41-8.

Haak R (2003b) 'Japanisches Produktionsmanagement – Organisationales Lernen als strategischer Erfolgsfaktor', *Zeitschrift für wirtschaftlichen Fabrikbetrieb* (ZWF), 98 (2003) 7-8, pp. 67-73.

Haak R (2004a) 'Japanese Supplier Network System in Transition - Survival Strategies', in *Innovation: Management, Policy & Practice*, 6, (1), pp. 45-9.

Haak R (2004b) *Theory and Management of Collective Strategies in International Business – The Impact of Globalization on Japanese-German Business Collaboration in Asia*, Basingstoke: Palgrave.

Hanft A (1996) 'Organisationales Lernen und Macht - Über den Zusammenhang von Wissen, Lernen, Macht und Struktur', in Schreyögg G and Conrad P (Eds), *Wissensmanagement*, Berlin and New York: de Gruyter, pp. 133-62.

Hayashi S (1991) *Culture and Management in Japan*, Tokyo: University of Tokyo Press.

Hemmert M and Lützeler R (1994): Einleitung: Landeskunde und wirtschaftliche Entwicklung seit 1945, in *Die japanische Wirtschaft heute*. Miscellanea, Nr. 10, Tôkyô, DIJ, pp. 23-44.

Hirsch-Kreinsen H (1989) 'Entwicklung einer Basistechnik. NC-Steuerung von Werkzeugmaschinen in den USA und der BRD', in Düll K and Lutz B (Eds): *Technikentwicklung und Arbeitsteilung im internationalen Vergleich*, Munich: Hanser.

Hirsch-Kreinsen H (1993) *NC-Entwicklung als gesellschaftlicher Prozeß. Amerikanische und deutsche Innovationsmuster der Fertigungstechnik*. Frankfurt and New York: Campus-Verlag.

Hitachi Seki Kabushiki Kaisha: hito ni yasashii gijutsu – Chie to sôi no 55 nen – Sôritsu 55 shûnen (1991). (Hitachi Seki Co., Ldt. Menschenfreundliche Technologie – 55 Jahre Erfahrung und Kreativität, Schrift zum 55 jährigen Unternehmensbestehen). Tôkyô: Hitachi Seki.

Hoffmann J (1990) *Erfolgsbedingungen des Innovationsprozesses der numerisch gesteuerten Werkzeugmaschine in Japan*. Diplomarbeit. Berlin TU IWF.

Hyodo T (1987) 'Participatory Management and Japanese Workers Consciousness', in Bergmann J and Tokunaga S (eds) *Economic and Social Aspects of Industrial Rela-*

tions. A Comparison of the German and the Japanese Systems, Frankfurt and New York: Campus-Verlag, pp. 261-70.

Imai M (1993) *Kaizen*, Frankfurt am Main: Ullstein.

Itô T (1992) *The Japanese Economy*, Cambridge, Mass.; London: MIT Press.

Jung HF (1992) Lean-Management. Arbeitswelt und Unternehmensethik in Japan in: Lean-Management. Ideen für die Praxis. *Dokumentation einer Informations- und Diskussionsreihe* (WiSo-Führungskräfte-Akademie Nürnberg), pp. 102-30.

Jürgens U (1991) *Kaizen – die Organisation von Verbesserungsaktivitäten zwischen Industrial Engineering und Qualitätszirkelaktivitäten*, Wissenschaftszentrum Berlin, Berlin.

Jürgens U (1994) 'Lean Production', in Corsten H (ed.) *Handbuch Produktionsmanagement*, Wiesbaden: Gabler, pp. 369-79.

Jürgens U, Malsch T, and Dohse K (1989) *Moderne Zeiten in der Automobilfabrik. Strategie der Produktmodernisierung im Länder- und Konzernvergleich*, Berlin, Heidelberg and New York: Springer.

Keizai Kikakuchô (1994) *Kokumin keizai keisan nenpô (Annual report on National Accounts),*Tôkyô, Keizai Kikakuchô keizai Kenkyujo, pp. 46-7.

Kennedy P (1954) 'Automatic Controls Takes Over in Automotive Manufacturing', *Automotive Industry* 111, pp. 62-7 and pp. 138-44.

Kief HB (1991) 'Von der NC zur CNC: Die Entwicklung der numerischen Steuerungen', *Werkstatt und Betrieb* 124 (5), pp. 385-91.

Koshiro K (1994) The Employment System and Human Resource Management, in Imai K and Koyama R (Eds) *Business Enterprises in Japan – Views of leading Japanese economists,* Cambridge, Massachusetts, London: MIT Press, pp. 247-49.

Liker JK (ed.) (1997) *Becoming Lean: Inside Stories of U.S. Manufactures*, Portland, OR: Productivity Press.

Liker JK (2004) *The Toyota Way*, New York: McGraw-Hill.

Matzky U (1994) 'Das Management des kontinuierlichen Verbesserungsprozesses in der japanischen Automobilindustrie', in Ostasiatisches Seminar der Freien Universität Berlin (Eds) *Soziale und Wirtschaftliche Studien über Japan/Ostasien. Occasional Paper*, 91.

Mommertz KH (1981) *Bohren, Drehen und Fräsen. Geschichte der Werkzeugmaschinen.* Reinbek bei Hamburg.

Monden Y (1983) *Toyota Production System*, Norcross, Ga.: Industrial Engineering and Management Press.

Nakamura K (1993) *Subcontracting System and Segmented Labor Market in Japan*, Musashi University, Tokyo.

Nakamura T (1996) *Lectures on Modern Japanese Economic History 1926-1994*. Tôkyô: The University of Tokyo Press.

Nihon Kôsaku Kikai Kôgyôkai (1982) *Haha-naru kikai: 30 nen no ayumi* [Japan Machine Tool Builders Association, The Mother of Machines: Thirty Years of History], Tokyo: Nihon Kôsaku Kikai Kôgyôkai, pp. 81-3.

Nihon Noritsu Kyokai (1978) *Toyota no Genba Kanri*, Tokyo: Nihon Noritsu Kyokai.

Nonaka I (1990) 'Redundant, Overlapping Organization: A Japanese Approach to Managing the Innovation Process', *California Management Review* 32 (3), pp. 27-38.

Nonaka I and Takeuchi H (1997) *Die Organisation des Wissens. Wie japanische Unternehmen eine brachliegende Ressource nutzbar machen*, Frankfurt am Main, New York: Campus-Verlag.

Ohno T (1988) *Toyota Production System: Beyond Large-Scale Production*, Cambridge: Productivity Press.

Park S-J (1975) 'Die Wirtschaft seit 1868', in Hammitz H (ed.) *Japan*, Nuremberg, pp. 123-44.

Park S-J (ed.) (1985) *Japanisches Management in der Praxis: Flexibilität oder Kontrolle im Prozess der Internationalisierung und Mikroelektronisierung*, Berlin: Express Edition.

Parker M und Slaughter J (1988) *Choosing Sides: Union and Team Concept*, Boston: South End Press.

Pfeiffer W and Weiß E (eds) (1990) *Technologie-Management*, Göttingen: Vandenhoeck & Ruprecht.

Reingold E (1999) *Toyota: People, Ideas, and the Challenge of the New*, London: Penguin Books.

Renkel H-P (1985) *Technologietransfer-Management in Japan. Gründung, Innovation und Beratung*, Bergisch Gladbach, Cologne: Eul.

Scherm M and Bischoff PR (1994) 'Lean Management - stereotype Sichtweisen japanischer Unternehmensphänomene', in Esser M and Kobayashi K (Eds) *Kaishain. Personalmanagement in Japan. Sinn und Werte statt Systeme, Psychologie für das Personalmanagement*, Göttingen: Verl. für Angewandte Psychologie, pp. 100-07.

Schmitt WW (1998) *Management japanischer Niederlassungen. Strukturen und Strategien*, Bonn: Institut für Wissenschaftliche Publikationen.

Schröder S (1995) *Innovation in der Produktion*. Berlin: IPK Berlin.

Sebestyén OG (1994) *Management-Geheimnis Kaizen. Der japanische Weg zur Innovation*, Vienna: Wirtschaftsverlag Ueberreuter.

Shimizu T (1988) 'Japanisches Management', in Busse von Colbe W, Chmielewicz K, Gaugler E, and Laßmann G (Eds) *Betriebswirtschaftslehre in Japan und Deutschland. Unternehmensführung, Rechnungswesen und Finanzierung*, Stuttgart: Poeschel, S. 173-91.

Simon W (ed.) (1969) Produktivitätsverbesserungen mit NC-Maschinen und Computern, Munich: Hanser.

Smitka M (1991) *Competitive Ties: Subcontracting in the Japanese Automotive Industry*, New York: Columbia University Press.

Spur G (1979) *Produktionstechnik im Wandel*, Munich and Vienna: Hanser.

Spur G (1991) *Vom Wandel der industriellen Welt durch Werkzeugmaschinen*, Munich and Vienna: Hanser.

Spur G (1998a) *Technologie und Management. Zum Selbstverständnis der Technikwissenschaften*, Munich and Vienna: Hanser.

Spur G (1998b) *Fabrikbetrieb*, Munich and Vienna: Hanser.

Spur G (ed.) (1994) *Fabrikbetrieb. Handbuch der Fertigungstechnik*, Munich and Vienna: Hanser.

Spur G and Specht D (1990) *Die Numerische Steuerung – Fallstudie einer erfolgreichen Innovation aus dem Bereich des Maschinenbaus*, Berlin: Akademie der Wissenschaften zu Berlin.

Spur G and Krause F-L (1997) *Das virtuelle Produkt*, Munich and Vienna: Hanser.

Staehle W (1999) *Management*, Munich: Vahlen.

Suzuki Y (1994) *Nihon Teki Seisan Shisutemu to Kigyo*, Sapporo: Hokkaido Daigaku Tosho Shuppan Kai.

Suzuki Y (2004) 'Structure of the Japanese Production System: Elusiveness and Reality', *Asian Business & Management*, 3, pp. 201-19.

Takayama K (1997) 'Machine Tool Industry', in Ifo Institute for Economic Research and Sakura Institute of Research (ed.) *A Comparative Analysis of Japanese and German Economic Success*, Tôkyô: Sakura Institute of Research, pp. 427-40.

Taylor FW (1903) *Shop Management*, New York: Harper & Brothers.

Taylor FW (1911) *The Principles of Scientific Management*, Westport, Conn.: Greenwood Press.

Toyoda E (1987) *Fifty Years in Motion*, Tokyo: Kodansha International.

Tsuruta T (1988) 'The Rapid Growth Era', in Komiya R, Okuno M, and Suzumura K (Eds) *Industrial Policy in Japan*, Orlando, FL: Academic Press, pp. 49-87.

Vestal JE (1993) *Planning for Change. Industrial Policy and Japanese Economic Development 1945-1990*, Oxford: Oxford University Press.

Waldenberger F (1994) 'Grundzüge der Wirtschaftspolitik', in Deutsches Institut für Japanstudien (ed.) *Die japanische Wirtschaft heute*, Munich: Iudicium, pp. 23-44.

Waldenberger F (1996) 'Die Montageindustrien als Träger des japanischen Wirtschaftswunders. Die Rolle der Industriepolitik', in Schaumann W (ed.) *Gewollt oder geworden? Planung, Zufall, natürliche Entwicklung in Japan*, Munich: Iudicium, pp. 259-71.

Waldenberger F (1998) 'Wirtschaftspolitik', in Deutsches Institut für Japanstudien (ed.) *Die Wirtschaft Japans. Strukturen zwischen Kontinuität und Wandel*, Berlin: Springer, pp. 19-54.

Womack JP, Jones DT, and Ross D (1990) *The Machine that Changed the World*: New York: Rawson.

Womack JP and Jones DT (1996) *Lean Thinking: Banish Waste and Create Wealth in Your Corporation*, New York: Simon&Schuster.

Yamashiro A (1997) *Japanische Managementlehre*, *Keieigaku*, Munich: Oldenbourg.

Yui T (1999) 'Japanese Management Practices in Historical Perspective', in Dirks D, Huchet JF, and Ribault T (Eds) *Japanese Management in the Low Growth Era. Between External Shocks and Internal Evolution*, Berlin, Heidelberg and New York: Springer, pp. 13-8.

Part III: Organizational Aspects

Reorientation in Product Development for Multi-project Management: The Toyota Case

Kentaro Nobeoka

Introduction

There are two primary purposes in this case study on Toyota. First, this study examines a new organizational form for product development, the one featuring the management of multiple projects and their interdependencies. Various authors suggest that the competitive environment in many industries has been changing in recent years as product life cycles have shortened and as customers have demanded increasing levels of product variety (Stalk and Hout 1990; Wheelwright and Clark 1992; Sanchez 1995). In the new environment, the strategic usage of economies of scope has become important as a competitive factor (Markides and Williamson 1994; Garud and Kumaraswamy 1995). In order to implement the scope strategy among multiple projects, the management of inter-project interfaces is necessary, which this study calls the multi-project management. This aspect of environmental change has demanded a new organizational structure and process. However, few studies have explored specific organizational arrangements that aim at the management of concurrent multiple projects.

A second purpose is this: By describing details of organizational transformation at Toyota, we explore processes and benefits of capability-based reorientation. Toyota's change from a single-project-oriented to a multi-project-oriented management is a major reorientation in many respects. In many cases, firms have to destroy existing capabilities when they try to implement major reorientation (Miller and Friesen 1980; Nelson and Winter 1982; Tushman and Romanelli 1985). Toyota, however, was successfully able to adapt to the new strategic direction, while at the same time enhancing its existing capabilities. This perspective contrasts with a distinction between continuous and discontinuous change (Hinings and Greewood 1988; Tushman and Romanelli 1985).

Specifically, this case study focuses on the objectives, inherent processes, and outcomes brought about by changes in product development organization implemented at Toyota in 1992 and 1993. The new organization strives for multi-project management. It consists of three vehicle development centers in which multiple projects are grouped together, in contrast to either traditional single-project-oriented or function-oriented organizations. The reorganization toward multi-project management was the most comprehensive change in product development organization implemented within Toyota since it established the Shusa (heavyweight product manager) organization system around 1965.

Firms such as Toyota that had been successful for a long time had accumulated bundles of unique capabilities or competencies over time. It is important to enhance the firm's existing capabilities to maintain a sustainable competitiveness (Wernerfelt 1984; Barney 1991; Amit and Schoemaker 1993). At the same time, organizations need to change in response to changes in their environment. A long-term organizational success, however, promotes the development of routines and inertia that make reorientation difficult to implement (Nelson and Winter 1982; Hannan and Freeman 1984). In addition, successful organizations tend to ignore changes in their external environment (Kiesler and Sproull 1982; Dutton and Duncan 1987).

Although the importance of utilizing the firm's unique capabilities to respond to a new external environment was widely discussed, there has been few studies that have described such processes (Leonard-Barton 1992; Garud and Nayyar 1994). In a changing competitive environment, firms have to develop and evolve their capabilities to sustain further their competitive advantage. The value of the firm's capabilities often depend on the combination of various capabilities (Black and Boal 1994). Firms may combine existing capabilities and newly developed capabilities to achieve major strategic reorientation, which Toyota seems to have done. It is also important for firms to search for new development of capabilities before their capabilities become totally obsolete in the competitive market (Itami 1987).

Toyota had accumulated unique organizational capabilities in the management of product development for a long time. In the 1960s, Toyota began to establish a project-based management system that aimed at coordinating activities in different functional areas into a well-integrated new product. Clark and Fujimoto (1991) have described this as an organization featuring "heavyweight" product managers. Toyota's organization encourages the exchange of information across functional boundaries within the firm and manages complex system products effectively. These organizational capabilities enabled Toyota to have been more successful than most other automobile firms.

Even in the early 1990s when Toyota made the reorganization into the Center organization, Toyota performed better than most competitors in the world. The reorganization was a fundamental reorientation with respect to both product strategy and organizational processes. Toyota, however, did not destroy its existing competencies or capabilities. On the contrary, while changing organizational goals, Toyota utilized and enhanced its capabilities. This case study describes details of processes and contents of Toyota's organizational changes.

Toyota has often been considered to be a leader in adopting new organizational structures and managerial processes in the areas of manufacturing and product development. For example, the Toyota production system, symbolized by its JIT and Kanban systems, has been targeted as one of the best practices in manufacturing by many firms, not only in automobile production but also in other industries. With respect to product development organization, Toyota seems to have taken initiative again in establishing the new development organization.

The paper first discusses the competitive importance and organizational requirements of multi-project management in Section 2. Section 3 explains the old organization, a heavyweight product manager organization, at Toyota, focusing on its history and emerging problems. It then turns to a description of changes into the new organization, the Center organization, in Section 4, and of its outcomes in Section 5. The final section will discuss conclusions and implications.

Multi-project Management: Framework

Existing studies on automobile product development have found that a project-oriented approach, rather than a function-oriented approach, leads to a higher performance in terms of lead time and efficiency for individual projects (Takeuchi and Nonaka 1986; Clark and Fujimoto 1991). Clark and Fujimoto (1991), for example, have found that in order to shorten lead time, to reduce engineering hours, and achieve excellent quality, product development projects need to utilize project-oriented management, led by heavyweight product managers. These managers, using their autonomous power throughout the entire product development activities, facilitate quick completion of a project by integrating different functions such as design engineering, manufacturing engineering, and marketing.

On the other hand, in addition to the efficient development of individual products, many studies have shown that Toyota as well as other leading Japanese automobile firms have been developing new products more frequently than U.S. or European competitors (Abegglen and Stalk 1985; Womack et al. 1990). Their capability in developing individual products efficiently through a project-oriented organization helped implement the strategy of prolific product introductions. This frequency has been considered as one of the sources of Japanese firms' competitive advantage in world markets (Fujimoto and Sheriff 1989, Nobeoka and Cusumano 1996).

In recent years, however, Japanese manufacturers including Toyota have been facing profitability problems that are related at least in part to the high costs of developing and manufacturing so many new products or product variations. Therefore, Japanese firms are attempting to develop new products more efficiently while maintaining both a high frequency of new product introductions and high design quality in individual projects. A project management system that assigns too much autonomy to each project may concentrate too heavily on developing multiple new products through relatively autonomous projects. This system tends to result in the development of many proprietary components for each project, and may require excessive financial and engineering resources.

In order to achieve economies of scale and scope in product development as well as in manufacturing, it is common for firms to leverage their financial and engineering resource investments by reusing existing technologies and designs in multiple projects (Nobeoka and Cusumano 1995; Garud and Kumaraswamy 1995). Firms also have to consider how to share many components among multiple projects without sacrificing an individual product's design quality and distinctiveness. A key challenge facing managers in terms of product development is how to share technology across multiple product lines and across multiple generations of products without overly compromising design quality and competitiveness.

In order to achieve this, product development organizations need to coordinate inter-project interfaces and interdependencies (Nobeoka and Cusumano 1995). Most product-management research that has focused on the management of single projects is not helpful for managers and researchers attempting to understand the complexity of coordinating multiple projects. It may seem that a traditional function-oriented, rather than project-oriented, organization may be more appropriate to manage inter-project interdependencies. Functional managers could oversee inter-project coordination at least within their functions. For example, firms could decrease autonomy of individual project managers and shift power back to functional managers to pursue scope strategy such as component sharing between multiple projects.

However, this type of structure is weak at cross-functional integration. Functional organizations also lack a mechanism to ensure that individual products retain distinctive features and a high degree of product integrity. A product development project is a system consisting of closely coupled multiple engineering functions (Rosenberg 1982; Henderson and Clark 1990), and an automobile is a typical example of complicated system product. Firms have to manage multiple projects, while recognizing the importance of "product integrity" in each project. Therefore, effective multi-project organizations may need a product development organization that achieves both cross-functional coordination and inter-project coordination.

One of the central issues most of the past studies have examined is the distinction between project-oriented versus function-oriented organizations (Davis and Lawrence 1977; Tushman 1978; Katz and Allen 1985; Clark and Fujimoto 1991). These studies have argued that product development organizations require two different coordination mechanisms to achieve two major goals. First, in order to increase the quality and quantity of inputs of technical knowledge, a high degree of coordination among technical specialties is needed. Second, in order to integrate all technical knowledge toward well-defined products, a high degree of coordination within a project is required. These two aspects of coordination requirements have primarily been discussed with respect to the balance between project and function orientations in the new product development organization.

These studies, however, have not paid much attention to the management of the inter-project interfaces except for resource-sharing efforts within each function. A primary issue regarding multi-project management organizations is the simultaneous achievement of cross-functional coordination and inter-project coordination through the way the firm organizes and controls multiple projects. Inter-project interdependencies must be coordinated within the context of a specific project as an integrated system. Cross-functional integrity in each project must be maintained. To share components while retaining the distinctiveness of individual products, firms also need organizational structures and processes that enable system-level coordination across multiple projects (Garud and Kumaraswamy 1995). Therefore, firms that consider a new multi-project management organization should use a new framework that moves beyond the balance between project and function orientated organizations.

Following sections examine that Toyota's reorganization into product development centers may represent one way to manage multiple projects. By establishing three centers, each of which contains several vehicle development projects, Toyota has improved inter-project coordination among technically related projects. At the same time, Toyota has enhanced its existing capabilities by strengthening the authority of product managers over functional managers, and this has improved cross-functional integration. This paper focuses on how Toyota's approach has solved the apparent contradiction between these two goals.

This case study is based on seven interview visits to Toyota between 1992 and 1996. The interviewees included four general managers who were involved in the planning and implementation of this reorganization, as well as four product managers, eighteen vehicle engineers, and three cost management planners. In two of the interviews, the general managers, utilizing internal documents, explained the purposes, processes, and outcomes inherent in the reorganization. In interviews with other development personnel, we made inquiries about their own perspectives regarding the reorganization including specific influences to their own tasks and processes. These procedures played an important role in detecting any potential personal biases of the interviewees.

Traditional Shusa Organization at Toyota

In 1953, Toyota assigned the first shusa, or product manager, to a new vehicle project (Ikari 1985)[1]. When Toyota started product development for the 1955 Crown, Kenya Nakamura became the first shusa to head a project. At that time he was a member of the Engineering Management Division. The shusa organization was strengthened in February 1965 when Toyota formally established the Product Planning Division to organize and support shusas. At that time, there were already ten shusas, and each shusa had five or six staff members, which totaled about 50 members in the division. The basic organizational structure with respect to the roles of the Product Planning Division and shusas did not fundamentally change until 1992, when Toyota introduced the center organization. One of the minor changes before that time was a change in the title name for a product manager from "shusa" to "chief engineer" in 1989. In order to avoid any confusion, the rest of this paper will consistently use the new term, chief engineer, to refer to this position, rather than shusa or (heavyweight) product manager.

After having maintained the same basic structure and processes for more than two decades, in 1990, Toyota decided to evaluate its entire product and technology development organization and to change it if necessary, so that the organization would fit the competitive environment at the end of the twentieth century. Toyota

---

[1]   I referred to Ikari's book with respect to the information regarding the early period of the Shusa organization in the 1950s and 1960s.

launched an initiative, called the Future Project 21 (FP21), to study any problems in its product development organizational structure and processes. The leader of the project was Yoshiro Kinbara, an executive vice president in charge of product and technology development. A manager at Toyota explained that no specific threats triggered this project. At that time, Toyota was actually doing better than most of its competitors. People at Toyota, however, recognized that organizations sometimes needed to be reviewed and overhauled to continue to be competitive in a changing environment. This belief helped Toyota improve problem sensing capabilities, while it was still relatively successful.

Soon after the FP21 started its studies, the team identified two potential problems for the future. These problems led Toyota to conclude that it would need a major reorganization. First, there was an organizational problem. A primary point was that Toyota's product development organization had become less efficient in communication and had come to need more coordination tasks than before to manage new product development. Second, the competitive environment for the Japanese automobile industry started changing drastically around 1990, which seemed to require Toyota to change its product development strategy and organization. The following sections discuss these two problems in more detail.

Organizational Problems

Figure 1 shows Toyota's product development organization before its reorganization in 1992. There were as many as sixteen design engineering functional divisions, and each had a functional manager. There were about fifteen projects proceeding concurrently, even though Figure 1, a simplified model, depicts only nine projects. Each project had a chief engineer, who was located in the Product Planning Division under general managers.

The product development organization was actually a huge matrix organization rather than a project-based organization. Chief engineers and general managers in the Product Planning Division did not directly oversee the engineering divisions in this organization structure. However, chief engineers at Toyota were supposed to have considerable authority over the entire product development process, including different engineering stages, manufacturing, and product concept creation. According to the definition by Clark and Fujimoto (1991), chief engineers at Toyota were supposed to be typical examples of heavyweight product managers.

However, the product development organization at Toyota had become much larger than before, and chief engineers started to find it difficult to control and integrate different functional divisions when developing a new product. As the number of product development projects increased, the number of engineers also increased. At the same time, the degree of specialization in the engineering divisions had become narrower, reflecting the increasing number of different engineering divisions. As of December 1991, there were about 7000 people in the sixteen product development engineering divisions. They were working, on average, on fifteen concurrent projects. In addition, Toyota had a Research and Advanced

Development Group located at the Higashi-Fuji Technical Center. This had about 2000 additional people[2].

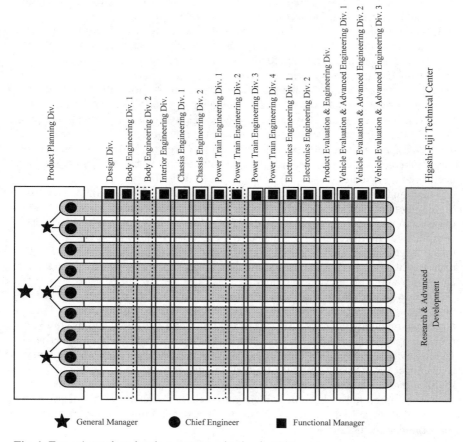

Fig. 1. Toyota's product development organization in 1991

In 1991, a chief engineer had to coordinate people in 48 departments in 12 divisions to manage new product development. This estimate comes from Toyota's internal data on the number of frequent participants in meetings a product manager held. In 1976, there were only 5000 people in the entire product development organization, as compared to 11,500 in 1991. A chief engineer had to coordinate

---

2   7000 people in the sixteen engineering divisions and 2000 people in the RAD group added up to 9000. There were, in total, about 11,500 people working on product development. The rest of the people were engaged in supporting activities such as patent management, certification process management, CAD system development, and prototype development.

only 23 departments in six divisions. At that time, a chief engineer generally needed to talk with only six division managers to integrate all the design engineering functions. This change indicated that, during the fifteen years, coordination tasks had become much more complicated for chief engineers.

In addition to this added complexity, there was another problem that made it difficult for some chief engineers to manage a new product development project. Some relatively junior chief engineers started to complain that they did not always have enough authority over senior functional managers. Originally, only a limited number of "charismatic" senior managers tended to rise to the position of chief engineer. Toyota people often considered them as "gods" within their projects. However, in recent years, Toyota has assigned relatively junior people to the position of chief engineer. There are two reasons for this change. First, the number of chief engineers required to cover all new vehicle projects had increased. Second, Toyota recognized that people needed particular talents to be excellent chief engineers, and their seniority was not as important as their ability.

Functional managers also found it difficult to spend sufficient time on managing engineering details of all the vehicle projects, because most managers had to oversee about fifteen different projects[3]. They did not have enough time to oversee complicated interfaces and interdependencies between these projects either. Due to the large number of functional divisions and vehicle projects, each chief engineer was able to arrange for regular meetings with all the relevant functional managers only about once every two months.

There was a problem also at the engineering level. Because of their narrow specialization, engineers did not have a "system view" of the entire product. For example, some engineers only knew about the inner body of doors and did not know much about the outer body because interior engineering and body engineering divisions were separate. This kind of excessively narrow specialization had a negative impact on the development of a well-integrated product. In addition, Toyota realized that the narrow specialization caused another problem for engineers when they were promoted to become a manager in charge of a larger engineering task such as the entire body. It was difficult to train general engineering managers in this organizational structure.

Engineers also found it difficult to have a strong sense of commitment to a specific vehicle development. Because of the narrow specialization and the large number of projects, each engineer frequently had to transfer between unrelated vehicle projects. This may sound useful to transfer technical know-how between different projects. In reality, however, despite the frequent transfer of engineers, Toyota found that it could not transfer system knowledge in this way. Nor was this structure particularly appropriate for inter-project knowledge transfer.

Toyota's rapid growth in size partially caused these organizational problems. One way to increase the chief engineer's authority and to eliminate problems

---

[3]   There were a few exceptions. For example, as of 1991, there were already two separate body engineering divisions, each of which was responsible for front-wheel-drive and rear-wheel-drive vehicles, respectively. Therefore, each functional manager was in charge of about a half of the entire vehicle projects.

caused by narrow specialization is to create a pure project team organization, such as the one Chrysler adopted for its LH and Neon projects[4]. In this organization, almost all engineers exclusively work for a single project for its entire duration. However, Toyota did not consider the project team organization efficient. This type of organization can work well for firms with a small number of projects and little technical interdependency between multiple products concurrently being developed. Because Toyota has many projects and a limited number of engineers, it cannot assign engineers to a specific project for the entire duration of the project. The peak period for design engineering work for engineers in a specific project lasts only about one and half or two years out of a four-year project. Therefore, when a project task is outside of the peak, engineers should be transferred to other projects to be utilized efficiently. In addition, a change in the competitive environment discussed in the next section also made the project team approach inappropriate. In the new environment, effective inter-project technology sharing has become more important.

Even the organization at Toyota prior to 1991 had problems with respect to inter-project coordination. One of the policies of Toyota's chief engineer organization was to encourage the autonomy of each chief engineer with respect to his own vehicle project. General managers in the Product Planning Division above chief engineers, therefore, did not supervise chief engineers in the details of individual projects. In addition, the number of vehicle projects was too large for managers to deal effectively with multi-project management issues such as resource allocation, technology transfer, and component sharing across all projects.

In summary, Toyota's product development organization had five problems. These caused difficulties in both project integration and inter-project coordination:

1. There were too many functional engineering divisions with too narrow specialization of engineers.
2. There were too many vehicle projects for each functional manager to manage the engineering details of each project as well as inter-project coordination.
3. It had become much more complicated and difficult for chief engineers to oversee all the engineering functions.
4. The chief engineer organization was not appropriate for inter-project coordination.

Change in the Competitive Environment

The competitive environment surrounding Japanese automobile firms started changing around 1991. There were two interrelated issues. First, rapid growth in domestic production levels at the Japanese firms virtually ended. The aggressive product strategy of Japanese automobile firms in the 1980's, such as frequent new

---

[4]   Many business magazines and industry journals have described the organizational change into the project team at Chrysler. Scott (1994) has summarized these articles and his own interviews at Chrysler.

product introductions and replacements, had been partially based on their assumption of continuous rapid growth. The new environment seemed to require some changes in this strategy, as well as in company organizations. Second, the importance of cost reduction became even more critical for international competition than before. In addition to the appreciation of the yen, Japanese advantages in development and manufacturing productivity have been diminishing. Both factors have had a strong negative impact on the cost advantages they had been enjoying.

Because of these changes, the traditional chief engineer system, which primarily focused on building the best individual products once at a time, needed to be fundamentally changed. Chief engineers always thought about the success of only their own projects. A general manager who used to be a chief engineer said, "Each product manager wanted to increase sales of his own project even by developing many new proprietary components and by expanding the target customer segments of his project into other product lines within Toyota." He explained that, during the period when Toyota's production volume was growing rapidly, these characteristics of Toyota's chief engineer system worked well for the Company. Because total production was growing rapidly, cannibalization of individual product lines was not a major problem. The market in each product segment also expanded, and this growth made it possible for each project to expand its target market.

In addition, Toyota was able to sell more of most new products than it had expected. Therefore, high development and production costs caused by many new proprietary components was not much of a problem either. A manager in charge of cost management admitted that, "Prior to 1991, few new products met an original target cost when it was introduced to the market. However, the sales volume for each new product was usually larger than its original plan. The large sales volume lowered the actual production cost compared to its original plan through scale economies. In the end, a new product usually reached the production cost that had been originally planned, when the entire production during its life cycle was fully considered." Because of a faster depreciation of manufacturing equipment than original plans, production costs also appeared to be lower than expected. Given this common pattern, a chief engineer primarily tried to develop a new product that would sell well, rather than a product that would meet a conservative cost target.

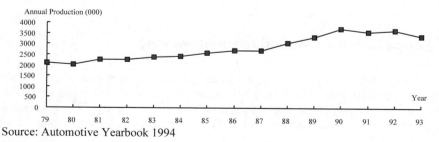

Source: Automotive Yearbook 1994

Fig. 2. Production units at Toyota

However, starting in 1990, Toyota's production volume stopped growing, as shown in Figure 2. Profit from each new product also started decreasing. Under these circumstances, Toyota needed a new product development strategy and organization, particularly with respect to cost management. One particular aspect of the chief engineer system was considered inappropriate in this new environment: The management of each individual project was too independent. Toyota concluded that multiple related projects needed more coordination.

First, in the stagnant market, new products should be more carefully positioned to each other so that any cannibalization would not occur. Within a limited total sales volume, the expansion strategy of one product line would easily cannibalize some portion of sales of neighboring products within Toyota. Second, in order to reduce production cost, Toyota needed to increase in commonalty of components and technologies among multiple new products. Sales increase, which used to help cover shortage in cost reduction efforts, could not be expected anymore. Under the Toyota's chief engineer system, there was a tendency that each project overly developed its proprietary components. There are many symptoms of the old product strategy and organization at Toyota. For example, there are now three distinctive platforms for three products that are similar in size and technology: the Corona/Carina, the Celica/Carina ED, and the Camry. A chief engineer for each project wanted to develop an ideal platform for each product.

In view of these organizational problems and changes in the competitive environmental, Toyota decided to change its product development organization extensively. A new organization needed both to strengthen the integration mechanisms for engineers in different functions so that they could create a well-integrated new product, as well as to facilitate coordination among different projects so that technologies and components can be effectively transferred and shared. These two objectives are in a sense contradictory, because Toyota needed both to strengthen its project orientation as opposed to function orientation, and to enhance inter-project coordination. For example, a project-oriented team approach might be appropriate for a strong project orientation, but might be inappropriate for inter-project coordination. On the other hand, strengthening the functional orientation to enhance the efficient usage of specific components throughout multiple vehicle projects would be totally unsuitable to enhance an individual product's level of integration or coherence. Therefore, Toyota decided to consider a new organization beyond the mere balance between these two alternatives. Thus, Toyota reached a conclusion that it would fundamentally change its organizational structure for product development.

Establishment of Development Centers

Toyota made two major changes in its product development organization. These changes did not reduce the total number of people working on product development at Toyota. At the end of 1991 before the reorganization, there were about 11,500 people in product development, and the number rose to about 12000 in

1993. Rather the changes specifically targeted the problems discussed in the previous section.

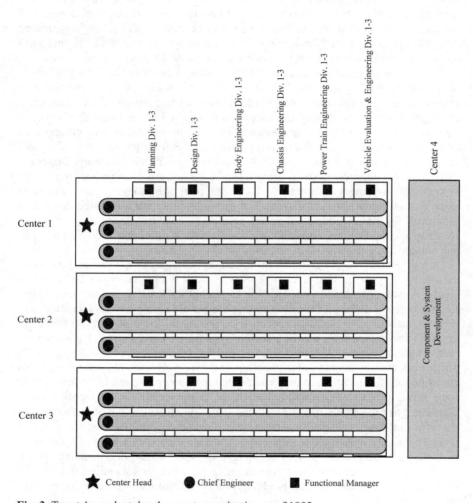

Fig. 3. Toyota's product development organization as of 1992

First, in 1992, Toyota divided all of its new product development projects into three centers as shown in Figure 3. The center grouping focuses on the similarity in platform design. Center 1 is responsible for rear-wheel-drive platforms and vehicles, Center 2 for front-wheel-drive platforms and vehicles, and Center 3 for utility vehicle/van platforms and vehicles. Each center has between 1500 and 1900 people, and works on about five different new vehicle projects simultaneously. Toyota had considered other grouping schemes, such as by product segment (luxury vs. economical vs. sporty cars, or small vs. medium vs. large cars). Toyota chose platform design similarity because this would lead to the highest level of inter-project design interdependencies within a center. In addition, because new platform development requires the most resources, sharing a platform design among multiple product lines would save the most in engineering investment and reduce production costs most effectively.

Second, in 1993, Toyota created Center 4 to develop components and systems for all vehicle projects. It reorganized the Research and Advanced Development Group (the RAD Group), and assigned most people from this to Center 4. While the RAD Group used to work on research and advanced development rather independently, Center 4 closely supports vehicle development by providing specific projects with components and systems. In addition to engineers in the RAD group, Center 4 added engineers working on some components such as electronics and new engines that did not need much daily coordination with a vehicle project.

As discussed earlier, the center organization changes were supposed to improve both project integration and inter-project coordination. This section specifically describes how some key aspects of the reorganization related to improvement in these two areas. Important features of this reorganization include:

1. Reduction of the number of functional engineering divisions.
2. Reduction of the number of projects for each functional manager.
3. Changes in the roles of the center head for multiple vehicle projects.
4. Establishment of planning divisions in each center.
5. Adoption of a hierarchical organization for chief engineers in related projects.
6. The roles of Center 4.

Reduction of Functional Engineering Divisions

In order to decrease coordination tasks required for a well-integrated vehicle project, Toyota reduced the number of functional divisions for design engineering. The complexity raised by the large number of functional divisions made it difficult for chief engineers to manage vehicle projects. While the old organization had sixteen different functional divisions, each new center has only six engineering divisions.

This simplification into the center organization prompted two other changes. First, specialization in each functional engineering division widened. For example, Toyota used to have two separate divisions for designing bodies and interior/exterior equipment: the Body Engineering Division and the Interior Engineering Division. In the new organization, the Interior Engineering Division merged with the Body Engineering Division. Another example is the merger of two different chassis engineering divisions, each of which had been separately responsible for suspension systems and brakes. Each design engineering division now has wider design responsibilities. An important point is that this did not enlarge the size of each functional division, because each functional division is now responsible for only a limited number of projects within the center.

Second, Toyota also reduced the number of functional divisions to be managed in a specific vehicle project through the usage of Center 4, the component and system development center. In order to simplify the work of the first three centers, Toyota separated development of some components and systems that can be managed outside specific vehicle projects. Toyota considered three factors to decide whether particular engineering functions should be in a vehicle project or the component center. First, managers decided that components that need to be extensively tailored to each vehicle project should be managed within a project. Second, components that have to be carefully coordinated with other parts of the vehicle design should also be developed within the project. On the other hand, some components with modular characteristics can be developed separately from specific vehicle projects and still be inserted into a product design relatively easily. These may be developed in Center 4. These types of components and systems tend to be shared by multiple vehicle projects, and it is not efficient to develop them in a specific project. Third, component development that needs much new technical knowledge should be developed in Center 4. Such development usually requires a group of technical specialists working together. These types of components also sometimes need a long time to develop and do not fit the time frame of specific vehicle projects.

Following these guidelines, Toyota allocated the development of some components or systems to Center 4. For example, the upper-body design directly visible to the customer has to be differentiated in each product. It should also be extensively interdependent with other parts of the automobile design, such as the chassis and interior. Therefore, the upper-body design should be managed within the project, and Toyota maintained this function within Centers 1-3. On the other hand, components like batteries, audio systems, and air conditioners do not usually need to be tailored to each different vehicle project. Therefore, Toyota moved the Electronics Engineering Divisions that developed these electronic components to Center 4.

The example of the Electronics Engineering Divisions is actually more complicated and indicates the extensive thought and analysis that Toyota put into implementing this reorganization. Toyota carefully examined characteristics and interdependencies of each component development, so that Centers 1-3 can be simplified and yet contain all relevant components that need extensive coordination within each vehicle project. For example, among the electronics components, the wire harness usually needs to be tailored to each vehicle project and has considerable interdependency with the body structure. Therefore, Toyota merged this engineering function into the Body Engineering Divisions and kept wire harness development within Centers 1-3.

Another example of eliminating activities from the vehicle project centers is the development of totally new engines, which is now located in Center 4. There are many engineering tasks involved in new engine development that are not related to integration tasks within a particular vehicle project. In addition, the time frame of new engine development does not fit that of specific vehicle projects. New engines usually need about six to eight years to develop, which is longer than the 4-year lead time of the average new vehicle project.

In this way, only component engineering that needs extensive project integration remains in the vehicle project centers. In the old organization, part of the product development organization was responsible for both vehicle projects and most component development. This mixture made the old organization complicated and difficult to manage.

In summary, by widening the engineering specialization within each division and by transferring some component development into Center 4, Toyota limited the number of functional divisions in Centers 1-3. In addition, because Toyota divided each function into three centers, the wider specialization did not require larger functional divisions.

Reduction of the Number of Projects for Each Functional Manager

Each functional manager is responsible for a smaller number of projects in the new center organization. For example, managers in Center 1 can focus only on vehicle projects with rear-wheel-drive platforms. Because, in some functional areas, there used to be too many projects for functional managers to oversee, it was difficult for them to pay careful attention to all the projects. For example, the functional manager for interior engineering was responsible for all different vehicle projects, which usually added up to about 15 concurrent projects. In the center organization, all functional managers are responsible for only about five product lines that are all technologically related to each other. Each functional manager now can spend sufficient time on the coordination with each chief engineer. In addition, this reduction of the management scope for each functional manager should result in more effective multi-project management in such areas as resource allocation and technology sharing. Each functional division can also focus on fewer types of vehicle technologies. This focus may lead to more efficient development and accumulation of technical knowledge as a division.

Roles of the Center Head for Multiple Vehicle Projects

Each head of Centers 1-3 officially supervises the entire product development operations, including both chief engineers and design engineering functions within the center. Equivalents to the center heads in the old organization were three deputy general managers above chief engineers in the Product Planning Division. Each of the deputy general managers was in charge of small cars, large cars, and trucks/vans. They reported to the general manager of the Product Planning Division. However, they officially managed only chief engineers, not functional managers and engineers as seen earlier in Figure 1. These general managers above the chief engineers, therefore, were not supposed to manage design engineering in detail. In addition, there were also general managers above the functional managers, and it was not often clear which general managers - those above chief engineers or those above functional managers - had more authority. In the center organization, each of the three center heads manages engineering details for multiple vehicle projects within the center. From these perspectives, while the old organization was officially a matrix organization both at the chief engineer level and at the general manager level, the new one is organized primarily around projects.

Using their positions, the center heads are supposed to play two important roles that have to be deliberately balanced. First, a center head helps each chief engineer integrate different functions. One of the key elements of the Toyota chief engineer system has been the strong leadership of a chief engineer. However, as discussed earlier, chief engineers recently found some difficulties in coordinating all the functional managers. In the center organization, chief engineers can use the center head's support to manage different functions. Second, each center head is responsible for the coordination of different vehicle projects within the center. A center head can now effectively implement this because he manages all the operations in the center. The separate planning division in each center, discussed next, also helps the center head coordinate projects.

Establishment of Planning Divisions in Each Center

Each center has a planning division to support the management of each center. The Planning Division consists of staff members and three departments: the administration department, the cost planning department, and the product audit department. There are about 170 to 200 people in each planning division of the three centers. The administration department is responsible for personnel management, resource allocation, and the long-term product portfolio planning within each center. It also conducts an advanced concept study for individual projects, before these projects become a formal project and a chief engineer is assigned.

The equivalent of the Planning Divisions in the old organization was the Product Planning Division. One of the major structural differences is that chief engineers used to be located within the Product Planning Division. Most members in the Product Planning Division directly worked for individual chief engineers. For example, most cost management people in the division used to be divided by vehicle project and primarily reported to individual chief engineers. On the other hand, in the new organization, cost management people are more independent of chief engineers and report to the planning division manager and the center head in each center, although they continue to work closely with chief engineers. This reflects one of the central concerns at Toyota, which is that each center needs to reduce development and product costs by efficiently leveraging resources and components across multiple projects.

Each center also does long-term product portfolio planning. The management scope used to be so large in the old organization that the project portfolio planning and resource allocation for each project were too complicated to be effectively managed. Now the Planning Division in each center can consider technology sharing and resource allocation among multiple projects in the present and the future more carefully than before, by focusing on a limited number of closely related projects. This type of center-oriented management support may be critically important to the effective operation of the center organization.

Hierarchical Organization of Chief Engineers

Another feature in the center organization is the hierarchical chief engineer structure for managing product families as shown in Figure 4. This structure also helps strengthen the multi-project perspective of the center organization. For example, there used to be two separate chief engineers for the LS 300 and the Supra projects. Now, there continue to be two chief engineers, but one of the two supervises both the LS 300 and the Supra projects, and primarily manages the LS 300 project. The other chief engineer manages the Supra project and reports to the chief engineer of the LS 300. Toyota also made the same kind of change for another pair of projects: the Tercel and the Starlet. Although this type of structure is not adopted for all projects, Toyota appears to be moving the organization in this direction.

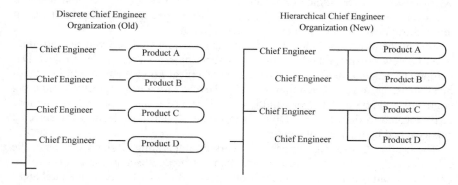

Fig. 4. Hierarchical chief engineer organization for multi-project management

Each of these pairs of projects share almost identical platform and drive train designs, even though these two projects target completely different customer segments and have separate product concepts. For example, the LS 300 is a luxury personal car and the Supra is a sports car. Therefore, it is important to manage the two projects separately, so that each project develops a product that fits with its own customer needs. A planning division manger at Toyota says that it is difficult for a single chief engineer to develop two products with widely separate concepts and to give the same level of commitment to each of these. However, at the same time, because these two projects should share the same platform design, they need extensive coordination. Therefore, the projects have to achieve differentiation in product characteristics and integration in product development at the same time.

The hierarchical chief engineer organization is one way to pursue these two goals simultaneously.

Roles of Center 4

As explained earlier, Toyota based Center 4 primarily on the RAD group in the old organization. The basic structure of the organization and technical areas have not significantly changed. Technical areas of both the old and new organizations include vehicle (body and chassis), engine and drive train, electronics, and materials. The most important aspect of the change was that, while Center 4 focuses on developing components and systems for vehicle projects, the RAD Group was relatively research-oriented. The relationship between the RAD group and vehicle projects was that between upstream and downstream organizations. Center 4 has virtually become a part of the vehicle development organization, and is responsible for system components that could be better developed outside specific vehicle projects.

The RAD group had about 2000 people, while there are about 4000 in Center 4. As discussed earlier, some components or systems like electronics and new engines can be developed more appropriately outside specific vehicle projects. Centers 1-3 can now focus on achieving project integrity.

One of the most significant improvements regarding Center 4 was the introduction of a new organizational mechanism, called the cross-area system project. Development of some new systems need new technical knowledge in multiple technical areas. To develop such new systems, Toyota forms project teams containing engineers and researchers from multiple technical areas. These projects are temporarily located in the Planning Division in Center 4, and their leaders are selected and assigned by the head of Center 4.

The head of Center 4 is supposed to work on integrating all the divisions of the different technical areas more actively than his predecessor in the old organization. In the old organization, the division managers of the different technical areas were relatively independent. Because in the RAD group, technical inventions within each technical area were important, top management gave each division relatively strong autonomy with respect to research agenda and time frame. The introduction of the cross-area system projects represents the new orientation of Center 4, as well as the important role of its center head.

In summary, the product development group was simplified in two ways by the new center organization. First, it excluded some areas of component and system development in order to focus on the integration of product development activities, rather than component and system development. This change reduced the number of people in the core product development organization from about 7000 to 5000. Second, the entire organization was divided into three centers. As a result, each center has only about 1500 to 1900 people. It is a drastic change with respect to management scope, if compared with the original size of 7000 people.

Outcomes of the Organizational Changes

Because of the introduction of the center organization, Toyota achieved significant improvements in several areas. In particular, it simultaneously improved both cross-functional project integration and multi-project integration. This section discusses some important outcomes of the reorganization, focusing on these two perspectives, as well as some potential problems of the reorganization.

Project Integration Through Streamlined Structure

Figure 5 summarizes the outcomes of the reorganization with respect to the reduction of coordination tasks for chief engineers to manage different functional groups. As discussed earlier, before the reorganization, each chief manager had to coordinate, on average, 48 departments in 12 divisions to manage new vehicle development. Primarily because of the reduction in the number of functional divisions and departments, in the new organization a chief engineer has to manage only 15 departments in 6 divisions. Toyota also compared these numbers with those back in 1976, when there were only about 5000 people working for product development. At that time, each chief engineer had to communicate with 23 departments in 6 divisions. The change into the new organization reduced the communication complexity down to the level in 1976, when the Shusa organization worked more effectively than the time just before the reorganization.

Number of Divisions/Departments

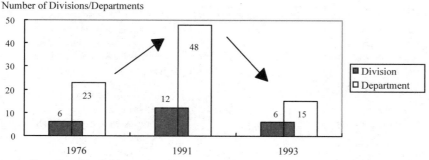

Source: Based on "Activities and Achievements of FP21", Toyota internal document, 1994

Fig. 5. Changes in the number of divisions to be coordinated

Each functional manager and engineer now covers a wider portion of the automobile design. Because of this, cross-functional coordination tasks had naturally decreased among chief engineers as well as engineers, which directly affected the effectiveness and the efficiency of project integration. In addition, it has become relatively easy for functional managers and engineers to see the entire picture of a vehicle project. This change also solved some other problems in the old organization. Engineers can train on the job for the time when they will be promoted to a manager, because they can now obtain knowledge of a broad scope of component engineering. Engineers can now also obtain more sense of achievement regarding specific vehicle projects. This seems to have positively affected the level of engineers' commitment and job satisfaction.

Because each functional manager is responsible for fewer vehicle projects than before, it has become easier for a chief engineer to communicate frequently with functional managers. There used to be regular meetings among a chief engineer and the entire functional managers only about once every two months. Now, chief engineers and the six functional managers, as well as the center head, have weekly meetings, called the Center Management Meeting.

The introduction of the center heads also greatly contributed to the improvement of project integrity. Chief engineers both in the old and the new organizations have not assumed formal authority over functional managers. On the other hand, center heads oversee all product development projects, including the work of functional managers. The center heads can work directly on integrating different engineering functions. Using this position, they also support chief engineers to coordinate different functions. For example, when a chief engineer encounters difficulty in negotiating with a strong functional manager, he can discuss the issue in the Center Management Meeting, and the center head may support the chief engineer. Decisions made as a center can be smoothly and quickly implemented. In this sense, through the combination with the center head, chief engineers regained the strong authority that the original Shusas used to enjoy.

Table 1. Outcomes of the reorganization to the center

	Performance change	Major factors
Development cost (average project)	-30%	• Reduction of prototypes • Increase in component sharing
Number of prototypes (average project)	-40%	• Intensive coordination between different engineering and testing functions • Increase in CAE usage
Lead time (average project)	Shortened by a few months	• Reduction of prototypes • More extensive simultaneous engineering

Source: Based on "Activities and Achievements of FP21", Toyota internal document, 1994

Table 1 summarizes achievements on some important measurements. The new organization helped reduce development costs on the average project by 30 percent. The number of testing prototypes used in an average product development project decreased by 40 percent. This reduction of prototypes was a primary source for the reduction in development costs. The reduction of the number of testing prototypes has reflected the effective communication in the organization. In order to test many different items in one prototype, an intensive coordination among different design divisions and testing divisions is needed. For example, without appropriate communication, it is difficult to install the testing items for interior equipment and chassis into a single prototype. Because of the simplification of the line of communication and project coordination, Toyota has also increased the extent of simultaneous engineering, which has helped cut project lead time by a few months. Stronger project management supported by the center head may also have contributed to quicker decision making and development processes.

Multi-Project Integration Within a Center

The new organization strengthened the multi-project management perspective with the strong leadership of the center head and strong support from the center-oriented planning division. Because of the large number of vehicle projects, it was difficult to manage Toyota's entire project portfolio and inter-project coordination. Now, the weekly Center Management Meetings discuss the details of multi-project management. In addition, each center now has its own building so that all members within a center can be co-located. Co-location at Toyota emphasizes the geographical integration of the center members rather than just the members of an individual project, which is becoming common in the U.S.

In order to achieve the integration within a center, to begin with, each center defines its own vision and theme for product development. Sharing a basic vision that focuses on projects within the center helps members effectively coordinate engineering activities. The current development themes of each center are:

- Center 1: Development of luxury and high-quality vehicles
- Center 2: Development of innovative low-cost vehicles
- Center 3: Development of recreational vehicles that create new markets.

One example of the changes can be seen in cost management activities. Targets for development and product costs used to be set and managed mostly at the individual project level, led by individual chief engineers. Most cost management staff members used to work directly for chief engineers and their orientation was the cost performance of individual projects. In the new organization, in addition to the cost management at the project level, each center manages the cost target of all the projects within the center, led by the center head. Cost management staff members are now located in the Planning Division in each center and report to the planning division manager and the center head. Through this new organizational setting, cost management is supposed to add the multi-project management perspective. Specifically, each center has been working on more component-sharing among multiple vehicle projects, which is one of the most effective ways to reduce product costs. In order to achieve this, project-level management alone was not sufficient.

With respect to component sharing, one critical issue each center is now working on is the reduction of the number of basic platforms utilized among multiple products. For example, in Center 2, currently there are five distinctive platforms: 1. Celica / Carina ED / Caren, 2. Camry / Vista, 3. Corona/ Carina, 4. Corolla / Sprinter, and 5. Tercel / Corsa / Starlet. The planning division manager in Center 2 believes that five different platforms for these compact-size front-wheel-drive models are too many. Center 2 is planning to significantly reduce the number of the platform designs within several years.

People at Toyota tended to think that, because each of the five platform designs had been produced at the level of more than 200,000 units/year, a distinctive design could be justified by economies of scale. This is true with a distinctive die that is needed for different platform designs, because at that level of production, each die is fully used for its life cycle. However, there are many other areas that could benefit from the reduction of platform designs. Some areas that could expect much cost reduction from platform sharing include prototype production, testing, designing, and component handling. The planning division manager concludes that one of the major challenges for the center in general is to develop multiple products that use as many common components as possible, and still enable each product to provide customers with as much differentiated functions and values as possible. The focus of each Planning Division on the limited number of technically related projects within the firm has facilitated more careful project portfolio management within the center.

With respect to component systems smaller than the platform design, Toyota has started a component sharing program that monitors component and system usage in individual projects. Toyota chose 290 different component systems for this program, which ranges from a system assembly like an instrumental panel to a small component like a door regulator. A center makes a list of a limited number of component variations for each component group. A new product development project is then supposed to choose a component from the list. When a vehicle project wants to invest in the development of a new component design, it must come up with a new design with a better cost-value ratio than any of the existing components on the list. When a new component design meets the requirement, it replaces one of the components on the list, so that the total number of variations will not increase within the firm. Because of the center organization, management of this program has become practical and effective. In the old organization, because of the large management scope, this type of sharing was not managed properly.

One of the other signs of the integration of center members is a sense of inter-center competition that center heads and members have begun to possess. The three centers have been competing with each other regarding the percentage of cost reduction compared to past projects that had been developed before the reorganization. This competition has a positive impact on organizational learning. The center head encourages engineers to learn any superior processes from other centers. The competition may have a negative impact on organizational learning in some other firms, if each center tries not to transfer its good processes. At Toyota, this does not seem to be the case. Each center has its own engineering functional divisions such as body engineering and chassis engineering. Three engineering divisions for the same type of technologies and components are competing. For example, when one body engineering division comes up with an effective idea for cost reduction, the other two divisions are strongly encouraged to learn the idea, so that they will not stay behind other centers.

Other activities have started within each center to strengthen the center integration, which directly or indirectly helps multi-project coordination within the center. For example, Center 1 held a design and engineering competition in which groups of young designers and engineers compete with innovative cars for a motor show. Center 3 has started a program called the "Let's Challenge Program," which encourages center members to submit any interesting and useful ideas for new models. Each center also publishes its own newsletter. These activities and programs enhance the intra-center integration.

Potential Problems of the Center Organization

The planning division manager of Center 2 raised two challenging problems. First, it is difficult to balance the chief engineer's autonomy and the center integration. Extensive guidelines given to each chief engineer from the center management may cause a negative impact on the motivation and commitment of chief engineers. Toyota doesn't want chief engineers to think that they should work only on what the center decides. This planning manager believes that the center management provides basic and critical guidelines, in which chief engineers maintain authority. There are six people who play a critical role in the center management: three center heads and three planning division managers. Except for the planning division manager of Center 3, who used to be an engine design manager, five of the six used to be chief engineers. This personnel assignment may help avoid any unnecessary misunderstanding between the center management and chief engineers.

Second, there may be some problems regarding inter-center coordination. The center grouping based on technology and design relatedness aimed at minimizing the inter-center coordination requirements. For example, the old GM organization, which was based on divisions such as Chevrolet and Buick, created difficulties because similar designs and technologies were utilized by products in different divisions and resulted in excessively similar products. Compared to that kind of grouping, the center organization at Toyota is more appropriate for a product development organization that tries to share components and produce distinctive products. However, there are still some problems. The planning manager in Center 2 mentioned one example. When sports-utility vehicles became a hot segment, all three centers proposed the development of such models. Because Toyota doesn't need to develop three sports-utility vehicles in parallel, inter-center coordination was required. Although inter-center coordination could become the next problem for Toyota, benefits from the inter-project integration within the center seem to surpass the potential problems at this point of time.

Discussion and Conclusion

This case study has discussed a new organizational structure that pursues multi-project management by analyzing changes in product development organization at Toyota. This paper confirms that while enhancing and utilizing its existing capabilities, Toyota has shifted beyond a traditional product development organization that is oriented towards either single project or engineering functions.

Figure 6 describes this evolution pattern with respect to the organizational orientation in product development. Toyota shifted from a function-oriented to project-oriented matrix structure in the 1960s (Ikari 1985). It maintained its heavyweight product management system until early 1990s. During 1992 and 1993, Toyota shifted from project-oriented management to multi-project management. In order to strengthen inter-project coordination, which was becoming important in the new competitive environment, Toyota could have weakened authority of individual product managers relative to functional managers who could have effectively managed inter-project coordination at least within their functions. However, one of the most important aspects of effective multi-project management is to improve both cross-functional and inter-project integration simultaneously. Therefore, Toyota decided to strengthen both integration mechanisms at the same time.

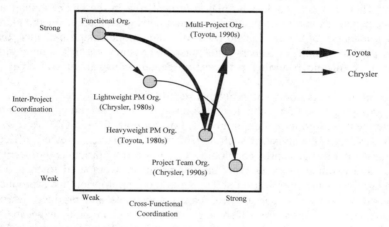

Fig. 6. Evolution pattern to multi-project management

While developing inter-project coordination mechanisms and processes, Toyota also enhanced its capabilities that had been accumulated in the heavyweight product management organization. The center organization at Toyota significantly improved inter-project coordination among technically related projects. At the same time, Toyota has improved cross-functional integration by strengthening the authority of product managers, who are supported by center heads, over functional managers. Cross-functional integration tasks were also streamlined so that additional tasks for inter-project integration can be carried out more effectively.

Effective multi-project organization cannot be established without capabilities in strong project management that is to coordinate functional boundaries. Heavy-weight product management organization at Toyota played a role as an organizational platform (Ciborra 1996) that enabled the changes into multi-project organization. The new competitive environment required an additional coordination mechanism that specifically targets inter-project coordination. Because of Toyota's capabilities regarding cross-functional integration that had been enhanced and nurtured for a long time, the firm was able to respond to the new requirements without penalizing cross-functional integration. These capabilities were firmly embedded within Toyota as patterns of routines and informal communication lines as well as culture.

With respect to organizational evolution, Toyota's movement can be contrasted with the one at Chrysler, which is also described in Figure 6. A primary issue for Chrysler in the 1980s was a lack of cross-functional coordination and integrity. Because Chrysler wanted to strengthen cross-functional integrity, in 1989 it changed the organization from one with lightweight product manager to a project team organization by discarding barriers between engineering functions. Scott (1994) has argued that the new Chrysler organization worked effectively to optimize the development of individual products such as the LH and the Neon. Using these organizational processes, Chrysler is currently developing capabilities in cross-functional coordination. Without these capabilities, it may be difficult to employ new additional coordination requirements such as inter-project coordination. In order to implement flexible strategic reorientation, firms need to accumulate capabilities in advance that may be combined to target new strategic directions (Ciborra 1996). Major reorientations without any capability base tend to result in organizational failure (Hannan and Freeman 1984; Tushman and Romanell, 1985; Singh et. al. 1986).

This in-depth case study has also offered evidence that in order to benefit from the center organization, a structural change of simply grouping some projects together is not sufficient in itself. Other automobile firms in the world also employ some type of product grouping. However, grouping alone does not necessarily lead to effective multi-project management, and organizations at other firms do not seem to work as effectively as at Toyota[5]. Toyota made several important changes along with the introduction of the multi-project center organization. For example, first, it reduced the number of engineering functions in Centers 1, 2 and 3, and added the component and system development center (Center 4). In this way, each center is simplified enough to simultaneously manage multiple projects within the center. The management scope of center heads and planning division managers is small enough to oversee all activities within the center. Second, a powerful planning division with more than 150 people in each center also seems

---

[5]   This statement is based on interviews at Nissan, Mitsubishi, and Mazda. At these firms, one example of the differences from Toyota is that some key functions such as planning, chassis/engine engineering, and cost management are not divided into centers. In this sense, it seems that these firms have been changing organizations in the same direction as Toyota, but has reached only incomplete multi-project organization.

essential to support the center head. Third, clear goal-setting specific to each center helps integrate center activities. Fourth, each center is encouraged to compete with other centers in performance, which leads to effective learning within the firm. The center organization at Toyota works effectively because all of these supporting mechanisms have been carefully designed.

The international competitive environment facing Japanese automobile firms has been in a transitional period (Fujimoto and Takeishi 1994). Toyota has taken the initiative in adopting a new organizational form. Historically, during periods of transition, a few leading firms that achieved an early tight fit with the new competitive environment by pioneering a new organizational form were successful (Miles and Snow 1994). Toyota may have established an organizational structure and process for product development that will set new standards for large international automobile manufacturers. This change has come at an appropriate time. Because many other competitors were adopting a heavyweight product manager system, in which Toyota had enjoyed leadership in the 1980's, Toyota's advantage over its competitors had started to diminish (Ellison, et. al. 1995). Toyota needed new unique capabilities to maintain its competitiveness.

Even though this study has provided a detailed description of an emerging organizational form that Toyota has adopted, there are many questions that remain for further study. First, this paper cannot concisely conclude whether Toyota's approach is the most effective among other organizational options in this new competitive environment. Now, competitors may or may not be following Toyota and adopting a similar style center organization. We need to continue to study similar organizational changes in other automobile firms to be able to carry out more systematic comparative studies. Second, it is also important to examine details of organizational evolution patterns from functional to project, or from project to multi-project organizations. These patterns most likely depend on various factors, including competitive environment and product strategy. The role played by management in organizational transitions may also affect the adoption of a new structure and processes.

In terms of general theory for organizational change, this study emphasizes the benefits and processes of capability-based reorientation. In order to sustain competitiveness, it may not be sufficient for a firm to have unique capabilities that create competitiveness in the market at a certain time, because competitive environment also changes. Firms need to adapt to a new environment. Sticking to existing capabilities per se may not provide a firm with long-lasting competitiveness. It may not be appropriate either to destroy existing capabilities and develop new capabilities from scratch. Firms need to have appropriate capabilities within the firm that can be utilized or supplemented in a new organization that fits a new competitive environment. This case study has shown one example of capability-based reorientation. Further studies are needed to provide more evidence that support this perspective.

References

Abegglen JC and Stalk G (1985): *Kaisha: The Japanese Corporation*, New York, Basic Books

Amit R and Schoemaker P (1993): "Strategic Assets and Organizational Rent," *Strategic Management Journal*, 14, 1, 33-46

Barney J (1991): "Firm Resources and Sustained Competitive Advantage," *Journal of Management*, 17, 1, 99-120

Black JA and Boal KB (1994): "Strategic Resources: Traits, Configurations and Paths to Sustainable Competitive Advantage," *Strategic Management Journal*, 15, 131-148

Clark KB and Fujimoto T (1991): *Product Development Performance: Strategy, Organization, and Management in the World Auto Industry*, Boston, MA, Harvard Business School Press

Davis SM and Lawrence PR (1977): *Matrix*, Massachusetts, Addison-Wesley

Dutton J and Duncan R (1987): "The Creation of Momentum for Change Through the Process of Strategic Issue Diagnosis," Strategic Management Journal, 8, 279-295

Ellison D, Clark K, Fujimoto T, and Hyun Y (1995): "Product Development Performance in the Auto Industry: 1990s Update," Working Paper, Harvard Business School, 95-66

Fujimoto T and Sheriff A (1989): "Consistent Patterns in Automotive Product Strategy, Product Development, and Manufacturing Performance - Road Map for the 1990s," Cambridge, MA, MIT International Motor Vehicle Program, International Policy Forum

Fujimoto T and Takeishi A (1994): *Jidoshasangyo 21-Seiki eno Sinario* (Scenarios of the Automobile Industry toward the Twenty First Century) in Japanese, Sisansei-Shuppan, Tokyo, Japan

Garud R and Nayyar PR (1994): "Transformative Capacity: Continual Structuring by Intertemporal Technology Transfer," *Strategic Management Journal*, 15, 365-385

Garud R and Kumaraswamy A (1995): "Technological and Organizational Designs for Economies of Substitution," *Strategic Management Journal*, Summer Special Issue, 16, 93-109

Hannan MT and Freeman JH (1984): "Structural Inertia and Organizational Change," *American Sociological Review*, 49, 149-164

Henderson RM and Clark KB (1990): "Architectural Innovation: The Reconfiguration of Existing Product Technologies and the Failure of Established Firms," *Administrative Science Quarterly*, 35, 9-30

Hinings CR and Greenwood R (1988): *The Dynamics of Strategic Change*, Oxford, England, Basil Blackwell

Ikari Y (1985): *Toyota tai Nissan: Shinsha Kaihatsu no Saizensen* (Toyota versus Nissan: The Front Line of New Car Development). Tokyo, Diamond

Itami H (1987): *Mobilizing Invisible Assets*, Harvard University Press, Cambridge, MA

Katz R and Allen TJ (1985): "Project Performance and the Locus of Influence in the R&D Matrix", *Academy of Management Journal*, 28, 1, 67-87

Kiesler S and Sproull L (1982): "Managerial Responses to Changing Environments: Perspectives on Problem Sensing from Social Cognition, *Administrative Science Quarterly*, 27, 548-570

Leonard-Barton D (1992): "Core Capabilities and Core Rigidities: A Paradox in Managing New Product Development," *Strategic Management Journal*, 13, 111-125

Markides C and Williamson P (1994): "Related Diversification, core competencies and corporate performance," *Strategic Management Journal*, Summer Special Issue, 15, pp. 149-165

Miles RE and Snow CC (1994): *Fit, Failure & The Hall of Fame*, New York, NY, The Free Press

Miller D and Friesen PH (1980): "Momentum and Revolution in Organizational Adaptation," *Academy of Management Journal*, 23, 591-614

Nelson RR and Winter SG (1982): *An Evolutionary Theory of Economics*, Cambridge, MA, Belknap Press

Nobeoka K and Cusumano M (1995): "Multi-Project Strategy, Design Transfer, and Project Performance: A Survey of Automobile Development Projects in the U.S. and Japan," *IEEE Transactions on Engineering Management*, 42, 397-409

Nobeoka K and Cusumano M (1997): "Multi-Project Strategy and Sales Growth: The Benefits of Rapid Design Transfer in New Product Development", *Strategic Management Journal*, 18, 3, pp. 169-186

Rosenberg N (1982): *Inside the Black Box: Technology and Economics*, Cambridge, MA, Cambridge University Press

Sanchez R (1995): "Strategic flexibility in product competition," *Strategic Management Journal*, Summer Special Issue, 16, pp. 135-159

Scott G (1994): "IMVP New Product Development Series: The Chrysler Corporation," Working Paper, International Motor Vehicle Program, Massachusetts Institute of Technology

Singh JV, House RJ, and Tucker DJ (1986): "Organizational Change and Organizational Mortality," Administrative Science Quarterly, 31, 587-611

Stalk G and Hout T (1990): *Competing Against Time*, Free Press, New York

Takeuchi H and Nonaka I (1986): "The New New Product Development Game," Harvard Business Review, vol. 64, Jan.-Feb

Toyota Motor Corporation (1992) and (1993): "Outline of Toyota Technical Center."

Toyota Motor Corporation (1994): "Activities and Achievements of FP21," in Japanese: "FP21 no Katsudo to Seika", Internal document

Tushman ML (1978): "Technical Communication in R&D Laboratories: The Impact of Project Work Characteristics", *Academy of Management Journal*, Vol. 21, No. 4, 624-645

Tushman ML and Romanelli E (1985): "Organizational Evolution: A Metamorphosis Model of Convergence and Reorientation," In Cummings LL and Staw BM (Eds), *Research in Organizational Behavior*, vol. 7, 171-222. Greenwich, CT: JAI Press

Wernerfelt B (1984): "A Resource-Based View of the Firm", *Strategic Management Journal*, 5, 171-180

Wheelwright S and Clark K (1992): *Revolutionizing Product Development*, The Free Press, New York

Womack J, Jones D, and Roos D (1990): *The Machine that Changed the World*, New York, Rawson Associates

Suppliers' Involvement in New Product Development in the Japanese Auto Industry – A Case Study from a Product Architecture Perspective

Dongsheng Ge and Takahiro Fujimoto

Introduction

Involving suppliers into new product development process has been widely recognized by auto makers as an efficient way to be agile and lean (Womack et al. 1990; Clark and Fujimoto 1991; Nishiguchi 1994). While American and European companies adopted design-in with the Japanese auto makers as the benchmark during 1980s and then turned to the outsourcing of big scale modules to suppliers in late 1990s, the continuing endeavor of the Japanese auto makers to improve the lean product development by incorporating information technology and modularization into their supply chain management still makes them take the lead at the turn of the new century. In this case study, we attempt to see more details about how suppliers are involved into the upstream of value chain in the Japanese auto industry.

Previous research on suppliers' involvement in new product development has provided an available taxonomy of systems (Asanuma 1989; Clark and Fujimoto 1991; Fujimoto 1997). Focusing on the ownership allocation of detailed design drawings of auto parts, we use here the drawing-supplied (DS) system, the drawing-entrusted (DE) system and the drawing-approved (DA) system as the subjects of our analysis.

Under the DS system, an auto assembler makes the detailed design of auto part and calls for suppliers to manufacture according to the design drawing. This is identical with the "detail-controlled parts" in Clark and Fujimoto's study (1991). In contrast, under the DA system, it is the supplier that makes the detailed design based on general blueprint requirements received from an auto assembler. In this case, through the procurement of auto parts, an auto assembler in effect buys the design drawings of auto parts, which are embodied in the final product where design is bundled with other tasks such as manufacturing and quality assurance (Fujimoto 1997, 2001). Finally, under the DE system, an auto assembler entrusts the making of the detailed design to a supplier, but on the other hand, claims the property right of the design drawings. This system can be considered as an intermediate mode between the contrasting cases of the DS system and the DA system. By the criterion of design's outsourcing, the DE system is the same as the DA system in that it is the supplier that makes the detailed design. While by the criterion of ownership of design drawings, the DE system is identical with the DS system; since it is the auto assembler which holds the property rights in both cases. Therefore, we can define two dimensions of the taxonomy of transaction patterns - the boundary lines of design task assignment and ownership of design drawings. As shown in the Figure 1, the three patterns can be put into a 2x2 table.[1]

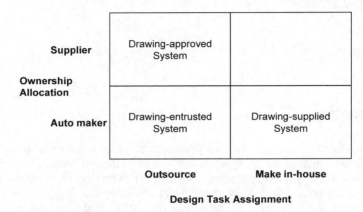

Fig. 1. Taxonomy of transaction patterns of detailed design drawings

Our main inquiry in this case study is that under what conditions that suppliers are involved in new product development in different ways. This inquiry especially becomes overwhelming when we look at a transaction dyad between one representative Japanese auto maker and one of its suppliers in which various patterns for different auto parts are adopted during development stage. Asanuma proposes that "relation-specific skill" is the underlying force to drive the classification of supplier's roles, which is defined as "the skill required on the part of the supplier to the specific needs of auto maker".[2] But in our case setting, the sup-

---

[1]   The so-called "black-box parts" in Clark and Fujimoto (1991) contain both the DA and DE systems and they are further ramified by Fujimoto (1997). Their empirical studies showed that in the mid- to late 1980s, the black box parts amounted to 62% of the overall transactions between auto assemblers and their suppliers in Japan, while in U.S., the detail-supplied parts had the dominant share of 81% (Clark and Fujimoto 1991, p.148). This difference was mapped to a gap in lead time of four to five months between the two regions.

[2]   Asanuma (1989, pp. 22-24) divides relation-specific skills into four factors and arrays them in a vector presentation (X1, X2, X3, X4). In detail, the four capabilities required by auto assemblers are:
X1: development capability in response to the specifications from an auto assembler and the ability to make proposals on specification improvement,
X2: process development capability and cost reduction capability through value engineering efforts,
X3: quality and timely delivery assurance capability, and

plier's relation-specific skill is very likely to be constant and can hardly explain the existence of different patterns. The intuition that some other factors may influence the pattern choice decision makes us attempt to examine the attributes of auto parts which can be made tractable from the perspective of product architecture.

Architectural Attributes of Auto Parts

Product architecture is a system design concept referring to the configuration or layout of how the components are arranged within a system (Henderson and Clark 1990). Defined in more rigorous terms, product architecture is "the scheme by which the function of a product is allocated to physical components and by which the components interact" (Ulrich 1995, p. 420). From the viewpoint of engineering design, first, it contains the arrangement of functional elements. Second, it reflects the mapping from these functional elements or design parameters to physical components. Third, it defines the interfaces among interacting physical components, which specify how they fit together, connect, communicate and so forth (Ulrich 1995; Baldwin and Clark 2000).

Modularity is one dimension to measure the way of decomposition and interface specification in the design process. It is a continuum describing the mapping structure of the functional parameters to the physical components and the degree to which components are independent from each other. The typical modular product is characterized as (1) each component implements a single function (the so-called "one-to-one mapping"), and (2) the interfaces between the components are well defined or standardized (Ulrich 1995). As a result, the product system tends to be of the loosely coupled kind and the mixing and matching of components can be carried out (Schilling 2000). In contrast, a product with extremely low modularity has the properties that (1) its components always implement multiple functions (function sharing) or a single function requires multiple components working together to be achieved (the so-called "complex mapping"), and (2) interfaces among tightly coupled components are ill defined (Ulrich 1995; Sanchez and Mahoney 1996).

We borrow the definition of product architecture of Ulrich (1995) that the mapping from functional elements to physical components and the interface specifications are two essential aspects. Product, then, can be viewed as the hierarchy of both functional parameters and physical components (Gopfert and Steinbrecher 1999). The interactions among components are clarified here into two types. One is the functional interaction, which refers to the relationships among components to implement functions. This is embodied in the mapping process from functional elements to physical components. The other is the structural interaction, which refers to the relationship among components reflected in the physical interfaces.

The architectural attributes of auto parts are defined as the features of both functional and structural interactions among auto parts. As such, the concept

---

X4: cost reduction capability in the production stage.

shares the same fundamental spirit of product architecture and can be regarded as a redefinition of product architecture on the component level. In particular, the architectural attributes of one auto part are specified to refer to:

1. The degree of interaction with other auto parts to achieve a given function, and
2. The degree of interaction with other auto parts in terms of physical intervention.

Modularity can also be applied here as a dimension to measure the architectural attributes of auto parts in a continuum manner. Along our logic, modularity can also be decomposed into two sub-concepts, a functional one and a structural one. Auto parts with higher functional modularity are those parts that implement simple functions and achieve their specified functions in a manner independent of other parts. Auto parts with higher structural modularity are the parts with relatively standardized physical interfaces with other parts. Contrarily, auto parts with lower functional and structural modularity are those parts that implement functional sharing with other parts and with physical interfaces that are tightly coupled and ill defined.

Furthermore, to make the concept of architectural attribute operational for empirical study, we construct eight indicators to capture both functional and structural modularity among auto parts, which can be measured on a 5-point scale.

1. Functional Integration (FIN) – the extent to which an auto part can implement its function independently.
2. Performance Measurability (PME) – the degree of ease with which design quality problems caused by the sample auto part can be correctly identified in the testing and assembly process.
3. Interface Commonality (ICM) – the extent to which the structural interface design of the sample auto part can be shared across different auto models.
4. Interface Complexity (ICP) – the degree to which the structural interface design of the sample auto part is coupled with other parts in terms of the number of joint points.
5. Design Independence (DIN) – the extent to which the design of the sample auto part can be carried out independently and concurrently with other parts. This variable contains both functional and structural aspects of the auto part design.
6. Design Commonality (DCM) – the degree to which the design drawing of the sample auto parts can be reused in other auto models. DCM can be considered as an indirect indicator of both functional and structural aspects of auto parts design since the more modular a design is, the more likely the design can be mixed and matched in other models.
7. Proximity to Core Function Sections of an Automobile (PCF) – the degree of structural proximity between the sample auto part and the core functional sections of an automobile such as the body, engine and chassis.
8. Proximity to Exterior/Interior Design of an Automobile (PEI) – the degree of structural proximity between the sample auto part and the exterior and interior designs of an automobile.

In addition, three indicators are designed to measure the internal complexity of auto parts.

9. Functional Multiplicity (FMU) – the assessment of how many functions the sample auto part contributes.
10. Structural Complexity (SCM) – the assessment of how complex the sample auto parts are in terms of their internal structure such as the number of parts used and the engineering hour used for manufacturing.
11. Technologically Advanced Degree (TAD) – the assessment of how advanced is the technology required to design the sample auto part. TAD also reflects the technological uncertainty related to the sample part. The number of patents related to the design and manufacturing of the auto part is one measure used for this indicator.

Case Study on Pattern Choices of Suppliers' Involvement into New Product Development

The setting of our case study is specified as a transaction dyad in which only auto maker A and one of its first-tier suppliers B are present. After receiving the approval from a senior manager at the supplier B to conduct our study on the basis of a confidentiality agreement at the end of 1998, we sent him the questionnaire on the supplier's roles during auto maker A's new product development and the architectural attributes of auto parts that were to be measured on 11 indicators mentioned above. After review and confirmation about the question items, our respondent randomly chose 33 parts and measured their attributes on a 5-point scale (with 1 indicating a "very low" level and 5 indicating a "very high" level) using his subjective perceptions. Although it may raise concerns about bias and the reliability of the responses, the judgment of the respondent based on his long career experience and receiving confirmation from other engineers of the validity of the responses to be an appropriate approximation for the purposes this exploratory empirical study.

Our processing of data base began with a correlation analysis. Table 1 shows the correlation coefficients matrix. A relatively strong positive correlation exists between FIN and PME. This result supported our intention of using these indicators as the variables for reflecting the functional interdependence between auto parts. To our surprise, there was no correlation between ICP and ICM which were used to measure the physical interfaces between auto parts. This could suggest that there may be more than one dimension of the interface being measured. Additionally, consistent with our expectation, an extremely high correlation is observed among the variables indicating the internal features of auto parts design.

Table 1. Descriptive statistics and correlation matrix

	FIN	PME	ICM	ICP	PCF	PEI	DIN	DCM	FMU	SCM	TAD
FIN	1										
PME	0.3946*	1									
ICM	0.2267	0.168	1								
ICP	0.1485	0.0371	0.0967	1							
PCF	-0.0381	0.1001	-0.3364	0.4172	1						
PEI	-0.315	0.2251	-0.4128*	-0.1457	0.2942	1					
DIN	0.1899	0.4763*	0.1351	-0.2461	-0.228	-0.0169	1				
DCM	0.09601	-0.1053	0.4592*	-0.41**	-0.6304**	-0.3466*	0.3679	1			
FMU	-0.4614*	-0.4168*	-0.3574	0.0914	0.1686	0.199	-0.0904	-0.1922	1		
SCM	-0.2812	0.1543	-0.4251**	0.0491	0.1622	0.3069	0.3787	-0.2159	0.6149**	1	
TAD	-0.3249*	0.2131	-0.1254	0.019	-0.1439	0.1289	0.4234	-0.0728	0.4722**	0.8001**	1
Mean	2.6669	4.1515	2.6061	2.1515	3.6667	3.2424	1.9394	3.3939	3	3.4545	3.5455
S.D.	0.2741	0.2	0.2645	0.2	0.2671	3.258	0.1991	0.2381	0.1628	0.2503	0.1986

*: Significant at 0.1 level
**: Significant at 0.05 level
Sample Size: N=33
Variable Measures: 1: very low; 2: fairly low; 3: average; 4: fairly high; 5: very high.

Next, to better understand the latent constructs in the measured variables, a factor analysis was conducted. Four factors were extracted that accounted for 66 percent of the variance, as is shown in Table 2.

Table 2. Results of factor analysis

	Factor1	Factor2	Factor3	Factor4
FIN	0.497	0.128	-0.301	-0.298
PME	0.881	8.61E-02	0.211	2.09E-02
ICM	7.60E-02	-0.17	-0.538	-0.304
ICP	-1.99E-02	0.778	-0.301	5.82E-02
PCF	8.57E-02	0.704	0.311	-4.99E-02
PEI	8.04E-02	4.53E-02	0.756	8.87E-02
DIN	0.538	-0.401	-4.68E-02	0.37
DCM	5.52E-03	-0.761	-0.47	-0.109
FMU	-0.409	0.115	9.47E-02	0.684
SCM	0.142	7.66E-02	0.251	0.935
TAD	4.51E-02	-7.99E-02	0.105	0.881

The first factor consists of the FIN, PME and DIN variables, which captures the functional independence of the sample part. This factor shows that the auto parts in the sample implement their functions with few interactions with other parts, that their functional performance can be well measured and that a higher degree of freedom can be enjoyed during the design process. Therefore, we label this factor the *functional modularity factor*.

Factor 2 also contains three variables - ICP, PCF and DCM. It reflects the complexity of the physical interfaces between the auto parts and the spatial proximity between the sample parts and the core functional sections of an automobile like the engine, body and chassis. It shows that the design commonality of auto parts across different car models is low. We can call this factor the *structural coupling factor*.

The third factor, which includes ICM, PEI and DCM, shows that auto parts are located close to the exterior and interior design of an automobile and both the interface and configuration designs of the auto parts are not likely to be shared among different car models. Due to the substantially high loading on variable PEI, we name Factor 3, the *styling design factor*.

Finally, the variables contained in Factor 4 have high positive values for the number of functions implemented by the sample parts (FMU), on the internal structural complexity of the sample parts (SCM) and on the advanced degree of technology required by the design and manufacturing of the sample parts (TAD). Since the factor apparently indicates the functional and structural complexity of the auto parts internally, we define this factor as the *internal complexity factor*. It is consistent with our expectation to use the internal features of the auto parts as a control variable.

Based on the results of factor analysis, a logistic regression of the four explanatory factors on the patterns of supplier involvement was finally conducted. Instead of using the factor scores directly, the means of the representative variables that have high weights for the same factor are used as the independent variables in the logistic regression models. Meanwhile, since the dependent variables in the logistic regression model are conventionally of the dichotomous kind, we ran five models for use in applying the logistic regression technique to analyze the choice of three transaction patterns. Table 3 shows the results.

Table 3. Results of logistic regression

	Model 1	Model2	Model 3	Model 4	Model 5
	The DS system	The DA system	The DA system	The DE system	The DE system
			(vs. the DS system)	(vs. the DA system)	(vs. the DS system)
Number of samples	N=33	N=33	N=22	N=25	N=19
Functional modularity factor	-1.9660 (1.3551)	0.8714* (0.4830)	2.2851* (1.2888)	-0.9752 (0.6017)	1.2358 (1.1688)
Structural coupling factor	2.5081 (1.8671)	-0.2638 (0.8818)	-0.6245 (1.1213)	-0.3367 (1.0916)	-2.0680 (1.6632)
Styling design factor	-1.1956 (1.0504)	0.7132 (0.6512)	-2.3127 (1.5956)	-0.4714 (0.6648)	0.3596 (1.0788)
Internal complexity factor	-2.3211 (1.1952)	0.9381* (0.501)	2.2982* (1.2717)	-0.4960 (0.5129)	1.6599* (1.0015)
Constant	6.3799 (5.2143)	-7.4522 (5.3052)	4.1612 (4.0620)	6.9113 (5.7777)	-2.1215 (5.1748)
Log. likelihood	22.666	34.916	14.731	29.791	19.199

In Model 1, the DS system is the dependent variable with the DE system and the DA system combined as the default. According to our logic, this model can be viewed as revealing the determination of the detailed design task outsourcing, since the DE and DA systems are the outsourcing cases while the DS system is case where the designing is done in-house. In Model 2, the DA system is the dependent variable with the DE and DS systems combined as the default. In this model, the determination of the ownership allocation of the detailed design drawings is examined since it is only under the DA system that suppliers claim the property rights of the design drawings. In Model 3, we left out the auto parts that were transacted under the DE system and studied the contrasting cases of the DS and DA systems using 22 of the sample auto parts. In Models 4 and 5, we focused on the choice of the DE system. Because of its intermediate nature, the DE system is studied separately first with the DS system, and then with the DA system as the defaults. The sample size was 25 in Model 4 after deleting the DS parts. In the same vein, 19 sample auto parts were used in Model 5 when the DA parts were left out.

Results of Model 1 show that only the "internal complexity factor" has a significantly negative influence on the choice of the DS system, when compared with the DE and DA systems (the so-called "black-box" systems). This indicates that the DS system is likely to be adopted when auto parts are less complex internally. In Model 2, the coefficients of the "functional modularity factor" and "the internal complexity factor" are positive and significant. The same results were obtained in Model 3. Both of these results indicate that the choice of the DA system is positively associated with auto parts that are internally complex and functionally independent from other parts.

Predicting the choice of the DE system, Model 4 shows the results when compared with the DA system. The DE system is associated with auto parts for which functional modularity is relatively low. On the other hand, when compared with the DS system in Model 5, "the internal complexity factor" significantly influenced the choice of the DE system.

The results of the empirical study can be summarized in Figure 2, with functional modularity factor and internal complexity factor as two explanatory dimensions for the DA, DE and DS systems.

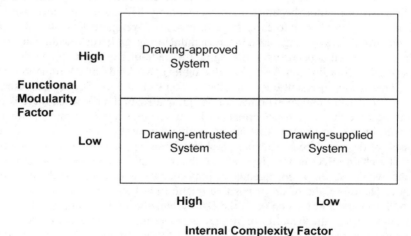

Fig. 2. Results of empirical study

Discussion

By looking at both matrices of supplier involvement patterns and the empirical study results, we can arrive at the following conclusions. First, functional modularity of auto parts but no structural one has positive influence on supplier B's ownership of design drawings while being involved in new product development of auto maker A. Put differently, the DA system is very likely to be chosen under the condition of high functional modularity among auto parts. Second, the internal complexity of auto parts positively impact the design outsourcing decision of auto maker A either adopt the DA system or choose the DE system. This result is correspondent to the term of "black-box" parts, although the cost structure of the supplier derived from product and process design of auto parts are not so hidden from the eyes of auto maker A during their long-term transaction relationship. Third, the DE system, which is a hybrid system between the DA and DS systems, is likely to be adopted under the conditions of high internal complexity and low functional modularity.

Functional Modularity and the Choice of the DA and DS System

As we know, subject to the constraint of the bounded rationality, new product development is in nature a searching process in which iterative efforts of trial-and-error are made to explore the necessary cause-effect linkages that lead to one possible solution. When such complicated tasks are conducted across the boundaries of firms, coordination becomes more demanding. Therefore, the successful involvement of suppliers into early stage of product development to take advantage of concurrent engineering, design-for-manufacturing and front-loading of problems to be solved depends upon managing the trade-offs between the productivity benefits and coordination costs. We distinguish two kinds of coordination costs here. One is measurement cost, the other is adjustment cost. The former refers to the cost to detect the responsibility for design quality problems when there is failure to achieve the desired performances in the testing stage. The latter is the cost incurred by design changes that are inevitable during the iterative trial-and-error process of design. Whether the design changes can be localized in a limited scope so that a chain effect is not triggered and the need for change does not spread out to the whole development agenda is important to inter-firm coordination efficiency. Therefore, the result of positive relationship between functional modularity of auto parts and the choice of the DA system shows that compared to the coordination costs, the benefits of design outsourcing are more dominant in this situation. The well defined interfaces of functional parameters of auto parts make it easy to identify the problems and pinpoint the responsibility and to conduct design changes without incurring a long chain reaction as well. The high-powered incentive is then offered to supplier by letting them claim the ownership of design drawings. While taking more responsibilities for design quality, supplier has more motivation to make innovations and to expand its transaction network.

On the other hand, the negative relationship between functional modularity and the choice of the DS system shows that even when supplier has been equipped with high level capability of designing auto parts, the ill-defined functional inter-dependence among auto parts tends to increase the coordination costs during the development process. Auto maker would rather like to design the parts themselves and internalize the likely adverse externalities in this situation. As we can see that the DS parts are not complicated ones, the in-house making of design drawings of these parts is not considered to cost large amount of engineering hours.

It is also interesting to see that variables reflecting structural modularity showed no impact on the choice of supplier involvement patterns, which implies that even when the physical interfaces between auto parts are ill-defined, they will not pose a severe challenge to the inter-firm coordination. This point was confirmed during the interview with the respondent who commented that the interface complexity of auto parts seldom posed problems during the design process. The reasons for this result may lie in the routine practices of auto maker A and supplier B in Japan. After establishing a very solid collaborative relationship, time-consuming negotiations during design changes of physical interfaces are likely to be replaced by collective problem solving as long as the functional interfaces and correspondingly, the responsibility boundaries are defined clearly beforehand. As one result, such practice is very likely to assure the optimal structural design to be achieved.

Internal Complexity of Auto Parts and the Choice of DA and DE System

The result that the internal complexity of auto parts, also as an indicator of supplier's capability, is positively associated with the outsourcing of detailed designing is compatible with the argument by Asanuma (1989) that the more know-how suppliers accumulate for designing auto parts, the greater the likelihood that design outsourcing will be done by the auto makers. It also backs up the analysis of Fujimoto on the supplier system in Japanese auto industry that "bundled outsourcing" to first-tier suppliers are conducted together with long-term transaction and fierce capability competition among small number of suppliers. By using the term of bundled outsourcing, Fujimoto points out that not only the first-tier suppliers conduct subassembly of the parts procured from the second-tier, but also they carry out a bundle of tasks such as design, testing, manufacturing and inspection-free delivery (Fujimoto 1997). When comparing such routine practices by the Japanese auto makers to the modularization trend from 1990s in Europe and America, we can interestingly find that the fundamental thought of modularization to reduce complexity and promote parallel engineering has been embodied in the supply chain management of the representative Japanese auto makers since 1970s (Fujimoto 2001). The major difference is that relative larger unit of modules are procured in European and American auto makers and the physical interface determination is given priority to facilitate the reorganization of their supplier system. The results from logistic regression analysis here show that the bundled outsourcing is likely to be adopted while the functional modularity is high among auto parts. The unit of module in this auto maker is not determined by the pursuit of larger scale through a top-down repartition of automobile, but is decided by the functional integration of auto parts through continuing improvement activities (Takeishi and Fujimoto 2001). To iterate, the point is that functional consideration is given the ultimate priority while deciding the supplier involvement of new product development process.

The Choice of the DE System

The results that auto parts with low functional modularity and high internal complexity are likely to be transacted as the DE parts while other variables are controlled are consistent with the hybrid feature of the DE system. The separation of design drawing ownership and design task outsourcing can be explained along the logic mentioned above. In the situation that functional modularity of auto parts is low, the auto maker has difficulties in measuring the design quality of supplier. If letting supplier to own the design drawings, coordination costs tend to increase when design problems are found and modification has to be done since no one would like to acknowledge that it is his fault. On the other hand, the internal complexity of auto parts is relatively high which means the expertise of suppliers can be possibly utilized. Therefore, the DE system is adopted like an institutional innovation that achieves the reduction of in-house engineering hours while avoid incurring too high coordination costs. Auto maker changes the transaction of design drawings into a one-spot deal by paying the design fees to supplier once the drawings are completed while taking the sequential responsibilities in the further development process. Our interviews with the respondent confirm that the main purpose of adopting the DE system is to take advantage of specialized know-how in suppliers to tackle complex and uncertain design problems.

Since the confidential agreement with the company does not allow the names of auto parts to go public, we refer to a case study in Fujimoto (1997) on the supply chain management of Toyota, in which weather strips are transacted under the DE system. He pointes out that although the spatial design parameters of the weather strip can be specified ex ante when the specifications of the body frame and the window glass parameters are determined, there is a high interdependence among the body frame, window glass, and weather strip to fulfill the sealing function. When a leakage problem occurs, it is hard to tell which part should be held responsible. However, if the auto maker internalizes this coordination problem by taking the responsibility for design defects, complicated intervention across firms can be greatly reduced.

Conclusion

Choosing a transaction dyad in the Japanese auto industry, we attempt to relate the architectural attributes of auto parts and the patterns of supplier's involvement in new product development process. The high functional modularity of auto parts which means the interfaces of auto parts' functional parameters are well defined, is shown to have positive relationship with the drawing-approved system, while the low functional modularity of auto parts tends to make the auto maker to claim the ownership of detailed design drawings of auto parts even when supplier has high level design capability. We arrive at the conclusion that balance should be secured between providing a high-powered incentive to a supplier, clearly defining responsibility and coordinating costs, and the matching between architectural attributes and the division of labor should be emphasized during the decision making of design outsourcing.

The priority of functional consideration in the supply chain management in the Japanese auto maker is also a conspicuous contrast with the practices by European and American companies. Having emerged much earlier and developed into a systematic practice, the delivery of functional modules with good design quality and cost efficiency in the Japanese auto industry continues to be improved by incorporating advanced integration technology and by optimizing the size of module. This function oriented thinking of the Japanese auto maker is consistent with its stance to construct a win-win relationship with suppliers and can be said as one source of its competitiveness in the global automobile industry.

References

Asanuma B (1989): "Manufacturer-supplier relationships in Japan and the concept of relation-specific skill," *Journal of the Japanese and International Economies,* Vol. 3, pp 1-30

Asanuma B (1997): *The Organization of the Japanese Firms: the Innovative Adjustment Mechanism.* Toyo Keizai Shinbu Sha (In Japanese)

Baldwin CY and Clark KB (2000): *Design Rules. Volume 1: The power of modularity.* Cambridge, MA: MIT Press

Clark KB and Fujimoto T (1991): *Product Development performance*, Harvard Business School Press, Boston

Fujimoto T (1997): *The Evolution of Production System: the Organizational Capability and Emergent Process in Toyota.* You hi gaku (In Japanese)

Fujimoto T (2001): "The Japanese automobile parts supplier system: the triplet of effective inter-firm routines," *International Journal of Automotive Technology and Management,* Vol. 1, No. 1, pp 1-34

Gopfert J and Steinbrecher M (1999): "Modular product development: Managing technical and organizational independencies," mimeo

Henderson RM and Clark KB (1990): "Architectural innovation: the reconfiguration of existing product technologies and the failure of established firms," *Administrative Science Quarterly*, 35, pp 9-30

Nishiguchi T (1994): *Strategic Industrial Outsourcing*, Oxford University Press, New York

Pahl G and Beitz W (1984): *Engineering Design*, in Wallace K (ed.), The Design Council, London

Sanchez R and Mahoney JT (1996): "Modularity, Flexibility, and Knowledge management in product and organization design," *Strategic Management Journal,* Vol.17, pp 63-76

Schilling MA (2000): "Toward a general modular systems theory and its application to interfirm product modularity," *Academy of Management Review,* 25(2), pp 312-334

Takeiishi A and Fujimoto T (2001): "Modularization in the auto industry: interlinked multiple hierarchies of product, production and supplier system," International Journal of Automobile Technology and Management, Vol.1, No.4, pp 379-396

Thomke SH and Fujimoto T (1999): "The effect of front-loading problem-solving on product development performance", *Harvard Business School Working Paper* 98-103 (Revised May 1999), Cambridge (Mass)

Ulrich K (1995): "The role of product architecture in the manufacturing firm," *Research Policy*, Vol. 24, pp 419-440

Womack D, Jones D, and Roos D (1990): *The Machine that Changed the World,* Rawson/MacMillan, New York

NPD-Process and Planning in Japanese Engineering Companies – Findings from an Interview Research

Cornelius Herstatt, Christoph Stockstrom, and Akio Nagahira

Introduction

In new product development (NPD) companies often struggle to achieve both, efficiency as well as flexibility due to their often opposing implications for organizing and managing NPD projects.

In this context, planning plays a central role. In NPD, one can distinguish between two different perspectives on planning (Verganti 1999). One stream of research strongly emphasizes the importance of the early phases of a NPD project as decisions taken at this stage are unlikely to be changed later on and if they are, then often only at considerable cost (Verganti 1999). The importance of these initial planning activities is documented in a number of studies (Cooper and Kleinschmidt 1986; Cooper and Kleinschmidt 1987a, 1987b; Gupta and Wilemon 1990; Khurana and Rosenthal 1998). A second stream of research more recently questions the effectiveness of elaborated initial planning and contends that the ability to rapidly react to changes later in the process and to improvise may lead to success in NPD (Eisenhardt and Tabrizi 1995; Ward et al. 1995; Brown and Eisenhardt 1997; Moorman and Miner 1998; Miner et al. 2001). This study aims at achieving a better understanding of these two management principles by investigating initial planning activities as well as planning carried out throughout the course of the project.

The literature provides a number of findings that suggest Japanese R&D management practices to be a fruitful object of study for the aims of our research: NPD process in Japan have been reported to be highly adaptive and oriented towards external circumstances (Song and Montoya-Weiss 2001). For example, it has been found that Japanese NPD project managers manage the process differently, depending on the degree of perceived technological uncertainty (Brown and Eisenhardt 1995). In addition, Rogers (1990) notes that Japanese companies give much greater care to planning for implementation than their American counterparts for example.

The Study

Aim of the Study

Research has shown that advanced planning in NPD projects positively contributes to a number of success measures, such as time, reduction of failure rates, financial returns and innovation levels (Moorman and Miner 1998). However, traditional planning efforts have also been criticized for exerting too much formalism and control, and thereby hindering creativity (Bart 1993). In addition, Song and Montoya-Weiss (1998) point out the need to better align planning activities to the degree of newness of the innovation.

Aside from the acknowledged relevance of planning in NPD most existing studies do not look in any greater detail into the various aspects related to planning and present them collectively under one heading such as "schedules / plans" (Pinto and Slevin 1988) or "planning methods" (Shenhar et al. 2002). Consequently, there is a call for research into what exactly constitutes good planning (Thieme et al. 2003). This study tries to contribute to developing a deeper understanding of NPD planning. To achieve this, general NPD planning practices in Japanese companies including the in-depth planning of innovation projects in these companies were analyzed. The following issues have been addressed: Are Japanese companies using a formal innovation process ("Stage-Gate") including detailed regulations concerning activities, decision procedures, and functional participation? If yes, which preferred process models are found, and what specific practices are applied? Which aspects are planned and in what detail during the initial project planning as well as over the course of the innovation process? How does planning evolve over the course of the project? How do the companies account for the uncertainty inherent in NPD and balance between the need to achieve both efficiency and flexibility? How do they deal with changes that occur during project execution? How to companies manage the trade off between the quality of planning and flexibility? In order to at least partially answer these questions, we investigated the processes underlying NPD projects in 15 Japanese companies. In the following sections we will report about these as well as all major related planning activities and management styles.

Methodology

We reviewed literature that is concerned with planning activities in NPD (e.g. Thieme et al. 2003; MacCormack and Verganti 2003; Miner et al. 2001; Song and Montoya-Weiss 1998; Moorman and Miner 1998) and drew on propositions from our previous research findings (Herstatt et al. 2004a, 2004b) to develop a standardized questionnaire.

Our questionnaire was translated in Japan and the interpretation of all questions was verified in a number of discussion rounds before companies were visited. For this research project, MOST (Management of Science and Technology Department) at Tohoku University in Sendai identified a total of 30 mechanical and electrical engineering companies that already took part in a large scale research project, conducted in 2003 by the authors (Herstatt et al. 2004b). For this study, we focused on the most innovative companies from the aforementioned sample. The selection was based on self-assessment of the companies carried out during the previous project and the contribution of new products to company sales. All in all, 16 companies finally agreed to participate. One company was excluded from the analysis as all new product development efforts turned out to be entirely controlled by the founder, owner and CEO of the company. (Although this is not an unusual finding in Japan, we decided to eliminate the interview results from this analysis because they were not comparable to the remainder of the sample.)

Sample

The Sample contains companies ranging in size from 400 employees to large corporations, one of which has more than 34,000 employees. The average number of employees is around 6500. The structure of our sample is further reflected in annual sales which vary between 1.8 billion and 2.78 trillion Yen. Here the average is approximately 500 billion Yen.

10 of the 15 companies are independent, while 5 describe themselves as dependent subsidiaries of larger corporations. Our interview partners were located in the planning and new product development departments. Further information on the companies and the projects we investigated can be found in the appendix.

NPD Project Processes

Despite carrying out some unique procedures during their NPD processes and sometimes using a slightly different terminology, most companies we interviewed generally followed an innovation process as depicted in Figure 1. The innovation process is based upon distinct phases. The average duration of the overall NPD process varied between a minimum of 4 months and a maximum of 60 months, with an average duration of approximately 33 months over all companies and projects.

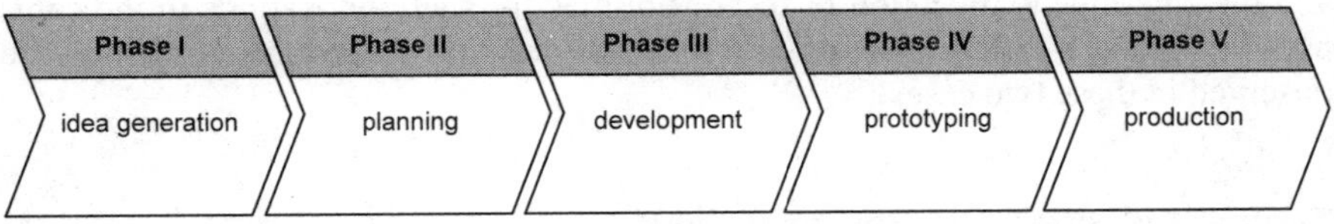

Phase I	Phase II	Phase III	Phase IV	Phase V
idea generation	planning	development	prototyping	production

Fig. 1. The new product development process

The number of phases or process steps varied between four and six. One company did not explicitly employ a prototyping stage but considered this to be a part of the prior development phase. The sixth process stage that some of the companies specified was devoted to marketing and sales efforts by all except one firm. This company, which produces various high tech glass products, does not use the production stage to manufacture at full capacity but delays this decision until the sixth phase during which is decides about a scaling up of production based upon how production samples were evaluated by potential customers.

In all but two cases, companies followed a standard Stage-gate approach for different kinds of innovation projects. A manufacturer of power distribution devices and various control equipment reported on having different procedures for long-term and short-term projects which are usually associated with radical and incremental innovation projects respectively. For short-term projects (incremental innovations), the planning phase is left out and product ideas which are usually derived from evaluating customer needs or an improved understanding of technology are screened by the development team and people from the marketing department. For long-term projects (truly new products), ideas are screened prior to the planning phase. Here, R&D works together with top management including the CEO of the company and for extremely high-stake projects, even the president of the holding company is involved in the screening process. After the planning stage, there is a second gate for long-term projects during which the business group's top management and the company CEO decide about the further continuation of the project.

The second company, a manufacturer of electronic components and information equipment employs two different process models for incremental and radical innovations. For incremental projects with clear customer needs, the company pursues the aim of improving its products accordingly and can therefore come up with a concept very early in the process. This concept is then developed into a prototype which is shown to potential customers to receive feedback. According to the feedback, the prototype is either revised or cleared for production. For radical innovation projects, the process is similar to the one depicted in Figure 1 but concludes with marketing as a sixth stage.

While researchers have emphasized the need for different management styles, strategic actions and organizational capabilities for radical and incremental innovation projects (Trauffler et al. 2004; Kessler and Chakrabarti 1999), an explicit differentiation between short-term/ incremental and long-term/radical innovation and the consequent allocation of responsibilities for such innovations in the company including a different set of activities and decision procedures could only be observed in these two cases.

Typical Activities and Parties Involved

The first stage of the innovation process described above, idea generation, first of all consists of information gathering activities such as market research, trend forecast, need and demand analyses and brainstorming sessions. Then, ideas are assessed and some rough first planning steps are carried out. All but one of the participating firms employ multifunctional teams consisting of R&D and marketing personnel at this stage. One company, a manufacturer of special metals and various equipment used in power transmission, telecommunications, and construction, has an especially interesting approach to this stage: The company maintains various R&D units worldwide which are allowed to decide which projects they want to pursue and with what priority. This autonomy is further supported by assigning each unit a R&D budget of its own a large percentage of which can be used very flexibly by the respective team. These efforts are coordinated by a central R&D planning team. Ideas may be shared between the different R&D units and the central R&D planning team has the authority to direct research to other teams if problems occur.

During the planning phase, stage 2 in Figure 1, the idea is scrutinized as technical feasibility is analyzed, business plans are developed, product objectives are formed and project planning is carried out. In one company, customers were already included in this early stage of the process to discuss the new product idea. This stage typically ends with the development of some first product concepts. With the exception of the company mentioned above, this stage is also carried out by multifunctional teams which in many cases are increased in terms of the number of people and corporate functions involved. The manufacturing department is frequently included and in some cases top management is involved in the planning efforts.

In stage 3, the development phase, the product concept and criteria it has to meet are refined. Profit, product and cost plans are further developed. As the project unfolds, product design and reliability are reviewed and checked. One of the companies already distributes samples of the product to selected potential customers at this stage. We did not observe any changes in the involved personnel in comparison to the preceding stage.

During prototyping, the 4th stage, one or more potential prototypes of the final product are developed and are subject to final quality tests and checks for manufacturability. At this stage, customers are frequently integrated into the process to receive feedback about the product's quality and customer acceptance. In one case, product samples are sold to potential customers who test them for a period of one year before the company finally decides about mass-manufacturing the product or not. With the exception of one company which includes top management in the prototyping and mass production stages, no other firm reported about any further changes to the functions assigned to the project in this or later phases of the project.

In stage 5, mass production, only two of the companies still carry out some final checks with regard to manufacturability and screen existing intellectual property rights (IPR). Frequently, this stage is divided into two sub-stages: Many companies begin with small-scale mass production to gain further information about customer acceptance and market performance of the product before scaling up and committing considerable financial resources into large-scale mass production lines.

Decision Gates

The companies we interviewed structure their NPD processes with a minimum of two and a maximum of five gates between process steps. The distribution of gates is even: 9 companies have a gate between idea generation and planning, 10 have a gate between planning and development, 9 have a gate between development and prototyping and finally 10 have a gate between prototyping and production.

With regard to the criteria employed at those decision gates, we identified two recurring practices: Several companies changed the evaluation criteria from technically oriented aspects during the early decision gates to economic and financial criteria as the project matured. Another set of companies did not change their evaluation criteria but rather changed the performance levels and information requirements the projects had to meet with more stringent performance levels and exhaustive business case analyses in the end.

One of our interview partners depicted an especially comprehensive approach to project evaluation at the gates. The company applies a so-called radar chart that is known to every employee in the company. The radar chart visualizes the level of performance of the project along certain dimensions. In this case, the company judges the originality of the project, its alignment with the corporate strategy and the current product portfolio, its feasibility, the IPR situation with regard to the technologies incorporated in the new product as well as financial data. Each of these dimensions is measured with several variables turning this approach into a very detailed and demanding scheme of analysis.

Problems

Not surprisingly, especially considering the example we described above, a frequent problem that the companies encountered during their NPD processes was the elimination of new ideas as they were not able to meet the specified targets or the team was not able to apply the criteria or gain meaningful information for them for very new products.

Aside from this issue, two other categories of problems were mentioned repeatedly: the collaboration of R&D and marketing personnel was considered suboptimal in many cases. Oftentimes, the teams felt that marketing was integrated too late and that therefore crucial information was missing. But also the communication between the people of the different departments was often prone to problems and they tended to have different expectations towards the product or couldn't agree on the number of functions it should incorporate. Finally, timing was often considered to be of vital importance and some companies stated that their installed processes sometimes were too cumbersome and didn't allow them to develop new products as fast as they would like.

General Planning Activities in NPD

Research has shown that product development cycle times are faster (Griffin 1997), failure rates are lower (Cooper and Kleinschmidt 1986), financial returns are greater (Ittner and Larcker 1997; Song and Parry 1997), and innovation levels are higher (Olson et al. 1995) when companies carefully plan and use advanced planning techniques. Besides, Dvir et al. (1999) found that the preparation of formal design and planning documents has a strong positive effect on meeting the project's time and budget objectives and further significantly contributes to end-customers' benefits.

All companies in our sample reported on having well-defined procedures, usually in the form of written documents, which are being followed during NPD projects. Accordingly, the companies do not plan the process for NPD projects from scratch individually. However, they widely agreed to plan NPD projects differently according to the degree of newness. During the interviews we frequently found that our interview partners resorted to planning different phases of the NPD process in different detail. A practice which they attributed to the uncertainty inherent in NPD that is especially pronounced during the early stages of the front-end of innovation ("Fuzzy Front End"). The need for flexibility at this point prevails over gains in efficiency associated with more detailed planning. During the later stages, however, when a major part of the uncertainty is already reduced, the need for flexibility is less pronounced and companies strive for more efficiency. This finding is summarized in Figure 2.

**What phases do you plan at the beginning
of an NPD-project and in what detail?**

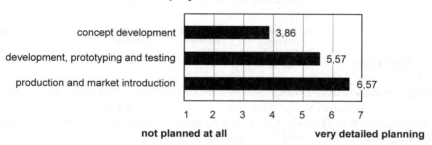

not planned at all   **very detailed planning**

Fig. 2. Level of detail of process planning

In all the companies we interviewed, planning was carried out by a multifunctional group. It consists of the project leader – who in the projects we investigated always had a technical background – and team members from the marketing department. Out of the 15 companies, 9 at least sometimes include external parties in the planning of their R&D projects. These parties often are technical advisors, consultants, market researchers or designers who are brought in to complement the market and/or technical knowledge available in the company. Oftentimes, these external parties were former employees of the company. Two of our interview partners reported on including university researchers in order to be up to date about the latest findings in engineering and management. One company, with one very large and important customer, reported that staff of this customer is frequently included in the planning of new products, especially when the company develops exclusively for this client.

Project-Related Planning

To assess project related planning issues, we asked the companies to select a successful and a less successful NPD project that they recently completed. Project success was measured in terms of profit level, sales volume, market share, competitive advantage and customer satisfaction (Figure 3).

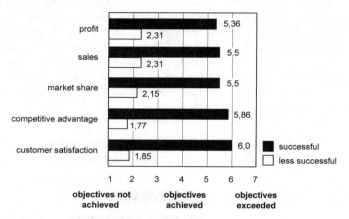

Fig. 3. Project success

The respondents were asked to assess whether the projects fell short of their objectives, met them or even exceeded them on a seven-point Likert scale. In doing so, we followed the notion of evaluating success by comparing the actual outcome of the companies' activities with the organizations' planned objectives (Zhang and Doll 2001, p. 102). This allows for a comparison of companies operating in different industries (Verganti 1997).

One of the key problems of traditional approaches of planning and controlling R&D projects is that they exert too much formal control which curtails creativity (Bart 1993). In addition, early planning efforts suffer from great uncertainty during the early phases. Consequently, crucial information such as customer needs, competitive product offerings, technological risks and opportunities and the regulatory environment is hard to anticipate at this stage (Verganti 1997). While being culturally inclined towards planning (confer e.g. Nakata and Sivakumar 1996),

Japanese managers have been shown to be highly adaptive towards external circumstances (Song and Montoya-Weiss 2001) and to give great care to the process of planning for implementation (Rogers 1990).

We asked our interview partners to assess both, the initial planning of the project as well as the planning activities that continued throughout the course of the project following the notion, that planning is not a one-time activity but rather a continuous effort (Lechler 1997): The current performance should frequently be compared to specified targets which may have to be re-specified from time to time.

With respect to initial planning, we asked the companies about the level of detail of their plans, whether milestones were planned, about the autonomy of the team and the participation of team members in the planning process and finally if responsibilities were assigned and whether contingency plans were devised in case the environment changed in ways not anticipated by the original plan. Surprisingly, with the exception of the level of detail of the initial plan and the planning of milestones, we could not find any differences between the more and the less successful projects. Teams were rather free to decide how to reach milestones, all project team members participated in the project planning process, and responsibilities of team members were assigned at the beginning of the project. But successful projects were planned in more detail than less successful ones and milestones were more often set. This is in line with findings of Ittner and Larcker (1997) as well as Dvir et al. (1999). The results are summarized in Figure 4.

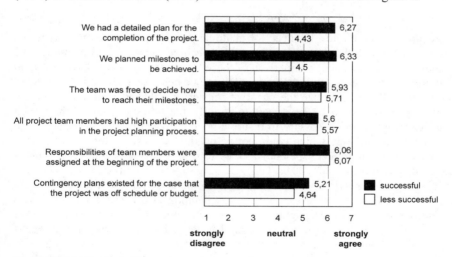

Fig. 4. Initial planning efforts

Another noticeable difference between successful and less successful projects can be found when looking at the state of the environment or "environmental turbulence" (Moorman and Miner 1998, p. 5) in which the project was carried out. Again, there is little difference between the two categories of projects (successful vs. non-successful) with regard to changes within the team or within the company. However, when looking at the changes in the environment, we find that the successful projects were carried out in a much more stable environment than the less successful ones. In a turbulent environment, the benefit of formal planning is reduced, as many changes occur which oftentimes cannot be properly anticipated beforehand. Consequently, plans are frequently outdated as the assumptions underlying them do not hold up anymore. This is emphasized by the fact that each project is a unique endeavor, making it impossible to know all the tasks that have to be carried out beforehand (Andersen 1996). For such environments, an emergent style of planning is recommended and improvisation may become necessary to avoid sticking to outdated plans (Eisenhardt and Tabrizi 1995).

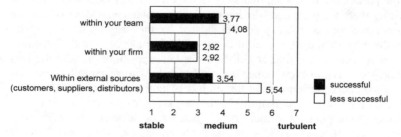

Fig. 5. Environmental turbulence during project planning

As the project unfolds, the need for planning persists and actual progress needs to be monitored and compared to the goals specified during initial planning. We argue here that a frequent comparison of these two states forms the basis for good planning, as deviations from the initial plan can be detected early and be corrected timely in order to minimize the negative impact of outdated plans. In doing so, firms may discover that they need to modify their initial plans. While such changes may become necessary to insure a good market fit for the product, or to substitute a technology which could not be handled as desired, they often have a negative effect on project efficiency as they lead to prolonged cycle-times and increase cost (Ahmadi et al. 2001). This again highlights the importance of constant monitoring and enacting necessary changes to plans as early as possible. In this context, focusing on milestones during the planning effort leaves the team with greater freedom to decide how to reach the milestones and will c.p. cause fewer changes than planning specific activities. The same argument holds for an emergent style of planning. However, if companies find that the project progresses without major deviations from the original plan, activity planning may reap additional efficiencies by optimizing the process.

As Figure 6 shows, there is no noticeable difference between the successful and the less successful projects concerning planning styles. In both cases, there were some changes to the original plan which resulted from a frequent comparison of actual progress against the project schedule. The companies relied on formal planning rather than an emergent style of planning, however, focusing on milestones provided the teams with freedom and flexibility to proceed as they deemed necessary.

All in all, our findings suggest that the most noticeable difference between successful and less successful projects is based on the initial planning efforts undertaken by the company and the turbulence of the environment. These findings are supported by prior research which has shown that many of the changes made during NPD projects and therefore a considerable amount of cost could have been avoided had the initial planning been carried out more thoroughly (Bullinger 1990). Our interview partners confirmed this, often stating that market related data which the plans were based upon was poorly researched or had changed in the meantime. This also underscores the influence of environmental turbulence on NPD which requires companies to react rapidly to the ever changing environment and highlights the importance of high-quality initial planning and the correct anticipation of future developments (Calantone et al. 2003; Verganti 1999; MacCormack and Verganti 2003).

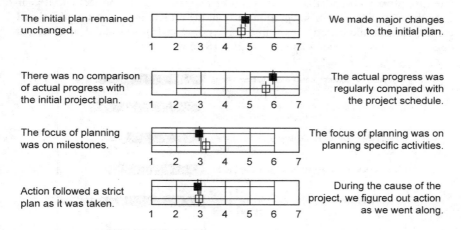

Fig. 6. Planning throughout the course of the project

Changes

As has been described above, companies may often feel the need to amend their plans. However, careful analysis is necessary to determine whether such changes are indeed required or not. For example, it is not always necessary or even advisable to integrate the newest technologies into a product which just became available during development (Gupta and Wilemon 1990). Such avoidable changes may add up to one third of total development cost (Bullinger 1990). Consequently, successful companies only perform necessary changes that may already have been anticipated in advance and have undergone a thorough examination with regard to their necessity (Keplinger 1991; Geschka 1993; Fricke and Lohse 1997; Brennecke et al. 2001). Dvir and Lechler (2004) found that both, changes made to the process as well as to the desired outcome of a project, have a negative effect on success. According to Wiskow (1999), 37% of the disturbances leading to changes can fully be influenced by the project team, while another 25% can be partially influenced. This again underscores the importance of careful planning activities.

We asked the respondents to assess changes to the technical concept, to project objectives, and to the core team as well as whether a lot of new elements emerged during the execution of the project, and if the team had to diverge from planned procedures. Finally we wanted to know, if other people or staff from other functions were integrated into the project during its course. An increasing integration of corporate functions such as marketing, operations or procurement over the course of the project, known as "dynamic integration", has been shown to contribute to success (Salomo et al. 2003). Olson et al. (2001) observe that the need for interdisciplinary co-operation increases over the course of the project and it is argued that a high degree of integration early in the project incurs cost, without generating comparable benefits, as teams may end up in fruitless and premature discussions because of incomplete information (Salomo et al. 2003).

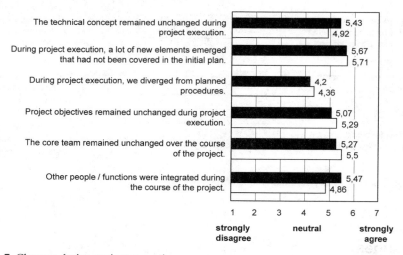

Fig. 7. Changes during project execution

As depicted in Figure 7, there is no noticeable difference between the successful and the less successful projects. However for all questions, the deviations between the respective mean values exhibit the expected directions.

In sum, our findings suggest that changes during project execution do not seem to exert as strong an influence on project success as the initial planning activities. This is contrary to the findings of Dvir and Lechler (2004) and may stem from the fact that the aforementioned authors drew their sample from a variety of projects ranging – aside from product development – from construction to software projects and reorganization. Our sample exclusively includes NPD projects which may not be subject to such negative influences from project changes as other types of projects. Of course, the exploratory nature of our research and the small sample size limit the generalizability of our results.

Project Management

With regard to project management, we interviewed the participants about the management style that was exerted as well as about the team staff and the resources that were used for the project.

Management Styles

Management style may be described along the dimension of formality and participation (confer e.g. Thieme et al. 2003), where formality is "the degree to which rules, policies and procedures govern the role behavior and activities of organizations (van de Ven and Ferry 1980, p. 303). These differing management styles reflect varied managerial assumptions and goals (Lewis et al. 2002).

In new product development, "formality occurs via utilization of structured processes for managing the project" (Tatikonda and Rosenthal 2000) and is associated with the assumption that NPD is predictable and rational enough to be planned and managed top-down (Lewis et al. 2002).

A participative management style is usually associated with less formal control mechanisms such as ad hoc management reviews or few structured progress reviews (Tatikonda and Rosenthal 2000) and fosters learning (Lewis et al. 2002) and communication (Gupta et al. 1986) among team members.

However, research by Lewis et al. (2002) has shown that such seemingly contradictory behaviors and requirements and the resulting paradox (Lewis 2000) are frequently united in practice, as elements of both approaches are mixed.

While there appears to be no significant difference between the successful and less successful projects with regard to the management styles involved, open and extensive communication seems to be more prevalent in the successful projects as the willingness to let all parties contribute to the project is higher. Our findings do not show differences in the evolvement of management style between successful and less successful projects. In both cases, management style remained the same and did neither become more formal nor more participative.

Staff and Resources

While it may be both, an antecedent to or a consequence of project performance, team motivation was considerably lower in the less successful projects than in their successful counterparts. Project performance influenced the level of motivation inasmuch as motivation in successful projects remained constant or increased slightly, while it radically decreased in unsuccessful projects.

As has been described above, our interview partners were of the opinion that many of the less successful projects particularly suffered from the environmental turbulence in which they were carried out. The most frequent explanations that we were given were that customer needs and market trends had not been correctly anticipated or that competitors had entered the market either earlier than the company, or with a superior product. Consequently, in these cases, the interviewees rated the marketing and management skills of the project team considerably lower than for their successful counterparts.

For both groups of projects, the teams had substantial access to management and resources, both within and outside the company. We found no pronounced differences here.

Conclusions

Companies achieve a balance by formulating rules for standard approaches but also employing a participative management style to insure extensive communication flows among the parties involved in the project.

With the exception of two companies, the processes employed for radical and incremental innovation projects are equal. Decision gates are equally distributed across. We found companies to follow two approaches with respect to the criteria applied for decision making. One strategy was to change the content of the criteria. In this case, the focus shifted from technically oriented aspects during the early decision gates to economic and financial criteria applied during later gates. The second approach was to apply the same criteria throughout the process but to increase the level of performance the project has to meet. Following these procedures a number of problems were frequently cited by our interview partners. Their major concerns were the killing of new ideas at decision gates and difficult communication as well as differing expectations between the departments involved.

With regard to the planning efforts undertaken by the companies initial planning and environmental turbulence seem to be the most influential factors for project success. While it is true that for about half of the successful projects environmental turbulence was lower than for their less successful counterparts, the other half of the projects was carried out under approximately equal conditions of environmental turbulence. As aggregate scores for initial planning activities in these cases are also virtually identical, we conclude that in these cases the responsible parties have been better at anticipating the future developments and changes. This is underlined by the slightly higher prevalence of contingency plans for the successful projects. Our findings support the notion of planned flexibility as developed by Verganti (1997, 1999): It is not sufficient for companies to rely solely on initial planning and trying to anticipate as many of the possible changes during the course of the project but it is equally important to maintain flexibility in order to be able to introduce changes late in the project without suffering considerable cost disadvantages.

Future Research

Future research should try to work on the interaction between initial planning, planning changes and process management style. Further research is needed to determine the impact of product novelty on planning activities and the present findings regarding the interplay of anticipation and flexibility should be subjected to large scale research endeavors. Another worthwhile avenue of research to pursue would be to study NPD project planning activities across different cultural backgrounds to find out how the balance is struck.

References

Ahmadi R, Roemer TA, and Wang RH (2001) Structuring product development processes, *European Journal of Operational Research*, **130**, 3, 539-558

Andersen ES (1996) Warning: Activity planning is hazardous to your project's health, *International Journal of Project Management*, **14**, 2, 89

Bart CK (1993) Controlling new product R&D projects, *R & D Management*, **23**, 3, 187-197

Brennecke VM, Drüner M, Gemünden HG, Kassner S, Langen R, Richter K, Salomo S, Schwarz P, and Trommsdorff V (2001) *Innovationskompass 2001*, Düsseldorf: VDI-Verlag

Brown, SL and Eisenhardt KM (1995) Product Development: Past Research, Present Findings, and Future Directions, *The Academy of Management Review*, **20**, 2, 343-378

Brown, SL and Eisenhardt KM (1997) The art of continuous change: Linking complexity theory and time-paced evolution in relentlessly shifting organizations, *Administrative Science Quarterly*, **42**, 1, 1-34

Bullinger H-J (1990) *IAO-Studie: F&E heute - Industrielle Forschung und Entwicklung in der Bundesrepublik Deutschland*, München: Gesellschaft für Management und Technologie Verlag

Calantone R, Garcia R, and Droge C (2003) The effects of environmental turbulence on new product development strategy planning, *The Journal of Product Innovation Management*, **20**, 2, 90

Cooper RG and Kleinschmidt EJ (1986) An investigation into the new product process: steps, deficiencies, and impact, *Journal of Product Innovation Management*, **3**, 2, 71-85

Cooper RG and Kleinschmidt EJ (1987a) Success factors in product innovation, *Industrial Marketing Management*, **16**, 3, 215-223

Cooper RG and Kleinschmidt EJ (1987b) What makes a new product a winner: success factors at the project level, *R&D Management*, **17**, 3, 175-189

Dvir D and Lechler T (2004) Plans are nothing, changing plans is everything: the impact of changes on project success, *Research Policy*, **33**, 1, 1-15

Dvir D, Lipovetsky S, Shenhar AJ, and Tishler A (1999) Common managerial factors affecting project success. Working paper, Tel Aviv University, School of Management No. 2/99, Tel Aviv

Eisenhardt KM and Tabrizi BN (1995) Accelerating Adaptive Processes: Product Innovation in the Global Computer Industry, *Administrative Science Quarterly*, **40 (March 1995)**, 1, 84-110

Fricke G and Lohse G (1997) *Entwicklungsmanagement: mit methodischer Produktentwicklung zum Unternehmenserfolg*, Berlin et al.: Springer

Geschka H (1993) *Wettbewerbsfaktor Zeit: Beschleunigung von Innovationsprozessen*, Landsberg: Moderne Industrie

Griffin A (1997) The effect of project and process characteristics on product development cycle time, *JMR, Journal of Marketing Research*, **34**, 1, 24-35

Gupta AK, Raj SP, and Wilemon D (1986) A Model for Studying R&D-Marketing Interface in the Product Innovation Process, *Journal of Marketing*, **50**, 2, 7-17

Gupta AK and Wilemon DL (1990) Accelerating The Development Of Technology-Based New Products, *California Management Review*, **32**, 2, 24-44

Herstatt C, Verworn B, and Nagahira A (2004a) Reducing project related uncertainty in the "fuzzy front end" of innovation - A comparison of German and Japanese product innovation projects, *International Journal of Product Development*, **1**, 1, 43-65

Herstatt C, Verworn B, Stockstrom C, Nagahira A and Takahashi O (2004b) "Fuzzy front end" practices in innovating Japanese companies. In: Proceedings of the R&D Management Conference 2004, 07 - 09 July, Sesimbra (Portugal)

Ittner CD and Larcker DF (1997) Product development cycle time and organizational performance, *JMR, Journal of Marketing Research*, **34**, 1, 13-23

Keplinger W (1991) *Merkmale erfolgreichen Projektmanagements*, Graz: dbv-Verlag

Kessler EH and Chakrabarti AK (1999) Speeding Up the Pace of New Product Development., *Journal of Product Innovation Management*, **16**, 3, 231-247

Khurana A and Rosenthal SR (1998) Towards holistic "front ends" in new product development, *The Journal of Product Innovation Management*, **15**, 1, 57-74

Lechler T (1997) *Erfolgsfaktoren des Projektmanagements*, Frankfurt am Main et al.: Lang

Lewis MW (2000) Exploring paradox: Toward a more comprehensive guide, *Academy of Management. The Academy of Management Review*, **25**, 4, 760

Lewis MW, Welsh MA, Dehler GE, and Green SG (2002) Product development tensions: Exploring contrasting styles of project management, *Academy of Management Journal*, **45**, 3, 546

MacCormack A and Verganti R (2003) Managing the sources of uncertainty: Matching process and context in software development, *The Journal of Product Innovation Management*, **20**, 3, 217

Miner AS, Bassoff P, and Moorman C (2001) Organizational improvisation and learning: A Field study, *Administrative Science Quarterly*, **46**, 2, 304-337

Moorman C and Miner AS (1998) The Convergence of Planning an Execution: Improvisation in New Product Development, *Journal of Marketing*, **62**, 3 (July 1998), 1-20

Nakata C and Sivakumar K (1996) National Culture and New Product Development: An Integrative View, *Journal of Marketing*, **60**, 1, 61-72

Olson EM, Walker OC, Ruekert RW, and Bonner JM (2001) Patterns of cooperation during new product development among marketing, operations and R&D: Implications for project performance, *The Journal of Product Innovation Management*, **18**, 4, 258-271

Olson EM, Walker OC, and Ruekert RW (1995) Organizing for Effective New Product Development: The Moderating Role of Product Innovativeness, *Journal of Marketing*, **59 (January 1995)**, 1, 48-62

Pinto JK and Slevin DP (1988) Critical Success Factors in Effective Project Implementation. In: Cleland DI and King WR (eds) *Project Management Handbook*, New York: Van Nostrand Reinhold, 479-512

Rogers EM (1990) The R&D/Marketing Interface In The Technological Innovation Process. In: Saghafi MM and Gupta AK (eds) *Managing The R&D Marketing Interface For Product Success: The Telecommunications Focus*, Greenwich and London: JAI Press, 5-14

Salomo S, Gemünden HG, and Billing F (2003) Dynamisches Schnittstellenmanagement radikaler Innovationsvorhaben. In: Herstatt C and Verworn B (eds) *Management der frühen Innovationsphasen - Grundlagen, Methoden, Neue Ansätze*, Wiesbaden: Gabler, 161-194

Shenhar AJ, Tishler A, Dvir D, Lipovetsky S, and Lechler T (2002) Refining the search for project success factors: A multivariate, typological approach, *R & D Management*, **32**, 2, 111

Song M and Montoya-Weiss MM (2001) The effects of perceived technological uncertainty on Japanese new product development, *Academy of Management Journal*, **44**, 1, 61

Song MX and Montoya-Weiss MM (1998) Critical development activities for really new versus incremental products, *The Journal of Product Innovation Management*, **15**, 2, 124-135

Song MX and Parry ME (1997) The determinants of Japanese new product successes, *JMR, Journal of Marketing Research*, **34**, 1, 64

Tatikonda MV and Rosenthal SR (2000) Successful execution of product development projects: Balancing firmness and flexibility in the innovation process, *Journal of Operations Management*, **18**, 4, 401-425

Thieme JR, Song M, and Shin G-C (2003) Project Management Characteristics and New Product Survival, *The Journal of Product Innovation Management*, **20**, 104-119

Trauffler G, Herstatt C, and Tschirky H (2004) How to transfer discontinuous technology into radical innovation – Some evidence from three nanotech cases. TU Hamburg-Harburg AB Technology and Innovation Management Working Paper No. 26, Hamburg

van de Ven AH and Ferry DL (1980) *Measuring and Assessing Organizations*, New York: Wiley-Interscience

Verganti R (1997) Leveraging on systemic learning to manage the early phases of product innovation projects, *R & D Management*, **27**, 4, 377-392

Verganti R (1999) Planned Flexibility: Linking Anticipation and Reaction in Product Development Projects., *Journal of Product Innovation Management*, **16**, 4, 363-376

Ward A, Liker JK, Cristiano JJ, and Sobeck DK, II (1995) The second Toyota paradox: How delaying decisions can make better cars faster, *Sloan Management Review*, **36**, 3, 43-61

Wiskow B (1999) *Die Verkürzung der Produktentwicklungszeit aus anreiztheoretischer Sicht*, München et al.: Hampp

Zhang Q and Doll WJ (2001) The fuzzy front end and success of new product development: a causal model, *European Journal of Innovation Management*, **4**, 2, 95-112

Part IV: Cultural Aspects

Japanese New Product Advantage: A Comparative Examination

Cheryl Nakata and Subin Im

Introduction

Over the last few decades, Japanese companies have been at the cusp of innovation, introducing new products to receptive buyers throughout the world. Toyota's Prius, a hybrid gas-electric car, and Casio's Exilim, a palm-sized digital camera, are just a few of the products recently developed and successfully marketed from Japan. The key reason for these products' popularity appears to be built-in advantage, or superiority, over rival offerings. For example, the Prius saves on fuel costs, emits almost no fumes, requires little maintenance, and sells at an affordable price. Despite such successes, Japanese companies are unable to rest on any laurels. Nipping at their heels are South Korean firms, which are vying with Japanese businesses in their traditionally strong sectors of consumer electronics and automotives. Samsung is perhaps the most notable challenger. The firm has introduced a flood of new products in the last several years, winning design accolades and many new customers for its premium cell phones, plasma flat-screen TVs, and ultra-thin computer monitors, among other innovations. In several of these categories, the firm is the global market leader or is a close second in sales. Along with several other companies based in South Korea (referred hereafter as Korea), Samsung is making great strides in innovation, mastering the ability to create advantageous new products.

Given this dynamic rivalry between Japanese and Korean businesses, we thought it timely to investigate new product advantage comparatively across the two countries. Specifically, we pursue these questions: 1) "how do Japanese companies create new product advantage and in what ways may the approach differ or be similar to that of Korean counterparts?" and 2) "does greater advantage necessarily lead to higher sales, profitability, and market share for Japanese companies, i.e. stronger new product performance, and is the relationship between advantage and performance different or the same for Korean firms?" It is interesting to note that despite the significance of the Japanese and Korean economies, whose combined GNP of $4.5 trillion ranks only second after that of the U.S., there is limited understanding of how these countries have come to excel in export-led growth, particularly through the sales of new products to foreign markets. Our search of the literature indicates few investigations have been conducted on new product advantage among Asia-based businesses. There is only one published study on new product development in Korean enterprises (Mishra, Kim and Lee 1996), but it is not specific to the topic of advantage. In other words, the above questions have not been previously addressed as best we can tell. Hence, we believe our study will be of interest and value to managers and researchers who are aware of, and wanting to fathom, the tremendous rise of innovation capabilities outside the West.

We began our study by proposing a conceptual model of new product advantage, with differences and similarities noted between Japanese and Korean approaches in terms of drivers and performance outcomes. We then tested the model by conducting a survey of over 200 new product development managers in Japanese and Korean firms. In the following sections, we present the conceptual model, followed by the research hypotheses. Thereafter, we describe the methodology and findings, and conclude with implications for managers and researchers.

Conceptual Model

Two related theories serve as the basis for our conceptual model: the Resource-Based View and the Source Position Performance paradigm. According to the Resource Based View, firms possess productive resources, which - if rare, valuable, and not easily imitable, substitutable, or transferable - generate sustainable competitive advantage and thereby superior business performance (Barney 1991; Barney and Ketchen 2001). Resources with these desired traits are deemed to be strategic, and their possession differs from firm to firm, explaining why some businesses outperform others. Similarly, the Source Position Performance paradigm argues that when companies possess superior skills and resources, they develop positional advantages relative to competitors, such as deeper customer loyalty and lower operating costs (Day and Wensley 1988). These advantages then lead to performance gains such as higher sales, profits, and market share.

Translating the two theories into the context of new product development, as has been done previously (Han et al. 1998; Song and Parry 1997a), we propose that firms with better skills and resources are more able to inject superiorities into new products. Customers, noticing these attractive qualities, prefer the products and vote with their pocketbooks. In the end superior products outperform alternative offerings, delivering higher market and financial returns for the firms that develop and market them. But what are these skills and resources that produce new product advantage, which in turn generates superior new product performance? According to Montoya-Weiss and Calatone (1994), the skills and resources pertinent to new product development fall into four categories: strategic, organizational, process, and market-environmental. Of the four, the most critical is process-centered. The reason is that process factors represent the primary and most direct form of managerial control over new product development projects (Henard and Szymanski 2001). Process factors are of three types: ones tied to interactions and communications among project participants (e.g. functional integration), ones based on the knowledge or skills residing in the organization and dedicated to projects (e.g. technological proficiency), and ones reflecting tasks undertaken to initiate and bring a project to successful completion (e.g. conducting market research with potential buyers).

In view of the above, we develop a conceptual framework focused on process factors, and posit that these factors facilitate the creation of new product advantage, subsequently benefiting new product performance. More specifically, we propose the following variables as influences on advantage, with each representing one of the three types of process factors: cross-functional integration (interactions and communications), new product team proficiency (knowledge and skills), and initiation process (specific tasks). Although other process variables may also be antecedents of advantage, we selected these three given their acknowledged importance in new product development, as will be elaborated in the next section. We do note that, while these process factors are generally believed to influence new product advantage, differences and similarities likely occur between the Japanese firm and Korean firm contexts. These differences and similarities will be detailed and explained in the section hereafter.

For the sake of clarity at this juncture, we define the core construct of our study - new product advantage - since it has taken on a range of meanings in the literature. Rogers (1983) may have been the first to observe that users embrace an innovation when it has a noticeable advantage over existing options. Since then advantage has been widely recognized as a desirable quality in new products. Various terms have been used to refer to it, including positional product differentiation (Song and Parry 1997a), product differentiation (Cooper and Kleinschmidt 1993), product competitive advantage (Song and Parry 1997a; Song and Parry 1999) and new product advantage (Li and Calantone 1998). Because "new product advantage" most succinctly captures the idea of a cluster of traits setting a new product apart from and ahead of others, we apply it in this study. Additionally, we adopt Song and Montoya-Weiss' definition: "a product's perceived superiority relative to competitive products" (2001, p. 65). Advantage encompasses a product's uniqueness, quality, problem-solving capability, innovativeness, technical performance, and ability to meet customers' needs compared to rival offerings (Li and Calantone 1998; Cooper 1983).

Research Hypotheses

Cross-Functional Integration

Typically, the more innovative and unique a new product, the greater the need for different kinds of expertise to create that product (Lindman 2000). However, as suggested by Madhavan and Grover (1998), the mere presence of an array of specialists does not guarantee this end, only the potential. This is where integration is the key. By synergistically melding together specialists, for example from R&D and marketing, integration exploits their disparate talents and knowledge toward developing advantageous new products. Lynn et al. (1999) in a study of 700 new product teams found that only 7% succeeded in developing truly superior products, such as Colgate's Total Toothpaste. Interestingly, the researchers observed that two of the five practices generating superior products are integration-related: information exchange and collaboration among team members. Also several studies by Song and his colleagues in Japan and the U.S. isolated cross-functional integration as an indirect antecedent of advantage (Song and Parry 1997a, 1997b; Song and Montoya-Weiss 2001).

While the above studies are suggestive, there are reasons to study formally the antecedent role of cross-functional integration in new product advantage. One reason is that the direct relationship of integration to advantage, incorporating all aspects of advantage - from innovativeness and quality to uniqueness and problemsolving capability - has not been investigated. A second reason is that the relationship may be contingent on where product development takes place. Japan and Korea are both known as highly collectivistic countries, so it would seem crossfunctional integration would be culturally valued, unlike perhaps in more individualistic countries like the U.S (Song and Parry 1997a, 1997b; Song and Montoya-Weiss 2001). The culture-based emphasis on cross-functional integration in Japan and Korea should in turn foster new product advantage. Yet as remarked on by social scientists, apparently similar countries can be distinct in historical and socio-cultural milieus, and hence in managerial and innovation practices (Fukuyama 1995; Hattori 1989).

Japanese companies have been described as consensual and decentralized, with an emphasis on information gathering and continuous learning in an open, iterative manner (Song and Parry 1997a; Song and Xie 2000; Yoshimura and Anderson 1997). Managers tend to state ambiguous goals and are non-directive, relying on social controls to achieve targeted outcomes. Girding these practices is a cultural force, namely *amae*, or the unwillingness of group members to take advantage of each other's weaknesses. *Amae* breeds mutual dependence, forming a communal solidarity among workers. *Amae*-based solidarity is pervasive in Japanese corporations but almost absent in Korean ones (Fukuyama 1995, p. 135). Because Japanese managers can rely on *amae* to bring about cooperation, crossfunctional integration as a formal policy or structure is less necessary than in Korea. If integration happens without emphasis or coercion, it may explain why this mechanism is not as consciously valued in Japan compared to Korea.

On the other hand, Korean firms are managed in a more centralized, top-down fashion. The managerial style is rooted in the country's history. Korea was forcibly occupied by Japan from 1910 to 1945. One vestige of the long period of military rule is a more authoritarian, paternalistic style of management, reinforced by centralized structures, formalized procedures, and vertical communications (Hattori 1989; Chung et al. 1997, p. 156). Tall organizational hierarchies are common in Korean businesses, with control firmly held by owner-managers. It is notable that *chaebols* such as Hyundai and LG Electronics, which till recently dominated all industrial sectors, behave more like family concerns: decisions come from owner-managers and are not vetted at lower levels (Fukuyama 1995, pp.133-135). One implication is that functional and hierarchical boundaries are not easily crossed when working on innovation projects. Deeply held inclinations to respect demarcations, denoting rings of power, restrain employees from participating in the give and take that typifies new product development projects in Japan (Chang and Chang 1994, p. 154). Therefore in Korean firms, formal mechanisms such as cross-functional teams may be imposed to sanction and spur cooperation. The imposition of such structures heightens sensitivities toward integration. We thus hypothesize a distinction in the role of cross-functional integration to new product advantage in Japan versus Korea:

H1: Higher cross-functional integration is associated with greater new product advantage in Korea but not in Japan.

New Product Team Proficiency

The new product team is the epicenter of innovation work (Brown and Eisenhardt 1995). Therefore creating a successful new product depends on the abilities of the group most responsible for its conceptualization, creation, and market introduction (Cooper 1979; Maidique and Zirger 1984). The group needs to be skilled in and knowledgeable about a host of tasks, from market opportunity identification and product design to sales forecasting and manufacturing planning. We are interested specifically in the capability of a new product team rather than an individual function to carry out these complex tasks, and thus propose the construct of new product team proficiency. This is defined as a team's skills, knowledge, and efficacy in carrying out new product development activities, which has not been previously investigated in relation to new product advantage.

An early study that acknowledged the role of functional proficiency was Cooper's NewProd project (Cooper 1979). Surveying several hundred Canadian firms about their innovation processes, Cooper identified marketing proficiency as one of the highest discriminators between successful and failed new products. Consistent with these results, the Stanford Innovation Project (Maidique and Zirger 1984) determined that a company's R&D and marketing skills are strong drivers of innovation results. The association between marketing or technical proficiency and new product success has been found in a range of countries, including China, Spain, Canada, Japan, the U.S., and Taiwan (Calantone et al. 1996; Cooper and Kleinschmidt 1995; Song et al. 1997; Souder and Song 1998).

Yet we are interested not in functional proficiency but rather in team proficiency, a more global or encompassing construct centered on the organizational unit responsible for delivering new products. Cooper and Kleinschmidt (1995) observed that the formation and use of a team for new product development in and of itself has little bearing on the product's ultimate success or failure; instead, the quality of teams makes all the difference. The researchers noted that higher quality teams - ones in which decisions are made efficiently and there is an emphasis on strong execution from idea generation through market launch - generate more profitable and impactful innovations. Separately, Lynn, Abel, Valentine, and Wright (1999) learned that optimal team skills are critical for generating successful high tech products in the computer and electronics industries. Without this capability at the collective level, a team is unable to discern distinctive needs among customers and fulfill those vis-à-vis technically appropriate, financially feasible, and observably better products. Logic dictates, then, that new product team proficiency corresponds with new product advantage.

But do the contexts of Japan and Korea make a difference? We note that some of the above studies - albeit focused on functional, not team, proficiency - have been conducted in a diverse set of countries, from developed (e.g. Canada) to less developed (e.g. China), and from West (e.g. Spain) to East (e.g. Taiwan). Hence the contextual variable has been incorporated, and the results suggest that proficiency is tied to advantage regardless of geography. Additionally, in Japan as well as Korea, teams are routinely employed for new product development work (Song and Parry 1997a), with presumably more skillful teams generating better products. Economic or socio-cultural forces are not expected to mitigate this influence, leading us to forward the following hypothesis:

H2: New product team proficiency is associated with new product advantage in both Japan and Korea.

Initiation Process

In the overall process of new product development, it is widely believed that the most important activities occur in the initiation, or front-end, stage (Cooper 1994; Moenaert et al. 1995; Nobelius and Trygg 2002; Reid and de Brentani 2004; Verganti 1997). Among these activities are idea generation and screening, concept development, market research to assess concepts, market and business analyses, and initial prototype creation and testing. The reason these activities are arguably the most important is twofold: 1) tasks performed during the initiation stage determine those that follow in the implementation, or back-end, stage (this is true even if recursive paths are taken to loop back through these phases more than once), and 2) initiation tasks generate the greatest improvements at the least cost for the product that ultimately emerges (implementation tasks in contrast make only incremental improvements to an already fixed idea and targeted market). Due to the importance of initiation tasks, they constitute a key process variable that deserves examination for its potential effects on advantage and new product performance.

The notion that initiation activities have a sizable influence on new product outcomes is well established in the literature. The Harvard Auto Study, an examination of 29 developmental projects in the automotive industry in the U.S., Japan, and Europe, determined that pre-development planning and other front-end actions significantly predict the quality, speed, and productivity of new product development (Clark and Fujimoto 1991). One way these actions benefit new product development is by resolving organizational conflicts and honing a clear project vision early on in a project, facilitating the many steps that follow thereafter (Brown and Eisenhardt 1995).

Two recent studies reinforce the positive role of initiation in general, and suggest its contribution to new product advantage in particular. Khurana and Rosenthal (1998) conducted case studies in American and Japanese business units, and learned that it is in the front end that the product definition is formulated, such that desired features based on customer need analysis are correctly identified and deliberately inserted into the product concept. In other words, the advantages of a new product are consciously considered and incorporated during initiation, better ensuring meaningful advantages materialize in the final product. In nearly 200 new product project cases, Goldenberg, Lehman, and Mazursky (2001) determined that the idea or concept itself is a significant predictor of a product's success, more so than many other factors. More specifically, a product idea must be seen as new and innovative (aspects of advantage) but still be familiar in some characteristics to existing products to be preferred by buyers. Given the potency of the product concept, the researchers recommended expending organizational time and resources at the initiation stage, and estimating the potential of a new product early in the developmental cycle in order to maximize the probability of success.

Although the above studies point to better initiation coinciding with stronger new product advantage, there is reason to believe this effect may not be universal. In particular, we posit that the relationship holds in Japan but not in Korea. We turn to Khurana and Rosenthal's study (1998) for insights on a potential difference. The researchers made the intriguing observation that the Japanese companies they studied used a more informal and culture-based approach to managing the front-end stage. While other companies (notably American and European) preferred to formalize the steps comprising initiation, Japanese firms relied on a more ambiguous but holistic approach that simultaneously considered business vision, technical feasibility, customer focus, scheduling, resources, and coordination. In Japanese companies, there was an implicit understanding of what needed to be done without anyone having to spell it out or use a rule book. Imai, Nonaka, and Takeuchi (1985) described this as a form of subtle control prevalent in Japanese firms, and argued that it is appropriate given the inherent complexity and uncertainty of innovation projects - characteristics that are most acute in the front end and for radical new products.

In contrast, Korean firms prefer formal control, as already discussed. Culture, history, and corporate structures have resulted in a reliance on explicit and overt supervisory styles. While this preference is gradually changing, notably among more globally oriented businesses such as Samsung, we would expect that the traditional mode is still widely practiced. This would mean that the initiation process, though important, may not have the full impact on exploring and creatively inserting advantage into new products as it does in Japan. In many regards, Korean firms may excel less in initiation tasks and more in implementation activities, where tight control is necessary to meet schedules, fulfill market commitments, and corral critical resources. The above leads us to propose a difference between Japan and Korea in the relationship of initiation to advantage:

H3: Initiation process is positively associated with new product advantage in Japan but not Korea.

New Product Advantage

As discussed by Hult and Ketchen (2001), a positional advantage held by a firm should be rewarded with market share and/or profitability exceeding competitors'. The reasoning is that customers perceive the firm offers greater value in its products and services, and consequently shift purchases away from rivals. Therefore, in relation to innovation efforts, when advantages are built into new products, the products should be more strongly received in the marketplace, or have higher new product performance. Researchers have found evidence of this effect in the U.S., Canada, Europe, and Japan. One of the earliest studies was conducted by Cooper and Kleinschmidt (1987), who identified product advantage as one of nine drivers for new product success among Canadian firms. Similarly, the researchers conducted a study of chemical businesses in four North American and European countries, and isolated superior quality, value, uniqueness, and need fulfillment as the strongest predictors of new product success (Cooper and Kleinschmidt 1993). More recently, Li and Calantone (1998) determined that advantage is significantly linked to new product performance for American software firms. Also, surveys of Japanese manufacturers indicate new product advantage correlates positively with new product performance (Song and Parry 1997a; Song and Montoya-Weiss 2001).

Although the advantage-performance link appears robust and uniform, does it hold in both Japan and Korea? Researchers have proposed that the relationship depends on market conditions (Song and Parry 1997b; Cooper 1979). In mature economies like Japan, an advantage tends to be of shorter duration due to market saturation, responsive competition, and demanding customers (Kodama 1995). Companies face severe competition even domestically, and have learned to introduce new products in rapid succession simply to survive. Buyers face a constant barrage of new offerings, but their choices continue to be based on what they perceive as preferable qualities in one product over all others. However, in developing countries such as Korea, new products are not always met with fast and adroit responses from local competitors. There are simply fewer firms that have developed superb innovation capabilities, making new product advantages more salient and persistent. Yet in both countries, despite a difference in the duration of advantages, the underlying market response to new product advantage is consistent: greater advantage is recognized and preferred, leading to greater sales and profits for the products that are superior. Therefore, we posit Japan and Korea are similar with respect to the advantage-performance relationship:

H4: Higher new product advantage is associated with greater new product performance in both Japan and Korea.

Methodology

Per Douglas' and Craig's recommendations for cross-cultural research (1983), we avoided assuming emic concepts were etic by conducting exploratory interviews in the two target countries. Product developers were interviewed in an open-ended fashion in Japan and Korea. The interview findings in combination with the literature were used to generate a questionnaire in Korean. Four academicians reviewed the questionnaire and minor revisions were made. The Korean questionnaire was then translated into a Japanese version using parallel-translation and double-translation methods (Song and Parry 1997a). Specifically, a Japanese business professional proficient in Korean translated the original questionnaire into Japanese; then two Korean bilingual business professionals translated the Japanese version back into Korean. Along with translation equivalence, we checked for measurement and administration equivalence.

Two pretests were conducted using the questionnaires, one in Japan and the other in Korea. Twenty new product development managers in Korea were asked to complete the questionnaire as well as provide feedback on the instrument's wording and appropriateness of the administration method; the same was done with twenty new product development managers in Japan. The questionnaire focused on the new product development process in the firm (the unit of analysis), more specifically the development of new products launched in the prior 12 months and their subsequent performance.

The sampling frame was created by obtaining a list of manufacturing firms on the Nikkei Stock Exchange and separately a list of manufacturing firms on the Korea Stock Exchange. The lists reflected a range of industries. From each list, firms were randomly selected to receive a mailing. Before the mailing, phone calls were placed to each firm to identify a marketing or product manager informed about recent new products to minimize the distortion of memory bias. These managers were then pre-notified by phone of the mail survey and requested to participate. Next, the survey was mailed out, followed by reminder phone calls and faxes. A total of 110 and 149 complete responses were collected in Japan and Korea, respectively, representing corresponding usable response rates of 68% and 93%. Research assistants collected data on-site after they hand-delivered the follow-up survey to managers in the metropolitan areas of Tokyo and Seoul.

To assess non-response bias, we conducted t-tests on major measures in order to compare early and late respondents as well as respondents versus non-respondents. No significant differences were found, indicating that non-response did not inhibit the generalization of findings (Armstrong and Overton 1997). Multi-collinearity diagnostic tests confirmed there was no serious multi-collinearity present in the individual country samples: all condition indices fell below 30, and Variance Influence Factors (VIFs) were all under 10 (Belsley et al. 1980).

Measures

We followed recommendations by Churchill (1979) to develop and validate the measures for major constructs. Multiple-item measures, with 5-point Likert-type scales (1 for "strongly disagree" to 5 for "strongly agree"), were collected from the literature and used to assess the major constructs. After data collection, we subjected the items to a purification process, keeping those that exhibited desirable psychometric properties. Final measures for each country showed acceptable internal consistency based on coefficient alphas of .70 or higher (see Appendix 1 for the scales and reliability levels).

Cross-functional Integration (CFI). We adopted Song and Xie's definition of cross-functional integration: "effective unity of effort by R&D, manufacturing, and marketing in new product development" (2000, p.64). For this construct, we used a three-item measure adapted from Song and Parry (1997a) that examines the overall goodness of integration and communications among R&D, marketing, and manufacturing.

New Product Team Proficiency (NPTP). This is a new construct referring to the abilities, skills, knowledge, and efficacy of a new product team in carrying out innovation activities. Based on the interviews as well as extant research on new product teams, we created a five-item measure encompassing dimensions such as technical skills, marketing knowledge, and team efficiency in the group responsible for developing a new product.

Initiation Process (IP). Following Zaltman, Duncan, and Holbek (1973), we define initiation process as the conceptual and pre-developmental tasks in new product development, including idea generation, concept evaluation, market research, screening, and prototype testing. We incorporated six items for initiation tasks from studies by Song and Parry (1997a) and Cooper (1979).

New Product Advantage (NPA). This construct refers to "a product's perceived superiority relative to competitive products" (Song and Montoya-Weiss 2001, p. 65). In keeping with this rather encompassing definition, we combined several measures of advantage current in the literature (Song and Parry 1997a; Song and Parry 1999; Song and Montoya-Weiss 2001;, Song and Parry 1997b). Our eight-item measure of new product advantage focuses on the new product's uniqueness, need fulfillment, utility, quality, benefits, problem-solving capability, innovativeness, and radical difference relative to competitive offerings.

New Product Performance (NPP). As recommended by new product strategy researchers (Song and Parry 1997a; Montoya-Weiss and Calantone 1994; Song and Parry 1997b; Churchill 1979), we incorporated multiple dimensions for this construct. A five-item measure was adapted from Cooper and Kleinschmidt (1995) and Song and Parry (1997a) to assess NPP in terms of relative market share, relative sales, and relative profitability of all new products in the last 12 months. The items represented the most critical and often used NPP measures, termed "core success/failure measures": customer acceptance (e.g. meeting sales goals), financial performance (e.g. profitability), and firm-level measures (e.g. firm sales volume) (Griffin and Page 1993).

Model Estimation and Results

Prior to testing the proposed hypotheses in the model, we examined the correlation matrix of the composite scales for the constructs. The signs of the correlation coefficients appeared to be consistent with the hypothesized relationships. In addition, means and standard deviations for composite scales for major constructs indicated enough variability in the construct measures. The correlation matrix and descriptive statistics are provided in Table 1.

Table 1. Correlation matrix and descriptive statistics

	CFI	NPTP	IP	NPA	NPP	Mean	S.D.
Cross-functional integration (CFI)	1					11.13/ 11.22	2.84/ 2.10
New product team proficiency (NPTP)	.41**/ .56**	1				15.75/ 17.18	3.62/ 3.08
Initiation process (IP)	.38**/ .49**	.48**/ .57**	1			21.37/ 18.82	3.97/ 4.47
New product advantage (NPA)	.18/ .41**	.41**/ .40**	.31**/ .40**	1		25.06/ 24.98	3.06/ 4.09
New product performance (NPP)	.21**/ .25**	.48**/ .53**	.35**/ .26**	.33**/ .33**	1	15.61/ 17.57	3.41/ 3.78

(Japan: N = 111/Korea: N = 149)
*   significant at p<.05 level
** significant at p<.01 level

Following Baldauf, Cravens, and Piercy (2001) and Piercy, Cravens, and Morgan (1999), we used simple path analysis, where path coefficients were estimated with ordinary least squares (OLS) regressions from the country-specific data on Korea and Japan. Although structural equation modeling analysis could have provided simultaneous estimations of all relationships, the sample size in each country was inadequate for such purposes (e.g. the Japanese sample included 110 respondents, considerably short of the 200 generally required to estimate all parameters). For this path analysis using OLS regressions, we performed the data analysis in two steps for each country.[1] First, we regressed new product advantage on the three antecedents of cross-functional integration, new product team proficiency, and initiation process (F = 10.59/13.24, p's < .01, R^2 = .23/.22 for Japan/Korea samples). Second, NPP was regressed on new product advantage (F = 12.96/18.13, p's < .01, R^2 = .11/.11 for Japan/Korea samples).

Main Findings

The results of the simple path analyses are summarized in Figure 1. The following country-specific results pointed out important similarities and differences in Japanese and Korean new product development.

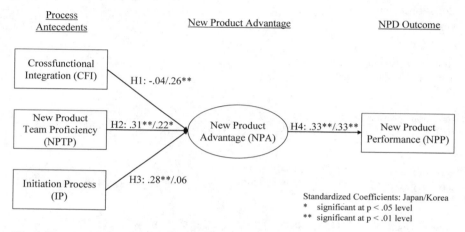

Fig. 1. Conceptual framework and estimation results

In H1 cross-functional integration (CFI) was posited to be an antecedent of new product advantage in Korea but not Japan. The standardized coefficient of .26 was significant ($p<.01$) in Korea; however, the coefficient of -.04 was conversely non-significant ($p>.05$) in Japan. The findings supported H1.

We had also hypothesized through H2 that a second antecedent, new product team proficiency (NPTP), is positively tied to new product advantage in Japan as well as Korea. The relationship was significant and positive based on the corresponding standardized coefficients of .31 ($p<.01$) and .22 ($p<.05$) for Japan and Korea, respectively. The findings provided evidence for H2.

---

[1] We also performed regressions with a country dummy variable (0 for Japan, 1 for Korea) as an alternate way of testing the model. We found the results to be very comparable, so we report here only the results of the original path analyses.

H3 predicted that initiation process is positively associated with new product advantage only in Japan. As expected, the standardized coefficient in Japan was significant .28 ($p<.01$), whereas in Korea the coefficient was .06 ($p>.05$) and non-significant.

Finally, we postulated in H4 that greater new product advantage corresponds with higher new product performance (NPP) in Japan and Korea. This relationship was found to be positive and significant for both countries: the standardized coefficient was .33 ($p<.01$). Hence H4 was supported.

To determine if new product advantage indeed plays a mediating role, we performed the test of mediation recommended by Baron and Kenny (1986) and Jap and Ganesan (2000). In the first step, we regressed NPP on three antecedents (F = 11.69/19.35, p's < .01, R^2 = .25/.31 for Japan/Korea samples). In the next step, NPP was regressed on the three antecedents along with new product advantage (F = 9.26/ 16.06, p's < .01, R^2 = .26/.31 for Japan/Korea samples). When we added the advantage variable in the second step, the effects of the three antecedents on NPP were reduced, and the overall fit based on R square value was improved in Japan as well as Korea.[2] These results suggested mediation though advantage.

Discussion

The purpose of our study was to shed light on Japanese new product advantage compared to Korean new product advantage. Specifically, we ask two questions: 1) "how do Japanese companies create new product advantage and in what ways may the approach differ or be similar to that of Korean counterparts?" and 2) "does greater advantage necessarily lead to higher sales, profitability, and market share for Japanese companies, i.e. stronger new product performance, and is the relationship between advantage and performance different or the same for Korean firms?" To answer the questions, we conducted a survey of Japanese and Korean innovation managers. That survey showed us that with respect to the first question, Japanese companies create new product advantage by excelling in the initiation process and new product team proficiency, whereas Korean businesses build new product advantage through cross-functional integration and new product team proficiency. In other words, there are country-based differences as well as similarities in approach to generating advantage. The survey also revealed that in relation to the second question, greater advantage does lead to higher new product performance in Japan as well as Korea.

---

[2]   Following Jap and Ganesan, we interpreted the magnitude of change as indicating fit improvement.

Managerial Implications

Our study has several managerial implications. Foremost is that this study points to the value of creating new product advantage in Japan and Korea. Henard and Szymanski (2001) concluded in the most recent meta-analysis of the new product literature that advantage is the most important determinant of new product success. Our study underscores this insight by demonstrating that advantage is clearly linked to the market and financial performance of a new product across both geographies. Therefore, to ensure the development of high performing new products, focusing on advantage is a potent and beneficial course. Industry leaders in Japan and Korea, such as Sharp and Hyundai, appear to be acting on this knowledge already, emphasizing multiple forms of superiority in new products in order to woo and keep customers.

The second managerial implication is that our model of process antecedents is a useful description and guide for developing new product advantage in Japan and Korea. Cross-functional integration, new product team proficiency, and initiation process are three critical levers that managers can manipulate to create superior new products. It would be useful, then, for managers to regularly assess the degree to which these levers or factors are in place and make adjustments accordingly. For example, if managers in a Japanese company determine that the initiation process is weak, they can draw more attention to the need for thoughtful initiation activities such as deep customer need analysis, leveraging culture-based controls as *amae*. In Korea, managers in a firm may determine that cross-functional integration is poor, impeding the development of new product advantage. In this case, the managers can establish more mechanisms to encourage interactions and communications among diverse functions, including imposing a formal team structure, offering team-based rewards, and providing computer platforms for information sharing.

A third managerial implication is the need to observe distinctions in product development by country. It is important to anticipate such differences, such as the greater role of initiation process in Japan versus cross-functional integration in Korea. If a multinational company is operating an R&D or innovation center in these countries, or is collaborating, say, in a strategic alliance with a Japanese or Korean company to develop new products, it may be counterproductive to impose a uniform approach. The mistake can easily be made since Japanese and Korean companies are both in Asia; however, presuming their approaches to innovation work are exactly the same would be ill-advised, as clearly demonstrated in our study. Interestingly, Japanese companies are entering into strategic alliances with Korean firms (e.g. Sony with Samsung to develop and sell products for the LCD market), so it is critical to be cognizant and accommodate country-based differences in innovation methods.

A fourth implication is that the knowledge and skill proficiency of the new product team is vital to the creation of advantage in both Japan and Korea. This process factor, which previously had not been studied, has the greatest and only uniformly positive impact on advantage (based on higher beta values over those for cross-functional integration and initiation process). This means it is worth the time and effort to carefully select members of a new product team, assembling the appropriate knowledge and skill set in the first place so that the end result is a truly superior new product. While integrating across functions and completing initiation tasks are important, team proficiency ensures the quality of human resources dedicated to the innovation enterprise is sufficient for success. The team proficiency scale from this study can be used to assess quality. If quality is thereby judged to be inadequate, the team may re-constitute or new leadership assigned to increase the likelihood of exploiting the team's capabilities. Additionally, training in innovation and group endeavors can be provided so that the talents and energies of individuals are properly harnessed, increasing collective proficiency over time.

Limitations and Research Implications

Our conclusions are qualified in several regards. First, data was collected in just two countries, Japan and Korea, so generalizing the hypothesized model beyond these settings is limited. Future research should examine the model in more countries. But we chose Japan and then Korea due to their importance in the world economy and because of the salience of their innovation output. Other countries that are worth exploring in regard to new product advantage are Germany, the U.K., Sweden, and the U.S.

Another limitation is that only three specific process antecedents were investigated - ones that, based on the literature, warranted examination. Future studies can investigate other precursors to advantage, as well as compare their direct and interactive influences. One particularly intriguing variable is cross-functional integration. This study showed it has paradoxical or mixed effects, so it would be worthwhile understanding more of its influences and the conditions under which they alter.

Another variable worth further probing is new product team proficiency. As this was the first study to conceptualize and measure this construct, it is deserving of additional study. Moreover, it was demonstrated to be the most influential driver of advantage. As firms move increasingly toward team-based new product development, it would be critical to understand exactly how this proficiency is cultivated and applied toward innovation endeavors. Although we did not examine it in this study, a team's culture may be a major factor.

The final limitation is our conjectural explanation for the contrasting approaches to innovation work between Japan and Korea. Although we propose stage of industrialization and culture act as possible influences, later studies can explicitly model and empirically test these effects. It would be particularly useful in relation to the culture variable to go beyond the well-known Hofstede treatment, which categorizes Japan and Korea as similarly collectivistic; other researchers have argued that Japan and Korea are distant on this and other cultural dimensions (Fukuyama 1995). Finer grained research tools may be required to capture such nuances. All in all, we hope that this study has produced greater understanding on the role of advantage in new products produced in Japanese firms compared to Korean companies, and how firms in both national settings may achieve higher performing new products.

Appendix: Measurement Items and Coefficient Alphas (Japan/Korea)

Variable (Japan/Korea alphas)	Items
Cross-functional integration (CFI) (.89/.83)	Integration and communication between R&D and manufacturing were very good in the new product development process. Integration and communication between marketing and R&D were very good in the new product development process. Integration and communication between marketing and manufacturing were very good in the new product development process.
New product team proficiency (NPTP) (.86/.86)	Our new product development team was efficient. We had accurate forecasts for market demand. Our predictions about customers' needs were accurate. Our knowledge of the market was accurate. Our technical skills fit the needs of the products.
Initiation process (IP) (.71/.74)	A systematic idea screening procedure was used. We used an elaborate product concept development procedure. We performed market research regarding potential customers in order to test the product concept. We conducted business analysis (e.g. demand forecast) for the new product concept. We performed a prototype or sample test in house. We performed a prototype or sample test with customers.
New product advantage (NPA) (.87/.87)	Our new product offered unique features or attributes. Our new product was superior in meeting customers' needs. Our new product contained useful functions that could not be found in competing products. Our new product offered better quality to customers compared to competing products. Our new product offered unique benefits to customers. Our new product solved problems that customers had before with competing products. Our new product was highly innovative, replacing vastly inferior products. Our new product was radically different from competing products.
New product performance (NPP) (.87/.93)	Sales volume relative to competitors Sales volume relative to a firm's original objectives Profitability relative to competitors Profitability relative to a firm's original objectives Market share relative to competitors

References

Armstrong JS and Overton TS (1997): 'Estimating nonresponse bias in mail surveys' *Journal of Marketing Research*, Vol. 14, pp. 396-402

Baldauf A, Cravens DW, and Piercy NF (2001): 'Examining business strategy, sales management, and salesperson antecedents of sales organization effectiveness' *Journal of Personal Selling & Sales Management*, Vol. 21 (2), pp. 109-122

Barney JB (1991): 'Firm resources and sustained competitive advantage' *Journal of Management*, Vol.17 (1), pp.99-120

Barney JB, Ketchen Jr. MW (2001): 'Resource-based theories of competitive advantage: a ten-year retrospective on the resource-based view' *Journal of Management*, Vol. 27(6), pp.625-642

Baron RM and Kenny DA (1986): 'The moderator-mediator variable distinction in social psychological research' *Journal of Personality and Social Psychology*, Vol. 51, pp. 1173-1182

Belsley DA, Kuh E, and Welsch RE (1980): *Regression Diagnostics*, New York: John Wiley and Sons

Brown SL and Eisenhardt KE (1995): 'Product development: past research, present findings, and future directions' *Academy of Management Review*, Vol.20 (2), pp. 343-378

Calantone RJ, Schmidt JB, and Song XM (1996): 'Controllable factors of new product success: a cross-national comparison' *Marketing Science*, Vol. 15 (4), pp. 15: 341-358

Chang CS and Chang NJ (1994): *The Korean Management System*. Westport: Quorum Books

Chung KH, Lee HC, and Jung KH (1997): *Korean Management: Global Strategy and Cultural Transformation*. Berlin: Walter de Gruyter

Churchill GA (1979): 'A paradigm for developing better measures of marketing constructs' *Journal of Marketing Research*, Vol. 16 (February), pp. 64-73

Clark KB and Fujimoto T (1991): *Product Development Performance*. Boston: Harvard Business School Press

Cooper RG (1979): 'The dimensions of industrial new product success' *Journal of Marketing*, Vol. 43 (3), pp. 93-103

Cooper RG (1983): ' The impact of new product strategies' *Industrial Marketing Management*, Vol.12, pp. 243-256

Cooper RG (1994): 'New products: the factors that drive success' *International Marketing Review*, Vol. 11, pp. 60-76

Cooper RG and Kleinschmidt EJ (1987): ‚New products: what separates winners from losers' *Journal of Product Innovation Management*, Vol. 4 (3), pp.169-184

Cooper RG and Kleinschmidt EJ (1993): 'Major new products: what distinguishes the winners in the chemical industry?' *Journal of Product Innovation Management*, Vol.10 (2), pp. 90-11

Cooper RG and Kleinschmidt EJ (1995): 'Benchmarking the firm's critical success factors in new product development' *Journal of Product Innovation Management*, Vol. 12 (5), pp. 374-391

Day GS and Wensley R (1988): 'Assessing advantage: a framework for diagnosing competitive superiority' *Journal of Marketing*, Vol.52 (2), pp. 1-20

Douglas S and Craig CS (1983): *International Marketing Research*, Englewood Cliffs: Prentice-Hall

Fukuyama F (1995): *Trust: The Social Virtues and the Creation of Prosperity*. New York: Free Press

Goldenberg J, Lehman DR, and Mazursky D (2001): 'The idea itself and the circumstances of its emergence as predictors of new product success' *Management Science*, Vol. 47 (1), pp. 69-84

Griffin A and Page AL (1993): 'An interim report on measuring product development success and failure' *Journal of Product Innovation Management*, Vol. 10, pp. 291-308

Han JK, Kim N, and Srivastava RK (1998): 'Market orientation and organizational performance: is innovation a missing link?' *Journal of Marketing*, Vol.62 (October), pp. 30-45

Hattori T (1989): 'Japanese zaibatsu and Korea chaebol' in Chung KH and Lee HC (Eds.) *Korean Managerial Dynamics*, New York, NY: Praeger, pp.79-95

Henard DH and Szymanski DM (2001): 'Why some new products are more successful than others' Journal *of Marketing Research*, Vol. 38 (August), pp. 362-375

Hult GT and Ketchen Jr. DJ (2001): 'Does market orientation matter? A test of the relationship between positional advantage and performance' *Strategic Management Journal*, Vol. 22, pp. 899-906

Imai K, Nonaka I, and Takeuchi H (1985): 'Managing the new product development process: how Japanese companies learn and unlearn' in Hayes RH, Clark K, and Lorenz C (Eds.), *The Uneasy Alliance: Managing the Productivity-Technology Dilemma*, Harvard Business School Press, pp.337-375

Jap SD and Ganesan S (2000): 'Control mechanisms and relationship life cycle: implications for safeguarding specific investments and developing commitment' *Journal of Marketing Research*, Vol. 37 (2), pp. 227-245

Khurana A and Rosenthal SR (1998): 'Toward holistic front ends in new product development' *Journal of Product Innovation Management*, Vol. 15 (1), pp. 57-74

Kodama F (1995): *Emerging Patterns of Innovation: Sources of Japan's Technological Edge*. Boston: Harvard Business School Press

Li T and Calantone RJ (1998): 'The impact of market knowledge competence on new product advantage: conceptualization and empirical examination' *Journal of Marketing*, Vol.29 (4), pp.13-29

Lindman M (2000): 'New product uniqueness in the context of industrial product development' *Journal of Marketing Management*, Vol. 16, pp. 247-271

Lynn GS, Abel KD, Valentine WS, and Wright RC (1999): 'Key factors in increasing speed to market and improving new product success rates' *Industrial Marketing Management*, Vol. 28 (4), pp. 319-326

Madhavan R and Grover R (1998): 'From embedded knowledge to embodied knowledge: new product development as knowledge management' *Journal of Marketing*, Vol. 62 (October), pp. 1-12

Maidique MA and Zirger BJ (1984): 'The new product learning cycle' *Research Report Series*, Innovation and Entrepreneurship Institute, School of Business Administration, University of Miami, Coral Gables, FL, February, pp. 85-101

Mishra S, Kim D, and Lee DH (1996): 'Factors affecting new product success: cross-country comparisons' *Journal of Product Innovation Management*, Vol. 13 (6), pp.530-550

Moenaert RK, De Meyer A, Souder WE, and Deschoolmeester D (1995): 'R&D-marketing communications during fuzzy front end' *IEEE Transactions on Engineering Management*, Vol. 42 (3), pp. 243-258

Montoya-Weiss MM and Calantone R (1994): 'Determinants of new product performance: a review and meta-analysis' *Journal of Product Innovation Management*, Vol. 11, pp. 397-417

Nobelius D and Trygg L (2002): 'Stop chasing the front end process-management of the early phases in product development projects' *International Journal of Project Management*, Vol. 20, pp. 331-340

Piercy NF, Cravens DW, and Morgan NA (1999): 'Relationships between sales management control, territory design, salesforce performance and sales organization effectiveness' *British Journal of Management*, Vol. 10, pp. 95-111

Reid SE and de Brentani U (2004): 'The fuzzy front end of new product development for discontinuous innovations: a theoretical model' *Journal of Product Innovation Management*, Vol. 21, pp.170-184

Rogers E (1983): *Diffusion of Innovations*. New York: Free Press

Song M and Montoya-Weiss MM (2001): 'The effect of perceived technological uncertainty on Japanese new product development' *Academy of Management Journal*, Vol. 44 (February), pp. 61-80

Song XM, Montoya-Weiss MM, and Schmidt JB (1997): 'The role of marketing in developing successful new products in South Korea and Taiwan' *Journal of International Marketing*, Vol. 69 (3), pp. 47-69

Song XM and Parry ME (1997a): 'The determinants of Japanese new product success' *Journal of Marketing Research*, Vol.34, pp. 64-76

Song XM and Parry ME (1997b): 'A cross-national comparative study of new product development processes: Japan and the United States' *Journal of Marketing*, Vol. 61 (April), pp. 1-18

Song XM and Parry ME (1999): 'Challenges of managing the development of breakthrough products in Japan' *Journal of Operations Management*, Vol.17, pp. 665-688

Song M and Xie J (2000): 'Does innovativeness moderate the relationship between cross-functional integration and product performance?' *Journal of International Marketing*, Vol. 8, pp. 61-89

Souder WE and Song XM (1998): 'Analyses of US and Japanese management processes associated with new product success and failure in high and low familiarity markets' *Journal of Product Innovation Management*, Vol. 15 (3), pp. 208-223

Verganti R (1997): 'Leveraging on systematic learning to manage the early phases of product innovation projects' *R&D Management*, Vol. 27 (4), pp. 377-392

Yoshimura N and Anderson P (1997): *Inside the Kaisha: Demystifying Japanese Business Behavior*, Boston: Harvard Business School Press

Zaltman G, Duncan R, and Holbek J (1973): *Innovations and Organizations*, New York: John Wiley

Differences in the Internationalization of Industrial R&D in the Triad

Guido Reger

Introduction

Internationalization of research and development (R&D) is a major topic within the business community, as well as for academic researchers and decision-makers in government since the 90s. These interests from various perspectives have stimulated a growing number of economic, policy- and management-oriented literature (Boutellier et al. 2000; Gerybadze et al. 1997; Meyer-Krahmer 1999; Brockhoff 1998; OECD 1998; Commission of the European Communities (CEC) 1998). An overview of this literature is published as a special issue in Research Policy (Niosi 1999)[1]. Another bunch of studies analyzed the differences of the internationalization strategies and the management of R&D and technological knowledge especially between Japanese, US and western European companies (Bartlett and Yoshihara 1988; Cairncross 1994; Fujita and Ishii 1994; Hedlund and Nonaka 1993; Kenney and Florida 1994; Sakakibara and Westney 1992; Westney 1994). This research was driven by the growing investment of Japanese firms in the United States and in countries of the European Union in the 80s and the beginning of the 90s as well as the growing internationalization of R&D of European multinationals since the 80s.

The internationalization of R&D and technology consists of complex processes and could be characterized by three main types of activities (Archibugi and Michie 1995):

1. *International exploitation of technology produced on a national basis,* which includes exports, granting of licenses and patents, and foreign manufacturing of innovations generated in the home country, carried out by profit-seeking organizations and individuals.
2. *International techno-scientific collaboration* between partners in more than one country for the development of know-how and innovations, whereby each partner retains his own institutional identity and ownership remains unaltered. Actors here are enterprises as well as other research performing institutions (universities, public R&D institutes).
3. *International generation of innovation and technology* carried out by multinational enterprises, which develop R&D strategies to create innovations across borders by building up research networks. R&D and innovation activities which

---

[1] *Research Policy*, Special Issue on "The Internationalization of Industrial R&D", edited by Jorge Niosi, Vol. 28, 1999

are carried out simultaneously in the home and host country, the acquisition of foreign R&D and the establishment of new R&D units in the host countries, are all means to this end.

This contribution builds on a survey on the practices in the strategic management of technology of large R&D intensive corporations. It focuses on the differences of the internationalization of R&D in North American, Japanese and western European corporations. First, it analyses the differences in the monitoring and acquisition of external technology (2nd type of the above mentioned category) and, second, in the international generation of innovation and technology (3rd type of the above mentioned category).

Methodology

Our survey aims at establishing a series of global benchmarks on the strategic management of technology from the personal points-of-view of the senior R&D/ technology officers of the world's most technology-intensive corporations. It is a follow-up to a similar study carried out in 1992 at the Massachusetts Institute of Technology by Ed Roberts (1995a, 1995b). Our research was jointly conducted by a team of researchers from the MIT in Cambridge, Massachusetts, the National Institute for Science and Technology Policy (NISTEP) in Japan and a research team from Germany. Our approach has been the following. First, we compiled a list of companies whose R&D expenditures totaled $100 million or more for inclusion in the sample. The geographical scope of the survey includes the countries of the Triad, i.e., the U.S. and Canada (North America), western European countries, and Japan. The assignment of a corporation's nationality was based on the location of its headquarters. The sample comprised 438 companies: 182 companies in North America, 126 in Japan, and 130 in Western Europe. This list of corporations whose R&D expenditures totaled $100 million or more was compiled from various sources and includes the main global players worldwide. Second, a joint questionnaire was developed and sent to senior R&D or technology officers of all the companies in our sample. We asked questions regarding the strategic technology management on both the corporate level and the largest or most representative business unit of the corporation. Since the questionnaire was sent to the person responsible for R&D/ technology on the corporate level, the answers naturally have a bias to the corporate view. An English-language questionnaire was mailed to the North American companies by MIT and to the western European firms by the German research team. An exact Japanese translation was created by NISTEP and mailed to the Japanese companies. Third, the companies were reminded by mail or phone to complete and return the questionnaire, so that we might collect data from a fairly representative number of corporations. The analyses reported here are based on data provided by 209 companies, which represents a rather high overall response rate of 48%. Our questionnaire was answered by 98 companies from Japan, 58 from North America, and 53 from Western Europe. In the coding of the questionnaires by the receiving institutes, all company-related information was omitted, so that the resulting database was a collection of anonymous information. Since nearly half of the responses are from Japanese corporations (which made up 29% of the entire sample), our data have a strong geographical bias. However, we differentiated the results presented here between the three regions – North America, Japan, and Western Europe. Overall, the responding firms were quite representative of the sample firms within each region, in terms of the data collected regarding sector, annual sales, and R&D expenditures. The responding firms can be briefly characterized as follows:

- *Annual sales volume*: The Japanese companies are the largest, with an average annual sales volume of $67 billion in 1997, compared to average annual sales of around $18 billion for both the Western European and North American corporations.
- *R&D intensity*: The North American firms have the highest R&D intensity (percentage of annual sales spent on R&D), with a mean of 7.4%, compared to the Japanese (5.3%) and the western European (4.7%) companies. Most companies with an R&D intensity of 10% or more are from North America.
- *Sales revenue from abroad*: If one takes the percentage of sales revenues from non-domestic countries as a measure of the degree of internationalization, the western European firms are on average highly internationalized (51% of sales revenue from abroad) compared to the North American (41%) and the Japanese (23%) companies.

This research focuses on large multidivisional and technology-intensive corporations that are internationally active. Since one selection criterion was R&D expenditure, our sample covers all industrial sectors in which the generation and use of technology plays an important role for competition. The results presented here include only aspects of the internationalization of research and development.

Monitoring and Acquiring Technology Internationally

Mechanisms to Monitor Technology

In our survey we have been interested in how companies monitor and acquire the requisite technologies and skills to ensure success in the markets in which they compete. The dynamics of environmental alterations may lead to radical changes of the foundations on which the technology strategy of a company is based. Therefore, at least, foresight of future technologies is explicitly an important part of the corporate-level technology strategy of the companies investigated. Which mechanisms are relied on to monitor technology? The companies investigated rely mostly on the following ones (average value of 3.0 or more, see Fig. 1):

1. Person responsible for core technology/ research program
2. Internal technology steering group
3. Participation in technical professional societies
4. Customer panels or input
5. Industry-based consortia

6. Participation in standard bodies

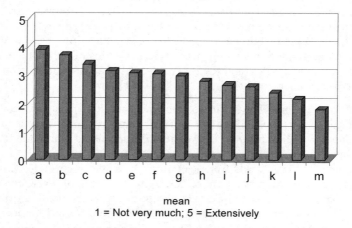

mean
1 = Not very much; 5 = Extensively

a: Responsible person for core technology/research program, b: Internal technology steering groups, c: Participation in technical professional societies, d: Customer panels or input, e: Industry-based consortia, f: Participation in standard bodies, g: University liaison/affiliate programs, h: Participating in publicly-funded R&D programs, i: University research consortia, j: Specialized internal monitoring unit, k: External science/technology advisory boards, m: Venture capital funds

Fig. 1. Reliance on various mechanisms to monitor technology – whole sample

The great reliance on the persons responsible for the core technologies or core research programs seems to reflect the growing importance of concentrating the company's research activities and their technologies on certain fields relevant for their businesses. The person responsible for a core technology/ research program is an excellent partner in the corporate technology foresight activities on two counts. First, he or she has utmost interest in latest and regular information on the specific topic of responsibility. Second, the responsible person is the 'technological gatekeeper' in his or her field and an excellent internal point of contact, who distributes information and may enter data in the company-wide technology foresight system. Regional differences in the use of mechanisms to monitor technology between the firms investigated are moderate. However, the Japanese companies seem to put more emphasis on customer panels or input, and the North American firms rely more on technical professional societies than the other companies investigated.

Given the variety of instruments and the growing importance of internationalization of R&D, companies also use a whole range of instruments to monitor technological developments around the globe, ranging from own laboratories abroad to sponsored research at foreign universities (see Fig. 2). For the sample as a whole, attending international conferences, company's staff liaison in other countries and newsletters/ reports are the most important monitoring instruments, formal panels of outsiders and affiliate programs at foreign universities are the least important ones. Differences between regions exist. The North American companies prefer attending foreign conferences, participating in standards groups and consultants from other countries. The Japanese companies consider as most important instruments the company's own staff liaison abroad as technology scout, conferences and newsletters/ reports. The western European firms prefer conferences, internet and newsletters/ reports.

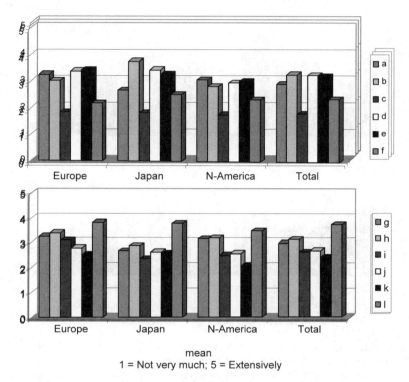

mean
1 = Not very much; 5 = Extensively

a: Our own labs in other countries, b: Our company's staff liaison in other countries, c: Formal technical panels of outsiders, d: Newsletters, reports, e: Internet, online databank analyses, f: Consultants from other countries, g: Participation in international consortia, h: Participation in international standards groups, i: Participation in publicly-funded R&D programs, j: Sponsored research at foreign universities, k: Liaison/affiliate programs at foreign universities, l: Attendance at foreign technical conferences

Fig. 2. Importance of mechanisms to monitor technology developments in other countries

Acquisition of Technology

In contrast to the *monitoring* of technology we wanted to know to what extent the companies rely on mechanisms to *obtain* technology in their *research work*. The answers focus on less mechanisms compared with those used for technology monitoring and point out the following instruments mostly relied on (average mean value 3.0 or more, see Fig. 3):

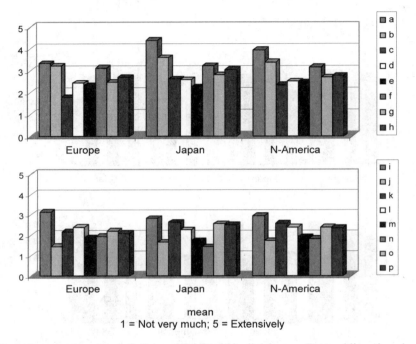

mean
1 = Not very much; 5 = Extensively

a: Central corporate research, b: Internal R&D within divisions, c: External licensing, d: Joint ventures or other alliances with other large companies, e: Consortia, f: Sponsored university research, g: University liaison/affiliate programs, h: Continuing education, i: Recruiting students, j: Equity investments in smaller firms, k: Consultants/contract R&D, l: Acquisition of: technologies, m: Acquisition of: products, n: Acquisition of: companies, o: Incorporation of supplier's technology, p: Incorporation of innovative customer's technology

Fig. 3. Reliance on various mechanisms to obtain technology for research work

1. Central corporate research
2. Internal R&D within divisions
3. Sponsored university research
4. Recruiting students.

The Japanese companies investigated rely heavily on their corporate research to generate technology, whereas R&D activities in the divisions seem not to be of such importance. Surprisingly, the same is true for the North American firms investigated as well, whereas the responding European companies consider R&D in their division only slightly less important to obtain technology than their central corporate research (the question was related to mechanisms to obtain technology for *research work*).

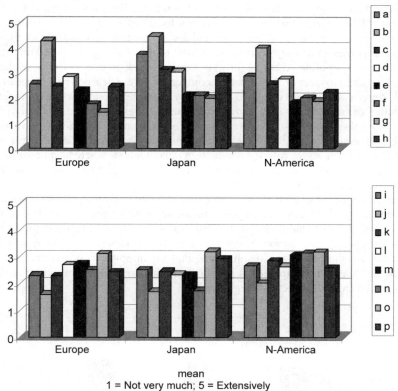

mean
1 = Not very much; 5 = Extensively

a: Central corporate research, b: Internal R&D within divisions, c: External licensing, d: Joint ventures or other alliances with other large companies, e: Consortia, f: Sponsored university research, g: University liaison/affiliate programs, h: Continuing education, i: Recruiting students, j: Equity investments in smaller firms, k: Consultants/contract R&D, l: Acquisition of: technologies, m: Acquisition of products, n: Acquisition of: companies, o: Incorporation of supplier's technology, p: Incorporation of innovative customer's technology

Fig. 4. Reliance on various mechanisms to obtain technology for development work

Studies on large Japanese corporations show that they have continuously invested in R&D and have still kept an eye on a strong corporate research organization and long-term research – despite the long-lasting economic recession in the 90s. Examples here are Hitachi, NEC, Matsushita Electronics, Sharp, Sony, Eisaij, Kao (Reger 1997; Nihon Keizai Shimbun 1998; Sômuchô Tôkeiyoku Tôkei Centâ 1998). Regarding regional differences, the Japanese firms investigated rely to a larger extent on continuing education as a mechanism to obtain technology for their research.

Further, we wanted to know to what extent the companies rely on mechanisms to obtain technology for their *development work*. Firstly, most important are the internal R&D activities within the divisions followed by corporate research, incorporation of supplier's technology, and joint ventures or other alliances with large companies (average mean value 3.0 or more, see Fig. 4). The still strong relevance of corporate research for *development* work is due to the overwhelmingly frequent answers of the Japanese companies here. Clearly, the European and North American firms investigated do not rely so strongly on their central research regarding development. This shows that the Japanese corporations still put a strong emphasis on long-term research and the generation of radical innovations. The incorporation of supplier's technology and joint ventures/ alliances with other large firms play a larger role for conducting *development*, whereas sponsored university research and recruiting students is of greater importance for *research* activities (cf. Fig. 3 and 4).

The extent of the overall reliance on external sources for technology acquisition will increase in the future according to our survey results (see Fig. 5). The companies with their headquarters in North America obviously paid less attention to external technology acquisition in the past than the European and Japanese firms. However, for the future, our results show that the importance of external sources for North American companies is growing stronger in comparison with the firms investigated from the other two regions.

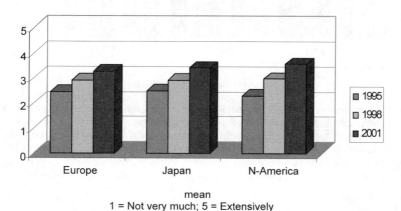

mean
1 = Not very much; 5 = Extensively

Fig. 5. Reliance on external sources for technology acquisition

Taking into account the results of the prior benchmarking survey (Roberts 1995a, 1995b), it can be stated that a very important change in technology management over the past decade is the increasing intensification of all companies' dependence upon external sources of technology. The number of companies which judged themselves as highly dependent on external sources to acquire technology dramatically increased: 35% of the Japanese firms (22% of the European and 10% of the North American firms) consider themselves to have high reliance on external sources in 1992, whereas 84% of the Japanese firms (86% of the European and 85% of the North American firms) made the same statement in 1998. The most dramatic trend can be seen for the North American companies.

The criteria for choosing between internal and external mechanisms for acquiring technology show significant differences regarding the regional origin of the companies investigated (see Fig. 6). The most important selection criteria for the European firms investigated are (1) external availability, (2) time and sense of urgency, (3) own familiarity with the technology, and (4) relative competence/ ability. In contrast, the Japanese firms investigated base their decisions especially on (1) time and sense of urgency, (2) intellectual property ownership, (3) relative competence/ ability, and (4) own familiarity with technology. The same ranking is mentioned by the North American firms investigated, with one difference regarding point (4): the firms with their home base in North America put slightly more emphasis on external availability than on own familiarity with the technology. However, it is obvious to say that the responding Japanese and North American companies take intellectual property ownership more into consideration than their European counterparts (see Fig. 6).

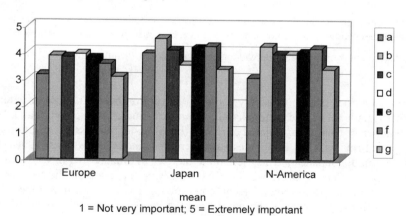

mean
1 = Not very important; 5 = Extremely important

a: Relative cost, b: Time and sense of urgency, c: Our own familiarity with the technology, d: External availability, e: Relative competence/ability, f: Intellectual property ownership, g: Industry fit/standards

Fig. 6. Decision parameters in choosing between internal and external mechanisms to acquire technology

There are different possible partners with whom a company can cooperate in technological innovation activities. Internal cooperation with other divisions of the company is mentioned as the most frequently sought partner from the firms investigated (see Fig. 7). Regarding external organizations, the most frequent partners are customers, suppliers and universities, followed by government laboratories, early-stage technology-based companies and competitors. Since this question explicitly asked for the frequency of the collaboration, a less frequent cooperation does not necessarily mean lesser importance of the partner. The regional differences between the responses of the firms are low, with the exception that the North American companies more frequently cooperate with young technology-based firms.

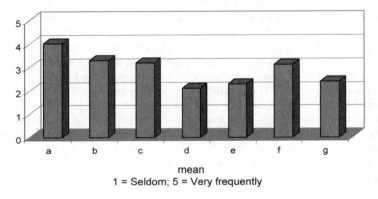

mean
1 = Seldom; 5 = Very frequently

a: Other divisions of your own company, b: Customers, c: Suppliers, d: Competitors, e: Early-stage technology-based companies, f: Universities, g: Government laboratories

Fig. 7. Frequency of collaboration with other organizations – whole sample

Our data does not convincingly show if the location of the internal or external partner is national or international. Other empirical studies pointed out that at least the number of technology-related alliances (business-to-business cooperations) of European firms with US companies have increased since the 80s (CEC 1998). The same is true for Japanese firms, herein the number of alliances with North American companies has also grown since the 80s. This indicates on the one hand a stronger internationalization of technology-related cooperation of European and Japanese firms, whereby on the other hand the cooperation seems to be oriented towards the United States.

International Generation of Research and Technology

Since *both* knowledge creation and exploitation *and* international competition are constantly gaining importance, the internationalization of R&D has increasing relevance for strategic management and thus for management research. To contribute to our understanding of the dynamics unfolding in the field of international R&D, the survey looked at strategies companies follow to respond to global technological issues.

Degree and Development of International R&D Activities

One way to get a notion of the importance of R&D internationalization in quantitative terms is to look at the degree of internationalization, defined as the share of the overall R&D budget spent for R&D beyond the borders of a company's home region. This figure includes R&D activities of a company's researchers abroad as well as the purchase of technology or technologically important products. A striking imbalance comes to the fore if one looks at the regional origin of the companies (see Tab 1). Japanese companies are much less inclined to generate technological knowledge abroad and to engage in international R&D activities than North American or Western European ones. The forward projection for the year 2001 from the point of view of the companies investigated indicates that the internationalization of R&D proceeds. Using the regression method a still growing trend towards internationalization of R&D for the year 2004 can be extrapolated.

Table 1. Percentage of R&D budget spent outside the home country

1995	1998	2001	Own estimation 2004	Investigated companies from
25.75	30.27	33.37	43.72	Western Europe
4.67	7.02	10.52	14.56	Japan
23.17	28.38	31.67	35.07	North America

Having had a look at the quantitative dimension of R&D internationalization, we now turn to the analysis of what activities companies perform internationally. Within a range from 1 (very little non-domestic activity) to 5 (significant non-domestic activity) there is a peak of 3.4 for joint technology development, followed by activities at own laboratories (3.1), license acquisition (3.06) and acquisition of products and companies (2.9) (see Fig. 8). Again, interesting differences between the regional clusters are obvious. For both Japanese and European companies international R&D collaboration is the most important strategic means in international R&D, whereas for North American companies the activities in own laboratories abroad are most important (mean of 3.2). In addition, Japanese companies are more active in acquiring foreign licenses (mean 3.5) than European (mean 2.8), and especially North American companies (mean 2.6) (see Fig. 8).

To find out how the various international R&D activities are spread around the globe, each company was asked to indicate which of four given R&D activities it performs within six different economic regions. These target regions are North America, western Europe, eastern Europe, Japan, Asia/Pacific other than Japan, and Latin America. Given the possibility of multiple response both for the target regions and the activities, the 209 companies of the sample most often mentioned joint technology development (435), followed by acquisition of licenses (408), acquisition of innovative foreign products and/ or companies (341) and finally research in own laboratories abroad (325).

As for the attractiveness of target regions, the sample as a whole mentioned western Europe most often, for each of the four activities, followed by North America. It is obvious that Japan is not as attractive as target region as it should be considering its economic and technological meaning. European companies mention North America as target region more than twice as often as Japan. North American companies mention Western Europe almost twice as often as Japan. At the same time, the so-called Asian Tigers seem to have gained some attractiveness, being mentioned by 22.9% of all companies of the sample for at least one of their international R&D activities. Not surprisingly, the remaining regions Latin America (9.5%) and Eastern Europe (11.7%) are still far less important.

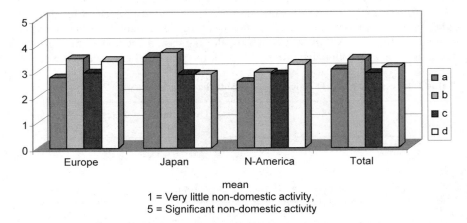

mean
1 = Very little non-domestic activity,
5 = Significant non-domestic activity

Fig. 8. Importance of various technology activities carried out outside the home region

Fig. 9 shows the global distribution of the four selected international R&D activities broken down by region of origin of the companies. The regional origin of the companies makes a difference. Just as Japanese companies spend relatively little R&D money abroad, compared to the rest of the sample, they obviously do not regionally diversify their international R&D activities that much. Companies from Japan most heavily concentrate on the two Triad regions Western Europe and North America, they spend almost no R&D money in Latin America and Eastern Europe. Moreover, they focus their efforts on the acquisition of licenses and technological cooperation.

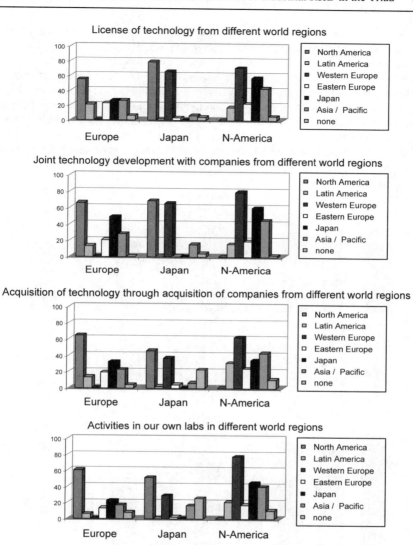

Fig. 9. The use of four different instruments to internationalize R&D activities

Motives for R&D Internationalization

To understand the nature of R&D internationalization, one has to look at the motives driving it. Nine possible motives were given in the survey and the most important observation might be that there is no single dominant reason. Still, there are some differences. In order of decreasing importance, the analysis of the sample as a whole shows the results in Fig. 10.

The three most important motives (mean over 3.4) are (1) the adaptation of products to local requirements, regulations, ingredients etc., (2) to get access to skilled researchers and talent and (3) to learn from foreign lead markets or lead customers. Of medium importance (mean between 3 and 3.3) for the internationalization of R&D is (1) to take advantage of technology developed by foreign companies, (2) to keep abreast of foreign technologies, (3) to support non-domestic production, and (4) to comply with local market access regulations or pressures. The two least important reasons (mean lower than 3.0) are (1) to take advantage of foreign public R&D programs and (2) the inappropriate environment at home.

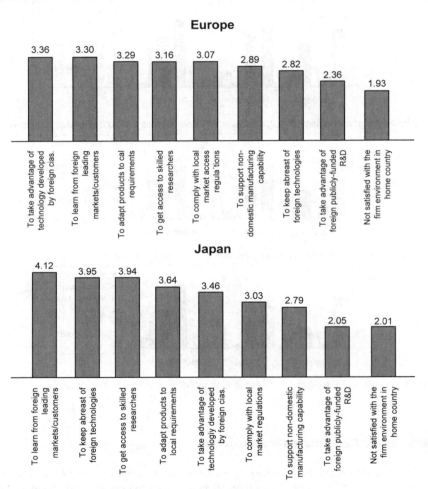

Fig. 10.a Importance of motives for non-domestic R&D activities

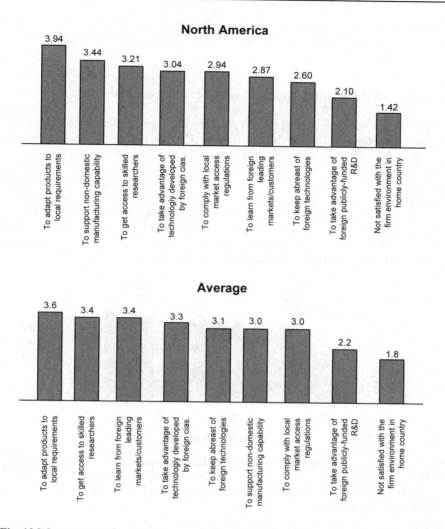

Fig. 10.b Importance of motives for non-domestic R&D activities

Obviously, internationalization of R&D in many companies follows the needs of adaptation to different local markets and is in principle not a reaction to inappropriate conditions at home. Again, the results on motives are more interesting if the regional origin of the companies is considered. Three strong motives for the European companies are to take advantage of technology developed by foreign companies, to learn from lead markets/ customers and to adapt products to local needs. Japanese companies want to learn from lead markets/ customers, to keep abreast of foreign technology and to have access to foreign researchers and talent.

North American companies are strongly motivated by adapting products to local requirements, supporting non-domestic manufacturing capability and to get access to skilled researchers.

Roles of R&D Facilities Abroad and Coordination Mechanisms

Those companies who perform R&D in their labs abroad were asked about the function and organization of these activities. The most striking result is that the concept of 'centers of excellence' had a breakthrough in recent years. Out of four possible characteristics of foreign laboratories, almost one third of the sample labeled their foreign laboratories as 'centers of excellence'. However, European companies much more tend to set up a centre of excellence with worldwide responsibility (43.6%) than North American (31.5%) and especially Japanese companies (21.4%) do (see Fig. 11). In contrast, 34.5% of the North American and 24.5% of the Japanese companies mentioned that their R&D units perform the same activities as domestic R&D facilities, but adapted to the local market.

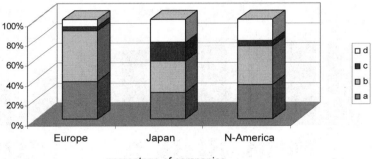

percentage of companies

a: They perform the same activities as domestic R&D facilities but adapted to local market,
b: They represent worldwide centers of excellence for a particular technology, discipline,
etc., c: They focus only on basic and/or applied research, d: They focus only on regional
technical support activities

Fig. 11. Most important functions of R&D facilities located abroad

As for the organization and independence of R&D facilities abroad, the analysis shows a resemblance for all regions. On a scale between 1 ('not very independent') to 5 ('totally independent'), the decisions about the content of R&D is ranked with a mean of 2.4, whereas the independence to internally organize the work has a mean of 3.1. It is interesting to note that for both the content and work organization the Japanese companies show the lowest value of independence from their foreign laboratories: for content the mean is only at 2.0 and for work organization 2.8. This shows that content is still more controlled by the headquarters than the mechanisms used to generate it. If foreign laboratories do not serve as centers of excellence, they are most likely to perform the same range of R&D as the laboratories at home, but adjust it to local standards. Only rarely do foreign and domestic laboratories complement each other on the basis of a division of labor. If so, it is mostly Japanese companies which have foreign laboratories concentrate on either applied or basic research, thus providing a service to their domestic laboratories.

Effective technology transfer mechanisms across borders are required to fully exploit all in-house R&D that is generated *within* multinational companies. Companies were asked to indicate three most important approaches (see Fig. 12). For the whole sample, the three most important mechanisms were the relocation of internal experts to the recipient countries, joint multi-country teams/ projects and the relocation of technical experts from recipient countries to the home country. Here regional differences are striking, especially joint projects and personnel transfer. Most obviously, North American companies stick much less to this idea, with only 9% of them indicating joint multinational teams as one of three important concepts, with only written reports and planning session being less important. North American companies rather rely on electronic means of communication even for technology transfer. The pattern of European companies, on the other hand, is just the other way round. They rely heavily on projects, more than 75% mention teams as important, by far the highest value. Here Japanese companies represent the middle ground, with some focus on relocation of internal experts and, most significantly, they count on education and training of their R&D personal abroad.

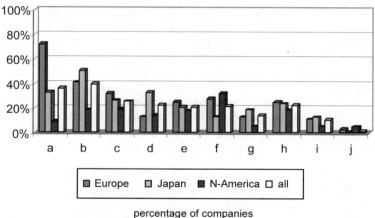

percentage of companies

a: joint multi-country teams, b: relocation of internal expert, c: relocation of foreign expert, d: training programs abroad, e: transfer of written documents, f: electronic communication, g: reports, h: conferences/workshops, i: planning sessions, j: other

Fig. 12. Mechanisms used for international technology transfer

Conclusions

The analyses presented here show the following main results: First, there is a growing tendency to acquire technology from external sources throughout our sample. The high reliance on external sources for technology of all companies investigated is a very important change in the strategic management of technology over the past decade and for the future. While there are very similar patterns of external technological cooperation – customers, suppliers and universities are most often mentioned – the motives to appropriate external technological knowledge differ between the three regions considered. Obviously, technology-related cooperations and horizontal and vertical networking even in core technologies have even gained in importance. However, acquiring technology from external sources has not been so familiar to the investigated North American firms in the past. Other empirical research shows that cross-border technology-related alliances are also of growing significance.

Second, the international generation of innovation and technology plays a very important role in the strategies of the large companies analyzed and the data show that this will gain further momentum in the future. The western European firms are in the forefront of this development, whereas the North American firms are catching up. Further, the internationalization of R&D is still strongly confined to the Triad regions and is not global – so the development regarding R&D is better described by 'triadization'. There are strong differences between the North American, Japanese and Western European companies investigated (see Tab. 2):

Firstly, Japanese companies still lag behind the overall trend of R&D investment in foreign countries: the share of R&D budget spent abroad is rather low compared with the other firms investigated. Further, the geographical diversification of R&D activities in own labs is limited strongly to North America as well as to Western Europe and Asia/ Pacific. The motives to invest abroad are driven by learning aspects (learning from lead markets/ customers and keeping abreast of technological know in foreign countries) and the wish to get access to skilled researchers. There seems to be no single dominant role for the R&D units – all four roles exist with the R&D unit performing the same activities as domestic R&D facilities is on the first rank. Compared to the companies from the other two regions R&D units which conduct basic and applied research play a more prominent role. Further, the R&D units abroad seem to be more strictly controlled: non-home-base R&D activities are not independent what and how they do their job. Technology transfer across borders is mainly done by using person-oriented coordination mechanisms.

Secondly, North American companies spent more of their R&D budget abroad. The geographical diversification is the highest among the companies investigated: North American firms have own R&D activities strongly in western Europe but also in Japan, Asia/ Pacific, Latin America, and Eastern Europe. The motives to invest abroad are driven by adapting products to local requirements, supporting production facilities abroad and the wish to get access to skilled researchers. The dominant roles for the R&D units abroad are performing the same activities as the domestic R&D facilities and the worldwide center of excellence; conducting basic or applied research plays no role. Further, the R&D units abroad seem to be controlled moderately: non-home-base R&D activities are independent what and how they do their job. Technology transfer across borders is mainly done by using electronic communication and relocating internal technical experts to recipient countries or from recipient countries to the home country.

Table 2. Differences in the internationalization of R&D between Western European, Japanese and North American multinationals

	North American firms	Japanese firms	Western European firms
Dependence on external sources of technology (in % of responses)	1992: 10% 1998: up to 85%	1992: 35% 1998: up to 84%	1992: 22% 1998: up to 84%
Partners in technology-related strategic alliances[a]	Numbers of newly established US-US strategic technology alliances increased from 286 (80-84) to 809 (90-94)	Numbers of newly established JP-US strategic technology alliances increased from 178 (80-84) to 213 (90-94)	Numbers of newly established EU-US strategic technology alliances increased from 221 (80-84) to 457 (90-94)
Degree of R&D internationalization (R&D budget spent abroad/ total R&D budget in %)	1995: 23.2% 1998: 28.4% 2001: 31.7% (estimated)	1995: 4.7% 1998: 7.0% 2001: 10.5% (estimated)	1995: 25.6% 1998: 30.3% 2001: 33.4% (estimated)
Geographical diversification of R&D activities in own labs abroad (more than 10% of responses)	(1) West. Europe (77.6%) (2) Japan (44.8%) (3) Asia/Pacific (39.7%) (4) Lat. America (20.7%) (5) East. Europe (13.2%)	(1) N. America (51.0%) (2) West. Europe (28.6%) (3) Asia/Pacific (16.3%)	(1) N. America (60.4%) (2) Japan (22.6%) (3) Asia/Pacific (17.0%) (4) East. Europe (13.2%)
Three most important motives for internationalizing R&T activities	(1) adapting products (2) supporting production (3) access to researchers	(1) learning from lead markets/ customers (2) keep abreast of foreign technologies (3) access to researchers	(1) learning from lead markets/ customers (2) technology developed by foreign firms (3) adapting products
Roles of R&D facilities abroad	(1) same activity (34.5%) (2) center of exc. (31.0%) (3) tech. support (19.0%) (4) research (5.2%)	(1) same activity (24.5%) (2) center of exc. (21.4%) (3) tech. support (18.4%) (4) research (15.3%)	(1) center of exc. (43.4%) (2) same activity (32.1%) (3) tech. support (5.7%) (4) research (3.8%)

Table 2. (Continued)

Independence of foreign R&D unit	- content ('what'): not independent - process ('how'): independent	- content ('what'): not independent - process ('how'): not independent	- content ('what'): not independent - process ('how'): independent
Three most important technology transfer mechanisms across borders (responses in %)	(1) electronic communication (32.0%) (2) relocation expert to home country (19%) (3) relocation expert to recipient count. (19%)	(1) relocation expert to recipient count. (51%) (2) joint projects (33%) (3) training programs abroad (33%)	(1) joint projects (72%) (2) relocation expert to recipient count. (41%) (3) relocation expert to home country (32%)

[a] See Narula (1998) and Narula and Hagedoorn (1997)

Western European companies spent a third of their R&D budget abroad which is the highest one compared to the other companies. The geographical diversification is moderate with a clear focus on North America; further R&D investment has been done in Japan, Asia/ Pacific, and Eastern Europe (whereas Latin America is neglected). The motives to invest abroad are driven by learning aspects (learning from lead markets/ customers and from foreign firms) and adapting products to local needs. The dominant role for the R&D units abroad is the worldwide center of excellence whereas performing the same activities is on the second rank; conducting basic or applied research or technical support activities play no role. Further, the R&D units abroad seem to be controlled moderately: non-home-base R&D activities are independent what and how they do their job. Technology transfer across borders is mainly done by using person-oriented coordination mechanisms with joint multi-country teams/ projects as the most prominent one.

All in all, the mode of internationalization of R&D in the Japanese multinationals investigated seems to be still strongly home-centered ('home-centered mode'): R&D units abroad learn from the markets and technological know how in foreign countries, transfer much information to the corporate R&D headquarters in Japan or use it for adapting products or technical support and tightly control their activities abroad. The North American multinationals investigated focus its international R&D activities on adapting products to local requirements and supporting manufacturing activities. The geographical diversification of the R&D units seems to be dedicated to the really global foreign direct investment of North American companies (adaptation/ technical support and geographical diversification mode'). The western European multinationals investigated seem to follow more a transnational mode of internationalization of research and technology with a geographical concentration on North America and Japan ('focused transnational mode'): learning as motive for internationalization of research and technology is in the foreground, R&D units as worldwide centers of excellence are relatively independent and the specialized and dispersed R&D activities are coordinated by joint multi-country projects and personal transfer in both directions.

Acknowledgment

This research would not have been possible without the vital contributions by Edward Roberts, Richard Lester and Richard Locke from the Massachusetts Institute of Technology (MIT) in Cambridge, Alexander Gerybadze from the University of Hohenheim, Ryo Hirosawa from the National Institute for Science and Technology Policy (NISTEP) in Tokyo, and my colleagues Frieder Meyer-Krahmer and Jakob Edler from the Fraunhofer Institute for Systems and Innovation Research (ISI) in Karlsruhe. All the data from the North American firms were collected by our colleagues from the MIT and all the data from the Japanese firms were collected by Ryo Hirosawa and his colleagues from NISTEP. In the coding of the questionnaires by the receiving institutions all company related information were omitted, leaving the resulting data base as an anonymous collection of information.

References

Archibugi D and Michie J (1995): "The globalization of technology: a new taxonomy", *Cambridge Journal of Economics*, vol. 19, pp. 121-140

Bartlett CA and Yoshihara H (1988): 'New Challenges for Japanese Multinationals: Is Organizational Adaptation Their Achilles Heel?' *Human Resource Management*, Vol. 27, 1, 19-43

Boutellier R, Gassmann O, and von Zedtwitz M (2000): *Managing Global Innovation. Uncovering the Secrets of Future Competitiveness.* 2nd Edition, Heidelberg: Springer

Brockhoff K (1998): *The internationalization of research and development.* Heidelberg: Springer

Cairncross D (1994): 'The Strategic Role of Japanese R&D Centres in the UK'; in: *Campbell N and Burton F (Eds.) 'Japanese Multinationals. Strategies and Management in the Global Kaisha.'* London, New York

Commission of the European Communities (CEC) (1998): "Internationalization of research and technology: trends, issues and implications for S&T policies in Europe". ETAN working paper prepared by an independent expert working group for the Commission of the European Communities, Directorate General XII. Brussels, Luxembourg: CEC

Fujita M and Ishii R (1994): *'Global Location Behavior and Organizational Dynamics of Japanese Electronics Firms and Their Impact on Regional Economies.'* Paper Presented at the Prince Bertil Symposium on 'The Dynamic Firm'. Stockholm, June 12-14

Gerybadze A, Meyer-Krahmer F, Reger G (1997): *Internationales Management und Innovation.* Stuttgart: Schaeffer-Poeschel Verlag

Hedlund G and Nonaka J (1993): Models of Knowledge Management in the West and Japan; in: *Lorange P, Chakravarthy B, Ros J, and Van de Veen A (Eds.): Implementing Strategic Processes: Change Learning and Cooperation.* Cambridge, MA

Kenney M and Florida R (1994): 'The Organization and Geography of Japanese R&D: Results from a Survey of Japanese Electronics and Biotechnological Firms'; in: *Research Policy*, vol. 23, 305-323

Meyer-Krahmer F (Ed.) (1999): *Globalization of R&D and technology markets - consequences for national innovation policies.* Heidelberg: Physica-Verlag

Narula R (1998): Strategic Technology Alliances by European Firms Since 1980: Questioning Integration? MERIT Research Memorandum. Maastricht, March 30

Narula R and Hagedoorn J (1997): Globalization, Organizational Modes and the Growth of International Strategic Technology Alliances. MERIT Research Memorandum. Maastricht, October

Niosi J (Ed.) (1999): *Research Policy*, Special Issue on "The Internationalization of Industrial R&D", Vol. 28

OECD (Ed.) (1998): *Globalization of industrial R&D: policy implications.* Working Group on Innovation and Technology Policy. Paris: OECD, June

Reger G (1997): *Koordination und strategisches Management internationaler Innovationsprozesse.* Heidelberg: Physica-Verlag

Roberts EB (1995): "Benchmarking the strategic management of technology (I)", *Research Technology Management*, vol. 38, pp. 44-56, January-February

Roberts EB (1995): "Benchmarking the strategic management of technology (II)", *Research Technology Management*, vol. 38, pp. 18-26, March-April

Sakakibara K and Westney DE (1992): 'Japan's Management of Global Innovation: Technology Management Crossing Borders'; *in: Rosenberg N, Landau R, and Mowery DC (Eds.): Technology and the Wealth of Nations.* Stanford

Westney DE (1994): 'The Evolution of Japan's Industrial Research and Development'; in: *Aoki M and Dore R (Eds.): The Japanese Firm. Sources of Competitive Strength. New York,* Oxford

Nihon Keizai Shimbun 06/03/1998, *Shuyô 20 sha no 98 nendo kenkyû kaihatsu - Setsubi tôshi.* Survey conducted on 06/03/1998

Sômuchô Tôkeiyoku - Tôkei Centâ (1998): *Heisei 10-nen kagaku gijutsu kenkyû chôsa kekka sokuhô (yôten),* 11/28/1998, http://www.stat.go.jp/

Global Innovation and Knowledge Flows in Japanese and European Corporations

Alexander Gerybadze

Global Innovation and Changing Patterns of Knowledge Production

The internationalization of research and development (R&D) and of other knowledge-intensive activities has been continuously increasing. Multinational corporations (MNCs) are the major engine of growth and international technology transfer. MNCs play a key role in the Japanese economy and in the European system of innovation. They are pushing the frontiers and they need to respond to the changing pattern of innovation in the global arena. Structural changes in global innovation and transnational technology transfer lead to great challenges for managers as well as for decision-makers in government agencies and within the research system. The following trends characterize international innovation activities and new modes of knowledge production.

1. The increased *intensity* and *speed* of innovation and accelerated product obsolescence. Cycle times in consumer electronics and mobile communications have been reduced to six months. Product development times have been shortened in several industries, often induced through competitive pressures of Japanese firms (e.g. in automobiles). More recently, other Asian countries are pushing the frontiers and exerting pressure on Japanese and European firms.
2. More and more countries are building up strong R&D capabilities and this has led to a greater global dispersion of innovation activities. The *increased globalization of R&D* and the concomitant international sourcing strategies of multinational corporations will be a core theme of this article.
3. A third important trend involves the stronger emphasis on application and demand-pull, and the reduced emphasis on basic research and technology-pull. We characterize this as "*innovation moving downstream*": the core of value-added in the innovation process moves towards the application system and end-user side of the spectrum.[1]
4. Finally, the so-called *Mode 2 of knowledge production* replaces Mode 1. Mode 2 is characterized by open innovation, the stronger role of cooperative ties between firms, greater multidisciplinarity and by problems and applications driving the research agenda. This is considerably different from Mode 1 of knowl-

---

[1] See Gerybadze (2004b, 106), Gerybadze, Reger (1999) and von Hippel (2005) for an analysis of this trend towards „downstream innovation".

edge production, which strongly emphasized intra-firm and intra-disciplinary work, with R&D typically preceding commercial applications.[2]

The first two trends can be observed in the most dynamic sectors which drive international R&D. Table 1 lists major high-technology industries with the highest business expenditures on R&D which are characterized by accelerated new product development. Almost 90 % of global business R&D expenditures are concentrated in nine sectors, with the rest distributed over 21 other industries. The most dynamic sectors are characterized by the predominance of transnational firms, which are forced to distribute their R&D activities globally. The extent of R&D globalization is particularly strong for pharmaceuticals, biotechnology and health, in information technology, in the chemical industry and in telecommunications. Other industries (automobiles & parts, electronics, aerospace & defense as well as engineering & machinery) are so far characterized by a medium degree of R&D globalization, but are under continuous pressure to increase their international innovation activities.

Table 1. Industries with highest R&D expenditures and the extend of R&D globalization

Industry / Sector	R&D expenditures in million $ 2003	R&D as % of revenues 2003	Extent of R&D globalization
Pharmaceutical, biotechnology & health	73,704	14.3	***
Information-technology (IT)-hardware	71,758	9.5	***
Automobiles & parts	68,718	4.3	**
Electronics & electrical	39,526	6.0	**
Software & IT-services	21,983	10.3	***
Chemicals	19,025	4.1	***
Aerospace & defense	13,699	4.6	**
Engineering & machinery	10,770	2.7	**
Telecommunication services	8,358	1.6	***
Other industries (sum of 21 sectors)	*38,688*		*
All companies / Total of 700 co.	366,229	4.2	**

*** High Degree of R&D Globalization
** Medium Degree of R&D Globalization
* Low Degree of R&D Globalization
Source: INTERIS-Database / University of Hohenheim; The 2004 R&D Scoreboard

There are significant differences in growth and innovation performance in these dynamic sectors between Japan and Western European countries. Japan has both been able to establish successful *new* industries (e.g. in information technology and electronics), while at the same time adapting technology to its *existing* set of industries (e.g. in automobiles and machine-tools). Meanwhile, European firms

---

[2]   See Gibbons, Limoges, Nowotny et al. (1994) and Nowotny, Scott and Gibbons (2001) for a more detailed analysis of this transfer process from Mode 1 to Mode 2 of knowledge production.

tended to concentrate innovation around areas of traditional strength and in established industries. In spite of heavy investments in some high-tech sectors (computers, semiconductors etc.), European firms and national governments have encountered great difficulties in attaining a viable position in the most promising growth fields, which were rather disconnected to existing strengths.

Moving from an established structure of industries to a new, more modern set of industries requires *dynamic capabilities*. These dynamic capabilities involve more than R&D investments and supplier-driven strategies. The following paper argues that there are three different "engines of innovation", and that countries as well as MNCs need to specialize on those types of innovation, for which they have organizational advantages. Multinational firms represent a critical asset and a core element for dynamic capabilities. For a nation state to be strong in innovation requires

- to build on a strong group of *large multinational firms* with strong embeddedness in the home country and in the national innovation system.
- *National firms* increasingly need to be strong in leveraging global innovation capabilities and in transferring knowledge from foreign sources to the home base.
- *Foreign multinational firms* are an important source of knowledge and will become ever more important for strengthening the innovation system in the host country.
- National strengths need to be built not just on R&D, but on a complex system of downstream innovation activities, including engineering, lead market capabilities and advanced services.

There are great differences between countries in terms of globalization strategies and the role of foreign MNCs. This can be seen in Table 2: the U.S. is a dominant home base for high-tech oriented MNCs and has attracted an increasing share of foreign MNCs to set up R&D facilities on its territory. Today, about 15 % of business expenditures on R&D (BERD) come from foreign sources and this percentage will rise over the next years.[3] For European countries, inward foreign direct investment plays a much stronger role for business R&D, with the United Kingdom and Ireland being very dependent on foreign MNCs (41 % and 65 % of BERD owned by foreign multinationals, respectively). Sweden, Italy, Spain, Germany and the Netherlands have also attracted significant R&D investments of foreign firms. Compared to European countries, Japan's innovation system is somewhat less interconnected with the outside world, with a few exceptions of some truly transnational firms and industries. On average, only 3.4 % of business expenditures of R&D in Japan represent investments of foreign MNCs. Outward-oriented R&D investments of Japanese MNCs are somewhat more important. Still, other forms of assimilating foreign technology and more targeted approaches of

---

[3]   Foreign-owned R&D expenditures in the U.S. grew at a real annual average rate of 10.8 % between 1994 and 2000, compared with an annual growth rate of 6.9 % for U.S. owned overseas R&D. Both growth rates exceed the annual growth rate for total business expenditures on R&D in the U.S. (NSF 2004, 4-69).

influencing the global innovation agenda are much more important and need to be studied in more depth at the industry or firm level.

Table 2. The role of foreign MNCs for business expenditures on R&D in the major OECD countries

Country	R&D expenditures of foreign MNCs (Million $ 2001)	Business enterprise expenditures on R&D (BERD) (Million $ 2001)	Share of foreign MNCs in BERD (Percent)
United States	29,638	200,525	14.8
Germany	8,108	36,763	24.8
United Kingdom	7,923	19,528	40.6
France	4,913	22,806	21.5
Sweden	4,194	7,943	38.2
Canada	3,355	11,011	30.5
Italy	2,647	8,033	33.0
Japan	2,598	76,570	3.4
Spain	1,330	4,294	31.0
Netherlands	1,251	5,063	19.6
Ireland	599	919	65.2

Source: OECD, Main Science and Technology Indicators, 2004

Downstream Innovation and New Sources of Knowledge

Due to the globalization of R&D and the increased international dispersion of knowledge, MNCs need to adapt their location strategies and the way they manage and organize the innovation process. There are still significant differences between Japanese and European corporations, and these will be described in more depth in the following sections. In addition, there are cognitive and strategic differences in the way the innovation process is addressed. In several European countries with a strong R&D and engineering tradition, we still follow a linear-sequential type of innovation process as described on the left-hand side in Figure 1. Corporations tend to invest in research facilities, they develop new products as an outcome of their R&D effort, and successively build on manufacturing and marketing capabilities. According to the OECD 1997 classification, this linear-sequential mode will continuously be outphased.

In many dynamic industries as well as in services, we observe a changing pattern of innovation, a reversed sequence of chain-links and different modes of knowledge flows. This has been described as a transformation from mode 1 to mode 2 of knowledge production (Gibbons et al. 1994; Nowotny, Scott and Gibbons 2001). Innovation is often induced through demanding customers and lead markets (Beise 2004; von Hippel 2005). These inducements lead to the search for refined products and improved processes, and to a more problem-driven build-up of R&D projects and advanced manufacturing (as described by a movement from right to left in Figure 1). Knowledge flows will often be reversed and this has profound implications on innovation strategies and on sourcing decisions within MNCs.

- **Key Issue 1:** Where is the *Core of Value Added* in the Innovation Process / The Functional Source of most advanced Knowledge? *Where is the **Engine** in the Innovation Process?*

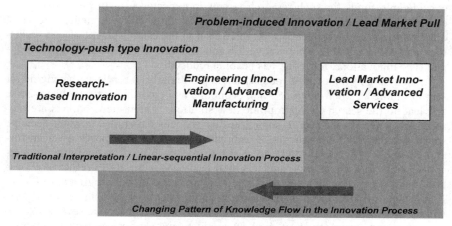

- **Key Issue 2:** Where is the *Geographical Center* / Locus of Innovation? *Where can we best learn about the Winning Combination?*

Fig. 1. Innovation moving downstream / Reversal of knowledge flows in the innovation process

In order to study knowledge flows within MNCs and effective new ways of structuring innovation processes across locations and functions, we have to address two key issues.

1. Where is the *core of value added* in the innovation process? Where is the functional source of innovation? Which type of knowledge is most critical for leveraging innovation? For illustrative purposes, we call this the *engine* or the driver of the innovation process.[4]
2. As a second key issue, we will ask: where is the *geographical center*, the best place to learn about and implement a particular innovation in the world? In which region or country do MNCs need to concentrate their most advanced innovation activities?

Let us first address *key issue # 1*, the analysis of the *core of value added* in the innovation process. Which factors or functional activities *drive* the innovation

---

[4]   For a more detailed description of functional sources of innovation see von Hippel (1988, 1994) and Gerybadze (2004a: 16 ff.).

process? The classical, technology-push type innovation model can be described as a *rear-drive engine*: knowledge is research-driven and leads to scientific advances; the outcome of the research process is often documented in scientific publications and patents. Successive stages of development and refinement lead to new products and to the establishment of emerging industries. Multinational corporations as well as governments in Asia, Europe and in North America invest considerable funds for such research targets in expected growth fields like high-energy physics, nanomaterials, superconductivity etc.. These strategies are valid only inasmuch as investments in research lead to the establishment of new industries and to sustainable comparative advantages. The importance of technology-pull type innovations, however, has become reduced.

In many highly-innovative industries and particularly in services, the engine resembles more a *"front-drive"*. Social, economic and environmental problems arise and lead to the search for appropriate new solutions. Latent new markets are created somewhere in the world, sometimes by chance, sometimes through decisive social and technical construction. Leading environments and more advanced foreign locations will attract MNCs to search for new solutions, to combine products and services in a novel way, and this again influences the R&D resource allocation, the research agenda as well as scientific and educational programs. In Figure 2, this type of *front-drive* or downstream inducement mechanism is called *lead market innovation*. An increasing number of industries and service sectors like information and communication, medical products and services as well as automotive electronics are strongly affected by lead market innovation. Innovative firms need to implement new business concepts, refined products and service configurations. This is most often done in close interaction with lead users, and here, geographical proximity and network externalities on the demand side are often critical. Knowledge generated in this interaction process is often much more critical than knowledge generated in research labs.

In addition to these two types of innovation (research driven vs. lead-market induced), there is a third mode of innovation often promoted in industries and countries with a strong engineering culture and a more technical tradition. For reasons of simplicity, we call this *engineering innovation*. The core of value added lies in quality and efficiency, and this requires an effective combination of product development, process engineering, supplier involvement and advanced logistics. Engineering innovation builds on a sophisticated network of manufacturers, suppliers and service providers, and also on an educational tradition of sophisticated skills, and workmanship across a wide range of related fields.[5] Innovation and comparative advantage in mechanical engineering, factory automation, mechatronics and transportation systems is largely explained by effectively integrating these skills, and this determines dynamic capabilities for engineering innovation. Nation states that are strong in engineering innovation, have often encountered great difficulties in dealing with research-based innovation or with lead market in-

---

[5]   The German and Swiss, as well as the Japanese tradition of skill-based learning and apprenticeship appears to be better suited for engineering innovation, than the Anglo-Saxon or French model of scientific education.

novation. In Germany, as an example, overemphasized engineering strength often works against market responsiveness and customer involvement.

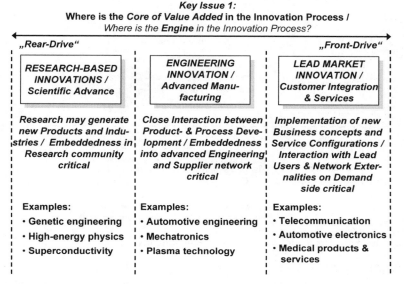

Fig. 2. Core of value-added in the innovation process / Three different types of innovations

Home-Base Augmenting vs. Home-Base Exploiting R&D Strategies

There is a growing literature on foreign R&D laboratories in MNCs, and on R&D offshoring decisions (Khan and Yoshihara 1994; Gerybadze and Reger 1999; Kümmerle 1997, 1999; Dalton and Serapio 1999; Narula and Zanfei 2004). Earlier studies of foreign R&D have concentrated on uni-directional knowledge flows: leading R&D activities were concentrated in the home-base of MNCs, often in close proximity to headquarters. Companies like BASF and Bayer built on strong capabilities in polymer chemistry and concentrated most of their advanced R&D projects in Ludwigshafen and Leverkusen, Germany respectively. Japanese electronics companies concentrated most of their leading R&D laboratories in the greater Tokyo region. Knowledge generated at home was later transferred to foreign R&D labs, and products and processes became adapted to local conditions. We call this process home-base exploiting R&D, as is illustrated on the left side in Figure 3.

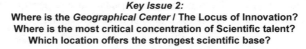

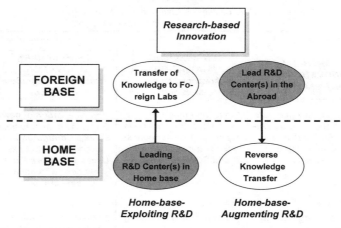

Fig. 3. Home-base augmenting vs. home-base exploiting R&D

Home-base exploiting R&D strategies are viable only as long as a particular country has a dominant position in research. For each industry and for each particular field of research, we need to ask: where does information break?[6] Where can we expect relevant discoveries and breakthroughs to happen? This depends on the most critical concentration of talent, and on the sophistication of the research system and the scientific base. Two parallel trends can be observed in the global research landscape and both will affect locational strategies in a different direction. (1) The strong upsurge of R&D investment in science-related fields in the U.S. after 1994. Parallel to this, we also observe (2) a growing number of countries which are investing heavily in specialized research capabilities and this second trend has led to a more distributed pattern in the global R&D landscape.[7]

Due to the first factor, North America has become a dominant target for foreign R&D investment decisions by European as well as Japanese MNCs. In 2000, foreign MNC were investing 26.1 billion $ in the U.S.; 22 % of this investment came from Germany, 19 % from the U.K., 12 % from Switzerland and 10 % from Japan. A certain percentage of this investment is still home-base exploiting in the classical sense, but more and more MNCs are adapting their innovation strategies and have established their lead research facilities in North America.

---

[6]   Following Stinchcombe (1995, 2), critical information in a project "breaks" at a particular location in the world. See also Gerybadze (2004a, 16 f.).

[7]   Around 1980, three source countries were responsible for 90 % of world R&D. Today, 90 % of world R&D expenditures are distributed among 15 countries.

Kümmerle (1999) has analyzed this new mode of *home-base augmenting R&D* for European, Japanese as well as U.S.-based corporations in electronics and pharmaceuticals. This trend for reversing knowledge flows in strategically relevant fields was particularly pronounced for German as well as Swiss pharmaceutical firms, who have encountered a significant challenge to their home research base. While more than 50% of major new drugs came from research labs in both countries until about 1980, more than 50 % of all new drugs are now being synthesized in research labs in North America. As a result, European pharmaceutical corporations have concentrated most of their prime R&D centers in biotech and health-related research in North America. In a related way, Japanese pharmaceutical firms have established offshore R&D centers in the U.S., often with a clear home-base augmenting strategy.

Due to the growing international dispersion of R&D capabilities mentioned above, an increasing number of countries have become targets for R&D offshoring decisions. About one third of this is home-base augmenting R&D,[8] with a clear trend to increase this percentage. And more and more of this investment is directed towards specialized centers of gravity (so-called lead R&D locations) in particular areas. Japan has become an important R&D location of European specialty electronics as well as specialty chemistry firms. Additional targets for home-base augmenting R&D of European electronics firms are now Korea, Taiwan and Singapore. Japanese corporations, apart from their prime emphasis on North America, have established advanced R&D centers in Germany, the United Kingdom and the Netherlands. Location decisions are primarily driven by the need to get access to advanced capabilities in automobile technology, telecommunication and factory automation.

Engineering Innovation and Knowledge Flows Within MNCs

Investment decisions for Japanese MNCs in Europe as well as foreign direct investment of European firms in Japan are primarily driven by the desire to get access to an attractive market and to become embedded in a sophisticated engineering environment. Quite in difference to R&D offshoring in the United States, where Japanese as well as European firms often set up R&D facilities with the primary intent to get access to advanced research results, R&D investment decisions in Europe and in Asia respectively only serve as a complement for other, more important value adding activities.

Japanese firms have established a total of 397 R&D and design centers in Europe at year-end 2003, the majority of which (76 %) is closely linked to offshore manufacturing facilities. They are concentrated in a few large and technically advanced countries (31 % in the U.K., 18 % in Germany and 16 % in

---

[8]   See Ambos (2005) for a detailed analysis of home-base augmenting and home-base exploiting foreign R&D strategies of German MNCs.

France), followed by Spain, Belgium, the Netherlands, Italy and Sweden; only recently have Japanese firms established a few R&D and design centers in Central and Eastern Europe.[9] A large percentage of subsidiaries in the larger European countries has been acquired with the target of getting access to manufacturing and engineering, to distribution channels and customer brands. R&D and design activities are closely linked to manufacturing and sales activities, and are directed towards adapting Japanese products to local markets.

Japanese innovation as well as Japanese FDI activity in Europe is most often concentrated on those industries where European countries have a particular competitive advantage: automobiles and automotive suppliers, machine tools, precision machinery, chemicals and chemical engineering. For R&D and innovation activities in new industries and high-tech fields (biotechnology, semiconductors, IT), Europe is much less of a target, due to limited visibility of research preeminence. As a result, with respect to leading-edge, research-based innovation, Japanese MNCs are much more active in North America, and in other uprising countries outside of Europe.

Sustainable European strengths in innovation are much more based on what we call *engineering innovation*, an often neglected dimension in innovation research. Industries and regions in continental Europe often display particular strengths not so much in high-tech and research based innovation. Instead, they rely on a strong home base in manufacturing, logistics, specialty-machinery and continuous product and process improvement. In Germany, Switzerland, and northern Italy as well as in other European regions, strengths in engineering innovation are the typical pattern of sustainable comparative advantage. In Germany, MNCs in automobiles, chemical and process engineering, machine tools and factory automation can build on a strong home-base of world-class manufacturing and engineering. Large firms are embedded in a strong network of suppliers, services as well as engineering and research facilities.

As can be seen in Figure 4, strengths in engineering innovation are closely interconnected with advanced R&D on one side and continuous product development and successful commercialization of new products at home. In addition, engineering capabilities are transferred to advanced foreign locations, and will be supported by successful export strategies as well as by R&D in foreign locations, most of which, however, is home-base exploiting.

There are close similarities in engineering innovation between Japanese German and Swiss MNCs, and this explains market success and high innovation performance in similar industries such as machine-tools, special purpose machinery, instrumentation as well as in automobiles. Engineering innovation builds on subtle and intricate mechanisms, for which both Japanese as well as European MNCs display similar strengths and capabilities. There are other areas, in which Japanese firms often outperform European rivals, and this often happens in fields for which engineering-innovation or research-based innovation is not at the center-stage.

---

[9]   JETRO (2004), Japanese Manufacturing Affiliates in Europe and Turkey – 2003 survey, Japan External Trade Organization, Tokyo.

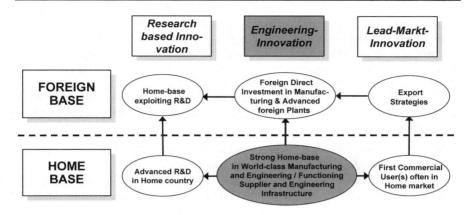

Examples: Automobiles, Process engineering, Special purpose machinery

Fig. 4. Home-base exploiting engineering innovation

Lead-Market Innovation and Knowledge Flows Within MNCs

Innovation moving downstream results in a growing role of innovation stimulated by problem-solving and value-enhancing activities in markets which are rather unstructured. We call this value innovation or *lead market innovation*. MNCs go to certain locations in which demanding customers exert pressure on offering intelligent new solutions, often combining refined products and services. They want to learn about social, economic or environmental problems which arise in specific regions and which induce search processes for new business concepts. Japanese firms are particularly strong for this type of innovation which is value-driven or lead market induced. A number of breakthrough innovations that were based on early discoveries in North America or Europe, were later successfully commercialized in Japan due to this value-engineering and lead-market effect: flat panel displays and the telefax are typical examples.[10] In most high-tech fields in which Japanese firms have become successful (personal computers, semiconductors, optoelectronics, electronic games etc.), innovation was largely triggered by demanding customers within a highly-sophisticated lead market in Japan.

Lead-market induced innovation is most effective, if corporations can build on demanding customers and strong network embeddedness with users, regulators and service providers in the home country. In Europe, there are only few success stories, where breakthrough innovations were effectively commercialized, but

---

10   See Gerybadze, Meyer-Krahmer and Reger (1997, chapter 3) for a detailed analysis of the role of Japanese lead markets in triggering innovation in flat panel displays.

some of these success stories have been explained through effective working of lead markets. Mobile communication and the evolution of the GSM standard in Scandinavia (Beise 2004), media and printing technology or automotive electronics in Germany are examples, where European MNCs have become successful in building on lead markets in their home country.

Similar to the differentiation between home-base augmenting and home-base exploiting R&D outlined in section 3, we can describe two different strategies that can be followed by MNCs, if lead markets drive innovation processes.

- *Home-base exploiting lead market strategies* build on demanding customers and·network embeddedness in the home country;
- *foreign lead market strategies* or home-base augmenting lead marketing are more difficult to deal with, but are becoming increasingly important for MNCs.

The literature on transnational innovation (Bartlett and Ghoshal 1998) has emphasized this new mode of leveraging innovation at distinct lead market locations. MNCs are reported to develop learning and sensing capabilities, and some companies, especially those from smaller countries, are particularly strong at this. However, the majority of MNCs from Japan and from larger European countries still encounter great difficulties when they have to deal with lead marketing in *distinct* locations (Gerybadze and Reger 1999; Sölvell 2004). There are few examples, of MNCs effectively implementing lead market innovation capabilities abroad. Nokia has been quite strong in developing novel products and services in Asia as well as in other European countries. Japanese firms (Sony, Matsushita) are more and more often generating new product and service concepts in sophisticated market environments in Europe, e.g. for automotive entertainment systems. However, managing foreign lead markets requires new management concepts and a new configuration of R&D and distributed teams within large MNCs. Apart from few effective cases, though, this new mode of transnational innovation still represents a great challenge for Japanese MNCs and European firms alike.[11]

---

[11]   See Gerybadze (2004b) for an analysis of team-building mechanisms and communication problems arising in transnational innovation.

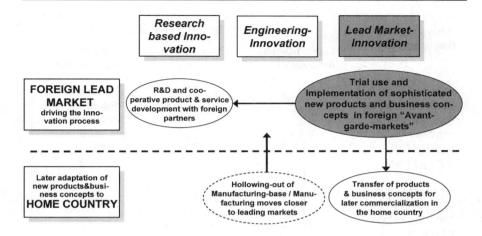

Examples: Mobile communication, Flat panel displays, Automotive electronics

Fig. 5. Innovation in foreign lead markets / Home-base augmenting lead marketing

Appropriate Mechanisms of Transnational Knowledge Flows: Comparing European and Japanese MNCs

There are still significant differences in the way the engine of innovation works in Japan and in different European countries, and this may help to explain persisting differences in innovation performance across countries and industries. Japan was very successful in the 1970s and 1980s to absorb foreign technology, and to adapt these to a combination of lead market capabilities and engineering innovation. In later periods, Japanese firms have strengthened their R&D capabilities in Japan, but with a clear focus of linking R&D projects to home-based strengths in engineering and lead marketing. Japanese MNCs are still less active in setting up foreign R&D, as compared to MNCs from other countries. Foreign R&D outposts often serve as a source of knowledge to strengthen R&D capabilities at home. They are much less embedded with the manufacturing and marketing network in the host country. Foreign factories are often more a user of Japanese process technology than a source of knowledge for advanced manufacturing know-how. Japanese firms are also much less active in lead marketing at foreign locations. Here, we see a recommended area for improvements within large Japanese MNCs.

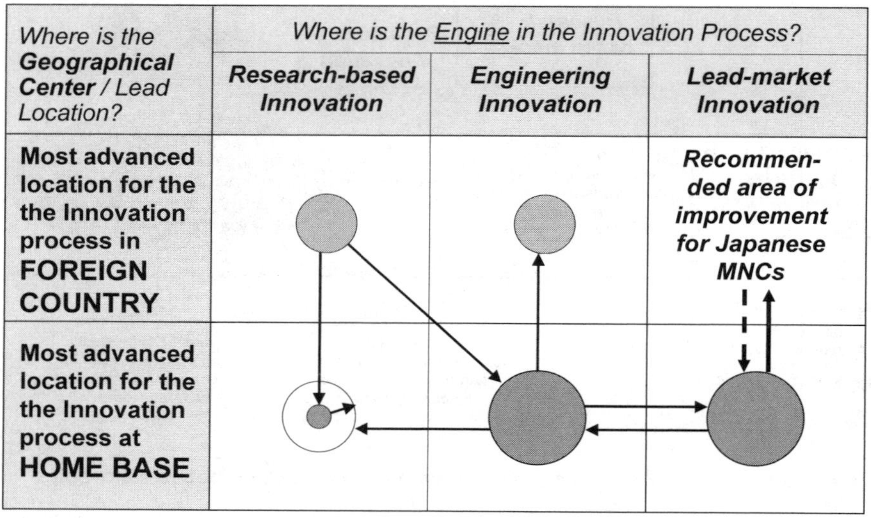

Where is the Geographical Center / Lead Location?	Where is the _Engine_ in the Innovation Process?		
	Research-based Innovation	Engineering Innovation	Lead-market Innovation
Most advanced location for the the Innovation process in FOREIGN COUNTRY			Recommen- ded area of improvement for Japanese MNCs
Most advanced location for the the Innovation process at HOME BASE			

Fig. 6. Source of knowledge and knowledge flows in Japanese MNCs

Innovation systems and the patterns of knowledge flows are still quite diverse in different European countries and need to be studied on a country-by-country and industry-by-industry basis. We will concentrate on the pattern of innovation observed in large German and Swiss MNCs. There is still a tendency to build on technology-pull, and to generate new products based on R&D in the home country, in combination with strong engineering capabilities. This is still the predominant pattern of innovation in mechanical engineering, automobiles and chemicals. German and Swiss firms have also set up R&D labs abroad and have invested in advanced manufacturing facilities. Competitive strengths can be explained by a functioning virtuous circle combining home-base augmenting and home-base exploiting R&D and advanced manufacturing, as is illustrated in Figure 6. Lead marketing capabilities are much less emphasized than in Japanese firms, and there are much fewer "success cases" where breakthrough products were triggered through home-based lead markets.

Innovation efforts outside this functioning circle, particularly in high-tech industries like information technology, computers, biotechnology etc. have often led to failures. European MNCs have invested considerable amounts of money for new products for which national or European markets turned out to be less advanced or over-regulated. Furthermore, German high-tech firms showed limited success rates, whenever the source of knowledge was concentrated in more advanced locations (like in the U.S.), and when they were lacking absorptive capabilities in R&D and manufacturing in the home country. Developing lead market innovation capabilities would be a recommended area for improvement for European MNCs. Learning from Japanese firms in managing home-based lead markets, as well as learning from successful examples of Scandinavian firms in leveraging foreign lead markets could be very useful for supply-driven MNCs from larger European countries.

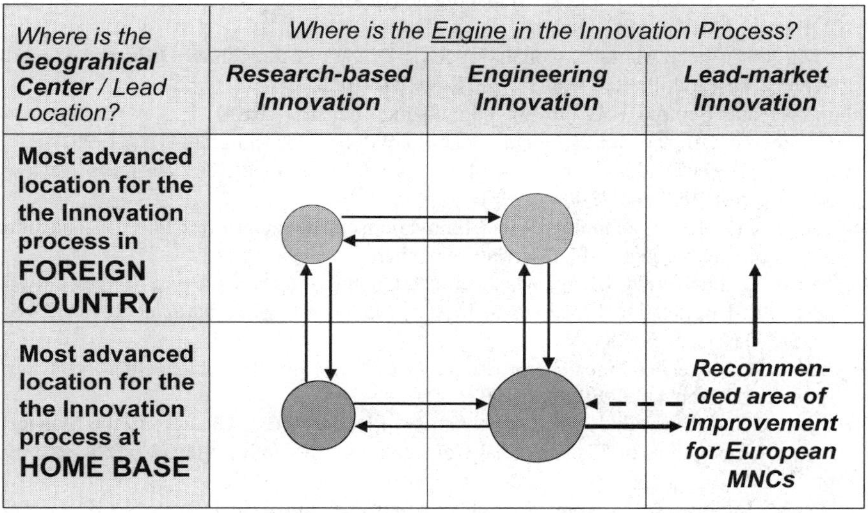

Where is the Geograhical Center / Lead Location?	Where is the _Engine_ in the Innovation Process?		
	Research-based Innovation	Engineering Innovation	Lead-market Innovation
Most advanced location for the the Innovation process in **FOREIGN COUNTRY**			
Most advanced location for the the Innovation process at **HOME BASE**			*Recommen-ded area of improvement for European MNCs*

Fig. 7. Source of knowledge and knowledge flows in German and Swiss MNCs

Compared to Japan and continental Europe, the innovation engine works differently in other nation states. The United States innovation engine builds on strong R&D in conjunction with strong lead market capabilities, and still builds much more on home-base exploiting strategies. MNCs from Scandinavian countries, by contrast, have emphasized R&D and lead market innovation, with much stronger capabilities to leverage foreign sources of knowledge. There are still persisting differences between countries in how they manage innovation across borders and across different business units and functions. Understanding persisting national differences and the structural and cultural reasons behind it is helpful in assessing which kind of investment is likely to succeed in a particular context.

References

Ambos B (2005): Foreign Direct Investment in Industrial Research and Development: A Study of German MNCs, Research Policy, forthcoming

Andersson U, Forsgren M, and Holm U (2001): Subsidiary Embeddedness and Competence Development in MNCs – A Multi-level Analysis, Organization Studies, Vol. 22, 6/2001, pp. 1013-1034

Andersson U, Forsgren M, and Holm U (2002): The Strategic Impact of External Networks: Subsidiary Performance and Competence Development in the Multinational Corporation, Strategic Management Journal, Vol. 23, 2002, pp. 979-996

Bartlett CA and Ghoshal S (1998): Managing across Borders, The Transnational Solution, 2. Edition, Boston, MA

Beise M (2004): Lead Markets: Country-specific Drivers of the Global Diffusion of Innovations, Research Policy, Vol. 33, 2004, pp. 997-1018

Dalton DH and Serapio MG (1999): Globalizing Industrial R&D, U.S. Department of Commerce, Office of International Technology Policy, Washington, D. C. 1999

Ferdows K (1997): Making the Most of Foreign Factories, Harvard Business Review, March-April 1997, pp. 73-88. (1997)

Gerybadze A (2004a): Technologie- und Innovationsmanagement. Strategie, Organisation und Implementierung, Vahlen-Verlag, München

Gerybadze A (2004b): Knowledge Management, Cognitive Coherence and Equivocality in Distributed Innovation Processes in MNCs, Management International Review, Vol. 44, 3/2004, pp. 103-128

Gerybadze A, Meyer-Krahmer F, and Reger G (1997): Globales Management von Forschung und Innovation, Stuttgart 1997

Gerybadze A and Reger G (1999): Globalization of R&D: Recent Changes in the Management of Innovation in Transnational Corporations, Research Policy, Vol. 28, 2/1999, pp. 252-274

Gibbons M, Limoges C, Nowotny H, Schwartzman S, Scott P, and Trow M (1994): The New Production of Knowledge. The Dynamics of Science and Research in Contemporary Societies, Sage Publications, London

Håkanson H and Nobel R (2001): Organizational Characteristics and Reverse Technology Transfer, Management International Review, Vol. 41, pp. 395-420

JETRO (2004): Japanese Manufacturing Affiliates in Europe and Turkey – 2003. Survey, Japan External Trade Organization, Tokyo

Khan S and Yoshihara H (1994): Strategy and Performance of Foreign Companies in Japan, Quorum Books, Westport, Conn. and London

Kümmerle W (1997): Building Effective R&D Capabilities Abroad, Harvard Business Review, March-April 1997, pp. 61-70

Kümmerle W (1999): Foreign Direct Investment in Industrial Research in the Pharmaceutical and Electronics Industry: Results from a Survey of Multinational Firms, Research Policy, Vol. 28, pp. 252-274

Management International Review (2000): Special Issue on the International Management of Technology: Theory, Evidence and Policy, ed. by Taggart JH and Pearce RD, Vol. 40

Narula R and Zanfei A (2004):, Globalization of Innovation: The Role of Multinational Enterprises, in: Faberberg J, Mowery DC, and Nelson RR (Eds.), The Oxford Handbook of Innovation, Oxford-New York, pp. 318-345

Nowotny H, Scott P, and Gibbons M (2001): Re-Thinking Science. Knowledge and the Public in an Age of Uncertainty, Blackwell, Oxford

OECD (1997): Oslo Manual, Proposed Guidelines for Collecting and Interpreting Technological Innovation Data, Organisation for Economic Cooperation and Development, Paris

OECD (2004): Main Science and Technology Indicators, I/2004, Paris

Research Policy (1999): Special Issue on Internationalization of Industrial R&D, Vol. 28, Nos. 2-3

Sölvell Ö (2003): The Multi-home-based Multinational: Combining Global Competitiveness and Local Innovativeness, in: Birkinshaw J, Ghoshal S, Markides C et al. (Eds.), the Future of the Multinational Company, Wiley, New York, pp. 34-44

Stinchcombe AL (1990): Information and Organizations, Berkeley, CA

von Hippel E (1994): Sticky Information and the Locus of Problem Solving: Implications for Innovation, Management Science, Vol. 4, 4/1994, pp. 429-439

von Hippel E (2005): Democratizing Innovation, MIT Press, Cambridge, MA

Reducing Project Related Uncertainty in the "Fuzzy Front End" of Innovation – A Comparison of German and Japanese Product Innovation Projects

Cornelius Herstatt, Birgit Verworn, and Akio Nagahira

Introduction

The Fuzzy Front End

Recently, researchers and practitioners in the field of innovation management are paying more attention to the so called "fuzzy front end" of product development, also known as the "pre-development" phase (Cooper and Kleinschmidt 1994), "pre-project activities" (Verganti 1997), or "pre-phase 0" (Khurana and Rosenthal 1997, 1998). Managers have identified the front end as being the greatest weakness in product innovation (Khurana and Rosenthal 1997, p. 103). Why? Because it strongly determines which projects will be executed, and furthermore the quality, costs, and time frame are to a large extent defined here. But research in this field has clearly demonstrated that efforts to optimize the innovation process at this stage in practice are minimal. In contrast, effects on the overall efficiency and effectiveness of the whole innovation process are significant (Moore and Pessemier 1993, p. 100). Consistent with these findings, an extensive empirical study by Cooper and Kleinschmidt showed that "the greatest differences between winners and losers were found in the quality of execution of pre-development activities" (Cooper and Kleinschmidt 1994, p. 26). Two factors were identified as playing a major role in product success: the quality of executing the pre-development activities, and a well defined product and project prior to the development phase (Cooper and Kleinschmidt 1990, p. 27)

A study of 788 new product launches in Japan confirmed that Japanese new product professionals view the importance of pre-development proficiency in much the same way as their American and European counterparts (Song and Parry 1996, pp. 422, 433).

In general, the front end ranges from the generation of an idea to either its approval for development or its termination (Murphy and Kumar 1997). Figure 1 shows a simplified figure of the product development process to demonstrate the stage in which the fuzzy front end plays a role in the innovation process. The product development process starts with an idea originating from basic research, customer based techniques, and creativity techniques (Cooper and Kleinschmidt 1990, p. 45). During phase I, the idea is evaluated. This could be an iterative process, where the idea is worked out in more detail and assessed in several steps. For instance, an initial rough assessment could be made according to "must meet" and "should meet" criteria such as strategic alignment, feasibility or company policy 'fit'. Following a more detailed investigation, it is typical for a quick and inexpensive assessment of the project in terms of market, technology, and financials to take place. Phase II tasks are the development of a more detailed product concept and the initial project planning. Output of the fuzzy front end is a detailed business plan which is the basis for the decision on a business case. The "later phases" commence with phase III, which is where the actual development of the product starts.

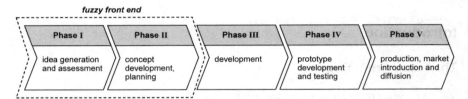

Fig. 1. The development process

Reducing Uncertainty in the Front End of Innovation

Product development and the processes behind it can be seen as a series of activities related to problem solving. The more radical the product or process innovation, the more complex and iterative the problem solving process or the innovation process behind it. Typical risks jeopardizing the success of innovation for example, include inaccurate estimates of the future market demand, failing to develop the technology as planned or in extreme cases, a combination of both.

In the product development process relevant information has to be gathered in order to reduce such risks and uncertainties (Moenaert et al. 1995, pp. 252–254; Mullins and Sutherland 1998, p. 228). Uncertainty is defined as "the difference between the amount of information required to perform a particular task, and the amount of information already possessed by the organization" (Galbraith 1973, p. 5). The more that a risk or uncertainty can be reduced during the front end of this process, the lower the deviations from front end specifications, during the following project execution phases and hence, the higher the product development success.

Uncertainties inherent in New Product Development projects relate to the market and technology (see Figure 2). The amount of information required very much depends on the type of New Product Development Project. Why? The highest level of newness to a firm is implied in the term *radical innovation* with an uncertainty in terms of both the market and the technology (upper right quadrant of Figure 2). In contrast, *incremental innovations* like small product improvements tend to rely on existing internal information. *Market and technical innovation* can revert to existing knowledge in one dimension, whilst the other dimension is highly uncertain. Examples of this are the penetration of new markets with existing products, or the replacement of an obsolete technology inherent in a product without changing product features or the target market.

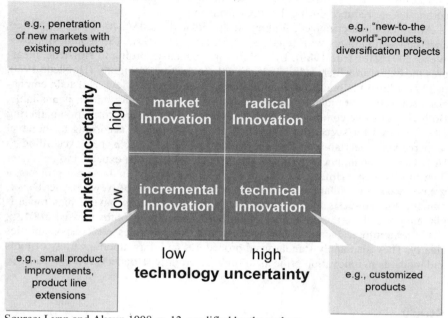

Source: Lynn and Akgun 1998, p. 13, modified by the authors

Fig. 2. Uncertainty matrix

Therefore, the degree of newness of a New Product Development project to a firm is an important contextual factor, which influences how uncertainties are reduced during the product development process (Balachandra and Friar 1997, p. 285; Mishra et al. 1996, pp. 536–539; Song and Montoya-Weiss 1998, p. 132; Moenaert et al., p. 253; Schlaak 1999, p. 304; Veryzer 1998, p. 318). If information is not yet available and has to be sought from secondary sources, a different approach is needed to acquire this information. For example, when the newness of the market and technology to the firm are high, identifying customer needs and translating them into a product's technical specifications are much more challenging, and these activities will require completely different marketing and technical capabilities than would be needed if the newness to the firm is low (Song and Montoya-Weiss 2001, p. 73).

Cultural Differences

In addition to the firm's perceived degree of newness of the planned product innovation, other factors such as branch specific or cultural differences might have an
impact on the new product development process and particularly on the way uncertainties are reduced during the fuzzy front end phase.

Although often criticized, findings from Hofstede and others indicate a difference between cultures with regard to uncertainty avoidance (Song and Montoya-
Weiss 2001; Hofstede 1980). Uncertainty avoidance according to Hofstede, measures the extent to which individuals are able to tolerate ambiguity (Hofstede 1980,
p. 112). Whilst Galbraith takes an information processing view, Hofstede emphasizes subjective attitudes towards situations where little information is available.
Both views can be combined to form the view that the basic information gathering
tasks required for successful innovation differ in emphasis according to the level
of perceived uncertainty (Song and Montoya-Weiss 2001, p. 65). According to
Hofstede, in Japan, uncertainty avoidance tendencies can be expected to be higher
than in Germany (Hofstede 1980, p. 122). Consequently, in Japanese projects, a
greater need to avoid ambiguity can be expected. In terms of New Product Development, this suggests that Japanese managers may tend to have a bias towards
planning to reduce the possibility of failures (Song and Montoya-Weiss 2001, p.
64). Furthermore, Japanese managers tend to define roles and responsibilities
clearly. They also apply standardized procedures and draw upon a variety of tools
and methods in innovation projects of high uncertainty (Hofstede 1980, p. 264).

Study

Aim of the Exploratory Study

Most of large scale empirical studies of the fuzzy front end, as well as large scale
cross-national comparative studies form part of the research on success factors for
New Product Development, where most of the activities during the fuzzy front end
were combined under one heading like "pre-development activities" (Cooper and
Kleinschmidt 1994, p. 26; Song and Parry 1996, p. 433; Song and Parry 1997, p.
3) but not outlined in any further detail. This exploratory study tries to develop a
deeper understanding of the major tasks to be undertaken during the fuzzy front
end – to reduce project uncertainties, e. g. related to market or technology. In addition, former studies indicate that besides company or project specific contextual
factors like company size or degree of newness of a project, cultural differences
might influence innovation related activities including the front end (Jürgens
2000, pp. 2–4; Mishra et al., p. 530; Song and Parry 1996, p. 432; Song and Xie
1996, p. 5; Souder and Song 1998, p. 222). Therefore, the second objective of our
exploratory study was to determine initial indicators of cultural differences in
terms of the way that uncertainties are reduced at the start the innovation process.
Germany and Japan were chosen because literature indicates differences in inno-

vation management practices, particularly with regard to uncertainty avoidance (Song and Montoya-Weiss 2001; Hofstede 1980; Jürgens 2000; Park 1996).

The aim and methodology of our study and a description of the samples are presented in the following section. The third section summarizes findings of our study. In chapter four, we formulate initial propositions, highlight managerial implications and make suggestions for future research.

Methodology

To reduce the complexity of our study, we focus on companies that are in similar industrial sectors and assume consistency in terms of sector related contextual factors. In Germany, we identified a total of 102 mechanical and electrical engineering companies located in the state of Hamburg by using the Hoppenstedt database[1]. All of these companies were contacted by telephone. Seven mechanical engineering companies and seven electrical engineering companies agreed to participate in our study. Finally, 14 in-depth interviews were conducted with the managers responsible for the development of new products during 2001.

In Japan, MOST (Management of Science and Technology Department) at the Tohoku University in Sendai contacted 28 mechanical and electrical engineering companies. 13 companies agreed to participate. In one large electrical engineering company, two projects were analyzed. In sum, 14 in-depth interviews were conducted in 2002 with three mechanical and nine electrical engineering companies. For pragmatic reasons, given that it was difficult to convince Japanese companies to participate in research from outside Japan, the sampling procedure in Japan differed from the procedure in Germany. Hence, although the Japanese companies in our sample operate in the same industry as the German companies and hence, products and markets are comparable, differences in our sampling methodology somewhat limited the impact of our comparative results.

Interviews lasted between two and three hours and were conducted by two interviewers in each country. The majority of the interviewees were directors of the Research and Development department (R&D) or general managers. In six companies, both, the R&D Director and Marketing Director were interviewed. In one of the Japanese companies, we were given the opportunity to interview the whole of the product development team. Interviews consisted of two parts: Firstly, interviewees were asked to briefly describe the development process and the outcome of the last product they had launched (last incident method) with the focus being on front end activities. The second part of the interview was solely based on a standardized questionnaire which was translated from German into Japanese for the interviews in Japan. The majority of the items were measured on a 7-point Likert scale. This two stage approach was designed to guarantee comparability of different interviews and to ensure that all of the issues perceived as being important by the interviewees could be addressed via the standardized questions.

---

[1]   www.firmendatenbank.de

Sample

A short description of all projects and respective companies is presented in the appendix to this paper.

Company size: The German sample contains three large companies with 11,000, 200,000, and 420,000 employees respectively and annual sales of over one billion Euros. However, the majority of the German sample consists of small and medium sized enterprises (SMEs) with 25 to 360 employees and annual sales between 2 and 77 million Euros.

The Japanese sample is split equally between large companies with 2,500 to 10,000 employees and annual sales mostly over one billion Euro and SMEs with 66 to 930 employees and annual sales from 7 to 708 million Euros. On average, the Japanese companies are larger than the German companies. Therefore, one must consider that in the following analysis, differences in innovation management could, in addition to cross-national differences, be attributed in part to company size.

Project scope: The average development time for new products developed was 20 months in Germany and 24 months in Japan.

Degree of newness: Interviewees in both countries classified the newness of their product concepts and assessed the overall degree of newness of the product concept to their company (see Figure 3).

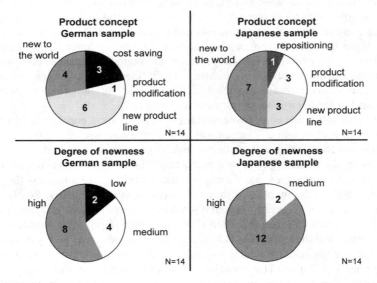

Fig. 3. Degree of newness

Firstly, ten of 14 projects were classified as new product lines in Germany as well as in Japan. Secondly, regardless of whether using the classification of the product concept or the subjective overall rating, the newness of the Japanese product development projects got higher ratings of newness than German projects did. Thirdly, in both countries, the overall subjective assessment of the degree of newness to the company did not correspond to the (rather objective) classification of categories used in our questionnaire. For example, two cost saving projects were rated as highly new to the company. We came to the conclusion that there seems to be a general tendency to overestimate the degree of newness in an overall assessment of innovations. This conclusion is mirrored to a large extent by a recent German large scale study by Schlaak, in which 117 product development projects, of which the assessment of the overall degree of newness lead to high and homogeneous values, whereas a multi-dimensional measurement lead to lower and more differentiated values (Schlaak 1999, p. 210).

Interviewees were asked to describe the major areas of uncertainty in the product development projects in more detail. As already indicated by the degree of newness of the product concept (see Figure 3), overall, uncertainties were perceived as higher in the Japanese projects. For the Japanese as well as the German projects, technology was the major source of uncertainty, but only on an average level in the German projects. In several of the German projects, there was a need to build new production lines, which was a further source of technological uncertainty. Corresponding to the fact that half of the Japanese projects were classified as new to the world (see Figure 3), the target market and customers for the new products differed from markets already served by the Japanese companies. Regarding the German projects, most of the new products were introduced to existing markets.

To summarize, the need to reduce uncertainties was lower for the German projects and was mostly restricted to technology. For more than half of the Japanese projects, a high technological uncertainty was accompanied by a high market uncertainty.

Project success: Although we asked interviewees to describe the development of the last product introduced to the market, regardless of whether it was a success or failure, most of the projects in our sample were indeed successful. To assess the effectiveness of the projects, interviewees were asked, if objectives existed and if yes, were they achieved? (see Figure 4). The five objectives we interviewed them about were relevant to the majority of the German projects (between 12 and 14) and all of the Japanese projects.

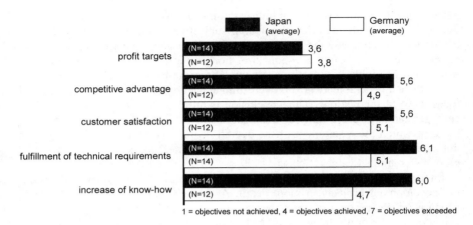

Fig. 4. Achievement of objectives

Overall, the effectiveness of the projects was fairly high regarding competitive advantage, customer satisfaction, fulfillment of technical requirements, and increased know-how. For these objectives, all Japanese and German projects either met or exceeded their targets. Deficiencies were only observed in terms of finance, where target profits were not reached in two of the German and six of the Japanese projects. In sum, all of the Japanese and German interviewees were satisfied with the outcome of the projects. Therefore, regardless of the way uncertainties were reduced, the respective approaches which are about to be outlined in the chapters that follow, were successful.

Results

This section summarizes our key findings about the fuzzy front end and tries to identify initial indicators for country specific differences. Firstly, we will describe how ideas were generated, assessed, and selected. Secondly, we will summarize to what extent market and technological uncertainty were reduced prior to project execution. Finally, we will describe the intensity of project planning activities as a further opportunity to reduce project related uncertainties and as a basis of controlling during the following steps of the product development process.

As already mentioned in the previous section, the findings of our research are affected by several limitations, e.g., different sampling procedures in Germany and Japan and a small sample size of 14 projects in each country. Therefore, we will only interpret differences between Japanese and German projects, but if having completed the interviews we are under the strong impression that a difference exists which can be explained, and the difference between average values is relatively high to confirm our impression, these will be included.

Idea Generation

The idea generation process is a combination of an organizational need, problem, or opportunity with the purpose of satisfying this need, solving a problem, or capitalizing on an opportunity. Although, the generation of ideas is often a complex and creative task, some researchers recommend reducing this uncertainty by assigning the tasks of systematic gathering, storing, and transferring all idea related information to specific individuals.

But since a greater number of ideas can often be more efficiently and systematically created by teams or groups, it is often recommended that systematic procedures like creativity techniques (see Geschka 1992 for an overview of creativity techniques) and team based techniques (like brainstorming) should be applied. On the other hand, some authors claim that individual idea generation produces more creative solutions than those from groups (Rochford 1991, p. 289). However, most authors favor an interdisciplinary group for idea generation (Baker et al. 1985, p. 40; Geschka 1992, pp. 284, 294–296; Rubinstein 1994, p. 656; Rochford 1991, p. 289; Song and Parry 1997, p. 9). R&D and marketing as well as other functions (e.g., production, customer service) should cooperate early on in this creative process. Such a multidisciplinary integration ensures that customer needs and technological capabilities are taken into sufficient consideration, even in the early stages of the innovation process (Rubinstein 1994, p. 656). A joint understanding and shared goals concerning the innovation, early in the process will have a positive influence on the project or even foster the information transfer between departments and therefore reduce uncertainties.

A general and vital precondition for all of these activities is that employees (individuals and teams) have sufficient time at their disposal to either collect relevant information or search for new ideas in addition to performing their regular business activities (Rochford 1991, p. 291; Baker et al. 1985, p. 41).

Our findings concerning idea generation in the context of companies in both countries are presented in Figure 5. They indicate differences in the way German and Japanese companies manage the idea creation process for new products.

Whereas the 14 Japanese projects were supported more in terms of systematic procedures and tools (such as a systematic information management process or the use of creativity techniques), the 14 German projects are characterized by a stronger emphasis on interdisciplinary teams and scope for the employees to generate new ideas.

Whilst only three of the 14 ideas in Germany, which suffered from limited resources in small enterprises, were not generated by an interdisciplinary team, six of the Japanese ideas were generated by one solitary function. These six ideas occurred in medium or large enterprises so that restriction to one function cannot be made accountable for, due to limited resources. Furthermore, the Japanese companies clearly favored allocating responsibility to a single competent person within one function, whilst the German companies clearly preferred a team approach to generating ideas for product development. This finding was somewhat surprising, since we had expected an equally or perhaps an even more team oriented approach in the case of information processing in the Japanese sample. One interpretation of these findings is that the Japanese Companies in our research try to encourage individuals and teams of people from various functions to collect and process ideas.

Our present study corresponds with former findings about the rare use of tools and methods to support generation of new ideas in the Western culture (Förderer et al. 1998, p. 13; Smith 1998, p. 114; Sowrey 1987, pp. 11–13) in contrast to the frequent use of brainstorming in Japan (Harryson 1996, p. 26). In 11 out of 14 German projects, creativity techniques were not used at all, whereas in 12 of the Japanese projects, brainstorming was applied. (In contrast, a comparative study in the chemical industry showed that creativity techniques were more often used in Germany than in Japan. Corresponding to our study, brainstorming was the most commonly used creativity technique (Park 1996, p. 129).)

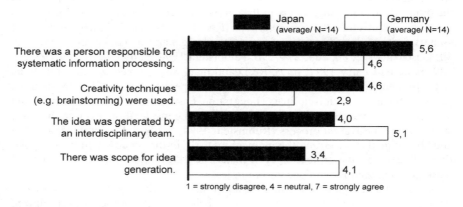

Fig. 5. Idea generation

Overall, our research indicates differences in the way Japanese and German companies organize their idea generation processes. Whilst the Japanese managers assigned clear responsibilities to individuals as well as to teams and made use of systematic procedures including creativity techniques to reduce uncertainties early in the process, in the case of the German projects, ideas were generated by interdisciplinary teams, mostly not applying any specific procedures or such techniques. Instead these teams had been allocated sufficient time (scope) to develop ideas for innovation.

Idea Assessment

Idea assessment is necessary to decide on the execution of an idea or to select the most promising idea from alternatives. The importance of this step within the product development process is empirically supported by studies in Western countries as well as in Japan and other countries (Cooper and Kleinschmidt 1986, p. 82, 1994, p. 25; Johne and Snelson 1988, p. 119; Mishra et al. 1996, p. 540; Song and Parry 1996, p. 431). Given that decisions frequently have to be made without having all of the relevant information to hand, idea assessment is a necessary step in the innovation process, but it is accompanied by a high degree of uncertainty. The more radical the innovation project, the more difficult an early assessment of an idea becomes.

As in the case of idea generation, some authors recommend taking an interdisciplinary approach to idea assessment to ensure that all facets and perspectives are taken into consideration and that uncertainties are reduced as far as is possible (Aggteleky and Bajina 1992, pp. 154–156; Song and Parry 1997, p. 9). In this case, such a team has to develop a rich set of criteria in order to effectively evaluate the list of ideas created by individuals or teams. Such criteria typically address technical and/or economical aspects. Furthermore, some studies have identified a proficient financial analysis to be a major success factor for innovation (Dwyer and Mellor 1991, p. 42; Mansfield and Wagner 1975, pp. 187–189; Mishra et al. 1996, p. 540). But such an analysis needs a minimum level of concrete ideas, of course. Unfortunately such rich data is hardly ever available for breakthrough type innovations during the early phase of the innovation process, the "fuzzy front end".

The results of our research paint the following picture: Firstly, six of the 14 companies in Germany (five of the 14 companies in Japan) were in a position where the New Product Development project was already scheduled anyway. One of the companies, e.g., had to adapt to a technical change in the target market. These six (five) companies assessed the idea but did not have to select between alternatives. Hence, in the following analysis, only the remaining eight (nine) companies which had built in a project selection step into their product development process have been considered.

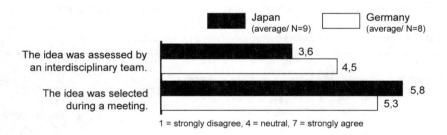

Fig. 6. Idea assessment

Regarding the interdisciplinary approach to idea assessment, as in the case for the German projects (see Figure 6), the findings are slightly misleading. All three projects managed by one function are included in the sample of 14 projects for idea generation and eight projects for idea assessment. The decrease in mean values in Figure 6 compared to Figure 5 is therefore caused by having a smaller sample. In Germany, all ideas that were selected by an interdisciplinary team were already generated by multiple functions. In Japan, similar to our results with regard to idea generation, the level of multidisciplinarity for idea assessment was slightly lower than in Germany.

In Germany, idea selection took place in meetings, where the various functions of the company were represented. Only one company held a meeting with participants from one department only. To the contrary, in Japan, five of the nine ideas were assessed during meetings with participants from one function only (like R&D, production or marketing/sales). This early assessment included discussions concerning the technical as well as economical attractiveness of the projects. At first glance, it seems surprising that although the Japanese culture is supposed to be more collectivist than the German culture, in our study the German projects were characterized by a more interdisciplinary team approach during the fuzzy front end. However, reconsidering the results, as the Japanese projects had a medium to high degree of newness to the firms, involving people from different functions may offer the opportunity to integrate diverse information and perspectives, but will also lengthen the process substantially, due to the collectivist element to be expected in such meetings. This view is supported by recent research that suggests that Japanese managers are willing to spend a substantial amount of time achieving group consensus in a harmonious setting (Song and Montoya-Weiss 2001, p. 66). But in order to run such evaluation sessions effectively, it makes sense that in the 14 Japanese projects, various meetings were held during the fuzzy front end, but mostly between people in one function: Implementing this approach, enables them to achieve a much faster consensus of opinion on development issues.

Table 1 shows the importance of technical and economical criteria for the assessment of an idea in Germany and Japan. Most of the companies considered technical as well as economical criteria (16 of 17) and therefore tried to base their decisions on minimum technological and market/economical uncertainty.

Table 1. Importance of technical and economical selection criteria

Germany		technical criteria				Japan		technical criteria			
		not important	neutral	very important	sum			not important	neutral	very important	sum
econo-mical criteria	not impor-tant	-	-	-	-	econo-mical criteria	not impor-tant	-	-	1	**1**
	neu-tral	-	-	3	**3**		neu-tral	-	-	1	**1**
	very impor-tant	-	2	3	**5**		very impor-tant	-	-	7	**7**
	sum	-	**2**	**6**	**8**		sum	-	-	**9**	**9**

Concerning the methodological support of idea assessment, in about half of the German as well as the Japanese projects, selection criteria used were weighted (see Figure 7). An analysis of cost effectiveness seems standard for Japanese projects regardless of company size. In Germany, only one medium sized and two larger companies carried out an analysis of cost effectiveness. A comparative study in the chemical industry showed different results. Whilst the weighting of criteria was more common in Japan than in Germany, no significant differences were found with regard to cost effectiveness analysis (Park 1996, pp. 140–142). Nevertheless, a stronger methodological support of idea assessment in Japan is a similarity that was also found in other studies from different industry sectors.

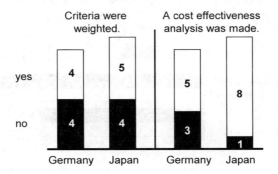

Fig. 7. Methodological support of idea assessment

To summarize, whereas in the German projects, ideas were often assessed during meetings with participants representing various functions, in the case of the Japanese projects, meetings were held with participants from one function only. In both countries, idea assessment relied on technical and economic criteria which were weighted in about half of the cases. Whilst a cost effectiveness analysis seems standard in Japan, only a few larger enterprises in Germany elaborately calculated costs. Again, as for idea generation, in the Japanese projects the use of methods was emphasized whereas in the German projects interdisciplinary teams were used to reduce uncertainties during decision making.

Reduction of Market Uncertainty Prior to Development

After selecting an idea to be worked out in more detail, market uncertainty has to be reduced further, which should lead to a more in-depth understanding of the market. The target market has to be defined and customer requirements integrated into the product concept, prior to development (Balbontin et al. 1999, p. 274; Cooper and Kleinschmidt 1990, p. 26, 1994, p. 26, Khurana and Rosenthal 1997, p. 113; Maidique and Zirger 1984, p. 198; Song and Parry 1996, p. 427). For new markets, it is more difficult to reduce market uncertainty as potential customers are often unable to articulate their needs or may not even be aware of them (Mullins and Sutherland 1998, p. 228). Therefore, we expected the challenge to be higher for the Japanese projects of our sample as they were characterized as "new to the world" products for at least half of the cases.

One possibility to reduce market uncertainty is to extensively use customer or user information for developing the new product concept. This type of information can either be gathered by direct contact with customers or by relying on functions operating closely with client organizations such as after sales/customer service.

The amount of information from these functions in our sample was similar in Japan and Germany, on average on a medium level (see Figure 8). Direct contact to customers was more important for the initiation of German as well as Japanese projects of our study.

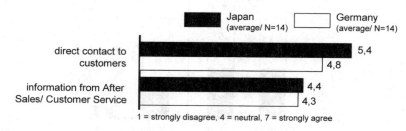

Fig. 8. Initiation

Overall, our findings with regard to initiation resemble the results of a large scale cross-national comparison between Germany, Japan, and the United States (Albach et al. 1991, pp. 311–313).

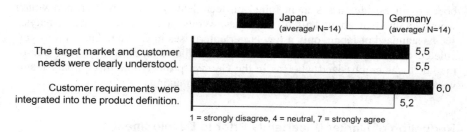

Fig. 9. Reduction of market uncertainty prior to development

Figure 9 reflects the results of our study with regard to the achieved market uncertainty reduction at the end of the "fuzzy front end". For the Japanese as well as for the German projects, the remaining market uncertainty prior to development was relatively low. The target market and customer needs were well understood before the proceeding with development. We are under the impression, that in the

Japanese projects the customer requirements played a slightly more important role in defining the product compared to the German projects. This might be explained by the fact, that the Japanese new product concepts were partly targeted at new customers.

To summarize, reduction of market uncertainty prior to development was achieved in the majority of projects both in Japan and Germany.

Reduction of Technical Uncertainty Prior to Development

Besides reducing market uncertainty, reducing technological uncertainty is a further key task during the fuzzy front end. For both samples this was a major task, as the 28 projects were characterized by a medium to high degree of newness. This means that interviewees felt unable to predict or completely understand some aspects of the technological environment at the very beginning (Song and Montoya-Weiss 2001, p. 61). For example, some interviewees perceived the product technology as under-developed and unknown and, thus, a trial and error research was considered unavoidable.

According to Moenaert et al., the amount of information acquired with regard to technology is a key differentiating factor between successful and unsuccessful projects (Moenaert et al. 1995, p. 249). The NewProd studies of Cooper and Kleinschmidt indicate a strong correlation between preliminary technical assessment and project outcomes (Cooper and Kleinschmidt 1986, p. 82). In Cooper and Kleinschmidt's measurement, preliminary technical assessment includes, among other things, a feasibility analysis and the definition of product specifications. In NewProd, preliminary technical assessment was undertaken in 85 % of projects and was regarded as effectively undertaken. Song and Parry likewise report a highly significant correlation between technological information prior to development (measured with six items) and project success in Japan (Song and Parry 1996, p. 431).

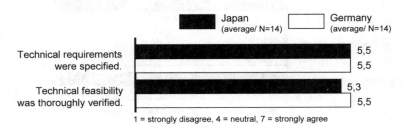

Fig. 10. Reduction of technical uncertainty prior to development

Our results paint a similar picture. Technical uncertainty prior to development was relatively low for the German and Japanese projects (see Figure 10). Technical requirements were not defined in two projects, and technical feasibility was not verified in one of fourteen German projects. In all of the Japanese projects requirements were defined and technical feasibility was checked at least to some extent.

To summarize, reduction of technical uncertainty prior to development was achieved in the majority of the projects studied with no indication for cultural differences.

Front End Project Planning

When the overall objective of a New Product Development project is clear, an initial planning before the start of the development of the new product translates the overall project goals into a series of activities and allocates resources to these activities. Although some information needed for the planning may at that point in time be difficult to forecast, overall uncertainties are reduced by laying out a rough process from development to product launch.

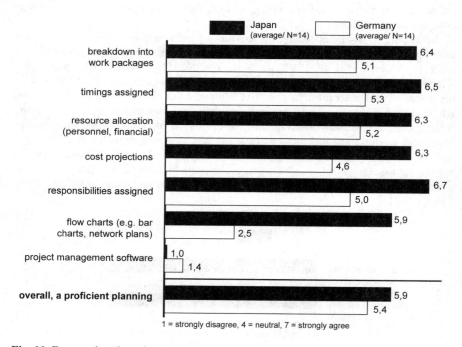

Fig. 11. Front end project planning

The first step of front end project planning is to break the product development project down into various work packages. Thereafter, timings, resources and overall responsibilities are allocated to the work packages. In addition, cost projections should be made and responsibilities should be assigned on an individual basis. The task of project planning can be supported by several tools and methods like bar charts, network plans, or project management software (Pinto and Slevin 1988, p. 73). Several large scale studies suggest that a proficient planning contributes significantly to the success of projects in Western countries (Balachandra and Friar 1997, p. 279; Pinto and Slevin 1988, p. 67; Maidique and Zirger 1984, p. 198). Song and Parry identified similar results for Japan (Song and Parry 1996, p. 432). Khurana and Rosenthal's exploratory study of incremental innovation projects in the U.S., Europe, and Japan observed deficiencies such as confusion about priorities and incomplete resource planning, which led to delays and product strategy mismatches (Khurana and Rosenthal 1997, p. 111). Results from Hofstede and Song et al. suggest that the intensity of the planning activities during the Japanese projects can be attributed to a higher level of uncertainty avoidance than is common in Germany (Hofstede 1980; Song and Montoya-Weiss 2001).

In our study, project planning is a front end activity that reveals clear differences in the management of Japanese and German projects and supports our proposition based on the studies from Hofstede and Song et al. (see Figure 11).

In every aspect of project planning, average values were higher for the 14 Japanese projects. Two of the German projects did not even have a front end project planning step at all. As expected, this was the case for product development projects in small firms (25/140 employees) and resulted in low project efficiency. The three large enterprises in our German sample carried out detailed planning for every aspect. Nevertheless, differences between German and Japanese projects cannot be explained by company size. In Japan, smaller enterprises had the same front end planning standard than larger enterprises. This country specific difference is abundantly clear for cost projections and flow charts, which were routinely utilized in all of the Japanese projects but in contrast, were an exception in Germany. This is consistent with our findings about the routine use of cost effective analysis in the Japanese sample compared to the German sample. Similarities between Japanese and German projects had already indicated in previous research that there is rarely project management software support for front end planning (Herstatt et al. 2001, pp. 155–157). In Germany, four companies used project management software, whereas, to our surprise, such software was not used at all in the Japanese companies, where in some cases they were completely unaware that such tools existed.

Interviewees were asked to assess not only the assessment of individual steps of front end planning, but also the overall proficiency of their front end planning. The average value for the German sample was surprisingly high compared to the assessment of individual planning issues, as well as compared to the overall assessment of the Japanese projects. Obviously, many of the German interviewees did not attach much importance to front end planning, whilst it was a routine step in the new product development process for the Japanese projects.

Overall, in our study, the most predominant differences between our Japanese and German sample was due to the management of fuzzy front end planning. Whilst proficient planning, including cost projections and flow charts seems standard for Japanese projects, regardless of firm size, the proficiency of front end planning is lower and divergent between the projects studied in Germany.

Given that the front end planning research revealed such interesting insights, we have decided to present the results of our study regarding controlling too, despite it not being a front end task. However, as controlling is based on deliverables defined during the fuzzy front end, differences between Japanese and German management practice can be expected to be found during controlling in the later phases of the process. In addition, as for planning, differences in uncertainty avoidance tendencies suggest a stricter approach to controlling in Japan than in Germany.

One of the principle controlling tasks is to detect deviations from the plans as early as possible. Furthermore, reasons for deviations should be ascertained, the impact assessed and a corrective action plan developed (Webb 2000, p. 216).

Consistent with our proposition and findings about project planning, the proficiency of controlling is significantly higher in our Japanese sample compared to our German sample (see Figure 12). Regardless of company size, the Japanese firms allocated substantially more effort in drawing up plans and controlling them.

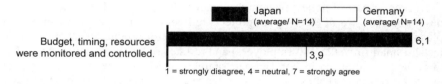

Fig. 12. Controlling

To summarize, similar to idea generation and assessment, initial planning is a more routine practice in the 14 Japanese projects of our study. Some of the 14 German projects did not have a front end planning step at all and support by methods and tools was the exception, whilst the Japanese interviewees drew flow charts for example as a matter of routine.

Conclusions

Despite the sample size being small and different sampling methods being utilized in Germany and Japan, our study revealed some interesting results. Contrary to former studies, the fuzzy front end of 14 projects studied in Japan and 14 projects studied in Germany were predominantly managed proficiently. Market uncertainty and technical uncertainty could have been substantially reduced prior to development. The majority of objectives were achieved for all projects. Yet, with regard to uncertainty reduction, in agreement with former findings about uncertainty avoidance in both countries, a different approach was identified in the Japanese sample, compared to the German projects. Whilst Japanese projects relied on a thorough planning and a strict regime of control to minimize deviations from front end specifications and enhance efficiency, in our German projects, functions were integrated early in the innovation process, in some cases already during idea generation phase, to ensure that all information and perspectives were taken into consideration right from the start. Responsibilities were assigned during the front end and rarely changed during project implementation to reduce deviations and enhance efficiency.

In summary, we suggest the following propositions for the "fuzzy front end":

Proposition 1: In Japanese New Product Development projects, project related uncertainties are reduced via strong methodological support and in particular a more elaborated planning model compared to German New Product Development projects.

Proposition 2: The early integration of corporate functions into the fuzzy front end of innovation to reduce project related uncertainty is more typical for German compared to Japanese innovation management style.

Proposition 3: Monitoring and controlling of budgets, timing and resources during the whole innovation process (including the fuzzy front end) is systematically carried out in Japanese companies and more elaborated in contrast to German companies.

For the management of innovation practice, our results indicate that there is no such thing as the "best" approach to reduce market and technological uncertainty and to successfully manage the fuzzy front end of innovation. In general, a company can choose either a more formal or a more interdisciplinary, informal approach. This decision will depend, besides other influencing factors, on the culture of the enterprise. When deciding on the most appropriate approach for a given company, one of the key points of consideration should be employee attitudes towards uncertainty. If employees tend to be risk averse, formal procedures and a tight planning/control process might be more appropriate than a rather informal network approach.

But due to the limited sample size of our study and different sampling procedures, our findings cannot be generalized. Nevertheless, initial indicators for country specific approaches to managing the fuzzy front of innovation were found. These findings suggest a contingency approach: The influence of contextual factors on the fuzzy front end should be considered in more detail and the sample size should be extended to enable a more elaborated analysis. Furthermore, studies of the fuzzy front end could be extended to other countries and industries. In particular, a comparison between countries with a more pronounced difference in terms of uncertainty avoidance tendencies, e.g., Japan and the U.S., would be promising. Another fruitful research area would be to explore the impact of uncertainty avoidance tendencies on individual behavior in more detail.

Appendix: List of Projects

No.	Type of company and size (number of employees)	Rough description of the project	Newness of the product concept to the firm and development time
1	Japanese manufacturer of electronic components (150)	Power resistor with temperature characteristics based on metal foil technology	New to the world, 12 months
2	Japanese manufacturer of electrical products (600)	Pointing device for personal computers ("mouse") for patients who suffer from muscle dysfunctions	New to the world, 2 months
3	Japanese manufacturer of electronic components (4000)	Three dimensional motion sensor, used for example to protect PCs or mobile phones from physical damages (e.g., via deactivating the device in the case of slipping from a table)	New product line, 12 months
4	Japanese manufacturer of transistors and IC products (930)	Switching element for communication products (e.g., telephones, mobile phones); triggering device for pulse ignitions	New product line, 4 months
5	Japanese producer of chemical products (2465)	Polymer used in the production of optical lenses or eye glasses	New to the world, 120 months
6	Japanese manufacturer of electronic components and products (123)	Electronic device to purify water for home and professional applications (e.g., laboratories, medical doctors or dentists)	New to the world, 10 months
7	Japanese industrial automation company (6000)	Production in-process control system with special characteristics (e.g., constant imaging)	New to the world, 12 months
8	Japanese manufacturer of tools (66)	Innovative tool for the effective manufacturing of airplane panels	New to the world, 5 months
9	Japanese manufacturer of tools (240)	New machine to produce ceramic and plastic components (used by manufacturers of electronic devices, e.g., mobile phones)	Repositioning in the market, 36 months
10	Japanese manufacturer of electronic components (8600)	Super capacitor	New product line, 36 months
11	Japanese manufacturer of electrical products (10.000)	eDRAM for PCs and digital cameras	Product modification, 24 months

12	Japanese manufac-turer of electrical components and products(10.000)	Laser machine for the semi-conductor industry (laser marker)	Product modifica-tion, 24 month
13	Japanese manufac-turer of process equip-ment (800)	Cleaning technology for LSI/FPD manufacturing (water treatment process)	New to the world, 24 months
14	Japanese manufac-turer of electrical products (10.000)	A new CVD technology, used to replace chemical and/or me-chanical edging of DRAMS and circuit design	Product modifica-tion, 24 months
15	German manufacturer of electrical and elec-tronic components and products (200000)	Sensor for measuring spark plug temperature	New to the world, 12 months
16	German automobile manufacturer (420000)	Low priced steering column (exchange of component)	Cost reduction, 6 months
17	German manufacturer of pumps (25)	Special pumps for industrial purposes	New to the world, 6 months
18	German manufacturer of equipment for printing machines (160)	Machine to dry printing ink	New to the world, 30 months
19	German manufacturer of pumps (125)	Rotary pump	Product modifica-tion, 12 months
20	German manufacturer of hearing aids (70)	Hearing aid with rechargeable battery	New product line, 6 months
21	German manufacturer of installation equip-ment for the shipping industry (50)	Headlights for the deck of a ship/ships	New product line, 42 months
22	German manufacturer of equipment for tire production (350)	Machine used for tire produc-tion	New product line, 30 months
23	German manufacturer of apparatus for gas analysis and level measuring (174)	Apparatus for gas analysis with special characteristics	New to the world, 24 months
24	German engineering company of equip-ment for bulk han-dling (75)	Low priced metering roller	Cost reduction, 6 months
25	German manufacturer of ships and off-shore equipment (360)	Fire protection device for air conditioning systems on ships	New product line, 18 months

26	German manufacturer of special drilling machines (140)	Laser machine (first laser machine developed in the firm)	New product line, 30 months
27	German manufacturer of medical technology (11000)	Low priced high voltage generator for X-ray equipment (exchange of component)	Cost reduction, 24 months
28	German manufacturer of power machines and drives (100)	Electric drives for ships	New product line, 36 months

References

Aggteleky B and Bajina N (1992): Projektplanung: ein Handbuch für Führungskräfte; Hanser, München, Wien

Albach H, de Pay D, and Rojas R (1991): Quellen, Zeiten und Kosten von Innovationen – Deutsche Unternehmen im Vergleich zu ihren japanischen und amerikanischen Konkurrenten; Zeitschrift für Betriebswirtschaft ZfB Vol. 61, No. 3: pp. 311–325

Baker NR, Green SG, and Bean AS (1985): How management can influence the generation of ideas; Research Management Vol. 28, No. 6: pp. 35–42

Balachandra R and Friar JH (1997): Factors for success in R&D projects and new product innovation: A contextual framework; IEEE Transactions on Engineering Management Vol. 44, No. 3: pp. 276–287

Balbontin A, Yazdani B, Cooper R, and Souder WE (1999): New product development success factors in American and British firms; International Journal of Technology Management Vol. 17, No. 3: pp. 259–280

Cooper RG and Kleinschmidt EJ (1994): Screening new products for potential winners; Institute of Electrical and Electronics Engineers IEEE engineering management review Vol. 22, No. 4: pp. 24–30

Cooper RG and Kleinschmidt EJ (1990): New products: The key factors in success; American Marketing Association, United States

Cooper RG and Kleinschmidt EJ (1986): An investigation into the new product process – steps, deficiencies, and impact; Journal of Product Innovation Management Vol. 3, No. 3: pp. 71–85

Dwyer L and Mellor R (1991): Organizational environment, new product process activities, and project outcomes; Journal of Product Innovation Management Vol. 8, No. 1: pp. 39–48

Förderer K, Krey K, and Palme K (1998): Innovation und Mittelstand: eine Umfrage bei 1871 mittelständischen Unternehmen; Deutscher Instituts-Verlag, Köln

Galbraith J (1973): Designing complex organizations; Addison-Wesley, Reading, Mass

Geschka H (1992): Creativity techniques in product planning and development: a view from West Germany; in: Parnes SJ (ed.): Source book of creative problem-solving; Creative Education Foundation Press, Buffalo, New York

Harryson S (1996): Improving R&D performance through networking – lessons from Canon and Sony; Arthur D. Little – Prism, Fourth Quarter

Herstatt C, Lüthje C, and Verworn B (2001): Die Gestaltung von Innovationsprozessen in kleinen und mittleren Unternehmen, in: Meyer J-A (ed.): Innovationsmanagement in kleinen und mittleren Unternehmen: Jahrbuch der KMU-Forschung 2001; Vahlen, München

Hofstede GH (1980): Culture's consequences, abridged edition; Sage, Newbury Park, London, New Delhi

Johne FA and Snelson PA (1988): Success factors in product innovation – a selective review of the literature; Journal of Product Innovation Management Vol. 5, No. 2: pp. 114–128

Jürgens U (2000): Restructuring product development and production networks: introduction to the book; in: Jürgens U (ed.): New product development and production networks: global industrial experience, pp. 1–19, Springer, Berlin, Heidelberg, New York

Khurana A and Rosenthal SR (1997): Integrating the fuzzy front end of new product development; Sloan Management Review Vol. 38, No. 2: pp. 103–120

Khurana A and Rosenthal SR (1998): Towards holistic "front ends" in new product development; Journal of Product Innovation Management Vol. 15, No. 1: pp. 57–74

Lynn GS and Akgun AE (1998): Innovation strategies under uncertainty: a contingency approach for new product development; Engineering Management Journal Vol. 10, No. 3: pp. 11–17

Maidique MA and Zirger BJ (1984): A study of success and failure in product innovation; IEEE Transactions on Engineering Management Vol. EM-31, No. 4: pp. 192–203

Mansfield E and Wagner S (1975): Organizational and strategic factors associated with probabilities of success in industrial R&D; Journal of Business Vol. 48: pp. 179–198

Mishra S, Kim D, and Lee DH (1996): Factors affecting new product success: crosscountry comparison; Journal of Product Innovation Management Vol. 13, No. 6: pp. 530–550

Moenaert RK, De Meyer A, Souder WE, and Deschoolmeester D (1995): R&D/Marketing communication during the fuzzy front-end; IEEE Transactions on Engineering Management Vol. 42, No. 3: pp. 243–258

Moore WL and Pessemier EA (1993): Product planning and management: designing and delivering value; McGraw-Hill, New York et al.

Mullins JW and Sutherland DJ (1998): New product development in rapidly changing markets: an exploratory study; Journal of Product Innovation Management Vol. 15, No. 3: pp. 224–236

Murphy SA and Kumar V (1997): The front end of new product development: a Canadian survey; R&D Management Vol. 27, No. 1: pp. 5–16

Park J-H (1996): Vergleich des Innovationsmanagements deutscher, japanischer und koreanischer Unternehmen: Eine empirische Untersuchung am Beispiel der chemischen Industrie; Dissertation, Universität Mannheim

Pinto JK and Slevin DP (1988): Critical success factors across the project life cycle; Project Management Journal Vol. 19: pp. 67–75

Rochford L (1991): Generating and screening new product ideas; Industrial Marketing Management Vol. 20, No. 4: pp. 287–296

Rubinstein AH (1994): At the front end of the R&D/innovation process – idea development and entrepreneurship; International Journal of Technology Management Vol. 9, No. 5, 6, 7: pp. 652–677

Schlaak TM (1999): Der Innovationsgrad als Schlüsselvariable: Perspektiven für das Management von Produktentwicklungen; Deutscher Universitäts-Verlag, Wiesbaden

Smith GF (1998): Idea generation techniques – a formulary of active ingredients; Journal of Creative Behavior Vol. 32, No. 2: pp. 107–134

Song XM and Montoya-Weiss MM (2001): The effect of perceived technological uncertainty on Japanese new product development; Academy of Management Journal Vol. 44, No. 1: pp. 61–80

Song XM and Montoya-Weiss MM (1998): Critical development activities for really new versus incremental products; Journal of Product Innovation Management Vol. 15, No. 2: pp. 124–135

Song XM and Parry ME (1997): A cross-national comparative study on new product development processes: Japan and the United States; Journal of Marketing Vol. 61, No. 2: pp. 1–18

Song XM and Parry ME (1996): What separates Japanese new product winners from losers; Journal of Product Innovation Management Vol. 13, No. 5: pp. 422–439

Song XM and Xie J (1996): The effect of R&D-Manufacturing Marketing integration on new product performance in Japanese and U.S. firms: A contingency perspective; Marketing Science Institute, Working Paper Report No. 96–117, Cambridge Massachusetts November

Souder WE and Song XM (1998): Analysis of U.S. and Japanese management processes associated with new product success and failure in high and low familiarity markets; Journal of Product Innovation Management Vol. 15, No. 3: pp. 208–223

Sowrey T (1987): The generation of ideas for new products; Kogan Page, London

Verganti R (1997): Leveraging on systematic learning to manage the early phases of product innovation projects; R&D Management Vol. 27, No. 4: pp. 377–392

Veryzer RW (1998): Discontinuous innovation and the new product development process; Journal of Product Innovation Management Vol. 15, No. 4: pp. 304–321

Webb A (2000): Project management for successful product innovation; Gower, Hampshire, Vermont

Part V: Implementational Aspects

From Practice: IP Management in Japanese Companies

Yonoshin Mori

Rapidly Changing IP Management Environment

The environment for IP management faced by Japanese companies is in the midst of considerable change. In 1999, the Japanese version of the Bayh-Dole Act came into force, which was followed by the Fundamental Principles for IP Management Strategy in 2002, and the establishment of the IP Promotion Plan under the guidance of the government in 2003. In the private sector, large-scale workplace invention lawsuits are occurring more frequently since the Blue Diode case. At universities, technology licensing organization (TLO) activities are becoming more energetic with the purpose of contributing to industrial development through the donation of IP to outside organizations. At the same time, business formats designed to encourage the distribution of intellectual assets are also being activated. In 2005, ten to twenty companies in Japan began releasing IP reports, based on the IP Information Disclosure Guidelines. In this way, the environment for IP management faced by Japanese companies has changed dramatically in recent years.

As part of our job, we meet many general managers in charge of IP management at Japanese manufacturers. They often explain to us that, "Although we have been dealing with IP management for many years, this is the first time that IP has gained so much attention in this form. Then, we are now changing our approach to IP management. However, there are still many gray policy areas, and the number of issues that need to be addressed is increasing."

Nevertheless, these changes in the Japanese IP management environment are still actually 20 years behind developments in the United States. In the US for example, the Bayh-Dole Act went into effect in 1980, and the Young Report, which recognized the importance of IP, was released in 1985.

In this part, we would like to look at how Japanese companies have managed their proprietary technologies until now, in light of the changing IP management environment.

Transformation of Technology Management

As shown in Figure 1, we have divided the technology management transition process into the following stages: the first, second, third, and next generations.

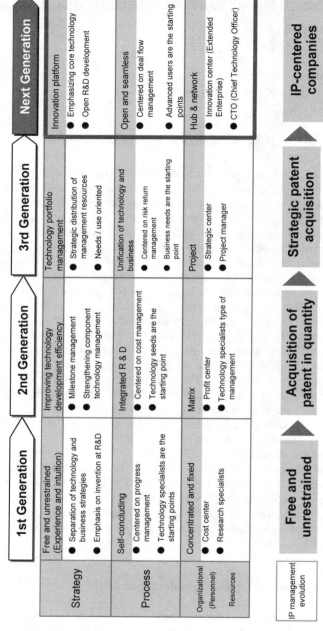

Fig. 1. Development of the technology management approach

In the first generation, or in the R&D management of the "good old days," there was a free and unrestrained approach to technology development management, in terms of strategy. For example, corporate R&D departments had many technology-seeds-driven R&D projects, which had no particular link to business strategies. These were self-concluding projects, and progress management formed the core of technology management. Furthermore, the R&D department was a cost center, and management was carried out through self administration by the research specialists themselves. This is called the free non-intervention form of IP management. Under this system, taking out a patent was left to the discretion of the individual technology specialist concerned, and the patent rights were considered to be no more than a certificate of achievement for the inventor. This was the first generation stage of technology and IP management.

Then came the second generation of technology management. There was the strategic intention to carry out technology development more efficiently, and milestone management was thoroughly applied by adopting an approach that would strengthen management for each component technology. Furthermore, management was carried out using a format where research and design were combined in R&D, and the entire development department team was managed as a profit center. This does not mean that the business and technical departments always carried out entirely combined activities. However, at least the importance of patents was well understood when promoting component technology development, and this meant that they sought to obtain patents so they could use more of their own patents. Therefore, in this case they tended to follow IP management based on the number of patents.

Although measuring success based on the number of patents was characteristic of the second-generation stage of IP management, there is data that shows remnants of this today. Among the top US patent holders in 2004, IBM was in first place, followed by Panasonic and Canon, while Hitachi was in eighth place, followed by Toshiba and Sony, thus demonstrating the penchant of Japanese companies for patents. Furthermore, looking at the number of international patent applications, in the last fiscal year, Japan was responsible for a record 20,000 patent applications, and by achieving a cumulative total of 100,000 international patent applications. Japan is second only to the United States in this endeavor. Therefore, we can see that even today, the IP management of patents that measures success based on the number of patents, as a result of the second-generation stage of technology management, is one of the mainstays of Japanese corporate policy.

In the third generation of technology management, companies have adopted the approach of theme prioritization and resource allocation based on strategies and targets shared by the technology development and business divisions. The theme evaluation criteria are composed of the perspective of scientific and engineering technology development and the perspective of the degree of contribution to problem resolution in the business. The value of the technology development themes is then evaluated by accurately weighing both sides. In this kind of case, the technology development organization is not a solitary island. Instead, the development organization and the business department work as partners, and in this way the so-called strategic patent acquisition type of IP management is carried out.

This is the format where the acquisition of the patents necessary for business execution is carried out systematically. Specifically, the company strengthens its own patent position, avoids other companies, and carries out patent application activities in order to increase the business's technology monopoly. Activities such as constructing patent networks using patent trees, infringement investigations, or detailed patent mapping in order to carry out patent applications that secure a level of freedom for the company's execution of its own business, are carried out regularly. IP management in this third generation stage of technology management is strategic, but the company's own technology specialists always obtain the IP for use by the company, and the IP department provides support for this.

After this comes the next generation of technology management. This indicates an open form of technology management that is based on an innovation platform (see Figure 2), and IP management is defined as functioning as an important medium for realizing this. Innovation platform is a term coined to indicate a management resource that unifies the continual creation of innovation. In other words, it expresses the concept that certain input information can be transformed into output information with a higher value, through a process that combines and changes resources within the platform. Therefore, from the standpoint of innovation creation, you can think of it as the transformation of the company's intangible assets.

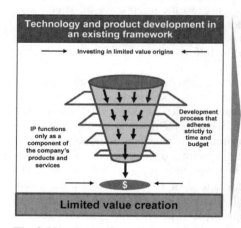 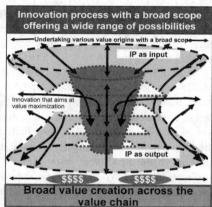

Fig. 2. Next generation technology management

Let us look at an example of an innovation platform. A set product manufacturer of consumer products, such as mobile phones or game machines, combines various component technologies and parts that are incorporated into its products, with the aim of developing, designing, producing, and selling products with a high level of function, quality and reliability. In this case there is no need for maintaining in-house the module component technology, or the electronic components always used in set products. Instead, the part and software manufacturers accurately manage the development process jointly, and skills for eliciting the maximum value from function parts and devices are more sought after. Rather than deciding on one component technology in detail, the source of innovation comes from skills for anticipating the needs of a changing market, and quickly designing, producing, and distributing the product.

From the standpoint of IP management, the IP management that the company should have is the user-interface and/or user-application type. For example, it is the ability to design the connecting function between devices which are procured from multiple suppliers. These are the "technologies" that can efficiently use technology or IP originating at other companies. In this case, the definition of innovation platform is the ability to quickly supply the product based on product planning skills that can anticipate the market needs, a wide range of component technologies, and IP integration skill.

In fact, many Japanese companies are taking the approach of creating new products and services by introducing technology from other companies based on this kind of innovation platform. For example, not just electronics product makers, but also home appliance, automobile, transportation equipment, construction machinery, and other industrial equipment manufacturers are all adopting this innovation platform model. Therefore, many Japanese manufacturers need to recognize the transition to the next generation of technology management, whether they are conscious of it or not.

If we want to perform this kind of next generation technology management, and are to define our own innovation platforms and expand the business, we have to understand the new role of IP. In other words, we have to combine and exchange not just our own IP, but also that of other companies. By jointly using and sharing IP we can create new value.

Up until the third generation, the core concept was to patent inventions which come along with technology development. However, in the next generation technology management, it will be important to have the ability to objectively analyze and understand the patents of one's own and other companies. This is due to the need to secure a degree of freedom for the business, improve the company's monopoly, and increase the efficiency of the company's product development through the active incorporation of IP from other companies. It is also necessary to promote superior cross-licensing, and create profit derived from using exclusive rights towards other companies.

In other words, in the next generation technology management, we will need to define relations with outside organizations, namely joint development partners and competitors, from the perspective of IP, and make management decisions relating to business and technology. Therefore, the systematic approaches needed to contribute to this will also have to be reconstructed. In this way, the IP management environment will change considerably, and as mentioned above, there are many issues facing the leaders of IP departments at Japanese companies.

Objective of IP Management

In the first part of this chapter, we discussed the necessary changes in approaches and methodologies for IP management in the transition process to the next generation of technology management. Nevertheless, in the midst of this environmental change, many Japanese companies are still in the process of defining their IP management policy and methodology. For example, here are some of the comments we have heard from various technical department people that we have met.

- There is no clear awareness that daily patent-related activities are contributing to the business.
- We have a lot of ideas in the product design stage. However, patent acquisition procedures are treated like just another chore, and there is no understanding of it as an activity that directly contributes to business profits.
- We have acquired quite a few patents. However, it seems that our IP management does not reflect the business strategies.
- The top management is not sending the message that there is business value in IP. Therefore, the R&D department does not actively follow up on requests from the IP department.
- There is no clear definition of the added value being created by the IP department.

Therefore, we divided IP management objectives into four types. Looking at Figure 3, you can see that there are four directions for IP management. Objective A is to secure the superiority of the company's business through IP portfolio. Objective B is to secure a degree of freedom in the company's business by avoiding utilizing other firms' IPs. Objective C is to create profits through utilizing IP beyond the existing business framework. Finally, Objective D is to improve the direct cost-efficiency of IP.

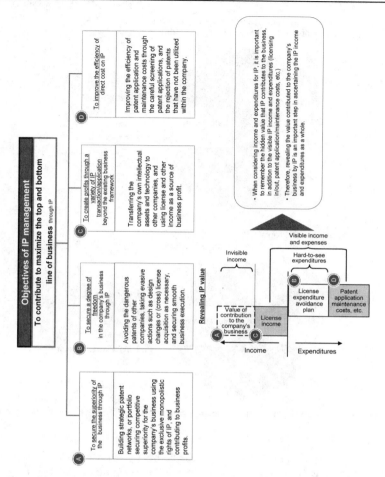

Fig. 3. Four objectives of IP management

Objective A

Let us look at these objectives, one by one. The activities for Objective A involve using the exclusive rights of one's own patents for the purpose of improving the monopolistic superiority of the business. Therefore, when there is the possibility for your business to obtain exclusivity, in other words when you have achieved superiority ahead of your competitors, or when the technology you possess has outstanding and innovative qualities, you need Objective A.

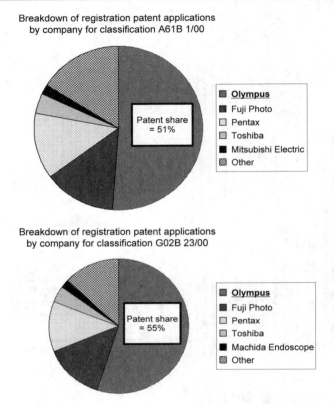

Fig. 4. Olympus: Example of securing the superiority of the company's business through IP

Let us look at one example of a Japanese company that fits into this case. Looking at the next diagram, Figure 4, you can see the example of the endoscope business at Olympus. Olympus has a 51% share of the registered patents for the IPC subclass of endoscopes, A61B1/00 (a device to perform diagnosis inside the cavities or tracts of the human body through visual or photographic inspection, e.g. endoscopes). It also has a 55% share of the registered patents for G02B23/00 (telescopes, periscopes, devices to observe inside openings (diagnostic device A61B), viewfinders, and optical sighting or observation devices). Within these shares, the company has acquired overwhelming shares of almost 70% domestically and 80% overseas. In other words, they have created a monopoly in the endoscope business through a portfolio of patents covering almost all the technologies at stake.

Olympus's medical endoscope business has been providing the world's most advanced products for the last 50 years. It has developed stomach cameras for imaging diagnosis, fiberscopes that can perform direct visual diagnosis, video scopes that enable small-scale operation with the addition of special tip attachments, and all kinds of medical devices that enable low-invasive treatments, which have allowed the company to gradually expand the revenue from the product lines. The driving force behind this effort has been a group of innovative technologies that were strongly protected by a patent portfolio. As a result, the company was able to realize the acquisition of an overwhelming share of patents and the market, as indicated above. Just like other Japanese companies with advanced IP, the IP managers at Olympus have been deeply involved in the technology development process from the beginning. They have been uncovering and surveying advanced technology, making effective suggestions for each research theme from the standpoint of IP, and carrying out activities to develop strength in patents themselves.

Here is a checklist of the points for Objective A (securing superiority of the company through IP).

1. Determining in which technology area to build a strong patent portfolio, and clarifying whether it will secure exclusive superiority for the company's business
2. Obtaining a portfolio of patents that include all peripheral patents necessary for execution of the business, and not just basic patents
3. Also obtaining patents that can impede or delay other companies from creating products that incorporate the same kind of invention, even if the company does not use them for the time being.
4. Investigating the possibility of purchasing or adopting patents of other companies necessary for completing the company's patent portfolio.
5. Properly updating patent maps, and developing a system to monitor the patent application status of both your company and competitors in real time.
6. Striving to obtain rights with a high level of security against lawsuits.
7. Having strong management policy and legal support for securing monopolies.

These seven points are necessary for securing Objective A.

Objective B

Next let us look at Objective B, or securing a degree of freedom for the company's business through IP. This enables the execution of business by avoiding the patents of other companies, and minimizing any payments required at such times. This is necessary when there is an uneven distribution of patents held by other companies surrounding the company's related technology. Since the company must continue to avoid infringing the patents of other companies in order to continue growing its own business, is why this objective of IP management exists. Therefore, when reducing or eliminating the risk of infringing other company patents, costs arise in order to minimize this risk. Consequently, reducing the following costs become specific targets in order to accomplish Objective B.

The first type of cost is for prevention. This is the cost in order to avoid infringement risk in a preventive way. For example, this includes the survey costs needed for the job of identifying patents that have the possibility of contravention, after setting conditions such as the applicant, target period, region, and patent type for each technology theme that the company is undertaking. Although this is usually carried out by the company's own technology and IP departments, it can also be consigned to an outside patent investigation company in some cases. At that time, it is necessary to acquire skills for designing the keyword search format in order to find infringements, as well as skills for using all kinds of databases. Japanese companies have been carrying out these investigations using various approaches. Some companies have their own patent investigation departments and perform the surveys using entirely in-house resources. Other companies outsource the entire job, and use patent investigation companies to carry out the infringement surveys for them. This depends greatly on the definition of the IP organization of the company.

The second type of cost is the legal cost at the time of infringement of another company's patent. This is the cost of legal action that should be taken when it is determined that the technology adopted by the company infringes upon the patent of another company, after performing the survey described above for the first type of cost. The cost of legal action includes the general activities for proving the invalid nature of the other company's patent. For example, it includes legal action such as a literature search of prior technology using public bulletins, filing a lawsuit, and a judgment of invalidity.

The third type of cost is technology related cost incurred at the time of infringement of another company's patent. For example, this includes the costs arising for infringement avoidance through design changes to parts that contravene the other company's patent. Generally, when the target specifications could not be achieved technically during technology product development stages, or when quality and reliability evaluation standards were not achieved, the design may very well have to be changed even if the deadline is extended. Depending on the company, this lost opportunity and supplementary cost is treated as a failure (F) cost and is added to the product cost. Under the same approach, if the fact of infringement of another company's patent is discovered during the product development or design processes, the design changes should be made, and it should be managed as an F (infringement avoidance) cost under IP management.

The fourth type of cost is the "use" cost needed to enable the patent of another company to be implemented by the company. For example, if it is determined that the patent of the other company cannot be avoided using the measures mentioned above, the company may take actions such as licensing-in the patent concerned, or buying the patent concerned. The running royalty and initial payment in this case become the company's own costs. Since the cost of licensing-in or buying the patent are clearly financial expenditure costs, most companies correctly manage these costs. However, putting it the other way around, the effective management of the other cost items given here is still weak. Even in the case of cross-licensing, when you consider paying with the IP that is a part of the company's management assets in order for the company to implement the patent of another company, the value of the asset transferred by the company becomes the cost arising from these actions. Furthermore, the out-payment generated at the time of cross-licensing with another powerful company, is a direct cost itself.

The fifth type of cost is the dispute cost relating to "battles" with other companies. In the case of a lawsuit arising from some infringement disputes, costs for damaged business for infringers and business suspension of infringers also arise. The amount of these compensations is based on the actual damage amount incurred by the patent rights holder (in other words the lost revenue/profit) or the revenue/profit obtained by the infringing party. All of these are large costs, and they will require careful attention. In addition, there are also potential costs related to loss of brand value arising from the publicity over the act of infringement, as well as compensation money arising from workplace invention lawsuits that have become numerous in recent years. However, since this paper is focused on technology management, these costs will not be dealt with here.

The costs above are the main cost items required for Objective B, securing a degree of freedom for the business. While technology is expected to become increasingly combined and complicated in the future, and the speed of technological development is intensifying, there will likely be more situations where the company needs to secure a degree of freedom while avoiding the IP of other companies. For this reason, the costs above should be carefully managed by every company.

Canon is an example of a Japanese company that has actually done a good job of addressing Objective B. Canon has secured a degree of freedom for its business primarily through cross-licensing schemes. For example, they realize that it is more important to obtain a license, secure freedom for design, and reduce the development period, rather than paying costs and spending time to avoid the patents of other companies. Therefore, even in the development stage before commercial application, if there is technology belonging to other companies that they need, they can reduce unnecessary costs in product creation and commercial application by forming cross-licensing agreements. However, they have a strong patent network to begin with, so they do not need to transfer the very core IP to their cross-licensing partners.

For example, when Canon finds an IP that it wants at another company, it first investigates whether the other company is infringing on any of Canon's own patents. If it discovers that there is a likely infringement, it notifies the company, and proposes the formation of a cross-licensing agreement. The result is that the company is able to use Canon's patent, and Canon is also able to use the patents held by the company. In addition, Canon with its strong patent network is also able to receive license fees through the cross-licensing agreement. Therefore, Canon is able to achieve its business and profit strategies simultaneously.

Objective C

Next, let us look at Objective C, the third objective of IP management, or profit creation through IP application that exceeds the existing business framework. This is a source of profit through the contribution of patents and technology held by the company to another company. For example, the company has IP and technology that it has accumulated through ongoing technology development activities. If it is discovered that this can be more effectively utilized outside rather than inside the company, the objective is to create direct and indirect profit by transferring these assets out to other companies, rather than using them inside the company. For this to work, the company must of course have technology and IP that would actually be useful for other companies.

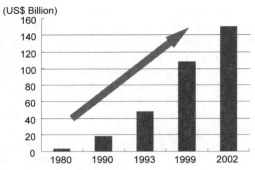

(In the US, patent applications grew from 100,000 to 357,000 in the same period)

Source: International income and expenditure estimates

Fig. 5. Rapidly expanding world IP transaction market

As shown in Figure 5 for example, regarding the model for external utilization of IP that exceeds the existing business model, the market scale for this is gradually expanding on a worldwide basis. The transaction market for IP in 2002 exceeded 150 billion dollars. Companies with advanced IP like IBM, achieved 1 billion dollar or more in income from IP, along with the increase in the number of patent acquisitions. Just like IBM, several Japanese research and development type companies such as Hitachi, are using in-house IP as a source of income by transferring it to outside companies. (see Figure 6)

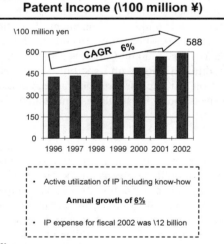

Source: ADL Interview

Fig. 6. Overview of Hitachi's patent income

Nevertheless, the indiscriminate transfer of proprietary IP outside the company, will weaken the company's legal binding force against the other companies, and might weaken the company's business position. Therefore, it is extremely important to ascertain which IP is to be transferred externally. Also, including not just patents but also technical expertise, human resource assets, and in some cases, trademarks, as part of the transfer can also be a direct source of income. With respect to patents, it is essential to design a deal that includes the attainment of not just implementation rights, but also patent transfer, and acquisition in the form of royalties, one-time payments, or stocks, as well as other business interests. Since the creation of schemes relating to Objective C requires a high degree of business skills, it will be necessary for Japanese companies to develop their abilities in this area in the future.

Objective D

Next, let us turn to Objective D, or the improvement of direct cost efficiency for intellectual assets. Simply put, this is the rational reduction of patent application and maintenance costs. The reason that this is necessary is, as stated above, that in the transition process for IP management at Japanese companies, much of companies' IP today is just sleeping and not being used. This is the situation after the period when companies were simply focused on applying for as many patents as possible as a measure of their success. Furthermore, it is even unclear at many companies who can make the decision on whether currently held patents can be used, and there really are companies where the patents are just lying dormant. Therefore, it may very well be necessary for companies in this situation to follow the classic example of Dow Chemicals. During 1993 and 1994, Dow took an inventory of all its IP, divided it into necessary and unnecessary patents, transferred the unnecessary ones to outside companies, and even abandoned some patents.

Leading Examples of IP Management at Individual Companies

In this part, let us look at some examples of how Japanese companies with advanced IP are carrying out IP management.

Hitachi

First we will look at Hitachi. As shown in Figure 6, the special characteristic of Hitachi is that it has extremely good patent income. Through utilization of IP including expertise, the company has achieved an annual patent income growth rate of 6%, and the income for 2002 reached 58.8 billion yen. Turning to the details, we can see that IP income from activities outside the Hitachi Group accounts for

70% of this type of income, and this demonstrates the superiority of their IP management.

Looking inside Hitachi's IP management, we can see that the company is maintaining its own profitability in the IP department while closely coordinating IP strategy with business strategy. Organizationally, Hitachi also posts top-tier personnel in its IP department, which shows the company's intention to achieve profitability from IP.

In order to sort patents strategically, a meticulous investigation of carefully screened patent applications is carried out at the time of invention. The company has established a process to strategically select inventions, and prepares detailed documents on inventions designed as strategic patents, and carries out priority processing of examinations of overseas applications. For example, in order to select strategic patents, Hitachi classifies patents for application into five levels, A through E. The A patents are considered to be the strategic patents, and these are further divided into the three ranks of gold, silver, and bronze.

Strategic patents are those fundamental and necessary inventions that cannot be avoided in terms of the principle products and technologies of the future. At the same time, they must be superior cutting edge technology and inventions that have been confirmed as technologically realizable. Furthermore, these patents must be inventions that can be reliably adopted on a large scale, and must be inventions that the company plans to adopt as part of major research themes. Therefore, they must also be given the highest priority for application processing. Hitachi has set targets for the number of these strategic patents: for example, 20 to 30 gold patents, 70 to 80 silver patents, and around 200 bronze patent applications.

The next most important patents are called basic patents, and these are the inventions that it will be difficult for other companies to avoid once the patents are registered. At the same time, these represent the favored technology in research and development planning, and must be inventions for which there is a fair degree of technological realization potential. These patent applications are given priority processing. Unlike strategic patents, the target numbers for these are in the thousands, in the range of 2,000 to 4,000 applications.

Next are the so-called regular patents. These are difficult for other companies to avoid, and are superior inventions compared to those of other companies. Efficient processing is carried out for these patents, and the target number of applications is in the range of 7,000 to 8,000.

Then comes the fourth group of patents, called public patents. These are somewhat difficult for other companies to avoid, and are fairly profitable inventions for the company. Although the rights are not necessary for the company, they serve the role of preventing other companies from utilizing the technology. These are also processed in an efficient way. The target number of applications is from 8,000 to 10,000 patents.

Finally, there is the deferred group of patent applications. This is technology that would be easy for other companies to avoid, and is not so different from existing technology. Furthermore, since they are not important patents, they can be postponed. Roughly several thousands of these patents are expected at Hitachi.

The company also has a strategic incentive system that works in conjunction with this patent ranking system.

Looking at the Hitachi's IP system organizationally, it is divided into head office staff and staff stationed at each of the business divisions. There are almost 200 head office staff, and over 200 staff in the divisions. The division staff is stationed at each of the research and development sites. However, the staff stationed at these sites belongs to the IP department. The division staff is comprised of staff that is in charge of patent application procedures and management, as well as technical staff that determines patent strategies for the technologies.

The division clerical staff is dispatched from the head office staff department, and the technical staff is technology specialists originally from the R&D department. However, since a lack of technical staff ability has been pointed out in the conventional system, in recent years, the patent strategy has been further strengthened through the addition of top-tier personnel from R&D division.

The existence of a licensing department is an example of the organizational uniqueness of the Hitachi's IP department. The licensing department serves the function of external sales and marketing for Hitachi's IP. It has several dozen people, who uncover infringements by other companies as one of their tasks. When a patent infringement is discovered, the licensing department follows the process of forcing the patent to be licensed out, or else carrying out an infringement dispute and exposure. Furthermore, the licensing department publishes the Hitachi patents on its own Website, and actively performs licensing-out activities.

Through these kinds of activities, Hitachi is carrying out the most advanced IP management among Japanese companies, and at the same time is substantially in the black with its IP income.

Canon

Now let us look at Canon's IP management. As stated above, the most unique aspect about Canon's IP activities is cross-licensing. This is carried out through the five steps shown in Figure 7.

First a technical information survey of competitor companies is carried out by the IP technology center or the research and development department. Then a check for infringement of Canon patents is made using the information on the competitors' technology. After that, the infringement details are gathered by the IP technical center, and the confirmed infringements are reported to the IP business center. The IP business center then instructs the contract and liaison center to start warning activities and this begins the warning activities by Canon regarding the patent infringements to the companies concerned.

In the case of negotiations with the company that received the warning, the contract and liaison center takes care of this work. The contract and liaison center investigates all the patents held by the other company, and checks whether that company and its divisions have any patents that would be useful for Canon. Then it examines the required cross-licensing agreement with those patents, and formulates a negotiation strategy. If the other company has no desirable patents, Canon negotiates towards signing a licensing out contract for its own patent. If the other company has some desirable patents at that time, Canon pursues negotiations to form a cross-licensing agreement. For very important cases, the contract and liaison center serves as the support base, but Canon directors carry out the negotiations. As a result, cross-licensing or licensing-out contracts are achieved with other companies.

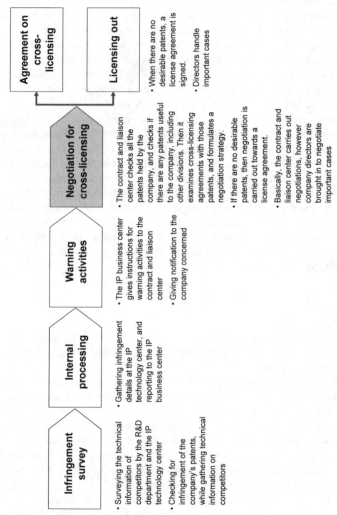

Source: ADL interview

Fig. 7. Canon's cross-licensing strategy

The person who has directed this patent management at Canon is Giichi Marushima, now retired and serving as an advisor at Canon. Mr. Marushima emphasized negotiation skills for Canon's IP management, and was the main proponent of personnel development in this area. He told me the following during a conversation:

At Canon, securing a degree of freedom for the company's business is the most important of the four objectives for IP management. In other words, I believe that having freedom for design and development gives the company control over its direction. In order to achieve this, it is important to take the stance of securing the company's superiority in relative problems and relative strength in relationships with competitors, rather than the digital world of ones and zeros. For example, the larger a company is, the harder it becomes to secure business superiority. In that case, lawsuits are the most undesirable method. In other words, small companies can pursue a lawsuit and benefit from a damage compensation award, while big companies usually only suffer losses through lawsuits.

I believe that IBM itself has never filed a lawsuit. This is because the company has confidence that it can steadily obtain the compensation money it wants without the need for a lawsuit. I think the ideal approach is to achieve a monetary objective without a lawsuit. This is the IBM style. In other words, the important point for negotiations is to take an approach where your company and the other company end up with a win-win situation as seen from the eyes of a third party. I believe that only those who are not good at negotiations cause situations which result in lawsuits.

Although the IP department plays a behind-the-scenes role in the business, its actions actually have a leading importance. In short, the IP department is the team that supports the execution of the business strategy. Its role is to eliminate the many obstacles that arise, and to execute the business according to plan. The work of this department is mainly to prevent the company's business from being eroded by other companies.

Our relationship with Hewlett Packard (HP) provides an example of IP providing backup for the business. The reason that we have had a long relationship with HP began with our IP strategy. Canon has a patent portfolio relating to the laser beam printer (LBP), and as a consequence other companies are not able to use this technology. Therefore, HP is forced to buy all their LBP engines from Canon. This is an example of an achievement made by Canon's IP strategy.

The idea of a license agreement with HP came from the IP department. While the division formulated the business plan, the IP department considered the best course of action from the standpoint of IP as the execution support measures. That is to say, a set-maker like HP usually goes with multiple sourcing at first. Considering what could be done with IP to avoid multiple sourcing by HP, we decided not to do licensing with our rival companies for essential core patents. This is one example of business support through IP. Using this IP strategy, we were able to prevent this kind of multiple sourcing for a long time.

Not limited to this example, we have to carry out technology development in order to steadily obtain patents for equipment produced for OEMs. Although cost reduction is also important, we have to create this kind of "protected" technology even if it means increasing costs. We also have to make strong patent portfolio. These become the links between intellectual assets and the business.

Looking at Canon's organization related to IP, it is made up of roughly three centers. The first is the IP business center, which is in charge of patent management, patent information system administration, and other application works. It employs about 170 people. The second is the contract and liaison center, which is in charge of lawsuits including patent infringement, cross-licensing agreements, and introduction of other-company licensing. This center employs over 70 people. The third is the IP technical center, which has the largest number of employees. This is where they survey and analyze patent and technology trends, and provide support to research in order to develop the company's own patents. As they say at Canon, this is the "core of the core" in the IP department. It is divided into specialists for each technology, and it provides IP support for each stage of the technology development. The center employs as many as 200 people.

Seiko Epson

As a third company example, let us look at Seiko Epson. As you may know, Seiko Epson is currently a printer manufacturer, and is also well known as an electronic device manufacturer. However, it got its start as a watchmaker. Incidentally, 90% of Epson's sales in 1970 were sales of wristwatches. By 2000 however, watches only made up 5% of its sales, while information equipment and electronic devices accounted for 65% and 30% of sales, respectively.

In a recent conversation, Mr. Kamiyanagi, the man who has led the IP management at Seiko Epson, told me the following.

"In 1980, Seiko Epson's sales were about 100 billion yen. However, 1 billion yen of that was from licensing income alone. That was the time when there was a growing awareness in the company of patents being extremely exciting and profitable. The number of patent applications at that time already exceeded 2,000. However, we did not remain content with this, and decided to diversify and branch into other markets besides watches.

Thanks to the implementation of this diversification strategy, our company, which had so far clung to the watch industry, began to realize how little it knew about the outside business world. As we entered into the realm of semiconductors, LCD, and computer technology, we became aware that we were coming under attack every day. Our current IP policy arose from a need to overcome this difficult experience. Around 1975, we had less than 20 people handling IP. Today this number has grown to 350.

There are various approaches to IP strategy, but it takes a suitable amount of time until the results are achieved. Also, we are aware that it takes time to develop personnel. Looking at it from this perspective, it is necessary to take immediate action by looking as far into the future as possible.

This philosophy is being applied in the building of all our IP strategies. In other words, medium and long-range vision is the most important thing for Epson's IP strategy. We envision what kind of company we want to have in three or five years and thoroughly discuss the best IP management approach at that point in time. Through repeated debate, various gaps with reality are exposed. By going through this process, we aim for the desired IP situation in five years, and adopt strategic measures to bridge the gap between the goal and the current situation. This is how Epson develops its IP strategy.

Let me tell you about the characteristics of Epson's IP organization. Currently, the IP headquarters is part of the head office organization. There are also IP organization departments in each of the company divisions. However, the top management of the IP organizations in each division also all serves as managers for the head office IP organization. There are four departments in the head office IP organization: the IP promotion department, the IP planning department, the patent technology department, and the licensing department. The patent technology department is the post that is in charge of the regular IP operations. However, there are quite a few general managers and section chiefs here, and most of these people also serve as top management for IP in the respective divisions.

As for the IP staff that carry out the work under these managers, there are the staff that belong to the head office IP department, as well as staff that belong to the division. Therefore, the division IP top management is in charge of both staff belonging to the head office and staff belonging to the division. For example, the section chief of an IP group in the production technology development center has to report to both the general manager of production technology development center, and the general manager of the head office IP headquarters.

The reason for this organizational structure is that the IP activities have to be as close to the divisions as possible. Also, the IP organizations in each division must be located in proximity to the head of the division. In other words, the objective is to create an IP organization in the division that is easy for the division head to use. However, by dividing up the IP organization into these divisions, unfortunately it becomes like a group of small and medium-sized businesses. In order to implement a company-wide strategy, it is necessary to use the head office IP organization as a unifying force.

This system is now functioning to promote the company's overall IP strategy, and to realize the IP profit in the divisions at the same time. However, in fact there are a fair number of cases where the head office IP objectives conflict with division profits, in addition to profit conflicts between divisions. The ability to sort out these differences depends on the skills of managers to pursue two goals at once, and so far it has worked out very well for us.

The IP organizations in the divisions are responsible for providing support to maximize the division's profits through IP. The company-wide IP organization is charged with building an IP foundation including infrastructure, and an IP base throughout the company to meet the needs three or five years into the future. At the same time, the greatest responsibility is to prepare an organization and personnel development that is ready for what lies ahead."

Theory for IP Organizational Ability

In this part, we will look at the theory of IP organizational function at Japanese companies. An important premise when considering the IP function and organization at Japanese companies is the concept of the company promoting management in a pro-patent environment for some time into the future. Therefore, it is necessary to strengthen the IP function in a way that is suitable for this environment.

Although it may seem a little round-about to return to the pro-patent discussion at this point, it is better to review this now so that the corporate policy to follow will be properly understood. Pro-patent policy usually means the protecting and strengthening of IP rights in general including patent rights. However, a more straightforward description of pro-patent from the standpoint of a company in a competitive environment is "the increasing role of patents (IP in a narrow sense) as weapons in the struggle to compete."

Therefore, in order to succeed in competition, the company must foster an awareness of organizational ability relating to IP. The importance of three organizational abilities will be discussed below.

Ability to Build Patent Networks and Portfolio

To build on the definition given above, pro-patent policy is the strengthening of relative positions between those that hold, and do not hold patent rights, through the protection and enforcement of "monopolistic exclusive rights" that are the characteristic feature of patents.

The important things for patent holders to strengthen their positions are patent portfolio and networks. Basically, patent holders can be thought of as those with patent portfolio or networks.

It is theoretically possible to construct the company's monopolistic position with a single basic patent (this is actually possible in fields like medicine and chemistry). However, due to the following reasons, if the company does not have a portfolio or network of patents, it is difficult to create/generate business power.

1. If a competitor obtains a group of peripheral technology-based patents, despite having the basic patent the company's own business becomes restricted by the competitor's patents
2. There is the danger that the sole basic patent owned by the company may become invalid.

However, once patents strengthened by "exclusive power" are held in a group, since the business execution of other companies in that field becomes rather restricted, the "business exclusive rights" of the patent network holder are strengthened. The expression "business, technology, and IP are the holy trinity" is often used here. However this does not simply mean that technology is needed for business, and technology is supported by IP. It is more accurate to say the superiority of the IP position dictates the superiority of the business position, at least partially.

Naturally, strong technical capability is essential to build a highly superior IP position, and there is no mistaking that technical strength can form a base for a strong business position. However, the organization that is in charge of IP functions has a large responsibility for creating the conditions that will allow the business to maintain its strength.

For advanced electronic part manufacturers such as above-mentioned Olympus and its endoscope business, or Sanyo and its lithium ion battery business, which have large shares of the global market, actually great pains are taken in vigorously maintaining their own patent networks. They are also very sensitive about any patents of other companies that may contravene their own patents. Top companies that maintain this kind of business with a high degree of monopoly in their fields do not hesitate to equate IP with their business. While concentrating their efforts on the improvement of sales strength, marketing, and technology and product development in a competitive environment, they are energetically investing in personnel and financial management assets in order to strengthen IP power through patent network building.

Ability to Utilize Patent Information

The IP organizational ability necessary to obtain a competitive superiority in a pro-patent environment is the skill to utilize publicly disclosed patent information.

Simply put, companies use the original objective of the patent system, which is to "contribute to industrial development," to their own advantage. This means that since patents articulate the technology development results after investment of management resources, this is a valuable technical information asset for anybody in the same industry and the companies following later. Therefore, through the referencing and analysis of this publicly disclosed patent information, it is possible to devise substitute technologies or new technical concepts, and uncover peripheral technology themes, while also being able to improve one's own relative technological level. This is also one of the aims of the patent system.

However, when companies take this policy it sends a strong message to the R&D department. This is because, as the premise for carrying out technology development activities, they learn about the technology of other companies (through patent information), and then develop even better technology for their own companies without contravening the original technology.

The important thing here is the skill to systematize technology and create technology themes. In other words, the company needs the organizational ability to systematize technology in the technical field concerned by creating technology trees, based on its own patent information and that of other companies. It then needs to decide how much emphasis to place on what level of the tree structure, and determine whether to pursue technology development in order to go beyond the technology of another company.

In particular, technology trees are important from the following standpoints.

a) Determining how to reach the upper levels of technology
b) Determining how to spread out and cover all the peripheral technologies

Regarding point a), innovative technology arises basically from defining the technology themes on the technology tree. This means, for a certain technology theme and area, defining the technology theme and focusing the development resources from the standpoints of what do you want to resolve with technology, what can you readily resolve, and what is the most suitable technology theme to elaborate for your company's own technology system. By doing this you can produce technology that is more advanced and innovative than that of other companies. As publicly disclosed information, patents are useful for determining the best direction.

However, here is the problem that can be found with technology development scenes in Japanese companies. Although a patent is a technical concept using natural laws, it cannot be established without concreteness and tangible action that can be repeated. For this reason, there is a tendency for the technology development sites to be content with technology that is only concrete, is a visibly applicable, or is a "peripheral" technology.

Therefore, the most important thing for future management of technology is now discovering new technology themes of the highest level through the creation of technology systems and trees based on patent information from all companies, while creating in the R&D divisions the climate to strategically and positively confirm innovative methods and technologies for those themes.

A key to succeeding against the competition in the pro-patent era is determining how the IP organization can support the identification of advanced concepts such as the highest level of inventive ideas and mental acts.

Ability to Utilize and Negotiate for the IP of Other Companies

The third organizational ability required is the ability to negotiate in order to efficiently and effectively utilize the patented technology of other companies by using the exclusive technology and proprietary patents as tools.

In the pro-patent environment, when advancing the business by infringing the IP rights of other companies, the consequence may be the immediate suspension of the company's own business, and the payment of a large damage compensation amount. For this reason, in order to avoid this kind of consequence, the company needs to carefully carry out infringement surveys in advance and prove the invalidity of other company patents. In addition, the company may need to negotiate with other companies. In other words, patent rights are like a game to obtain as much of the opponent's territory as possible in the unlimited field of technology. Therefore, it is important to have skills that allow the use of the opponent's positions (i.e. patents) by utilizing the positions already obtained by your own company.

In the pro-patent environment, since serious damage is incurred when infringement occurs, a strategic choice must be made at the negotiating table. A company can negotiate mutual entry into each other's territories, or it can secure new territory by jumping over to a completely different area and develop its business in the area surrounding the new territory. In reality, since it is expected that, led by the electronics industry, in the future there will be increasingly more combining of technology, standardization, and intensification and acceleration of competition in technology development, it will be more and more difficult to promote exclusive business in the company's own territory (excluding the fields of medical and chemical industry). Therefore, the ability to negotiate and build relationships that can profitably utilize IP belonging to other companies is becoming an extremely important element in the IP function. Specifically, there are leading cases such as the strategic cross-licensing being carried out by Canon and IBM, the global procurement of advanced patents that Samsung is trying out, and the building of leading positions in the global standardization process that many electronic companies are experimenting with.

Principles of IP Function

Now, let us discuss the role that corporate IP departments need to play in the pro-patent era. Generally, the company IP department has the following functions, irrespective of whether it is a corporate organization, a division organization, or a subsidiary organization.

A) Patent Technology Function

Having the function of promoting invention in the R&D department, and preparing invention reports and specifications. Also dealing with domestic and overseas patent applications, and so-called liaison activities.

B) Patent Management Function

Having the function of performing status management of the company's patents. Executing a series of tasks relating to application, midterm processing registration, and rights maintenance. Work includes application management, joint application management, publicly disclosed technical information management, outside agent management, examination request necessity management, midterm processing management, registration and rights maintenance, annuity management, as well as workplace invention compensation and bonus management.

C) Patent Survey Function

Being in charge of advanced technology surveys, infringement surveys, trend surveys in the specific technology fields, and the preparation of patent maps.

D) Liaison and Legal Function

Managing general technology contracts including licensing, infringement lawsuits, preventive legal affairs, maintenance of confidentiality agreements, joint application agreements, joint development and development of consignment agreements, and rights transfer agreements.

For the people now working in IP departments, the above work is common and not difficult at all.

However, for the IP function in the pro-patent environment, this kind of work forms the foundation and a more substantial IP function needs to be pursued. In particular, the improvement of the following three planning functions can increase the future value of IP (see Figure 8). Although these planning functions cannot always be strictly separated into three types, for the sake of explanation they have been classified this way.

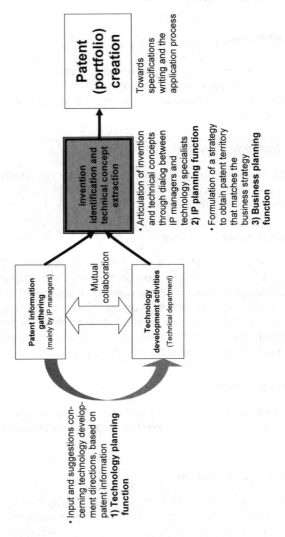

Fig. 8. IP upstream process and planning function

Technology Planning Function

With respect to advanced technology development activities, accumulating information from the standpoint of IP, and identifying ideas for technology development directions, themes, technical subjects, and technology approaches. Having the function of executing technology plans from the perspective of patent characteristics relating to the technology concerned (application trends, degree of control by other advanced companies, map density or open territory, etc.). Having the role of navigator or pilot to sort out the organized knowledge in the world and then elicit technology (implicit knowledge) creation activities in the company.

IP Planning Function

This is the more precise mission of the "patent technology function" in item A) above, and it involves entering providing support for the task of expressing individual technologies (tacit knowledge). At the same time, it strives to identify technical concepts and build a specification request scope, without being particular about individual technologies (regarded as practical applications or peripheral). This function aims to draw out universal concepts that indicate the essence of the technology from individual technology examples, through dialog with technology specialists, opinion exchange, and revision. As an analogy, you can think of it like the role of Socrates' use of conversations in the discovery of truths (later arranged by Hegel's dialectic as "thesis – antithesis – synthesis"). The main point is that the IP manager identifies the essential technological value through repeated opposition and questions, rather than simply accepting the claims of the technology specialists. IP managers are like the obstetricians of knowledge.

Business Planning Function

This function involves staying focused on the future of the business, and drafting strategy to obtain patents (patent networks) that support the business strategy. These are not merely the patents that can be obtained from the company's technology, but include the obtaining of patents necessary to succeed in the competitive environment. There are various methods to strengthen the company's business position including obtaining patents that restrict the business freedom of other companies, introducing patents from advanced patent holders, and eliminating the patents of other companies. In order to fulfill this function, the IP manager must carry out reliable business planning from the perspective of IP in order to strengthen the business through IP, while being thoroughly familiar with the business environment beyond the level of a technology specialist.

The above are the IP planning functions for high added value, in addition to maintaining the conventional functions of the IP department.

Hot IP Topics Now Faced by Japanese Companies

Lastly, let us look at recent IP topics in Japan.

Disclosure of IP Information

With the promotion of various policies based on the Japanese government's aim to create an IP nation, a debate has arisen over the intention to promote information disclosure for IP. After the start of investigations under the IP Strategy Outline in 2002, the IP Information Disclosure Subcommittee released IP disclosure guidelines in 2005, based on guidance by the Ministry of Economy, Trade and Industry. Already a dozen or so Japanese companies have disclosed information on their own IP, in the form of IP reports.

In the past, although independent IP management and administration was promoted at companies, it was unclear what information was needed by the market and investors in particular, and in what format it should be disclosed. This is one element of the background of this issue. At the same time, while the market was aware of the need for information relating to IP, as most companies did not disclose this information, there was a gap between companies and the market due to the uncertainty over the possible scope of disclosure by companies. In order to bridge the gap between the two sides, the IP Information Disclosure Guidelines were created for companies.

There are a total of 10 specific items in these IP Information Disclosure Guidelines, as follows: 1) Core technology and business model, 2) R&D segment and business strategy direction, 3) R&D segment and IP outline, 4) Technology marketability and market superiority analysis, 5) IP organizational chart, and R&D cooperation and tie-ups, 6) Policies for IP acquisition management, trade secret management, and technology outflow prevention, 7) Contribution to licensing activities and related activity business, 8) Contribution to patent group business, 9) Policies for IP portfolios, and 10) Information on risk.

The above is the basic details for information disclosure, and there are five principles in this approach. The first is that information disclosure must always be voluntary. In other words, the information disclosure guidelines are meant to serve as a guide for dialog between companies and the market relating to IP information. The second principle is the demonstration of IP management. The third principle is accompaniment of quantitative evidence and items of premise. The fourth principle is the use of a consolidated reporting basis in principle, and segment units. The fifth principle also applies to small and medium venture companies in addition to large companies. Based on these five principles, it is preferable that IP reports be prepared by organizational measures, as the disclosure medium.

In accordance with these disclosure guidelines, a dozen or so companies including Hitachi have issued IP reports. However, it is important to note that industry opinion is still divided regarding these IP reports. The argument of the companies opposing the guidelines is summed up in the following three points.

The first point of contention is the content of the IP reports. In other words, since the information relating to patents is already publicly disclosed, why is it necessary to re-summarize this information again? This is work best done by the market analysts, as there is no need for the companies to compile this, and no value is added.

The second point claims that IP, or the company's intellectual assets composed mainly of patents, is confidential in-house information. Publicizing this information in itself may result in a reduction in the company's value. For example, information such as important licensing facts, the position of the company's core patents, IP strategy, and technology strategy are all confidential, and announcing this to the market is very difficult.

The third point is similar to the second point. It says that rather than simply listing patents for disclosure like numerical data, it is more important for the company to have the corporate strength to produce IP in the first place, to have intellectual capital, and to have a basic company stance. For this reason, without the disclosure of this fundamental corporate information, it will not constitute true IP disclosure. This task is very difficult, and should be carried out inside the company, but it is not something to be announced outside the company. Based on these three reasons, many companies are against IP information disclosure.

Nevertheless, there are also companies that feel that IP reports are necessary. One of these companies is Asahi Kasei. Mr. Tsurumi, the former head of Asahi Kasei's IP center, explained it this way.

"I believe that one of the major premises behind the issue of IP reporting is the necessity for information disclosure. In my understanding, accounting information is no more than past information. However, institutional investors need to invest for the long term of five or ten years. Therefore, since they cannot make their judgments based on the past results of accounting information alone, they are looking for various kinds of information. IP reports are one type of this information. What kind of core technology and core competence does this company use to make a profit? Is the company thoroughly aware of this? It is also desirable for the company to use charts to show that it is applying an IP business model to earn profits.

In the case of Asahi Kasei, we do not yet prepare IP reports for each of our divisions and member companies. Although I had considerable discussions with the heads of materials departments at other companies in the process of preparing IP reports, now there are no business areas, companies, or member companies that are preparing clear stories in the format that I mentioned. Simply put, Japanese companies are not carrying out business development with an awareness of this kind of thing. Therefore, in order to be able to prepare a report, the company must first have a clear awareness of itself. By doing this, the company can properly develop its business. I understand that this is one way to set policy direction. We need to take this approach and prepare a story for the development of our business, and put this into writing. As there are many Japanese companies that cannot do this, the intention to keep pace by properly preparing this is actually a policy purpose, and Asahi Kasei has adopted this policy.

Therefore, I think that the IP reports that we have actually prepared are not always so concerned about IP details. Our format uses more of an awareness of how intellectual capital is being created, or how intangible assets are being produced as a whole."

This concludes the discussion of recent trends at Japanese companies relating to IP information disclosure. Simply put, companies have finally taken an interest in IP in recent years, and are beginning to inquire about methods and concepts for disclosure. Although there is still no single answer to the question of IP information disclosure, it seems that every company will have to distinguish its own stance on IP information disclosure in its own way.

System for Workplace Invention Compensation

In Article 35 of the Japanese Patent Law there is a unique regulation concerning workplace inventions. It states that, "In the case that an employee has rights to receive a patent for a workplace invention based on a contract, employment regulations, or other stipulation, or if the patent rights were transferred to the employer, or if exclusive implementation rights were established, the employee has the right to receive a reasonable compensation payment." The Supreme Court has indicated that the employee may seek the payment of a shortfall amount, when the compensation amount paid by the employer to the employee, according to the employment regulations, does not constitute a reasonable compensation.

Based on this "reasonable compensation" matter, there has been a recent sharp rise in lawsuits for achievement compensation based on a workplace invention. One famous case involved Shuji Nakamura, a professor at the University of California at Santa Barbara, who sued his former employer, Nichia Corporation. Initially the district court awarded him 20 billion yen. However, afterwards there were cases before the Tokyo High Court where the parties were advised to settle out of court and both sides agreed upon an amount of about 600 million yen. In addition, lawsuits have been launched by employees of Olympus, Hitachi, Hitachi Metals, Ajinomoto, Canon, Mitsubishi Electric, Toshiba, and other companies against their employers, seeking "reasonable compensation." All of these cases are still pending.

The Patent Law was revised due to this reason. However, there is the additional matter of the stipulation that "the compensation amount agreed upon by both parties should be respected." To this the stipulation that "it is important to respect the procedures for compensation determination and to ensure that this is rationally secured" was added. Therefore, we still have the argument of whether or not there is rationality, and the matter of "reasonable compensation" remains.

Various arguments have been raised concerning this issue. For example, the inventor technology specialist has an employment relationship with the company, and that person is responsible for producing knowledge in the form of inventions under consignment to the company. The companies argue that, since the company bears the risk for the equipment, funds, and the passing on of past skills and expertise for technology development, and the employee inventor is producing knowledge without any risk, it is unreasonable for the employee to request a compensation amount for an invention. In the case of important inventions that contribute to the company, the companies say it would be better to recognize this through incentives such as promotions, bonuses, and other rewards, rather than a legally stipulated "reasonable compensation." Therefore, they argue it is not a matter in which the courts should be involved in the first place, with regard to the "invention transfer compensation" of Article 35 of the Patent Law.

Even with the above-mentioned Blue Diode trial at the Tokyo High Court, there is the argument that the fact there was finally no court determination except for an out-of-court settlement shows the limitation of the judiciary in making determinations on transfer compensations in the first place.

There are three reasons for this, some of which I have already mentioned. The first reason is that, irrespective of whether there is a law or not, compensation is something that is first given to someone who achieves something at that person's own risk. In other words, a person who does not take the risk cannot expect to receive the returns from an enterprise. Therefore if a person that produces an invention under the security of employment in the company, and then makes a request for compensation based on legal requirement, since the company is only one-sidedly liable for that moment, it becomes very contradictory.

The second reason is that an individual claiming an invention compensation amount is in itself contradictory. When a certain employee produces an invention, as a precondition for this, the employee needs to have the technical background, facilities, equipment, and past data originally possessed by the company, as well as various other information and competence held by the company itself. For this reason, it is difficult to say that the employee produced the invention individually, except in a very limited sense. In other words, even if the employee makes an important invention, since this invention is based on the precondition of the employee being in the company, it is hard to say that the invention is a product of that individual.

Of course, we must not think that there is no relation between the excellence of the technology specialist's individual abilities and the value of the invention; in fact there is a substantial relation between the two. More generous incentives need to be provided to outstanding employees whose excellence as technology specialists raise the quality of inventions. It goes without saying the other technology specialists must also be rewarded correspondingly. However, this is different from the argument of whether or not employees have the right to seek "reasonable compensation" in the legal sense.

A third reason often comes up in this debate. The invention only produces business value once it reaches the market in the form of a product that is a practical application of the invention. Without this business value, there would be no reason for invention compensation amount. If the value of the invention is to be estimated from the perspective of contributing to the company's business, then the combined business value created by production, manufacturing, sales, distribution, marketing, branding, and a host of other functions also needs to be considered. In this sense the original invention itself is just one corresponding function. Therefore, it is very dangerous to claim that everything is solely the result of the invention, and ignore the corresponding value of the employees performing all the other functions. This would be very hazardous for company management.

On the one hand, when the company transfers IP to other companies through the format of licensing out, how does it compensate the inventor employee for the licensing fee that the company receives? This can be varied through the company's policy.

As in the previously stated argument, the IP itself exists in order to increase the company's monopoly and exclusive rights, and to strengthen the company's business, rather than for the purpose of transferring it to another company and obtaining profit. If considered this way, this argument states that the activity of licensing out to other companies is basically a diversion from the company's objective. Canon is one of the companies that take this view.

On the other hand, in the case of a research and development oriented company, IP is a source of income through the licensing out of inventions to other companies, rather than implementing them in the company's own business. In this case, the view is that an inventor employee should be duly compensated with a reward. Therefore, in this instance as well, it is an issue of providing the proper incentives to employees rather than a legal problem.

As shown above, there are various arguments regarding reasonable compensation for workplace inventions. However, as management consultants, we cannot help but feel that there is very little basis for stipulating the issue of reasonable compensation in law, for the reasons already explained.

This concludes our discussion of IP management in Japanese companies. In recent years, there has been a tendency to give priority to IP rights issues that are picked up by the mass media. However, as shown here, these issues are deeply rooted in innovation management. In the future therefore, Japanese companies will need to acquire a range of management tools that link business, technology, and IP, methodologies for utilization of the company's IP, measures to deal with workplace invention, proper organizational functions for IP as part of a pro-patent policy, and an approach that estimates the value of IP. There will likely be more and more issues that will need our attention and each company will have to develop its own special skills to address them.

MoT: From Academia to Management Practice – The MoT Implementation Case in a Traditional Japanese Company

Gaston Trauffler and Hugo Tschirky

Co-authors: Masaharu Kinoshita[*] and Keizo Okui[**]

Introduction

The present paper is a progress report describing the elaboration and implementation of basic strategic technology management concepts in a Japanese technology intensive company. The concepts were proposed and put into action during an academic consulting project where researchers form the Swiss Federal Institute of Technology, Zurich – Chair of Technology and Innovation Management - collaborated with the company for a of period of more than eighteen months.

As an initial position, the company did not have any technology and innovation management (MoT) processes, structures or methods in place, thus the conception and implementation of the latter needed to be started from scratch. From a research perspective this untainted initial position was most interesting for the purpose of studying the procedure and deployment of concepts that would be most effective when MoT were put in practice under such preliminary conditions.

As this research work generated a procedure for designing and implementing MoT within the company context, action research has been used. The aim of the research paper is to contribute to two aspects of MoT: First, it reports how MoT concepts were elaborated and implemented in a company that previously did not have any such concepts in use. It describes which MoT activities were introduced and implemented and in which order. Second, it describes a generalized and practitioner-oriented procedure derived from the experiences of this particular case. This procedure describes step by step the most important activities that enable in general a smooth implementation of MoT in a company that was unfamiliar with these concepts.

The paper closes with some general lessons learned from this case.

The Initial Position

The cooperating Japanese company, in this action research case was Nitta Corporation (Nitta) with its headquarters in Osaka. It is active in production and sales in

---

[*]Nitta Haas Incorporated, Nara, Japan, [**]Nitta Corporation, Nara, Japan

global markets. The company's most important products, in terms of sales, are mainly in the domains of belting, rubber joints, filter systems, mechatronics & sensor systems and hose & tubing systems. The company employs approximately 800 people. The income in percent of sales is about 3%.

The organization is divided into six independent business segments. These segments are responsible for their own sales, production and innovation. Recently the company formed a corporate technology center. However, the role of this center seems not yet to be clearly defined. At present it mainly supports research activities of different business segments that run out of the human resources' project schedule.

A rough analysis of the company's situation uncovered two major points. On the one hand, it was mainly selling mature products in stagnating or decreasing markets. On the other hand the company was lacking a clear innovation strategy that would point out innovation goals and establish organizational responsibilities needed in order to create a turn around situation oriented towards higher growth rates.

From a technology management perspective the company situation described above was difficult to overview at first sight: The organizational structures and the management processes had been mainly market oriented. However a strategic purpose focused link between the technologies the company was exploiting and the products it delivered to their markets was not given. The company's technologies had not been considered and managed as strategic assets by which a competitive advantage could be built up. Furthermore, there were no routines implemented that could be interpreted as technology and innovation management processes designed to leverage technologies and foster innovation.

Thus the academic consulting project's objective was to systematically identify and evaluate opportunities for innovation. In doing so, the focus was on developing and implementing strategic technology and innovation management routines, including processes, structures and tools. The ultimate goal of the project was three fold: First to leverage and reposition the present portfolio of technologies, second to find new growth fields and third to build up the innovative power to explore these growth fields.

Creating Transparency

The first activity in the project was directed towards creating transparency and reducing complexity in order to gain an overview of the company's MoT relevant assets. To create transparency, a tool called innovation architecture (Sauber 2004) was applied.

Innovation architecture (IA) is a tool that mirrors the company from a knowledge-based view. It shows the interplay between knowledge assets of the company, residing in products, technologies and scientific research as well as knowledge assets in the markets of those products. The link between products and technologies is established through functions. Functions are solution neutral descriptions of an operation that describe the constraints between an input, for example one ore more technologies and an output such as product variations. Companies should define their functions so that they create links between technologies or strategic aggregations of technologies, called technology platforms that fulfill these functions and address the market needs that need to be satisfied.

At Nitta an IA was drafted for the whole company in order to reflect the "as is" situation of its business. This was followed by a series of workshops, which were conducted in all divisions of the company, and where different IAs were elaborated. Participants of the workshops were collaborators from middle management, engineers, and researchers as well as people from marketing and sales. In these IAs, the divisions of the company were structured according to company functions. Functions defined in this company are for example: "Transmit power" and "transport objects" for the belting division, "transport fluids" for the tubing division, "separate molecules and particles" for the filtering division, etc.

Once the entire company was mapped in IAs, in order to reduce complexity it was decided to design and implement the MoT concepts first as a prototype to one single division instead of applying them to the whole company right from the beginning. Management decided the belting division should be the one to serve as the prototype.

Figure 1 displays part of the belting division's IA. It is built around the main functions of that division; one of these functions is the function "transmit power". The IA represents a knowledge-based view it shows that basic scientific knowledge of the belting division comes from joint ventures. The technology level comprises a technology platform, which is rubber-technology and other technologies that support the latter. The function "transmit power" links the business field level and its products to the technology level. The market level shows all the markets to which the division sells. Knowledge about markets, products and technologies is called object knowledge.

The leap from one level of the IA to another, for example from the business field level to the market level, is enabled through methodological knowledge, which is symbolized by broad arrows. The methodological knowledge needed for example, to bring products into a market is described as "market development knowledge".

By visualizing the elements and links between knowledge assets, the IA managed to considerably reduce the complexity and create transparency in the belting division. Besides this, a common basis was created for discussion as the IA had been elaborated in consensus between the different parts of the organization.

This "as-is" IA was used in order to critically reflect the present activities of the belting division. As all of the knowledge assets of the division were displayed in the IA, the strengths and weaknesses of those assets could be discussed. This way, room for improvement in existing technologies and products could be detected and new opportunities could be discussed, as the whole picture of the division became visible at one glance. Looking at the IA the head of the Nitta's Technical Center said that for the first time he had gained a complete and transparent overview of the division's technologies and products including their strength and weakness and their interrelation, but above all he knew now in which fields that he had a lot of work to do.

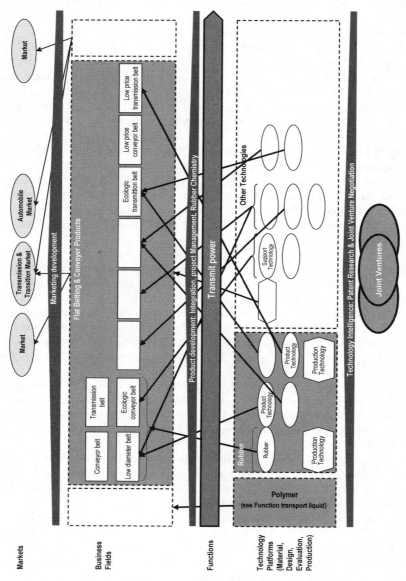

Fig. 1. Innovation architecture of the belting division built around the function "transmit power"

The IA had displayed the direct relation between market needs, products, and technologies to enable those products and the scientific research fields the technologies were based on. Out of an initially unstructured heap of technologies and out of an initially opaque product/market constellation, an initial structure was now visible. The rough assessment of the company's knowledge strength and weaknesses had already shown where further efforts were needed in order to reach the strategic goals that had been set in the previous year for this division.

The newly created transparency revealed that the division only had a weak strategic alignment in terms of strategic MoT. The technologies had not yet been grouped strategically or aligned to fully exploit their competitive potential. Thus in the next phase of the project, a proposal was elaborated which would regroup the division's technologies in groups of technology that were to be manageable as strategic entities.

Forming Strategically Manageable Technology Entities

The IA provided transparency in the knowledge assets of the company. In spite of the fact that all main technologies could be seen at one glance, it was not apparent how all those technologies should be rated and valued strategically. Displayed in the IA, all the technologies seemed to be equally important for the business' success. In order to find out which technologies were strategically critical for the business and which were less so, the technologies had to be grouped according to strategic importance. The ultimate aim of this endeavor was to group strategically important technologies in order to visualize the competencies they represented for the company. A competence is considered the ability of an organization to achieve its (strategic) goals (Sanchez 2001, p. 5). Those technologies that contribute to forming the competencies of a company are referred to as core technologies. Core technologies are "relevant theories, products, process and support technologies which grouped as a whole represent a strategic entity suitable for setting strategic priorities" (Tschirky 2003a, p. 71).

Making a company's competencies visible goes beyond just knowing what they are. It means to know in which business fields a competence is actually needed, how this competence could be used in the future, what the strategic impact of this competence is, how this competence will develop, and who the knowledge carriers are. The Strategic Impact Analysis method (see Figure 2) was used to make the competencies visible, to detect core technologies, and to show in which business field they play a strategically important role. This method aims to reduce the overall complexity of a company's technology and business interrelations by breaking down its interaction in three steps. First, the so-called Strategic Business Areas (SBA) are reflected. SBAs are dedicated sectors of the overall market place in which the company intends to position itself. The selection of SBAs includes strategic consideration of which markets and customer benefits to address, which product functions to fulfill and which concrete products and services to offer. The creation of SBAs follows the theory of the market based view which suggests that companies build up competitive advantage by positioning themselves in markets with the highest business potential (see Porter 1985). Once a company has selected its SBA it should try to align its internal business structures according to the chosen sectors of the market place. Usually creating business divisions and/or business division achieves this alignment. Second, from the large number of technologies available in a company, Strategic Technology Fields (STF) are created. They represent a specific competence of the company materialized through a set of identified core technologies of the company including their corresponding basic theories, product technologies, process technologies and support technologies. The creation of STF follows the theories of the knowledge based view that endorses companies creating competitive advantage through building up company internal core competencies that are valuated in the market (see Prahalad and Hamel 1990). In a third step, the STF are opposed to the business structure of the company so that so-called technology platforms can be created. Technology platforms emerge when a certain constellation of one or more core technologies with corresponding product, process and support technologies can be used as a fundament that creates value in many business division or units of a company.

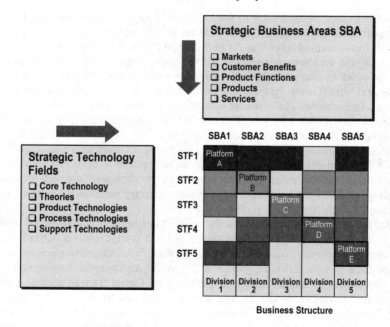

Fig. 2. The strategic impact analysis

Performing the Strategic Impact Analysis on the Nitta Case brought forth six technologies that could be considered as core technologies with corresponding platforms. The analysis well visualized how these core technologies could be cross-used in other business division of the company emphasizing a higher strategic priority compared to other technologies in use at Nitta. Knowing the actual strategic priority of a technology finally allowed the critical questioning of the present strategy and its implementation. For example the question arose if the technologies that the Strategic Impact Analysis had shown as most important for the company had indeed been the ones the company had planned to build upon in the future. Whether those technologies had been given enough resources compared to their strategic position in the company was also questioned. Furthermore, the question arose if the synergies that the technologies had shown to other businesses had been exploited efficiently?

Aside from the effect of stimulating management to discuss the concrete strategic questions described above, the Strategic Impact Analysis at Nitta showed that a clear and systematically elaborated technology and innovation strategy had been missing so far. The full scope that could be leveraged by systematically positioning the company's technological assets strategically had not yet been fully optimized. In order to do so a further phase of the academic consulting project was commissioned: the design of a MoT procedure that systematically lead to a technology and innovation strategy. In other words the project team was asked to design a strategic planning process to enable the systematic elaboration of a strategy formulation.

Designing a Holistic and Integrated MoT Process

The strategic planning process designed for Nitta was based on the generic process model of MoT, developed at the Swiss Federal Institute of Technology. According to this generic model, two fundamental principles of process design have to be followed: First, it has to be a holistic management process and second, it has to be an integrated management process (see Figure 3).

The holistic management of this process is insured through the interaction between the normative, strategic and operational levels. As an initial position for the strategic planning process, *the normative level* provides the guidelines through a corporate vision[1], a company policy[2] and an innovation policy. These three elements provide a raw but focused direction to the innovation activities on the strategic level. The direction given by the normative level influences the whole strategic process, which thus affects all phases of the strategy formulation as well as the strategy implementation.

---

[1]   Visions usually cover "long-term objectives, main areas of activities, geographical dimensions of businesses, major resources and competencies, innovative ambitions, the desired relationship with customers, attitude towards societal and ecological expectations, the role and development of human capital and the values which determine communication and collaboration." (Tschirky, 2003: 33)

[2]   According to Hunger (2002: 9) a policy "is a broad guideline for decision making that links the formulation of strategy with its implementation. Companies use policies to make sure that employees throughout the firm make decisions and take actions that support the corporation's mission, its objectives, and its strategies."

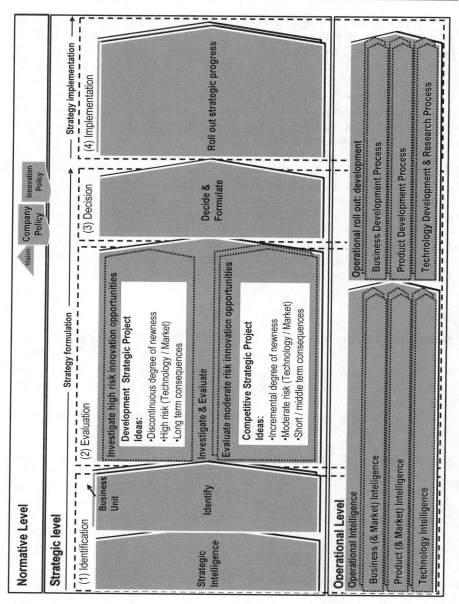

Fig. 3. Proposed process design

Once the strategic process is kicked off it works in close relation with the operational level. The relation between the strategic and operational level can be seen similarly to the relation between the normative and strategic level. However the directives given by the strategic level to the operational one are much more specific than the once directed from the normative to the operational level. Basically, the strategic level steers and decides which actions have to be carried out by the operational level and how that is to be done. For example, the very first phase of the strategic level - the strategic intelligence - fixes first which technology related information has to be gathered then the operational level is in charged with collecting this information.

The process design provides an integrated process: It is an integrated part of the corporate strategy run by each different business division as well as by the corporate division. The process phases run by the different business divisions are symbolized in Figure 3 by process symbols that are doubled as for example in the case of the "Identify" phase. When the symbols are not doubled, as is the case for the "Decide and Formulate" phase, the process phases have to be run by the corporate division alone. The actual integration of all strategic decisions from different divisions to one corporate strategy takes place in the phase "Decide and Formulate" where all the information elaborated during the process flows together.

On the strategic level the process is structured along successive process steps differentiating between strategy formulation and strategy implementation. The process is designed in four phases: (1) Identification, (2) Evaluation, (3) Decision and (4) Implementation. These phases are symbolized by the four dotted squares and within each of these squares the process steps are symbolized by the typical process arrows.

The "Identification" phase comprises the process parts "Strategic Intelligence" and "Identify". "Strategic Intelligence" comprises all strategic activities related to gathering information relevant for the best possible decision to be made.[3]"Identify" is charged with detecting innovation opportunities out of the information gathered.

The "Evaluation" phase comprises the process parts "Investigate & Evaluate". The upper process arm within the "Investigate & Evaluate" phase in Figure 3 takes care of high-risk innovation opportunities; it is called more specifically "Investigate High Risk Innovation Opportunities". These opportunities formulated in the form of project ideas are of the discontinuous degree of newness with long-term consequences for the company. If such project ideas are realized, they are for a company considered to be of a development strategic nature. They enable the company to evolve as an organization by developing its potential new strategic competencies which are meant to be deployed in products of the second next generation. Thus such projects ideas in the company are intend to initiate in the company learning about technologies that will develop future competencies. This learning is based on the "Investigate High Risk Innovation Opportunities" process arm. Therefore its ultimate task is to assess and eventually to select those new technologies project ideas that will lay the foundation for the company's changing competencies. As project ideas are often very uncertain and difficult to assess, they are handled differently from so-called competitive strategic innovation opportunities. Such opportunities are analyzed in the process called "Evaluate Mod-

---

erate Risk Innovation Opportunities" shown in the lower process arm of the phase "Evaluate" in Figure 3. The innovation opportunities analyzed in this process are of an incremental degree of newness, usually enhancing familiar applications and businesses of the company. The primary goal of this process is more straight-forward, it is not about developing new competencies for the future of the company but to yield next generation products that sell and that allow an existing market position to be expanded or strengthened. Project ideas at the basis of such goals should be of moderate risk and have rather short to mid term-consequences for the company.

The decision phase comprises the process part "Decide and Formulate" which reviews all the analysis done in the previous phase in order to formulate the inno-vation strategy.

The implementation phase comprises the process part "Roll Out Strategic Pro-gress". The tasks of this process are focused towards the successful implementa-tion of the strategy. These include the redesign of the innovation processes in the operational level, the controlling of the strategy implementation projects and the ongoing update of the strategy.

On the operational level there are two major process blocks "Operational Intel-ligence" and "Operational Roll Out" grouping operational processes for the simul-taneous and differentiated management of radical and incremental innovation. In the "Operational Intelligence" process block technology intelligence, product in-telligence and business intelligence are all handled separately. The separation has the main purpose of appropriately managing the different management contents and their various time horizons, priorities and strategic steering structures.

As a matter of fact the technology intelligence process in operational intelli-gence is mandated in the first place by strategic intelligence, identification and strategic evaluation structures in charge of high-risk innovation opportunities. This operational intelligence process collects technological information above all from radical innovation opportunities. For these kinds of innovation opportunities, technical feasibility and the assessment of technical risk is most important while product and market information are still scarce. In alignment with the strategic level this information is forwarded to the "Technology Development & Research Process" step in the "Operational Roll Out" process block. In this step that is initi-ated after the strategic level has passed its "Decide and Formulate" process step, the intention is to develop the technology to a level where it is technically mas-tered. The time horizon of such technology development projects is rather mid to long term as it takes most often five years and more as a result of being only of moderate priority.

As a contrast, the horizon of product development projects and its correspond-ing product and market intelligence is usually of a short-term horizon with a high priority. Such projects are driven by a time to market pressure built up by the competitive environment of the company (Petrick and Echols 2004, p. 85). In or-der for a company to be successful in such competition, the company should mas-ter the technology underlying the products, just as the risks and uncertainty of technical and market nature must also be mastered. Thus the operational processes of "Product Intelligence" and "Market Intelligence" as well as the "Product Development" processes should be mandated by the strategic evaluation structures for moderate risk innovation opportunities and only be fed with incremental innovation opportunities based on mastered technologies. Once the technology is mastered and the products are on their way to development, operational Business and Market Intelligence processes and „Business Development" processes can be run. These processes develop the business model for the product that is close to being fully developed. Table 1 summarizes what strategic process should be in charge of steering which operational level process. Furthermore it shows the differences in the management content: the various characters of the technologies and innovation opportunities that are managed according to various time horizons and levels of priority.

Table 1. Strategic processes in charge of corresponding operational level processes

Strategic level process	Corresponding operational level process	Character of technology and innovation opportunity managed	Time horizon / level of priority, goal of the process
• Strategic intelligence / identity • Investigate high risk innovation opportunity	1. Technology intelligence	1. Discontinuous technology / radical innovation	• Mid to long-term / moderate priority • Goal: Find technologies to build up future competencies & core competencies
• Strategic intelligence / identity • Investigate moderate risk innovation opportunity	1. Product intelligence 2. Business intelligence	1. Continuous or mastered technology / incremental innovation 2. Mastered product / incremental innovation	• Short term / priority driven by time to market pressure • Goal: find technologies to enhance existing products, strengthen existing markets
• Decide & formulate • Strategic roll out	1. Tech. develop. & res. 2. Product development 3. Business development	1. Discontinuous technology / radical innovation 2. Continuous or mastered technology / incremental innovation 3. Mastered product / incremental innovation	1. Mid to long-term / moderate priority 2. & 3. short term / priority driven by time to market pressure

Nitta rapidly accepted the process proposed above, however accepting it was far from implementing and customizing it to its own specific needs. To enable implementation an organizational structure had to be designed that could at the same time integrate the above process while also respecting the business structure shown in the Strategic Impact Analysis. Furthermore an implementation plan had to be elaborated that allowed the process to be customized.

Designing Organizational Company Structures

The organizational structures proposed to Nitta represented the first step towards bringing the analysis already conduced into action by concretely implementing the MoT concepts in the company. As already mentioned, the organizational company structures should be designed in a way to enable the implementation of the process shown in Figure 3 at the same time as the integration of the business structures are elaborated by the Strategic Impact Analysis (see Figure 2).

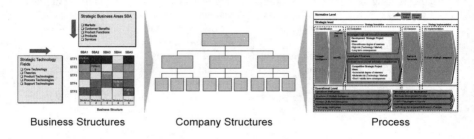

Business Structures   Company Structures   Process

Fig. 4. Organizational structures that respect business structures and managing processes

The structures designed for Nitta and the business structures had to respect the strong market orientation of the company in order for the implementation to be successful. An extract of the organizational structure suggested is shown in Figure 5. It was composed of two types of structures: business division oriented structures and a corporate division structure. Although both types of structures had specific competence areas, they work closely together. The specification in their competence areas was a distinction between various processes that they host along the management process as displayed in Figure 3. On the one hand the corporate division hosted the high-risk processes and on the other hand the business divisions hosted the moderate risk processes.

Starting with strategic intelligence, this process was to be hosted by a corporate division, the Nitta Technical Center, which took the role of a corporate R&D division. It was to decide which technology fields should be investigated then the researchers and engineers in the business divisions were to do the actual process of collecting the information in the selected fields. Therefore a network of gatekeepers[4] was suggested. Those gatekeepers were charged with gathering information across the whole company as well as outside it in different fields.

The "Identify" process was to be hosted in every business division and also in the corporate R&D division. Each division was responsible for finding its own innovation opportunities that were most interesting for their own business. Doing so, all innovation opportunities that were attractive on short- as well as long term perspectives had to be registered. In a subsequent step of consensus seeking, a responsible corporate manager together with business division managers discussed the risks involved in these innovation opportunities. According to the risk assessed, the opportunity was either directed towards corporate or to a business division for assessment.

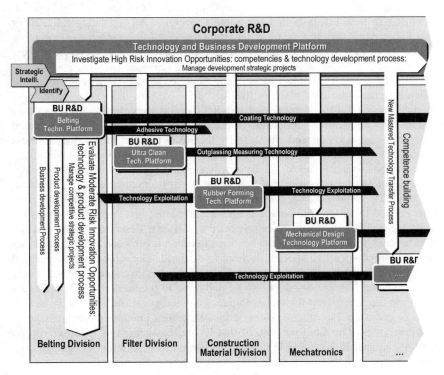

Fig. 5. Extract of the proposed MoT organizational structure

In the case of high-risk innovation opportunities, the "Investigate High Risk Innovation Opportunity" process that was to be hosted by the corporate R&D divi-

---

4   "A gatekeeper is a real person. He has numerous contacts to external experts, and he transfers knowledge from these contacts to the company. Thus, he informally pursues technology intelligence activities. However, he is not perceived as a 'formal' intelligence source by top management" (Savioz 2002, p. 98).

sion and lead by the CTO was in charge. The corporate division not being as strictly market driven was in charge of exploring new technologies in order to estimate their strategic and future market potential. These technologies did not necessarily have to be related to the company's familiar businesses; on the contrary, research done on the corporate level was to open the existing technological and business horizons of the company enabling it to enter into new and unexplored fields. Thus the main competence of corporate R&D division had to be to develop new technologies and businesses. This competence was to be regrouped in a virtual organizational structure called platform. A platform on the corporate level represents a collection of competencies serving one common purpose. In the Nitta case, the platform was designed to regroup all the competencies necessary to develop new technologies and to build up new businesses. It included skills from basic research to new business development. The generated technological and/ or market knowledge were not meant for internal use at the corporate level but in the first place to extend the knowledge of existing business divisions or to create new businesses. It has to be emphasized here that the deliverables of the corporate R&D division were in the first place, new knowledge, which was meant to be beneficial for the business division's R&D.

In the case of a low to moderate risk innovation opportunity the "Evaluate Moderate Risk Innovation Opportunity" process was in charge. It was conducted in every business division and was lead by the R&D responsible of that business division. The innovation opportunities evaluated in these business-oriented structures had to be easily related to the division's existing business and activities. Ideally these innovation opportunities had to be used to enhance existing products and markets by improving the technology incrementally. Such incremental innovations needed to fit into the competencies accumulated in a specific business division's technology platform. Similarly to the platform described earlier on the corporate level, the platforms on the business division level were to be regarded as centers of competence in a specific technological field. The innovations generated in these business division platforms can be twofold: One the one hand their new products and services are developed to be delivered to the markets of the business division, on the other hand the technological knowledge arising from these activities can be cross used in other business divisions and/or integrated into their products and services. The main purpose of this technology cross use is to exploit the technology as broadly as possible using it in many different fields. This allows the company to use technological synergies across different businesses.

Customizing the Process and Accelerating Its Implementation

The effective implementation of the structures proposed in the previous section including the creation of technology platforms, competence centers and corresponding responsibilities was a time consuming procedure that had to be pushed in the first place by Nitta management. However the implementation of the process including its customization to Nitta's situation could be accelerated by explicitly proposing an implementation plan describing which activity of the process had be executed when and by whom. In other words, laying down the process meant agreeing on a number of management meetings to be held throughout the year. In each of these meetings specific activities described in the process of Figure 3 had to be discussed and decided. Figure 6 shows how mapping it in an implementation plan with fixed date management meetings can customize the generic process.

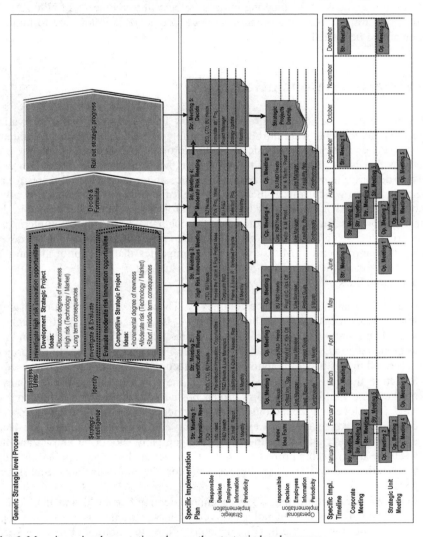

Fig. 6. Mapping a implementation plan on the strategic level process

The implementation plan at Nitta exactly described which meetings were necessary and when they were to take place. It also fixed responsibilities, the decisions to be taken, the participating employees; the information needed in order to take decisions as well how to document the information elaborated during the meetings and finally it fixed the frequency of the meetings. The customization of the process could be done by once running through the implementation plan in a scheduled calendar year and by adapting and changing activities, tasks, responsibilities and agendas of the meeting in order to best fit to the needs of Nitta. At the end of the strategic planning process, strategic project descriptions are formulated and ready to be started.

Summary and Conclusion

This article describes as a progress report how basic technology and innovation management concepts were introduced and implemented at the Japanese company Nitta in the course of an academic consulting project. The particularity of the project was that Nitta previously did not have any MoT concepts in place. However this particularity increased the freedom of choice about what MoT concepts to implement, and in which way. It increased at the same time the complexity involved in how to proceed at all in a very basic sense. From the experience obtained in this particular project, the authors deduced on the one hand, a generalized implementation procedure in five steps that should be taken as minimal guidelines for developing and implementing MoT concepts in companies that are not at all familiar with MoT and on the other hand overall lessons learned.

The guidelines:

- Create transparency and reduce complexity. These two tasks consist of classifying the knowledge assets of the company – assets related to scientific, technological and market knowledge - into structures that allows their purpose and use to be understood, and interrelated in an overall company context. In the project described in this paper the innovation architecture by Sauber (2004) was used.
- Structure the core technological assets of the company along the company's markets and build a technology driven business structure. One major goal of MoT is to leverage technological assets strategically in order to build up new competitive advantage or to extend existing competitive advantage; the technologies' impact on the businesses of the company should be known and actively be used. In this project technology impact analysis was applied in order to visualize and optimize the alignment of (core) technologies for business purposes.
- Elaborate a procedure that allows technological self-renewal and that fosters innovation. Taking the technology driven business structure as a base, the company should now be able to systematically follow technology change by keeping its portfolio of technologies updated and systematically deploying technologies in order to generate innovations. For this purpose the academic

consulting project described in this paper suggested a strategic MoT planning process including some management tools. (The management tools have not been described in the paper).

- Elaborate MoT oriented structures. In order to create a basis for the MoT concepts to be implemented, an organizational structure is necessary. The structures described in this paper proposed MoT oriented structures that could at the same time host the business structures and enable the technology self-renewing procedure. These structures suggest core technology platforms at each business divisional level that are on the one hand fed with new technological knowledge by corporate level MoT processes and on the other hand are cross divisionally exploited by corresponding divisional MoT processes.
- Actively support MoT implementation and company specific adoption. While the previous steps of these guidelines consisted of a generically designed MoT concept, this step discourages leaving any company on its own when implementing those concepts. Experience from the academic consulting project described in this paper shows that support for implementation bears considerable potential for accelerated action. Thus this project fixed specific MoT management meetings scheduled throughout the calendar year mapping the process as well as the tasks described in the process. Management meetings being closely linked to the planning process the process can well be adapted to the specific needs of the company.

Lessons learned:

- Support given by Top Management in favor of the academic consulting project at Nitta was essential for its success. Although Top Management had so far not been actively involved in the conception and implementation of MoT it showed high commitment to it. The signals from Top Management emphasizing the importance of MoT at Nitta helped to give the project a definite sense of urgency beneficial for its achievement. Indeed the MoT could be conducted as a strategic project within the company.
- Seminars and Teaching Workshops during the MoT introduction and implementation project, seminars and teaching workshops were given to middle management. The experience in the project showed that such practitioner oriented teaching work increases collaboration, active participation and understanding during the conception and implementation of MoT. The progress made in the present MoT project considerably increase during the project as the seminars and workshops were held in the company.

At the present time, the MoT implementation project at Nitta is still going on. The company has already implemented and used a great part of MoT concepts; it will be exciting to observe how the company will further deploy its newly acquired knowledge and how it will contribute to their future competitive advantage.

References

Hunger JD and Wheelen TL (2002). *Essentials of Strategic Management* (Third edition). New Jersey: Prentice Hall

Petrick IJ and Echols AE (2004). Technology roadmapping in review: A tool for making sustainable new product development decisions. *Technological Forecasting & Social Change* 71: 81-100

Porter ME (1985). *Competitive Advantage - Creating and Sustaining Superior Performance*. New-York: The Free Press

Prahalad CK and Hamel G (1990). The Core Competence of the Corporation. *Harvard Business Review*: 79 - 91

Sanchez R (2001). Managing Knowledge into Competence: The Five Learning Cycles of the Competent Organization. In Sanchez R (ed.), *Knowledge Management and organizational Competence*: 3 - 37. Oxford New York: Oxford University Press

Sauber T (2004). Design and Implementation of a Concept of Structured Innovation Strategy Formulation. Dissertation ETH, Zurich

Savioz P (2002). Technology Intelligence in Technology Based SMEs. Conceptual Design and Implementation. ETH Zurich

Savioz P (2004). *Technology Intelligence, Concept Design and Implementation in Technology-based SMEs*. Houndsmills: Palgrave Macmillan

Tschirky H (2003). The Technology Awareness Gap in General Management. In Tschirky H, Jung H-H, and Savioz P (eds.), *Technology and Innovation Management of the move*: 21-41. Zurich: Verlag Industrielle Organisation

Tschirky H (2003a). The Concept of the Integrated Technology and Innovation Management. In Tschirky H, Jung H-H, and Savioz P (eds.), *Technology and Innovation Management of the Move*: 43-105. Zurich: Verlag Industrielle Organisation

Index

Printing and Binding: Strauss GmbH, Mörlenbach